READING INSTRUCTION THROUGH DIAGNOSTIC TEACHING

Larry A. Harris
UNIVERSITY OF NORTH DAKOTA

Carl B. Smith
INDIANA UNIVERSITY

with a foreword by
Leo Fay   INDIANA UNIVERSITY

HOLT, RINEHART AND WINSTON, INC.
New York Chicago San Francisco
Atlanta Dallas Montreal Toronto
London Sydney

To Barbara and Virginia

Library of Congress Catalog Card Number: 70-175165
ISBN: 0-03-079480-3
Printed in the United States of America
    4 5   038   9 8 7 6 5 4

Design by Leslie Adalman

FOREWORD

Occasionally a book appears that approaches a topic in a new way and consequently creates new insights for its readers. This is such a book. Traditionally, texts concerned with the teaching of reading were usually classified as either developmental or remedial. Characteristically, developmental texts reviewed the teaching of reading in classroom situations by describing practices at various stages of development. Remedial texts on the other hand, discussed techniques for discovering and overcoming the specific weaknesses of individual children who were experiencing difficulty in learning to read. In either case the teacher tended to be the user of some prescribed system, set of materials, or approach.

The contribution of this book is that the classroom teacher is viewed not as the user of a particular system, but rather as a decision maker whose task it is to enhance the learning of his students. This difference in the conceptualization of the teacher's role is highly significant. In this book the reader will soon sense that the teacher is viewed as a professional who needs to be equipped to make the choices that will ensure all children will learn. Anything less than this is to relegate the teacher's role to that of a technician whose function is merely to apply a particular system as effectively as possible. The authors do not neglect the importance of technical competence for they do discuss instructional systems, procedures, and materials. They suggest, however, that as a teacher grows in his profession, these are tools to be used selectively to ensure that the learners are successful.

Viewed this way, teaching is a diagnostic activity, and the key to the teacher's success is his ability to assess the needs of his students. A particular strength of this book is the thorough treatment of what to assess and how to assess student needs. This element alone distinguishes this text from traditional ones that emphasize teaching methods and largely ignore assessing learner needs.

The text contains other noteworthy features which demonstrate the authors' concern for both the learning and teaching dimensions of reading instruction. It emphasizes practical guides to individualize instruction, learning modes, knowledge of the range of options available to the teacher in regard to instructional systems, approaches, materials, and assessment procedures.

The reader will be struck by the book's thoroughly modern approach to the teacher as a manager of learning and by the authors' sense of reality as they discuss the questions of both what to do and how to do it. This book will serve well instructors who are concerned that their students view themselves as diagnosticians—a term that suggests that a teacher's first responsibility is to know his students' needs in order to individualize instruction.

Indiana University   Leo Fay

December 1971

PREFACE

We have written this text to meet the needs of teachers who face a fast-changing educational system, one that demands accountability for individual students progress in reading, one that expects the teacher to know how to assess growth, one that is concerned with the reading process instead of isolated skills. We believe that diagnostic teaching separates effective teachers from teacher technicians. A well-trained technician can take the teacher's guide for a reading series and use it to make group assignments and carry out group activities. But it takes another kind of teacher to identify the strengths and deficiencies of each child and to plan instruction on the basis of these strengths and deficiencies.

The diagnostic concept has been preached quite often and for quite a few years. But the "how-to-do-it," the pedagogy, of that principle is a book with blank pages. We hope to fill some of those pages with this book. One of the reasons for the lack of attention to teaching diagnostically is that until recently American schools have not expected individualization beyond some kinds of homogeneous grouping. That picture is changing. Many school systems not only will permit individualization of instruction but will actually require it. This book is not only a presentation of various approaches to teaching children to read, it is a presentation of how to use those various approaches in teaching diagnostically.

This book is organized around the skills a reader needs to move from a beginning reader to one with the ability to evaluate and synthesize. The emphasis on skills eliminates the need to categorize children by grades. A diagnostic approach with an emphasis on skills and interests places a child on his own program. We realize, of course, that many schools will continue to be organized on a graded plan for years to come. Nonetheless, personalized instruction can take place in the classroom if the teacher assumes the role of a diagnostician.

This text is more than a commitment to scholarship and research. It is a synthesis and a point of view. It represents our feelings that a child needs to succeed in reading every day, and he needs to find joy in books. To accomplish that end, constant diagnosis and planning for the individual must take place. This means the attitudes, interests, and feelings of the child must be considered as well as the knowledge and skill. We discuss attitudes and interests in several places in the text, but the reader should keep the affective aspects of reading in mind throughout the book.

Part 1 presents an overview of the book and discusses the factors that promote individualization of instruction. A model of the reading process is also included in Part 1.

Part 2 deals with the four main components of a classroom reading program: instructional systems for teaching reading, instructional materials for the classroom reading program, organizational principles and plans for teaching children in the classroom, and a strategy for assessing student needs, including the techniques and instruments useful in this assessment.

The remainder of the book treats various reading skills. Part 3 focuses on the reading skills that are most important for the child to get started in reading. Thus there are chapters dealing with language and perception skills, visual memory skills, and decoding skills. Decoding skills include both the broad notion of decoding language and the narrow concern of the letter-sound relations.

Children do not complete the initial reading skills at any definitive point. As the materials children can read increase in complexity, however, greater demands are placed on their skills. By a matter of degree the reading program shifts from concern with initial reading skills to the broader range of skills necessary for functional reading.

Part 4 focuses on the skills that enable a reader to be functionally literate, for example, to read the daily newspaper. Several word-recognition skills are described, building on those skills presented in Part 3. Reading comprehension skills are described in this part as those needed to acquire what is traditionally called literal comprehension. Oral reading skills, as required in the elementary grades, and techniques for the development of reading interests and standards for choosing books are also presented in Part 4.

Part 5 considers the reading skills necessary for using reading as a tool to accomplish various purposes. Competencies of analysis, evaluation, synthesis, and application are discussed under the heading of critical and creative reading, reading in content fields, and study and reference skills.

A final chapter reviews the concepts presented and suggests means by which the classroom teacher can evaluate his own approach to the teaching of reading.

Beginning with Chapter 3, each chapter is preceded by a personal message to the reader which gives him a focus on the chapter. Questions which provide clues to the major issues in each chapter are included prior to each chapter. After each chapter, there is a list of key terms that enables the reader to review by checking on how clearly he can define them.

Some important features of this text that are not usually found elsewhere are an organization of reading methods into four major instructional systems, a strong section on reading in the content areas, a section on critical reading according to specific educational objectives, and a practical system of assessment techniques that makes it possible for a classroom teacher to personalize reading instruction through a continuing evaluation of student progress.

Many writers and researchers have provided ideas that contributed to our thinking in the development of this book. It is inevitable that acknowledgment of some will result in the omission of others who also deserve recognition. Yet the contributions of Mary Austin, Theodore Clymer, Leo Fay, and George Spache cannot be overlooked. Also instrumental in shaping our thinking have been Benjamin Bloom, Guy Bond, Dolores Durkin, Roger Farr, Kenneth S. Goodman, Albert Harris, William Labov, Nila Banton Smith, and Ruth Strickland. Special thanks are due Nancy Lee Roser and Margaret Griffin for their suggestions on the original manuscript. Special research assistance provided by Trinitia Meehan, Deborah Reagan, Georgia Binek, Nancy Vargus and Paula Blomenberg is greatly appreciated. Thanks are due also to the hundreds of students and teachers who have attended our classes and workshops for their suggestions and reactions to our ideas. Without the help of all these people this book would not have been possible.

University of North Dakota　　　　　　　　　　L.A.H.
Indiana University　　　　　　　　　　　　　　C.B.S.

December 1971

CONTENTS

PART I

DIAGNOSIS
IN THE TEACHING
OF READING

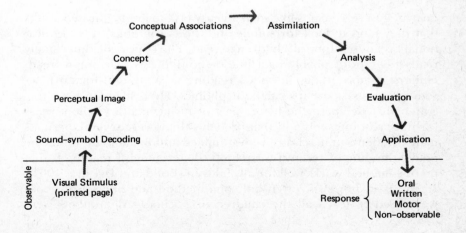

Chapter 1

Diagnosis: The Key to Individualizing Instruction

Anyone who has watched good and poor readers in various class-rooms knows that people walk many paths to acquire reading skills. Most of the children who fail to read in the elementary school have average or better intelligence; it is not stupidity that causes most reading failures. Evidence from studies on disabled readers reveals a multitude of causes, not the least of which is inadequate instruction (Strang, 1968). Undoubtedly there will always be youngsters who fail to learn to read under the best classroom conditions. Those children will need the help of specialists. But our concern in this text is the everyday student who has good days and poor, who grows in spurts physically and intellectually, and therefore needs a teacher who adjusts instruction to the hills and valleys of intellectual growth.

DETERMINING THE NEEDS OF LEARNERS

Learning to read seems like such an easy task to most educated adults that they tend to look for simple and direct solutions to the educational task of teaching all children to read. The educated adult usually reads well and probably had little or no difficulty learning to read. Understandably, then, he views reading as a straight-forward decoding process, perhaps calling it phonics. He is likely to have forgotten that he spent the better part of his elementary school years learning reading skills and that probably there were several, perhaps many, students in his classes who stumbled and failed to do well. One notable finding of recent research on the teaching of reading is that no one method works well for all children (Bond and Dykstra, 1967). In the past, however, often only one method and one set of books were used to teach all the children in a school. All students were moved from grade to grade and were given approximately the same material and the same instruction no matter what their background or ability. It should not be surprising, then, that some surveys have indicated that as many as 40 percent of U.S. high school graduates are functional illiterates in several major cities. In 1970 the U.S. Office of Education initiated a "Right To Read" campaign to drama-tize the need for differentiated instruction in order that all able students might learn to read to their capacity. That goal cannot be accomplished, however, through one method as exemplified in one set of books. With any given method there is a wide range of per-formance even among students of similar ability. One explanation for that range is that children vary in the ease with which they learn through any one sense. Some learn most easily through visual tech-niques, others primarily through auditory techniques, and still others through tactile or kinesthetic means (H. K. Smith, 1968). Some children do best when all of their senses are involved in mutual reinforcement in learning to read.

What happens to the child who learns most easily by auditory means when the system used to teach him to read emphasizes visual learning? If he is lucky, he will adjust and respond to the visual learning techniques. If he cannot apply himself to that extent, he may stumble into the wild guessing habits of some poor readers, saying *house* for *horse* and *farmer* for *flower*, for example. A teacher must be alert to cues that indicate the learning preference of the child. Though a methods test, the *Mills Learning Modalities Test* (Mills, 1964), may be used to check the learning of symbols through visual, audi-tory, kinesthetic, and combination means, most teachers prefer in-formal measures that are quicker and can be used in impromptu situations. A procedure for estimating a child's preferred sense is discussed in Chapter 3.

Most children learn readily through all of the senses—visual, auditory, kinesthetic, tactile. Every class contains a wide range of student abilities. To find the strengths and use them and to overcome weaknesses among learners requires observation, diagnosis, and care-ful planning. Techniques and considerations for accomplishing that purpose appear in succeeding chapters.

POPULATION DIFFERENCES

For many years educators have been aware of occasional lags in a child's development that affect his performance in reading. More recently there has been concern for the differences in student popu-lations. Privileged and underprivileged, native speakers and second-language speakers, gifted learners and slow learners, all approach reading with different language equipment and different cultural experiences. Teachers need to make a decided effort to diagnose these and other differences and then to provide for them in an instructional program.

Privileged children come to school with a wealth of experiences that assist them in reading and in all academic subjects. They have books, they visit the zoo, they go to the movies, they travel. These experiences operate as a kind of curriculum for them at home, leading them directly into the readers and social studies books they use in school. Compensation has to be made in the classroom for the underprivileged child who lacks these experiences. But the underprivileged and the innercity child should not be equated. The teacher needs to find ways to enable the innercity child to identify his own experiences and associations, for example, multifamily dwellings, traffic, and playgrounds in the streets.

The Language Factor

An intimate part of every child's experience is the language he uses; in a sense, a child's oral language is a record of his experiences. In the past educators tended to think only of foreign languages as an obvious barrier to reading American English. Linguists have pointed out, however, that there are many dialects in the English language, some of them associated with underprivileged groups, that hinder a child in learning the grammatical patterns and pronunciations acceptable in business and in educated society. Different patterns and pronunciations appear among Appalachian groups, Black American groups, southern groups, and isolated rural groups. Standard English is similar to a second language to these children. The teacher must become acquainted with the dialect of his pupils in order to understand them and gradually lead them to see and hear the language of the school and of books (Bloom, Davis, and Hess, 1965).

The bilingual student offers a similar challenge to the teacher. Historically, however, the bilingual child has fared better in having instruction adjusted to him because it is obvious that an English vocabulary has to be built and the sound-symbol relation has to be carefully explained in order for the child to read. That phase of his learning profile is easy to identify. On the other hand, teachers have often assumed that a native speaker has the necessary equipment to cope with standard English no matter what his dialect. Recent studies indicate that the use of a nonstandard dialect does not necessarily prepare a child to use standard English in school (Labov, 1967; Shuy, 1970).

Gifted Learners and Slow Learners

Gifted learners need different instructional approaches than their slower-learning counterparts. The difference should be more than merely the number of practice exercises each group engages in before mastering a reading skill. Gifted learners seem able to develop their own system of cues that enable them to handle the alphabet code whereas slow learners need a more structured explanation of the code. Gifted learners can often develop vocabulary and word-analysis skills inductively. They are able to generalize—for example, to ask themselves, "What features make these words alike: *thankful, prayerful, basketful?*" Slow learners are less able to arrive at generalizations about semantic patterns, spelling patterns, and syntactic patterns.

Besides his ability to figure out quickly and easily his own word-analysis system, the gifted learner shows other characteristics that enable him to leap ahead. He knows about many things, uses a large number of words easily, performs difficult mental tasks, asks questions, and is alert and observant. Thus it is a disservice to the fast child to make him do all of the exercises in the reading book whereas for the slow learner the practice may be necessary.

BELIEFS ABOUT THE READING PROCESS

What a teacher believes about how a person learns to read will affect the way he instructs different kinds of learners. Understanding the process called reading is so important that it might be well for you to stop here and formulate your own definition of what reading is. Write your definition on the last page of this text. When you have finished the book you can determine whether your concept has changed, been refined, or remains the same.

Since most people do not develop their own theory about how children learn to read, you will probably base your definition on one of the philosophies expressed in the books used to teach children to read. These philosophies vary, and this variety becomes helpful in light of the differences that exist among learners. Children's reading books follow a systematic procedure for introducing a child to the act of reading and for leading him toward competency and maturity in reading. The approach used in a series of readers is a highly organized set of procedures that can legitimately be called a system of instruction in reading.

One system views reading initially as a visual activity in which the learner responds to the visual symbol with a concept—he translates the visual symbol into a thought. Such a system starts reading instruction with a body of sight words, that is, a group of words taught as whole entities without reference to the parts or letters that make up the whole word.

Another system considers writing as a code for spoken sounds. This system begins by establishing the relation between the spoken sounds and the symbols used to represent these sounds. Printed symbols, or words, are then translated into sounds, or oral language, as a means of getting the message from the printed page.

Still another system is based on the belief that learning to read can be accomplished most effectively through trial and error with positive reinforcement for success. Such a system may use a computer that talks to the child and gets him to respond on an electric typewriter or some other electronic answering device. The computer directs the child to find some symbol, then rewards him with praise when he has located the correct symbol. On some of these machines the keys of the typewriter are locked so that only the correct response is open.

Another system sees learning to read as one of many ways to express thought. This system correlates several language skills. The correlation goes something like this: "I can think. What I think, I can say. What I can say, I can write. What I can write, I can read. A reader can then know my thoughts." Reading is thus an expression of thought with oral language as an intermediary. In this system the learner is trained to respond with all his senses.

Some systems seem designed to appeal to a specific sense. Though generally reading systems are not quite that simple, there is enough truth in the statement to merit a teacher's analyzing his instructional materials to determine which sense or combination of senses they emphasize. Systems for teaching reading are treated in detail in Chapter 3 and materials for instruction are discussed in Chapter 4.

CONTENT PHILOSOPHY

The content of a reading program is often dictated or at least controlled by the learning system on which the program is based. If the learning system emphasizes the decoding aspects of reading, the story content will likely be different from that in a program which emphasizes finding meaning in words. In a highly structured decoding system the early stories are limited to words that fit into the parts of the alphabet code the child has learned to date. An example is, "Bat the fat cat, Dan. Dan can bat a fat cat." As is apparent from the story, the consonants have been introduced as well as the sound of "a" as heard in *at*. Nothing beyond these sounds enters into the story, since the child has not learned the code with which to analyze and recognize other kinds of words.

FIGURE 1-1 A Talking Typewriter

A talking typewriter rewards a child immediately for an appropriate response. (Photo courtesy of Responsive Environments Corporation)

A system that emphasizes a meaning-getting process largely employs words that occur most frequently around the home, school, and neighborhood. The theory here is that meaningful content stimulates learning, and that which relates most closely to the child's life has the most meaning. Such a story might be, "Jane goes to school. Jane likes to go to school. School is fun. Mary goes to school, too. She is a friend of Jane. They both like school."

A system that says anything a child can think about is ideal content for his first books evidently encourages individual, self-made books. Under this system, often called the language experience approach, the child gets variety in his vocabulary and in the content by exchanging his stories with other members of the class. Class pressure builds to create more interesting stories and thus stimulates an expansion of the reading and writing vocabulary.

It is not necessary to consider all of the possible reading systems here. Chapter 3 will study this matter in more detail. The point should be made, however, that any one system does not fit all learners equally well. It should also be apparent that a learner who is placed in a system for which he is not suited has a strong chance of failing or of being severely retarded in reading.

To match the learner with an appropriate reading system requires two steps: (1) a diagnosis of the needs and learning styles of the child and (2) an analysis of the learning system used in the reading program adopted by the school.

MASTERING DIAGNOSTIC TECHNIQUES

In order to diagnose children's reading needs a teacher must be able to analyze the reading problems he meets and understand the instructional techniques and instruments that can help him in the classroom. He must be able to answer such questions as, What is the reading process? At what points might a student stumble or fail? What symptoms should I as a teacher look for at each stage in the development of a reader? Of course, the answers to questions like these can become extremely complex when a child has severe reading disabilities, but for the kinds of problems that the classroom teacher has the time and the knowledge to handle the answers can remain relatively simple. He has the opportunity to apply the proverbial ounce of prevention so that small problems do not become major reading difficulties. While today's classroom teacher cannot be expected to know all the symptoms and treatments for severe reading problems, he must know basic diagnostic techniques that he can apply routinely to the lifeline of reading activity. Chapter 5 will explore the techniques and instruments needed by the classroom teacher to assess children's progress and individual needs.

THE READING PROCESS: A MODEL

Reading is a process of communication between the writer and the reader. Hopefully, the reader receives from the communication all that the writer intended. Figure 1.1 indicates what the reader does with the written message to turn it into a complete communication. The reading process starts with word recognition and proceeds until a body of knowledge is synthesized and used according to the purposes of the reader.

The only observable physical activity that takes place is the reader's glancing at the printed page and later perhaps making some kind of response, such as an oral or written comment or a nod of the

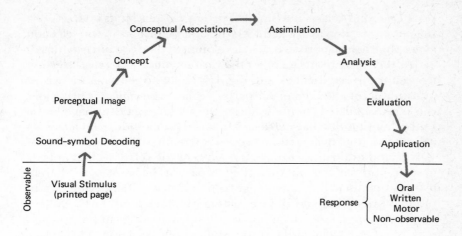

FIGURE 1-2   The Reading Process Model

This Reading Process Model indicates the variety of operations in an act of reading.

head. The response may also be an internal one that cannot be seen through casual observation. What happens between the time the reader looks at the page and the time he makes some kind of response is crucial to the analysis of the person's reading activity. The reading communication model shown in Figure 1.1 describes the internal operations that take place. Through this model a teacher can focus on specific elements of the reading act and discuss the instructional activities involved at any given step. In this way reading diagnosis can become more specific. In reality, of course, each step meshes with the next, and there are some extremely rapid exchanges with the memory system that enable the reading process to continue toward the goal of evaluation and application.

Follow the stages of the model as they are described. It will also be helpful to refer back to this model at various points in the text in order to identify the place a certain skill has in the development of reading competency. Start in the lower left-hand corner of the diagram. A *visual stimulus*, the printed page, has to be translated and related to spoken language. In the early stages of reading this process requires a decoding operation. The letters must be related to the sounds they stand for. A correct translation of symbol into sound should provide a basic recognition of the word provided the word has been part of the learner's listening vocabulary. The recognition of the word on a sensory level evokes what is sometimes called a perception or a *perceptual image*. This is a sense image at the threshold of abstraction. It is the learner's first step toward forming a *concept*. The reader's perception of *dog* is a rather specific image of a four-legged creature that barks. The concept of *dog* uses the image of a specific *dog* and relates it to animal, pet, or various kinds of dogs. The concept *dog* is then associated with the other concepts in the selection (conceptual association) so that a developing theme can be recognized.

As the learner puts together the various concepts from a selection he attempts to see them as a whole. His ability to see what the writer said with all of the connected parts is called *assimilation*. The reader who has assimilated the message of the writer is said to have literal comprehension of what he read. He has the main idea and a correct ordering of the main parts. From that point the competencies of analysis and evaluation are used. *Analysis* of the relations that appear in a selection is made and then used as part of the *evaluation*. Analysis involves operations such as categorizing elements, identifying organizational principles, and differentiating opinions from facts. Evaluation is that operation which applies designated criteria to a selection to arrive at a determination of the value of the selection. The reader must develop criteria based upon logic, empirical studies, or the subjective feelings he has about the issue. As he reads, he uses his criteria to make a judgment about the value of what he sees. The mature reader will finally decide to do something with the knowledge he has gained (*application*). Depending on his evaluation, he may reject the selection and the author who wrote it or he may look for a similar work to build additional knowledge. That decision may be observable and expressed orally, in writing, or through a gesture, or it may be an unobservable decision or response.

The reading-communication model serves to give the teacher a schema to diagnose a reader's progress at specific stages in the process of learning to read. He can ask about the reader's skill in decoding, in perceiving, in conceptualizing, in assimilating, in analyzing, in evaluating, and in applying. Means for testing and for teaching each of these steps in the reading process appear in succeeding chapters. Simply being aware that a reader may experience difficulty at any one of these stages gives the teacher an orientation toward analyzing and assisting each student's needs.

TERMS

perception	auditory
concept	kinesthetic
assimilation	sensory modality
functional illiterate	language experience approach
differentiated instruction	

Chapter 2

Current Factors Promoting Individualization

Educators have for many years urged, "Teach the individual." Outstanding teachers have always strived to individualize their instruction despite such odds as oversized classrooms, inadequate materials, and archaic administrative structures. But things are happening these days to loosen purse strings, cut down class size, and streamline organizational structures. What is happening is an influx of technology, a change in the role of the classroom teacher, a concern for linguistic and other factors that influence school learning, and an emphasis on training teachers to plot progress for individual learners.

INNOVATIONS AND TECHNOLOGY

Materials Explosion

The knowledge explosion that has occurred since World War II has been matched by an explosion of educational materials. Books, charts, games, films, transparencies, and machinery of every shape and description have appeared in abundance. Each year in the 1960s some 3000–4000 children's books were published, and probably more new reading series and more isolated reading skill texts appeared in these years than in the previous fifty. The appearance of all of these new materials for children reflects a desire not only to find better methods of presenting academic content but also to meet the learning needs of minority groups and to compete with the flash and color of television. Certainly the quantity of materials poses selection problems for the teacher and the supervisors, but this is a problem more easily overcome than not having available the kind of material needed to help a child learn to read.

Audiovisual equipment has become generally available; indeed it is not unusual to find an overhead projector and a tape recorder at the daily disposal of the classroom teacher. Most teachers find these two instruments extremely valuable in teaching reading skills or in motivating youngsters. Slide projectors and filmstrip projectors are now used not only for motivation but also for teaching word-attack skills, vocabulary, and some comprehension skills. It is common today for reading series to come with sets of slides or filmstrips that can be used to assist in the teaching of reading skills.

Most audiovisual equipment is easily adapted for individualized instruction. Children enjoy putting answers on transparencies and seeing their writing appear on the screen. A set of headphones turns the ordinary tape recorder into a private tutoring device. One school system encouraged teachers to set up a corner of the classroom as an audiovisual corner. The projector and screen were in constant readiness, as was the tape recorder. Individual students or small groups could go to that corner without disturbance and carry on activity that helped them make progress in reading.

Specialized machinery has been developed to help students learn some of the mechanical and repetitive operations involved in reading. A reading pacer leads the reader through a selection at a mechanically controlled rate. The text is revealed on a screen or a bar of light moves down the page to regulate the speed. Since rate is quite individually determined, these machines provide individual attention to meet the needs of the learner. Tachistoscopic devices flash symbols or words on a screen to train readers to focus quickly and accurately on words and phrases.

Auditory machines frequently are used with some of the techniques of programmed learning. A taped voice methodically leads the student through an exercise and gives him the opportunity to hear immediately whether or not he has responded correctly. A modified tape recorder called the language master uses cards with strips of tape on them. The cards contain prerecorded words, phrases, or sounds that the child can play over and over again. The learner can also record his own voice to try to match the recorded sound or to answer a question that has been posed. Such machinery can be of particular help with children who need motivation or many repetitions. Properly used, all of this equipment can help the teacher give each child specialized treatment and practice.

The Teacher's Role

Instructional materials may have changed but not any more than has the role of the teacher. In times past teachers often looked upon themselves as dispensers of knowledge, and in general society accepted this view of the teacher. Today, however, with certifica-

FIGURE 2-1 The Overhead Projector

With an overhead projector students and teachers can make illustrations that focus on specific reading skills. (Photo courtesy of 3M Company)

tion requirements becoming stricter and specialization more common, the classroom teacher is somewhat like the general practitioner in medicine. He puts his students on a general program for good learning. He knows the major symptoms indicating learning difficulty and can prescribe treatment for common learning ailments. When he identifies a problem that seems to involve complex learning disorders he sends the child to the appropriate specialist—the remedial reading teacher, the psychologist, the social therapist. Just as parents expect their doctor to explain physical problems to them and tell them what they can do to promote the health of their child, today they ask the classroom teacher the nature of their child's reading problem and how they can assist him at home.

Socially and economically the modern teacher has also assumed a new position. The teacher speaks out on social issues and asks boldly for compensation equal to the work of a professional person. Money and status have improved for today's teacher and justifiably the public looks for an improvement in the quality of instruction. Society and the teaching profession expect a teacher to be accountable for defined objectives and to apply learning theories and practices to the development of particular skills in individual children. Reading, more than any other academic skill, is held up for public inspection. Society expects every child to be able to read according to his capacity.

One big advantage that many teachers today have is the help of a classroom assistant. Teacher's aides are being employed in more and more communities to handle the routine duties of the classroom in order to give the teacher time for analyzing pupil performance, planning individualized programs, and evaluating instructional procedures. Reading teachers above all others have benefited from teacher's aides, according to a national survey of federally financed reading programs (Smith and Austin, 1969). One exemplary reading program used an aide to help students work on several kinds of repetitive tasks, such as listening to taped stories as they read them from a book. Under this plan the teacher met each student for direct instruction and then sent him to an aide with a plan for practice on the skill he needed. This is but one example of the emphasis school systems now place on the analysis of reading performance.

The reading teacher today has to be well versed in child growth and development theory and must understand the motivational aspects of learning and the sequence of skills needed for a child to read easily and maturely. The teacher who wishes to lead his pupils to their full potential in reading must be able to ask—and answer—such questions as: What level can this child work at? What are his interests? What can I do to get him to read with joy? What word and comprehension skills does he have and what does he not have? What tasks must be assigned immediately to keep him improving in his reading?

APPLYING NEW INSTRUCTIONAL THEORIES

Programmed Learning

Programmed learning techniques are in wide use today in the classroom teaching of reading. Not only are there programmed texts designed to teach reading but the principles of programming are exerting a profound effect on instruction in this area. Two principles of programmed learning are particularly suited for use in the teaching of reading: self-pacing and progression through carefully defined small steps. Whether it is a listening exercise by means of a tape recorder or a worksheet on prefixes, the observer will see the effect of programmed instruction in today's classrooms. The value of such an instructional approach is that it recognizes the need of the learner to follow his own time clock and not that set by the teacher for the entire class.

Reader Identification

Today's reading texts tend to be more realistic in content than the basal readers of the forties and fifties. Stories about Oriental Americans, American Indians, White Americans, Black Americans, Spanish Americans, and other groups abound. They are realistic without being depressing, and they express the social values of justice and brotherhood, values that American children a generation ago did not often find in their readers. Such stories aim at giving the young learner a content that gives him a sense of identification.

Teacher Judgment

All of these developments in school and in society point to one conclusion: today's teacher is expected to exercise judgment about the learning life of his pupils. He has the freedom of being able to choose strategies, techniques, and books to stimulate the individual learner, and he has the responsibility of setting up precise performance objectives for his students to achieve. When they do not measure up, it is his responsibility to decide why and to adjust his instruction accordingly.

LINGUISTIC STUDIES OF DIFFERENCES

In the early and middle sixties linguists charged into the arena of reading instruction, armed with their studies of language in different regions and among different groups in the United States. Language variation is strongly affected by environment; this has to be considered when choosing a system for teaching reading. As indicated earlier, some methods and their related materials make little allowance for differences between the language of the school and the language of the child. The problem may simply be that the child uses a vocabulary only slightly different from the teacher's, or there may be a wide difference between his pronunciation and response patterns and those of the teacher.

Researchers have found that some ghetto children find the language in school books inordinately difficult (Gordon and Wilkerson, 1966). These children have not been exposed to a variety of language patterns nor are they familiar with the pronunciation the teacher uses. For such learners some authorities recommend teaching reading almost as if it were a foreign language (Kasdon, 1962; Shuy, 1970). By taking that approach, the teacher says, in effect, "You may say this a different way at home, and that is fine for home, but in school and in books it is said this way."

In addition to stressing the regularity of English spelling and making it easier to build up the notion of decoding through a sound-symbol response, the linguists say that the language of the child's environment should be used in setting up his reading program (Baratz and Shuy, 1969). Environmental language, therefore, becomes one more variable for the reading teacher to weigh in making his diagnosis and in planning instruction for individuals and groups.

FEDERAL FUNDS FOR INNOVATION

In 1965 Congress passed the Elementary and Secondary Education Act (ESEA) to promote innovative instructional techniques in the nation's schools. This act provided funds for libraries and materials and supplied money for instructional programs for disadvantaged youth. The influx of a billion dollars a year of federal money into the nation's schools gave impetus to many programs that emphasize individualized reading instruction. In fact, according to one survey of the programs stimulated by this legislation, more than 70 percent dealt with reading instruction (Smith and Austin, 1969). Underprivileged children were given more individual attention than they had ever received under previous reading programs. Teacher's aides, educational machines, and reduction in class size were only a few of the ways school systems attempted to individualize reading instruction for poor children.

Federal money has likewise been spent on institutes for training teachers. A survey of these institutes reveals that most of them have focused on the diagnostic teaching of reading. The need for diagnostic teaching has become so evident that administrators and teachers develop many of their inservice training activities around the theme of individualizing reading instruction.

SPECIAL GROUPS

For individualized reading instruction to be effective the teacher must understand the learning strengths and weaknesses of specialized groups of children.

Disadvantaged Children

Disadvantaged children may be defined as those who come from homes where poor communication exists, where little general knowledge is gained through trips, books, and other contacts, and where the child is not stimulated to talk and develop concepts that will benefit him in school and in reading. It is apparent that these conditions as well as the lack of varied experiences directly affect the child's use of language. When a child is experiencing difficulty with language, reading instruction has to be adjusted accordingly. The teacher cannot assume that disadvantaged children possess a standard vocabulary. He has to check each student to determine what words he can hear and identify and what basic vocabulary has to be communicated as a foundation for reading books in school.

Some groups of inner-city children begin school with as few as 500 words in their listening vocabulary as opposed to several thousand for the average middle class youngster. In one major city the beginning first grade children identified as disadvantaged failed to recognize 50 percent of the words common to five of the popular basal readers. Language, vocabulary, common concepts, and confidence in the school are necessary ingredients in any instructional plan for a group of disadvantaged youngsters (Bloom, Davis, and Hess, 1965).

Bilingual Readers

In certain sections of the United States there are large concentrations of foreign-speaking families. In these homes English is a second language and may be used only when there are outsiders present. These students require still another approach to the teaching of reading. Often the teacher has to teach each word in the reading book as a word in a foreign language. The bilingual child must hear the word and see it so he can make the sound-symbol association, but he must also have a picture or a representation of what the word stands for. In effect, the teaching of reading to these students is a combination of teaching English at the same time reading skills are taught. Unless the learner is diagnosed, however, such an instructional plan might not be carried out.

The Slow Learner

In any heterogeneous class there may be a slow learner, that is, a child who scores below 80 on an intelligence measure and who does not easily grasp abstractions or generalizations. Some researchers have suggested that slow learners may show deficiencies in their muscular and motor responses (Kephart, 1960) and so encourage a program of motor coordination practice (walking a balance beam; tossing a bean bag) as a prerequisite for teaching reading and other academic skills. The precise value of motor coordination activities has not been determined but reading teachers must adjust to the slow learner by providing additional practice and a slower pace. Since everyone may be at a different point in learning the skills, the slow learner can take all the time he needs to make his way through reading tasks. Parents and teachers often form local groups to study the needs of slow learners. These groups have been instrumental in obtaining help for these students, especially in alerting educators to their need for time to learn.

The Gifted Learner

On the opposite side of the ledger is the learner sometimes described as gifted. Unfortunately, no specific I.Q. designation nor any measure of creativity or fluency adequately identifies him. However, one way to identify him is to compare his performance with that of others. He has many more interests, learns quickly, learns to read easily, and generally reads more and better books than does the average child. He is especially adept in handling comprehension questions after reading. The gifted learner requires less practice and less explanation and can carry on activities at a higher conceptual level than other members of the class. He may often enjoy doing creative exercises that follow reading. Gifted learners are prime candidates for individualized reading instruction.

Knowing some of the characteristics of typical groups of children enables the teacher to initiate instructional plans designed specifically for his students. In addition, the teacher has some direction for beginning a child's learning program. The plan can be modified as the teacher learns more about the individual from continuing contacts.

TOWARD INDIVIDUALIZING INSTRUCTION

Classroom diagnosis and the individualization of instruction did not appear on the educational scene all of a sudden. Since the beginning of this century education in general and reading instruction in particular have developed techniques and principles that focus on the individual learner. The development of standardized tests beginning with Thorndike's *Handwriting Scale* published in 1910 permitted the measurement of individual achievement on the basis of graded units and made possible a comparison of one individual's performance with another's. Equally important, the tests revealed that individuals respond differently at different age levels. Reading was the last of the tool subjects to yield to the testing movement. It proved extremely difficult to standardize oral reading, virtually the only way of teaching reading at the beginning of the twentieth century. The first standardized reading test was the *Gray Standardized Oral Reading Paragraphs*, published in 1915 (Smith, 1965).

With the introduction of standardized tests came the development of measurement techniques as we know them today. During World War I it was found that thousands of American men could not read well enough to perform military duties. Subsequently there was a rapid expansion of reading research and the development of many innovations in instruction, especially the movement from oral reading to silent reading and the development of remedial reading techniques. The upshot of all the research was, first, the appearance of many professional books and monographs and, second, the publication of elementary readers based on silent reading procedures. Silent reading had gained ascendancy because it was found to be the way people used reading in practical life. It also lent itself to mass testing whereas oral reading did not. At the same time the use of the child's dictated story (the experience-story technique) for teaching reading was initiated, though the method did not come into wide use.

Reading research in the twenties indicated that an analysis of comprehension errors served well as the basis for remedial work. To meet a variety of reading problems several remedial techniques were developed: an alphabet-spelling method for nonreaders (Smith, 1965); a phonics-kinesthetic (writing in the air) approach; and several methods dealing with treatment through bodily movements.

In the first half of the thirties two opposing philosophies dominated the teaching scene—one committed to teaching a sequence of skills; the other to directing the child to his own purposes, to problem-solving and the use of experiences. The former emphasized group instruction while the latter focused on the individual's personal style.

Textbooks reflected the educator's interest in reaching the child at various stages of his development. New texts tried to provide rich experiences, encouraged lifetime reading interests and habits, emphasized adjusting to individual needs, and encouraged an abundance of supplementary materials. Over 650 reading studies were conducted between 1924 and 1935, many of which were concerned with grouping and the handling of individual needs in the classroom. At this time the concept of readiness became a part of educational theory and teachers were expected to determine what concepts and skills a child brought with him to any new instructional task.

During the second half of the thirties the individualized approach to reading was promoted as a full-fledged method of reading instruction. It tried to mesh reading and child development in all areas—physical, social, intellectual, emotional, and linguistic—and was concerned with interests, attitudes, self-esteem, and satisfaction as well as achievement on a standardized reading test. In the terms of Willard Olson, the objectives of individualized reading were seeking, self-selection, and personal pacing (Smith, 1965).

The stage was set for the individualized approach to reading instruction to gain acceptance in U.S. schools. With the outbreak of World War II, however, teaching remained in a state of suspension for a decade. True, some significant research on learning was conducted during the war years but the results did not reach the schools until the fifties. What spurred developments in the teaching of reading and other educational areas more than anything else was the Russians' orbiting of Sputnik, the first successful space capsule, in 1957. The fact that the Communist ideology with which we were competing beat us into space shook up the public, educators, and politicians and shook loose a fair quantity of research and development money at the local and federal levels. Reading instruction came under special fire from influential laymen who felt that U.S. children were unable to cope with the modern knowledge explosion because the methods used in the schools to teach them to read were inadequate (Flesch, 1955).

SUMMARY

The trend toward the individualization of reading instruction is reflected in the variety of books and technologies available, in the changing status of teachers, in the research on learning techniques, and in the demands of society. Linguists have also encouraged individualized reading instruction because of language differences among students. Federal funds have been employed to meet the learning needs of special populations.

Numerous developments in education since 1900 have encouraged classroom diagnosis and the acceptance of individualized reading instruction.

TERMS

individualization	reading process
diagnosis	kinesthetic
reading skills	

PART II

INDIVIDUALIZING READING INSTRUCTION IN THE CLASSROOM

In order to teach reading diagnostically, a teacher needs specific knowledge and skills. He must know several systems for teaching reading and be able to apply them to benefit his students. He needs to be familiar with a wide variety of books and materials to use within the teaching systems. He must be able to organize his students for efficient learning and be able to assess their needs in order that his knowledge of systems, materials, and grouping plans may be applied to help the individuals in his class.

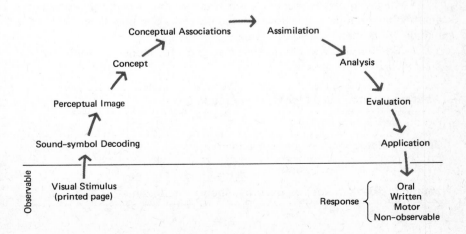

Chapter 3

Instructional Systems

Some people think of teaching reading as teaching a book. That attitude confuses the materials that are used for instruction with the teaching methods that are employed. It is essential to know the difference between methods and materials in order to know what each contributes to an effective reading program. This chapter will help you understand that distinction.

You know that various instructional methods are used in the teaching of reading. The task of selecting and using one of these methods looms just over the horizon for you. You may know something about several methods but be unable to tell how they differ from each other or how they work in the classroom. This chapter will help you understand the rationale underlying each instructional method.

Finally, you may wonder if one method can possibly fit the needs of all youngsters and, if not, how various methods can effectively be combined. This matter will also be treated.

In Chapter 3 you will find answers to such questions as the following:

What methods are used for teaching reading?

Which method is best?

Can all children learn by the same method?

What is individualized reading?

Should the basal reader be used by a beginning teacher?

American educators have been searching for the best approach to reading instruction since before 1900. Each year dozens of investigations are conducted which compare one teaching method with another. In 1965 the U.S. Office of Education invested $1 million in a search to determine what method was most effective for beginning reading instruction. The major finding of practically every such investigation, including the 1965 study, has been that no one method of reading instruction is best for all children.

A considerable amount of evidence indicates that people learn in different ways. It is therefore not surprising that studies which compare teaching methods are typically inconclusive. They often find a greater difference in achievement among learners taught by a single method than among those taught by different methods. Even when one teaching method is found to be equal to another as measured by group achievement, when individual learners are compared it is found that some youngsters do better with one method while others do better with the other method. The same is true for children who do poorly; each method is relatively ineffective with some youngsters.

LIMITATIONS OF METHODOLOGICAL STUDIES

Educational research is often limited because many important factors cannot be controlled. Unlike the scientist working in a laboratory, the educator cannot control a number of important variables. The teachers using a given method of reading instruction, for example, may have varying degrees of interest in its success. One teacher may be determined to make method A effective while another secretly hopes it will fail. Or the amount of time given to reading instruction can vary so much from one classroom to another that minutes of instruction become more important than the teaching method. Many such variables are at work in methodological research. It is possible to introduce some degree of control into these studies (Clymer, 1962), but research of this kind will probably be subject to such errors as long as human beings take part in it.

Another significant factor that limits the value of methodological comparisons is simply that "methods" are not clearly defined. For example, many investigations seek to compare the individualized approach to the basal reader approach. The "methods" employed in such studies are often primarily a set of instructional materials, not distinct instructional strategies. Furthermore, in true methodological research where a unique approach to teaching is the variable actually being studied, the teachers using a given method frequently personalize their teaching so much that no common method can be identified.

Teachers using the language experience approach, for example, vary their teaching not only from study to study but within the same study.

METHODS VERSUS MATERIALS

A variety of innovative reading programs are currently on the market. The initial teaching alphabet (ITA), Words in Color, linguistic readers, and numerous other devices have recently been the subject of much attention in professional and lay literature. Investigations have sought to determine the effectiveness of these approaches. Many of the limitations cited earlier have plagued these studies.

A more fundamental question needs to be raised for these innovative programs, however. Are real differences in teaching method introduced by ITA, for example, or is the main distinction simply a change in format? Educators have concluded that while some teaching changes are introduced by ITA, the primary difference is one of code, not method. Analysis of other programs such as Words in Color, the Merrill Linguistic Readers, and Unifon lead to the same conclusion.

This is not to dispute the potential value of the innovative reading programs. The point is simply that discussions and research must avoid confusing a teaching method with what is only a new set of instructional materials.

INSTRUCTIONAL SYSTEMS

Despite the criticisms that have been directed at methodological research and the confusion over what constitutes a teaching method, reading instruction must proceed according to some plan. Careful analysis of the existing literature indicates that there are four distinct systems* for teaching reading: (1) the controlled vocabulary approach, (2) the language experience approach, (3) the programmed approach, and (4) the individualized approach. None of these systems should be regarded as a panacea; rather, each should be viewed as an instructional strategy with specific characteristics.

Since individual youngsters have unique learning styles, one instructional system may be more appropriate than another for some children. Furthermore, the teacher has to adjust to the strengths and weaknesses of each system. Continued search for the best method

*The word *systems* is preferable to *methods* for two reasons: (1) *methods* has been widely and incorrectly applied to materials and nonmethods and therefore connotes incorrect associations, and (2) *systems* correctly implies a planned strategy for instruction with an underlying rationale.

of teaching reading appears to be a fruitless pursuit in the light of the evidence already in hand. The key to effective reading instruction is evidently the teacher. The skillful teacher can create a successful reading program when permitted to teach with a system he endorses and understands.

The Controlled Vocabulary Approach

The controlled vocabulary approach is a highly structured system for teaching reading. The teacher is provided with a manual or guide that contains suggested procedures and activities, and the learner reads from a book which is carefully graded in terms of reading difficulty and controlled from the standpoint of vocabulary, sentence length, sentence complexity, and story setting. Practice exercises are contained in an accompanying workbook. In this system the presentation and reinforcement of skills are organized into careful sequence. In many programs supplementary and enrichment materials as well as evaluation instruments are available. Often referred to as the *basal reader program,* this system is used in one form or another by 80 to 95 percent of U.S. schools (Staiger, 1958; Chall, 1967).

Learning to read is considered to be a difficult task by the proponents of this system. The rationale seems to be that the teacher as well as the child can easily experience difficulty and even failure with reading instruction. Therefore, the controlled vocabulary approach seeks to avoid problems by controlling the teaching-learning situation. Systematic controls are placed on the materials the child uses in learning the complex act of reading and specific directions are given to the teacher for planning learning activities. Each element in the scope and sequence of the total reading program is organized so that movement of the child through the system continually refines and broadens his skill in reading.

We prefer the label *controlled vocabulary approach* for two reasons: (1) the name focuses specifically on the distinctive aspect of the system and (2) the more usual label *basal reader program* is so closely associated with specific commercially prepared materials that numerous inappropriate connotations are unavoidable. The discussion here will turn on the teaching-learning principles that underlie the controlled vocabulary approach and the limitations of this approach. The elements of the typical basal program are discussed in Chapter 4.

Rationale

Controlled vocabulary stories employ words that are believed to be a part of the vocabulary of almost all children. Word lists based on frequency of usage, such as those compiled by Dolch, Dale, and Murphy, are used as word sources. The controlled vocabulary approach is based on a principle commonly accepted by educators: proceed from the known to the unknown. The content and setting of controlled vocabulary stories reflect the same idea: begin with what is familiar to the learner. Neighborhood scenes with family and pets as the central characters are frequently found in primary grade controlled vocabulary stories. This careful control of vocabulary and story is intended to help the child learn to read by eliminating potentially troublesome factors such as unfamiliar words and story characters.

The principle of systematic repetition of words is another central element in the controlled vocabulary approach. The research of Gates (1938) indicates that repeated exposure to a word is necessary for mastery. Indeed, it has been reported that the average child requires approximately thirty repetitions of a word before he recognizes it on sight. In the controlled vocabulary approach a small number of new words is introduced in each story, and each new word is repeated a number of times to provide practice and reinforcement.

The readability of stories in the controlled vocabulary approach is carefully graded to require more reading skill from story to story and book to book. Sentence length and complexity, the number of characters, the variety of story settings, and the length of stories all gradually increase. Stories gradually require more understanding of sequence and more inference on the part of the reader. The learner is asked to assume more sophisticated reading tasks but he is led to do so in a systematic, controlled fashion.

Reading skills are taught with the same degree of organization and planning. The principles of continued practice and movement from the simple to the complex are also important in skill development. Workbook and suggested teacher-directed activities regularly introduce and reinforce reading skills. Finding the main idea is an example of a skill introduced early and developed in more difficult stories. (See Fig. 4.1.)

The completeness of the program is another aspect of the controlled vocabulary approach that should not be overlooked. Materials are provided for the learner and the teacher as well. Teaching suggestions that have been developed by teams of reading experts, as well as tests and other evaluation tools, are provided for the teacher. References are given for supplementary and enrichment materials such as filmstrips and reading games; recently many of these materials have been included in the program itself. The controlled vocabulary approach is not regarded by its proponents as a program that can teach all aspects of reading, but it is decidedly more complete and self-contained than any of the other systems for teaching reading.

Limitations

Some authorities have criticized the controlled vocabulary approach on the basis of the highly controlled nature of the program. They argue that present controlled vocabulary programs destroy rather than create an interest in learning to read. The critics (Spache, 1969; Strickland, 1968) point out that today's youngsters are sophisticated learners. Such criticisms are valid. Television has catapulted four-year-olds into space, under the sea, and into the heart of a living man, fourth graders can watch the proceedings of Congress or the United Nations in color.

In addition to television, technology, the critics argue, has further expanded the horizons of youngsters today by making transcontinental travel a common occurrence. Some children in Pittsburgh and Nashville stand a good chance of seeing Disneyland or the Astrodome before they are six years old. Families have more leisure time, rapid modes of transportation, and the means necessary for such travel. (The fact that many children have none of these experiences is notable and will be pursued in detail in a later chapter.)

The critics suggest, therefore, that word lists such as the Dale list are antiquated when compared with the vocabulary of a typical first grader. Furthermore, they declare that stories about Dick and Jane or Tom and Betty playing store in their backyard are both boring and insulting to the beginning reader. Studies such as those by Strickland (1962) and Loban (1963) demonstrate that today's learner arrives in grade one with astounding verbal facility. While estimates vary, the evidence currently available indicates that a six-year-old has a speaking vocabulary of at least 5000 words. The initial stories in the controlled vocabulary system contain language that is quite unreal. The six-year-old uses every form of sentence, including complex, compound, and complex-compound structures (Strickland, 1962). Children's oral utterances have also increased in length.

It should be noted, however, that educators have sometimes incorrectly judged the interests and reactions of children. The "dry" stories of the primary reading program may well be entirely satisfactory from the child's standpoint. Repetition of a word may be more of a blessing than a bore to the youngster who struggles to decode each word he encounters. (See Appendix A to discover the feelings associated with reading a story in an unfamiliar alphabet much as a beginning reader.) The criticisms cited above merit careful consideration, but one must not ignore the overwhelming success which controlled vocabulary programs have enjoyed.

Other criticisms of the controlled vocabulary approach are directed more at the misuse of the system than at the system itself. Despite cautions to the contrary, many educators regard the controlled vocabulary package as a total reading program. In some cases children do practically all of their reading in the graded reader and are never allowed to skip sections of the book. The workbook is regularly assigned without regard to individual need. Every suggested activity in the teacher's manual is indiscriminately followed. If the controlled vocabulary program has any responsibilities for this misuse, it is largely an indirect guilt since it *appears* to be a complete program.

Another disadvantage that has been cited is that the structured nature of the controlled vocabulary approach makes reading instruction seem artificial when compared to the uncontrolled reading a child does for recreation or in his other subjects. In this sense the controlled vocabulary approach does not present a realistic reading task; consequently, the important transfer of skills from the instructional program to application in everyday reading may be hampered. For example, seldom does the child begin reading a news item or directions for assembling a model airplane by studying the new vocabulary he will encounter. Yet as a regular procedure the controlled vocabulary system introduces new words prior to reading. Again, this criticism is not entirely directed at the system but at least partly at the manner in which teachers use it. Teachers' manuals often recommend that children be given the opportunity to practice reading skills in real-life settings. The apparent completeness of the controlled vocabulary approach may account in part for unsatisfactory emphasis on the transfer of skills.

Forms of the Controlled Vocabulary Approach

Despite a great deal of similarity among all controlled vocabulary systems, distinct differences do exist. Basically the differences have to do with the emphasis that is placed in beginning reading on learning to decode the language as opposed to reading for meaning. The importance of gaining meaning from what is read has been debated among proponents of the controlled vocabulary approach. Jeanne Chall points out that the issue is not a matter of decoding versus meaning getting, or vice versa, but rather a difference in emphasis. As the child learns a system for decoding the language, how much attention should be given to gaining meaning? On this issue controlled vocabulary programs fall into two major groups, different but not necessarily conflicting in their emphasis: (1) the *sound-symbol emphasis* and (2) the *meaning emphasis*. The rationale and limitations for each approach follow.

Sound-Symbol Emphasis

Written English contains a large number of irregular words. That is, words with similar spellings may be pronounced differently, as *low* and *cow*, or *break* and *leak*. While many people regard this irregularity as an oddity with no logical explanation, linguists have found this view to be incorrect. They have traced the English language back to the Anglo-Saxons of the fifth century, and by studying the influences of various tongues on Old English they have identified the origins of many words that appear to be irregularities today. The Viking invasion of England was responsible for some changes in Anglo-Saxon; later, Greek and Latin terms were introduced by Christian missionaries to England; and the French invasion of Britain in 1066 introduced a Norman influence that can still be observed in modern English. American English reflects all of these influences and incorporates as well many words contributed by the various cultural groups who emigrated to this country.

The irregularity of the sound-symbol relation of English is largely due to the way the language has evolved. New words have been added from other tongues but given an English (or American) pronunciation. The spelling and meaning of these words often do not change. Consequently, words that have a spelling incongruent with their pronunciation are still used as part of the spoken language. For example, *sea* and *see* were pronounced differently at one time, thus making two spellings desirable. Today the difference in spelling seems strange since the words are pronounced the same (Laird, 1953). Down through the ages various attempts to introduce a new spelling system have failed, and it seems unlikely that a major spelling reform will occur in the foreseeable future.

Rationale The sound-symbol system teaches the child to read by helping him learn a technique for breaking the English code. Emphasis is placed on knowing what symbol is associated with a sound. The learner builds words out of the elements he is able to decode. This process is often called a synthetic approach to reading.

Sound-symbol systems do not deny the irregularity of English but instead emphasize the regular aspects of the language. Even though *low* and *cow* are pronounced as nonrhyming words and thus demonstrate an irregularity, *how, bow, now, wow, pow, sow,* and *cow* do follow a regular pattern. Proponents of a sound-symbol emphasis believe that children should learn the patterns that are consistent and be taught to apply the appropriate rules or generalizations to new words. Once the correct associations between sounds and symbols have been learned, the child becomes an independent reader. Complete agreement does not exist on what patterns should be learned, the sequence or techniques for teaching the patterns, or even the code that should be employed. These differences will be explored in a later chapter on word recognition. All sound-symbol proponents emphasize that learning a means for breaking the language code should be an initial step in learning to read.

Sound-symbol proponents generally attach less importance to

gaining meaning from the English code. Some suggest that meaning is completely unimportant, that only a decoding technique is required (Flesch, 1955; Fries, 1962). Others report that meaning is closely associated with decoding, since all words encountered in beginning reading are part of the child's own vocabulary (Lefevre, 1964; Chall, 1967), but that no special effort need be made to emphasize meaning. These differences illustrate the fact that two distinct camps on the matter of meaning cannot be identified. If we could visualize a continuum ranging from strict decoding at one extreme to strict meaning at the other we would find proponents of the sound-symbol system at many points along the line.

Limitations   The most obvious and frequently cited limitation of the sound-symbol emphasis is that with it youngsters are taught an approach to reading which may later interfere with understanding. Since the primary goal of reading is to gain meaning from the printed page, an instructional system that teaches and reinforces strict attention to word symbols may develop inefficient reading habits. The logic of this criticism is sound but is unsupported by research evidence. Until more definite answers are available, the possibility of developing overanalytic readers should be recognized as a danger but not a proved limitation of the sound-symbol emphasis.

One clear limitation of the sound-symbol emphasis, however, is an overreliance on a single approach to word recognition. Youngsters with hearing difficulties or a style of learning not suited to an auditory approach are severely handicapped because of the emphasis placed on the differences among sounds. The association between sound and symbol is not readily grasped by all youngsters. This limitation exists for every system of teaching reading that emphasizes one mode of learning to the exclusion of others.

Many irregularities do exist in English despite the fact that sound-symbol advocates choose to emphasize the regularity of the language. A study by Clymer (1963) illustrates the many exceptions to widely accepted rules in primary grade reading material. Sound-symbol systems not only fail to help the reader unlock a new word when it is irregular, but they actually mislead and confuse him. This is a limitation of considerable importance, especially for the beginning reader who cannot employ other word-recognition techniques. Controlled vocabulary systems that shield the child from irregular sound-symbol words in his reader cannot control every book in the library or home.

Analysis of a word symbol by symbol is a very slow technique. Furthermore, unless a word is one the reader has previously heard and understood, merely assigning the correct sounds to each symbol and pronouncing the word does not provide a clue to meaning. As will be seen later, several other word-attack techniques provide clues to meaning.

Meaning Emphasis

Horace Mann in the 1840s challenged a long-accepted approach to the teaching of reading. For generations children had learned to read by grunting their way through the alphabet, then two-letter syllables, three-letter syllables, and so forth. Only after several years of "reading" instruction were meaningful words encountered (Durkin, 1965). Mann suggested that a more logical procedure would be to begin instruction with words, since meaning is associated with whole words. With this approach children could immediately apply their skills to meaningful stories, and hopefully develop a lifelong interest in reading.

Mann's ideas became predominant during the period 1840–1890 and again in the 1920s (Emans, 1968). Word analysis was delayed so that initial reading would focus on whole words and be meaningful. Mislabeled the *look-say approach,* the myth grew that with this system children never learned to analyze words. The sound-symbol relation was completely ignored, according to critics of the look-say approach.

Rationale The meaning system teaches the child to read by helping him memorize whole words. Emphasis is placed on knowing what printed symbol is associated with a word. The learner eventually analyzes the words he knows to understand sound-symbol associations. This system is often called an analytic approach to reading.

The meaning emphasis is based on the logic stated by Horace Mann over one hundred years ago. Since meaning is associated with whole words, the child should first learn to read whole words. No system suggests that all reading be taught on a whole-word or sight basis. Obviously sheer memorization of all words is both impractical and inefficient. The meaning emphasis typically includes study of the relation between sound and symbol, patterns or families of words, and similar analytic procedures. The emphasis is different from that of the sound-symbol approach primarily in the placement of word-analysis studies.

Different systems of meaning emphasis vary somewhat with respect to timing and procedures, but all present word-analysis activities after a body of sight words has been taught. The words that a child has memorized and can recognize at sight are used to develop generalizations concerning sound-symbol relations. For example, vowels at the end of one-syllable words usually have a long sound. Even the young reader who knows *he, she, be,* and *me* can readily see the principle at work in familiar words.

A major strength of the meaning approach is that from the outset children are encouraged to expect meaning from what they read. This expectation is difficult to develop if children have inadvertently learned to ignore meaning.

Another advantage of the meaning approach is that words and stories with meaning are more interesting for the child and easier to learn than nonmeaningful material. With this approach a child is more likely to develop a positive attitude toward reading.

Limitations   Critics of the meaning approach usually create a straw man for their attacks with their claim that in this system analysis is typically ignored. They complain that children do not learn to "sound out" words. The learner must therefore guess wildly at words and has no system for refining or checking his guesses. Such assertions may have been true thirty years ago, but they do not bear up under present practices. It may be realistic to suggest, however, that for some students an emphasis on meaning puts undue stress on guessing words.

Too, since an emphasis on gaining meaning places much importance on visual factors, the child who learns best through other modes may be at a disadvantage with this approach.

THE LANGUAGE EXPERIENCE APPROACH

In contrast to the structure and organization of the controlled vocabulary approach, the language experience approach springs directly from the interests and needs of the child. The teacher is provided with little or no structure and children create or select their own reading materials with a minimum of supervision.

Rationale

In the language experience approach reading takes its place as one additional language skill that is essential in learning to communicate. Speaking, listening, reading, and writing form the foundation for the exchange of ideas and information. Both common sense and research evidence indicate the interdependence of these four language skills (Loban, 1963; Strickland, 1968).

Good teaching begins with what is known to the child. The oral language that a child brings to school is an excellent record of his past experiences. The child with numerous enriching activities in his background is likely to use language which accompanies such experiences. Other youngsters lack oral facility with language because of inadequate opportunity and stimulation. Reading instruction that utilizes the language of the child automatically builds on what is known. For example, the youngster who shares the antics of a pet dog with his classmates has a genuine involvement in the telling of an incident. The language experience approach to reading would capitalize on this opportunity by recording the child's story in print. The teacher with the help of the child writes a brief description of "My Dog Rex." In this way the child learns that what he thinks he can say; what he says he can write; and what he can write he can read (Van Allen, 1963). The story belongs to the child. His background, his experiences, and his self-image are all employed in teaching him to read.

Later the child records his own thoughts as he learns to write. The same personal involvement is retained and the correlation of the language skills is continually reinforced. Books that meet the interest of the child can be selected and later read to become the stimulus for additional oral and written activities.

The language experience approach is adaptable to individual, group, and class instruction. Activities can be devised that permit each child to write his own story, for example. Group activities are easily devised with dramatizations, sharing through oral reading, and instruction by the teacher on a specific skill—all samples of worthwhile exchange. Class projects could include book reports, reading a description of a recent field trip taken by the class, and listening to the teacher read orally.

Because so little structure and systematic skill development are incorporated into the language arts plan the teacher must continually evaluate and diagnose the needs of the students. While this method places a great deal of responsibility on the teacher, it also encourages careful assessment of each child with the result that the opportunity for individualized instruction is maximized. One major strength of the language experience approach is that each learner progresses at an individual rate. His interests can lead him in many directions and the freedom to explore promotes creativity.

Skill development is conducted in a meaningful context through the language experience approach. Since no set sequence must be followed, the teacher can use ongoing activities to introduce and reinforce skills as they are needed. The primary advantage of such an arrangement is its emphasis on reasoning and utilization of skills as opposed to memorization.

Especially important in this approach is the relation that is developed between the spoken word and its graphic form. In beginning reading the teacher writes out stories that usually come directly from the child's experiences. Introduced in this fashion, the child easily understands reading as a method of communications with an exchange of meaning being the primary goal.

Just as the interrelatedness of the language skills is a central

FIGURE 3-1 A Learning Chart

A child's knowledge of children's fables can also be the source of his language experience story. In this chart a child has given his interpretation of the story of the tortoise and the hare. (Photo by Carl B. Smith)

element of the language experience approach, the involvement of many senses is also an important feature of this system. The child is continually interrelating visual, oral, and auditory stimuli, frequently with some kinesthetic involvement as well. It follows that with this approach no learning modality is emphasized to the exclusion of others. The child having a strength in a particular learning mode is not handicapped when learning to read with this system since strengths can be emphasized and limitations circumvented. The child with poor auditory memory, for example, can overcome his deficiency through other learning channels more suited to him.

Limitations

The fundamental limitation of the language experience approach is the expertness required to make it operate. Because of the lack of structure and prepared materials, the classroom teacher assumes far more responsibility with this system than in the controlled vocabulary approach, for example. While the flexibility inherent in this plan makes the individualization of instruction more likely, it also raises the risk of creating a haphazard, incidental reading program.

The development of reading skills requires some organization in order to build readiness for subsequent skills. For example, following a sequence of events is a skill that depends on the ability to find main ideas and recognize transitions. Without instruction and practice on underlying skills, higher levels of competency are not attainable. A skillful teacher is capable of developing such a sequence for individual children. In order to instruct thirty individuals properly, however, superior ability and organization are required.

The language experience approach does not eliminate the use of commercially prepared materials, but it does place primary emphasis on teacher- or child-prepared materials. Again, this feature of the system maximizes the opportunity to individualize instruction, but it also places enormous demands on the teacher. It is commendable that with this system all the children do not use the same workbook which is regularly completed in spite of individual needs. On the other hand, practice exercises are highly desirable to reinforce skills and provide evidence of mastery. In the absence of a standardized workbook the teacher must develop or find appropriate materials. The same is true of books written with a desired reading difficulty or filmstrips helpful in supplementing a story.

Although not regarded as a limitation by some educators, the absence of structure with regard to vocabulary, sentence structure, and concept development inherent in the language experience system may be troublesome for some youngsters. The planned repetition evidently required by some children in order to learn to recognize a word at sight is difficult to achieve with the language experience approach. The large number of words introduced by the variety of incidents children experience and write about places an additional burden on the learner. While research evidence indicates that even young children have a remarkable grasp of oral language, it is not clear whether the same assumption concerning language can be made for learning to read. It is possible that concepts or sentence structures that a child easily grasps in an oral setting become much more difficult when the tasks of decoding and interpreting written symbols are added to that of understanding. Additional evidence gathered over a period of years is required on this matter.

THE PROGRAMMED APPROACH

Based on the work of behavioral psychologists (Skinner, 1954), programmed instruction teaches by taking the student through a series of carefully planned steps, often in the form of statements or questions, culminating in some predesignated terminal behavior. For example, a beginning reader can be led through a step-by-step procedure to recognize a family of words that rhyme with *cat*. Typically the terminal behavior is observable or behavioral. In this case the child would demonstrate his newly acquired skill or knowledge by correctly picking from a list of ten words the five that have the same spelling pattern as *cat*.

Programmed instruction often requires a series of responses on the part of the learner. The steps in a program are arranged so that correct responses are practically certain. Clues are often provided to help the learner. For example, only the last two letters may be missing from the correct response to a question or statement in the program. As the program proceeds the clues become fewer and the learner must provide more of the correct word or answer himself. Eventually the learner supplies an entire word without the benefit of prompts.

This process of gradual clue withdrawal is referred to as *successive approximation*, and it is by a series of such approximations that the learner's behavior is "shaped" (Skinner, 1961).

Most programmed instruction provides immediate feedback to the learner concerning the correctness of his responses. After the learner supplies a response the program provides the correct answer for comparison with the learner's response. Since each step is carefully designed to avoid incorrect responses, the learner is afforded immediate reinforcement. Proceeding a small step at a time, he can immediately know his progress and is rewarded for each correct response. These features make learning efficient and provide real support for the programmed approach. An example of a programmed exercise is presented below.

Self-pacing is another important aspect of programmed instruction. Each learner can progress through a program at his own rate. The able learner is not held back by slower classmates while very slow youngsters can take whatever time they need with each step

SAMPLE PROGRAM ON PHONICS

Directions: Place a piece of paper on the page below at the number 1. Read the statement and write in the word you think fits. Next move your paper down to line number 2. Compare your answer with the correct answer. If you are correct, go on to line 3 repeating the procedure. If you are incorrect, go back to see why your answer was wrong. Then proceed to line 3.

1	One approach to the teaching of reading is by emphasizing sound-symbol associations. Often called phonics, in this approach the child is taught to decode by associating a sound with a _____.	
2		symbol
3	Several strategies can be used to teach sound-symbol associations. Regardless of the strategy, the approach emphasizing sound-symbol is called _____.	
4		phonics
5	One phonics approach teaches the child by beginning with individual letters and the _____ associated with each letter.	
6		sound
7	By practicing the sound-symbol association, the child learns automatic responses that help him sound out words letter by _____.	
8		letter
9	Once the child has a sound for every letter he can sound out _____.	
10		words
11	This approach is called a synthetic approach to phonics. In the synthetic approach the child learns to associate individual letters and _____.	
12		sounds
13	Another approach has the child learn a small body of words at sight. Similarities among these words are then observed by the child. With this approach the child first reads whole _____.	
14		words

or frame. With the programmed approach the slow learner makes as many responses as the bright student and suffers fewer failures than he would in a typical classroom setting.

Programs are often written to develop specific skills and concepts. Since children work independently in programmed materials, the teacher can easily match the learner with a program that meets his individual needs. A youngster who experiences difficulty with short vowel sounds, for example, can be assigned to remedial work in a program suited specifically to this need. Too, children who are absent and might not otherwise be able to make up important lessons are able to do so with the programmed approach. The child simply begins where he left off before he was absent.

Perhaps most important, the programmed approach presents skills and concepts in a carefully organized, logically sequenced series of steps. Instructional goals are established ahead of time and each step contributes to the eventual achievement of the objectives. Those responsible for developing programs are alert to possible confusion or errors and anticipate them, and systematic research is conducted to guarantee that a program leads to the desired behavior.

Limitations

Such pains are taken to eliminate the possibility that the student will make an incorrect response in programmed materials that little challenge or interest may remain for the learner. We have found that once the novelty of this approach has worn off students may find it monotonous.

In addition, the step-by-step sequence of programmed materials tends to be extremely slow for most learners. The more able learner in particular may be bored by repetition of what to him is obvious. In a few programs an adjustment in sequence, often called *branching*, permits those who need less background to skip ahead and work at a faster rate. When branching is not provided, however, every student, fast or slow, goes through exactly the same steps. The argument that able students can pace themselves is not a satisfactory provision for individual needs.

The interaction between teacher and child is not completely obviated by the programmed approach. Indeed, freed from constant group work and paper correcting, the teacher may have more time for such interaction in a classroom using programmed materials. However, the impersonality of programmed instruction is an obvious limitation of this approach. Opportunities for discussion and exchange of ideas are decidedly reduced. The teacher is less responsible for instruction and therefore may know less about the needs of individual children.

At a time when many educators are urging greater freedom of thought and more creativity in the classroom the programmed approach, with its built-in emphasis on a single correct answer, may not be contributing to our educational goals. Certainly, for example, interpretive and creative reading are worthy segments of an instructional program, yet it seems unlikely that programmed materials as presently conceived can effectively stimulate students in these areas of learning.

Finally—and ironically—in most programmed approaches to the teaching of reading children must be able to read in order to respond. The child who has difficulty in reading is obviously at a disadvantage in such a program. The youngster with a weakness in one learning modality is particularly handicapped. A paper and pencil program, for example, places emphasis on the visual mode. While a tape recorded program could be employed with such a child, few are available. With most programmed instruction a premium is placed on the visual mode of learning.

THE INDIVIDUALIZED APPROACH

As the name implies, the individualized approach teaches reading by permitting each pupil to progress at his own rate. Nearly all reading is done in books that the child selects himself. Conferences between the teacher and the child are held regularly to check progress and identify needs. Grouping is seldom practiced, although occasionally interest groups are formed. Most skill instruction is provided during the conference or in small groups that meet over a short period of time on the basis of need. The students often present book reports as a means of sharing their experiences with classmates.

The idea behind the individualized approach is that given the opportunity to pursue his own interests, the child will be eager and willing to read. This view is in contrast to that of several other systems which impose on the child a series of stories, usually in the form of a graded reader. Self-selection of reading materials also provides the child with an opportunity to build a positive self-image by strengthening his own ego. His interests and desires are an important part of the reading program. The close association between pleasant personal experiences and reading activities is a powerful factor in developing lifelong readers.

Furthermore, a reading program based on self-selection closely approximates the reading activities of a nonschool setting. Outside of school adults as well as children usually read only what they choose to read for recreation or information. School reading programs emphasize assigned reading, follow-up discussions, and related skill activities do not resemble the reading demands of adult life. The strongest aspect of the individualized system may be that it bridges the gap between reading for school and reading for real life purposes.

Another outstanding feature of the individualized approach is the regular interaction that takes place between the teacher and the learner. This arrangement not only facilitates instruction that meets the unique needs of each child but it also guarantees the child an undivided segment of the teacher's attention. As the teacher comes to understand the personality of each child through such personal contacts the child grows both emotionally and educationally.

The individualized approach has much in common with the language experience approach. An important distinction between the two, however, is the role of writing. Individualized reading depends primarily on prepared materials such as library books while in the language experience approach children prepare much of their own reading materials.

Many aspects of the individualized approach fit into and supplement the broader language experience approach to reading instruction, however. For example, the teacher assumes a great deal of responsibility for organizing the instructional program in the individualized approach. From a positive standpoint the flexibility and freedom of such an arrangement enables the teacher to make whatever adjustments are necessary to individualize instruction. A premium is placed on being able to diagnose the needs of each student, and the opportunity to differentiate instruction is clearly available. Only the teacher's ability and the resources available to him limit the effectiveness of the instructional program.

LIMITATIONS

Essential to an effective individualized reading program is a wealth of imaginative reading materials. Each classroom must have a supply of books and other materials on a variety of topics written at several reading levels. The school library must include reference volumes and both fiction and nonfiction books. For this system of teaching reading Jeanette Veatch (1959) recommends that a school contain at least twenty to thirty books per child. Thus according to this formula a school with twenty classrooms requires 6000 volumes. A knowledgeable librarian who is present on a regular basis is also important to the success of the individualized approach. Obviously, one limitation of this system is the tremendous amount of resources necessary to implement it. Many school districts cannot meet this requirement and consequently cannot initiate an individualized system.

FIGURE 3-2   A Teacher-Pupil Conference

Valuable interaction can occur between teacher and pupil in a conference situation. Individual needs can be identified and instructional plans drawn when attention is focused specifically on one child. (Photo by Suzanne Szasz)

Like the language experience approach, the individualized method is characterized by flexibility and variation according to the needs of the learner. Here too an experienced classroom teacher is required who can assume considerable responsibility in planning imaginative learning activities and developing or locating materials appropriate to beginning readers.

To fulfill his role in the individualized approach the classroom teacher must know children's literature. Even though selection of materials is an important characteristic of this plan, it is the teacher who must guide and upgrade the child's tastes and interests. Too, in order to check his students' progress in comprehension and skills the teacher must be familiar with the book being discussed.

Given the resources required by the individualized approach to reading, a master teacher can truly meet the needs of the individual learner with this method. More than any other approach the effectiveness of the system is directly related to the ability of the teacher.

MODES OF LEARNING

The trend in modern education toward individualized instruction, as we mentioned earlier, is based on the fact that all children do not learn by the same means. Research literature focuses on four primary modes of learning: (1) visual, (2) auditory, (3) kinesthetic, and (4) multisensory (Mills, 1964; Figruel, 1968). Most children have relative strengths and weaknesses with regard to learning modes. Some youngsters learn more effectively when they see similarities and differences between stimuli (visual), others when they hear differences and similarities between stimuli (auditory) (Cooper, 1969). Most children are able to learn through all modes, though one is usually more efficient than the others.

The flexibility with which children learn is evidenced in the fact that for decades most teaching of reading was directed at the auditory mode. Children were expected to sound the letters of a word in order to read it. Certainly many kinesthetic and visual learners were at a disadvantage under these circumstances but managed to learn to read anyway. Later, emphasis on the visual mode favored another type of learner, but most children still learned to read. In effect, many children learned to read despite the instructional system, not because of it. This situation was particularly true in cases where the individual strengths of learners were ignored. Unfortunately, current reading instruction seldom takes into account the learning mode of youngsters, thus continuing an unsatisfactory practice from the past.

We know that no single system for teaching reading is superior for all learners. Rather, each learner has strengths and weaknesses that make one system preferable to another for his particular needs.

The role of the teacher is to match the learner and the instructional system. In order to match effectively the learner with an instructional system that emphasizes the appropriate learning mode, the teacher must (1) know which modes of learning are emphasized by each system and (2) be able to determine what mode is best for each child.

Learning Modes Emphasized by the Instructional Systems

No system of teaching reading depends on a single mode of learning. Each system includes some learning activities that appeal primarily to one mode and other activities that appeal to other modes. Overall, one learning mode is usually *emphasized* in a large majority of the instructional activities. The youngster having a strength in the learning mode emphasized by a given instructional system can be expected to benefit more than a youngster with a different strength.

The Controlled Vocabulary Approach

The controlled vocabulary approach with emphasis on sound-symbol relation has three distinct approaches to teaching the child to decode language. First, the phonics approach emphasizes the auditory learning mode. In this approach children must be able to hear the differences between sounds and associate each sound with a written symbol. Learners who experience difficulty with auditory discrimination or auditory memory are handicapped by this emphasis on the auditory mode (Bond and Tinker, 1967). Second, two other decoding methods, the linguistic approach and the new alphabet approach, emphasize the visual learning mode. Here one is expected to recognize differences and similarities among written symbols. Learners who are weak in visual discrimination or visual memory will find learning difficult with this approach.

The controlled vocabulary approach with emphasis on meaning, presents the learner with a primarily visual task. Words are learned as wholes with general shape and length being primary clues. Children who experience difficulty with visual learning tasks will be handicapped by this approach. Later, auditory and kinesthetic modes are often featured by many meaning-emphasis approaches.

The Language Experience Approach

The language experience approach utilizes all learning modes. Activities such as those described earlier which feature the interrelatedness of the language skills naturally involve all sensory channels. The learner uses the auditory mode as stories are dictated or read aloud. When the child writes a story or takes part in a field trip he uses kinesthetic mode. When the child reads a story written by himself or a friend he uses the visual mode. Most of these and similar activities require that each learning mode be used in some combination with other modes. The youngster with a weakness in a particular learning style can still be handicapped using this approach unless adjustments are made. However, the very nature of this approach to reading instruction facilitates such adjustments.

The Programmed Approach

Most programmed materials for reading instruction are in printed form. In such cases the learner is largely dependent on the visual mode. Since most programs of this type require a written response, the kinesthetic mode is often employed as well. Some programs feature tape recordings, talking typewriters, or computers to accompany or replace a printed workbook. The auditory mode, or more accurately a combination of modes, is employed in these programs. Since the involvement of many learning modes is desirable, this approach is preferable to a printed program only. As presently constituted, however, programmed materials for reading instruction lean heavily on the visual mode and handicap learners with deficiencies in this area.

The Individualized Approach

It is difficult to generalize concerning the learning mode emphasized in the individualized approach. Certainly the independent reading of library books is primarily a visual activity. However, skill-building activities can take nearly any form since in this system no structured program is followed. Thus the teacher determines in large part the learning mode that is emphasized.

In the usual individualized reading program all modes of learning are utilized. The activities related to sharing books require that children listen, write, and speak in addition to reading silently and orally. The skill-development program is likely to further utilize all modes, but this depends on the individual teacher.

Matching the Learner and the System

The matter of assessing a child's strengths and weaknesses with regard to learning mode is not an exact and simple process, yet the correct matching of the learner and an instructional system is dependent upon this assessment.

Given the time and opportunity, most classroom teachers could learn to administer the *Mills Learning Test* (1954). This test permits the examiner to determine the learning mode that is most effective for the child. A similar technique which the teacher can use in the classroom is described by Harris (1961). Basically the procedure requires the teacher to present several words to a child using different methods of presentation. Each method emphasizes a different learning mode. The method resulting in the most effective acquisition and retention of the stimulus words is taken to be the child's best learning mode. Instruction is then adjusted accordingly.

Ladd (n.d.) suggests the following procedure using nonsense words and numbers.

Informal Test of Learning Modalities

Any informal test must be considered only as a means of observing the learner, but it does give the teacher a chance to look at some specific behaviors of the child. The following technique indicates one way of observing what the child does while using several modes of learning.

The technique involves the child's learning five examples or symbols by having them presented through different senses. Since response is always in writing, it is possible to administer the test to a small group.

I. AUDITORY MEMORY

Say, "Listen to the numbers that I will say. When I am finished, pick up your pencil and write the numbers on your paper."

1. 3-4-1-7   "Write."
2. 8-4-2-3-9   "Write."
3. 3-8-9-1-7-4   "Write."
4. 5-1-7-4-2-3-8   "Write."
5. 1-6-4-5-9-7-6-3 "Write."

II. VISUAL MEMORY

Say, "I am going to show you some pictures and some words. I'll show you one at a time and then ask you to write the word that fits the picture."

	Picture Card	Word Card
1.	(Picture)	rac
2.	(Picture)	lisk
3.	(Picture)	ered
4.	(Picture)	iregt
5.	(Picture)	arechet

III. KINESTHETIC MEMORY

Say, "I am going to show you some word cards. I want you to look at the word and write it in the air. I will then put the card aside while you write the word on your paper."

Word Card

1. nma   "Write."
2. archi   "Write."
3. roflo   "Write."
4. lpneci   "Write."
5. tilapmal   "Write."

IV. COMBINATION MEMORY

Say, "I will say a word and ask you to repeat it after me. Then I will show the word to you and ask you to write it in the air. Finally you will write it on paper."

Listen	Say	Show	Air	Write
1. pmal	"	"	"	"
2. sifh	"	"	"	"
3. taniph	"	"	"	"
4. latlilma	"	"	"	"
5. uosehmo	"	"	"	"

The alert and skilled teacher can supplement these more formal procedures with careful observation during instructional activities. For example, the youngster who consistently fails to understand skill-building exercises in a workbook, worksheet, or other written form may be a poor visual learner. Noting this pattern of behavior, the teacher can experiment with auditory exercises taped and played for the child by means of a tape recorder and headphones. Or both types of exercises, visual and auditory, can be tried at the same time. The key to making the necessary adjustments is the teacher's attitude; the diagnostic teacher automatically suspects that failure to learn may be related to an inappropriate matching of instructional method and learning mode. Attempts at correction should involve experimenting with other modes of input. Ideally such experimentation will enable the teacher to identify a learning mode for each youngster and point the way to necessary adjustments in the choice of instructional systems.

COMBINING SYSTEMS FOR EFFECTIVE INSTRUCTION

There are four distinct approaches to the teaching of reading, each having unique strengths and weaknesses. Since no single system is superior for all children, it is necessary to match the preferred learning mode of the student learner with an appropriate instructional system.

We may appear to be suggesting that every classroom teacher must use all four systems to meet the needs of all her students. Actually, with some qualification, we are doing just that. The classroom teacher must select one system he endorses and understands. As his experience and expertness permit, he must supplement his chosen system with elements borrowed from the other systems.

Typically, the controlled vocabulary approach is the system a teacher will employ when he first teaches. Because of its structure and suggested teaching activities, this is an excellent system for the novice. At first the new teacher will no doubt follow the teacher's manual rather closely. The sequence of skills and wealth of prepared materials which it offers are necessities for the beginner. Soon, however, the teacher must begin to be selective in his use of suggested activities. The unique nature of his own students dictate certain adjustments. The authors of the controlled vocabulary materials cannot anticipate the tremendous variety of teachers and students who will use their products. Consequently they aim their materials at the "average" learner and usually admit that considerable adjustment will be necessary. After all, it is the teacher, not the textbook author, who requires every child to complete all the pages in his workbook rather than selecting appropriate ones.

Eventually the teacher should be adding and deleting so much from the controlled vocabulary materials that they hardly resemble the original program. How long does this transition take? One cannot say exactly; some teachers achieve the break from close adherence to the system by the end of their first year while others may follow the program rather closely for five or ten years.

A progression from the controlled vocabulary approach to the language experience approach seems quite natural. At one extreme is structure that approaches rigidity; at the opposite extreme is flexibility approaching randomness. Somewhere within this range the teacher must find a balance that suits his own abilities and meets the needs of his class. From year to year the exact nature of the balance should vary depending on the children being taught.

In addition, the teacher must incorporate in his program features of the individualized approach and the programmed approach as they are appropriate. All children require the opportunity to read in a setting that corresponds to real life. Therefore, elements of the individualized approach are employed in an effective reading program. Occasional self-selection of materials and individual pupil-teacher conferences are two aspects of the individualized system which merit special use. At the same time, programmed materials, used judiciously, can be an invaluable aid to students who benefit from this type of presentation. For example, series of programs designed to teach specific spelling patterns are an excellent resource to have available. The teacher could then draw on such a collection as the need occurred.

Figure 3.3 illustrates how a teacher can begin with a controlled vocabulary approach and gradually expand her techniques to incorporate useful aspects of other systems. The move from a structured to a nonstructured reading program will correspondingly increase the amount of individualized instruction the child will receive.

SUMMARY

The search for one reading method that is best for all children has been fruitless. A more realistic approach is to recognize that individual learners benefit from different instructional systems. Further research on instructional methods will continue to be plagued by a myriad of uncontrolled factors that severely limit the results of such studies.

There are four distinct systems of reading instruction: (1) the controlled vocabulary approach, (2) the language experience approach, (3) the programmed approach, and (4) the individualized approach. The rationale and limitations of each system were discussed in detail.

The controlled vocabulary approach is the most highly structured of the four systems. Constraints are placed on the vocabulary, sentence length, sentence complexity, and story setting in this system. The learner uses a textbook written at a specified difficulty level and a workbook containing practice exercises. The teacher is provided with a guide which contains teaching suggestions and activities. The careful control of all aspects of the system is designed to make the learning tasks manageable for the child. The complexity of the tasks gradually increases as the learner grows in his ability to handle them. A major criticism of this approach is that such a high degree of control is unnecessary for the sophisticated child entering school today. Two forms of the controlled vocabulary approach were discussed, the sound-symbol emphasis and the meaning emphasis.

The language experience approach builds the reading program around the child's own stories and interests. The interrelatedness of the language arts is emphasized by this system. Essentially the rationale of the approach is that what a child thinks he can say; what he says he can write; what he writes he can read. The early reading activities are based on stories created by the child. Later, books are used to stimulate and create activities which grow into language

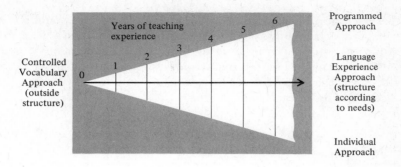

FIGURE 3-3   Combining Instructional Systems

As the teacher grows in experience he is able to move from the structure of the controlled vocabulary approach to a structure according to need, borrowing elements from various approaches.

arts experiences. The major limitation of this system is its lack of structure in terms of skill development and sequence. In this approach the teacher must assume a large measure of responsibility for providing his own structure.

The programmed approach teaches reading by taking the student through a series of highly organized, carefully planned steps. The learner makes an overt response at each step, and obtains immediate knowledge of his success or failure. The child works at his own pace in such materials and experiences almost constant success regardless of his ability. Programmed learning has not yet been used for creating a total reading program. The major limitations of this system are its impersonal nature and its failure to provide for creative, divergent thinking.

The individualized approach is essentially a reading program based on self-selection of library books. Each child selects his own reading material, reads it independently, and regularly meets individually with his teacher for discussion and skill activities. Personal interests and genuine ego involvement make motivation extremely high in this plan. For schools able to supply the enormous amount of materials necessary to implement it, this system offers definite advantages. The major limitation of this approach lies in the amount of responsibility placed on the classroom teacher for planning and executing the system. In particular the teacher must be capable of assessing and guiding a complete reading skills program for a whole class of children simultaneously.

Realistically the beginning teacher is likely to use the highly structured controlled vocabulary approach until his knowledge and skill enable him to shift toward less structure, as in the language experience approach. Ideally the best of each system is combined so that a teacher draws on the strengths of all systems. Since the learning styles of children differ and a variety of approaches should be used to avoid undue emphasis on a single learning mode. Procedures were discussed for discovering the mode of learning that is most efficient for each child.

TERMS

instructional systems	individualized approach
controlled vocabulary approach	sound-symbol emphasis
language experience approach	meaning emphasis
programmed approach	learning mode

Chapter 4

Selecting Materials for Instruction

The first time you open the cabinets in your new classroom you will probably find a large portion of books, charts, and games for use in the teaching of reading. After evaluating these materials you may find that you need additional ones. If you are lucky, you may have a budget to purchase materials. Intelligent selection and use of teaching materials requires an evaluation of the specific needs of the children in your class.

As a teacher you need to know what kinds of instructional materials are available, where you can get additional information about them, when to use particular types, and how to choose appropriate materials for your students. Certainly there is no dearth of books to choose from. Dozens of basic reading series have been published, many in the past few years, and thousands of supplementary items are produced each year. With this wealth of possibilities and with an ever-increasing school budget for materials, you must develop some guidelines to help you in making your selections. Answers to such questions as the following will aid you in your evaluation of instructional materials:

What is the difference between core reading materials and supplementary reading materials?

Are materials written to match specific instructional systems?

How does a teacher match materials with learners?

What criteria should be used in purchasing materials?

A knowledge of materials and guidelines for selecting materials are priorities for every teacher of reading. There are two reasons for this: first, today's teacher has a significant voice in the selection of classroom materials, both on text selection committees and in the purchase of supplementary books for use in his own classroom; second, the 1960s were marked by an explosion of educational materials. How to sift the valuable from the less valuable becomes a decision the classroom teacher frequently has to make.

This chapter reviews the various kinds of materials available for use with the four systems of teaching reading identified in the previous chapter, discusses their use for different types of students, and offers some principles for evaluating materials. For purposes of discussion, materials are classified here as basic, or core, materials and supplementary materials. Core materials are those that carry the basic sequence of reading skills within one of the systems. Supplementary materials are library books, games, practice readers, enrichment readers, newspapers, and magazines which are used to reinforce, enrich, and personalize reading instruction.

MAKING DECISIONS ABOUT MATERIALS

Instructional materials play an important role in teaching reading. But materials are only tools or means; they are not ends. Materials do not constitute a reading program, but they help to achieve a reading program. Since they are tools, decisions concerning the selection of materials should be based upon their capability to assist leaners in achieving specific reading tasks.

How does a teacher know what materials to use? The answer to this question involves five steps:

1. Collect data to identify the needs of the students.
2. Develop an instructional plan based on needs.
3. Review materials that seem to fit the plan.
4. Use general criteria to evaluate materials.
5. Select materials to meet the needs of the students.

How to identify the needs of students will be a continuing concern of this text. This chapter considers specifically the criteria which the teacher must use to evaluate available instructional materials.

Ideally, the teacher will find and use materials that match perfectly the needs of the student. Actually, perfect matching is not always possible to achieve. Assessment techniques are not always accurate; commercial materials are not always available for specific needs; money may not be available for the desired products; or school policy may limit a teacher's authority to use materials other than those provided by the school's official curriculum committee. Nonetheless, the teacher should do his best to reconcile the needs of the student reader and the materials available. At times he may find it necessary to improvise, to develop his own worksheets and exercises, and to enlist the children to bring in books and games that will lead them toward their instructional objectives.

CORE MATERIALS

Core materials are basic tools designed to give structure to reading and sequence to the reading skills. Most materials of this kind can be classified in one of the four systems for teaching reading, although some may be used in two or more instructional systems. It may not always be clear whether an item or a series of books belongs to core materials or to supplementary materials. Classification decisions between core and supplementary materials were not made arbitrarily, but are intended to give perspective and direction to the discussion of materials.

Materials for the Controlled Vocabulary System

The controlled vocabulary system offers a large quantity and variety of materials. That is due to the long history these materials have had and to the subcategories under the controlled vocabulary system. These materials are here presented in three groups: materials controlled by frequency of word use, sound-symbol materials, and new alphabet materials. The last category includes the initial teaching alphabet (ITA), Words In Color, and other unusual core materials that are related to the controlled vocabulary system.

Materials Controlled by Frequency of Word Use

Beginning reading series that generally apply a vocabulary control based on the frequency of word use usually contain books with a grade range from kindergarten through the sixth or eighth grade. Skill development ranges from readiness activities (skills and concepts needed prior to formal reading activity) to comprehension exercises using different kinds of expository selections. Between those two poles come word-recognition skills and meaning skills arranged in a sequence that corresponds to the physical and intellectual development of the child. The books and audio and visual aids that make up the program would fill a large closet and provide for a surprising number of different classroom activities. Harris' *Guide to Materials for Reading Instruction* (Harris, 1968) lists over one hundred different items for the reading series published by Ginn and Company, books fairly typical of those that control vocabulary on the basis of frequency of word use.

The results of using only a few high frequency words in the stories have been lampooned often. Especially in the very first stories, when the children know only a dozen or so words, the repetition and the story content seem ridiculous. Indeed, the controlled vocabulary approach is built with restraints that almost prohibit stimulating prose through most of the first grade books. Consider this sample story:

New words: *books, school*

Bob at School
Bob goes to *school.*
Each day Bob goes to *school.*
See Bob and Jane.
They like *school.*

There are *books* in *school.*
Bob has *books.*
Jane has *books.*
The read *books* in *school.*

Try writing a story for use in the first semester of the first grade and see if you can do better than other authors of such stories. Write a story using the following set of circumstances:

1.   Thirty-five words have been introduced. They are:

ride	look	you	come	something	pony	a
fast	work	balls	here	is	father	go
see	at	wants	airplane	dinner	apple	we
and	for	red	I	the	get	surprise
mother	said	chair	can	stop	toys	this

2.   Five new words are to be introduced in this story. You may select any additional five one- or two-syllable words that are frequently used. You may use the names of people without counting them as new words.
3.   Each of the five new words is to be repeated at least five times during the course of the story.
4.   Describe the illustrations for each of the six to eight pages of the story. The pictures must support the story at this point.

When you have finished your story compare it with others written under similar circumstances, for example, the last two stories in *My Little Green Story Book,* the third preprimer in the Ginn 100 basic reading series. This exercise should demonstrate that the stories in the early readers of a controlled vocabulary series do not spring from literary inspiration. To a large degree the usable vocabulary determines the content of the story. This fact should indicate how to use most of the early reading selections. They are designed for practice in word and sentence recognition and for getting meaning from short selections. When an interesting or stimulating story does appear the class should be encouraged to react to it and explore it. The higher the level of the core material, the more likely are the stories to have literary merit. In those instances, besides practice in word and sentence recognition, students practice some higher reading skills such as analysis, evaluation, and synthesis.

In the late 1960s publishers began to loosen the restrictions on the vocabulary introduced into the readers. Authors thus had more freedom in writing stories and in developing exercises to be included in the series.

Tests

An attractive feature of most controlled vocabulary reading series is the testing program. Tests are often included that are specifically oriented to the skills treated in a unit or in a book. These tests can be used for readiness or entry purposes, or they can be used to check on performance following a unit of instruction.

For example, before learning to read a simple story in a pre-primer a child learns how to "read" pictures. As a means of evaluating the student's sense of storytelling, a readiness test for the preprimers would ask him to look at a series of pictures and put them in the proper order. Most reading series tests concentrate on a set of specific skills and thus can be used as criteria for proceeding with instruction in new skills. Chapter 6 gives several examples of this kind of criterion testing.

A Complete Package of Materials

Though a large number of items is usually available with a controlled vocabulary basal series, only three items are here defined as core materials — a reader for the child, an activity book or workbook, and the teacher's guide. Some authorities object to the inclusion of a workbook because it is sometimes misused as busywork for the child. Practically speaking, however, workbooks contain many valuable practice exercises. The teacher's guide is used to determine the objectives the author of a series established for a given story, what procedures he recommends for teaching the skills, and the kinds of practice activities he believes will reinforce direct instruction by the teacher.

Books for Special Populations

One principle used in constructing readers controlled by frequency of word use is that early reading should center on situations and characters with which the children can easily identify. Thus the home and school are often used as a setting and young children as the primary characters in the stories. Until the 1960s the major reading series pictured blond Caucasian families living in middle class suburban homes. Obviously a large percentage of American youngsters do not fit into this picture and supposedly had difficulty identifying with the setting and the characters. Recently almost all of the major reading series began to include black faces and yellow faces in the illustrations. Some changed a few stories to reflect settings that inner-city children might recognize. In several instances entirely new series were written using vocabulary, settings, and characters that fit the inner-city child. One such series is the *Bank Street Readers*, named after the Bank Street College in New York City which experimented with the development of the materials and demonstrated their use for the schools of New York City. The vocabulary of the Bank Street series is quite different from that of the typical suburban reading program. In the list below you can see how the story selections in the first grade have affected the vocabulary used by the Bank Street Readers as compared with the vocabulary from the Ginn 100 series.

Bank Street Readers
Vocabulary 1:1

boats	drill	policeman	snowplow
books	highways	potatoes	store
boxes	lunchroom	sea	train
car	mailman	sidewalk	truck
cat	plane	skates	tugboat

Ginn Reading Series
Vocabulary 1:1

barn	ducks	mouse	quack
bunny	farm	paint	tree
cake	hen	party	turkey
candles	kitten	pets	wagon
cowboy	mill	plant	wheat

Use of Materials Controlled by Word Frequency

If the teacher, on the basis of an evaluation of the learning and environmental characteristics of his students, decides to use word-frequency materials, he should choose a specific series of books based on the content of the stories and the difficulty level of the vocabulary.

"Pull over!" calls the policeman.
The man stops his car.
"You were going too fast!"
says the policeman.

The man goes away in his car.
But this time, he goes slowly.

115

FIGURE 4-1   A Basal Reader Page

Reprinted with permission of The Macmillan Company from "My City," Bank Street
Reader *by Bank Street College of Education.* © *copyright 1966 by The Macmillan
Company.*

If you had the opportunity to choose, you would try to match
materials controlled by frequency of word use with learners who
demonstrated strength in learning through the visual sense, since
these materials rely heavily on a visual presentation and learning
through the visual memory. Created for use with both small and large
groups, these materials provide for a highly structured and systematic

approach to the teaching of reading. The stories and the vocabulary create an order and a control that fairly well govern the general teaching procedures and guide the child in his daily progress toward reading.

Word skills and comprehension skills are introduced inductively; that is, they are first based on the content of the story and then reinforced through activities in the workbook or in the teacher's guide. For example, consider the sentence,

Can the good goat get home safely?

Teacher's question: "Three words in that sentence are somewhat alike. What are they?"
        Answer: *"Good, goat, get."*

Teacher's question: "Why are they alike?"
        Answer: "All begin with the letter *g*."

Teacher's question: "Can you give another word that begins with the same sound?"

In this fashion the teacher uses the story to lead to an understanding of the sound represented by the consonant *g*.

These techniques and the philosophy of the word-frequency method emphasize meaning and thinking. Therein lies much of the appeal of the method and also its opportunity for individualization. Because of its highly structured nature these materials used with this method may seem to place some rather severe restrictions on the teacher and children, but the sense of self-discovery and the emphasis on meaning give individual children latitude in which to be themselves, to be individual learners. You must decide whether those characteristics match the characteristics of your students.

Sound-Symbol Materials

Some materials designed for use with the controlled vocabulary system use phonics or linguistics to control their vocabulary. As we have seen, in this approach children learn that there is a relation between the sounds within spoken words and the symbols used to spell the words. The symbol "b" is used to represent the sound one hears at the beginning of the words *bat, beggar,* and *bite.* This sound-symbol approach first identifies a sufficient number of sounds and symbols so that some words can be wholly constructed from the learned bits of sound. Once the children learn a half-dozen consonant sounds with their appropriate symbols and the sound /a/ as in *bat,* they can decipher a number of words that make use only of those sounds, for example, *A cat can bat a rat.* By analysis and manipulation the child should be able to deal with any words that do not go beyond those learned parts. *Pat the fat man* and *Dan ran fast past the cat* are words thus available for use in workbooks and readers. The vocabulary control does not rest on the word-use frequency but on the words that fit the learned sound-symbols and their various combinations.

There are different labels attached to the materials that make use of a sound-symbol vocabulary control. Some readers are called phonics readers, others linguistics readers. From the appearance of their practice books, it may be difficult to distinguish one from the other.

A phonics program usually presents a number of time-honored rules concerning the spelling and related sounds of English words. Thus the silent "e" rule says that an "e" at the end of a one-syllable word usually indicates the "e" is silent and that the preceding vowel says its own name, or has a long vowel sound, for example, *state, pope, bite.*

A linguistics program usually takes the findings of linguistic research concerning the regularity and patterns within the English sound-spelling code. Instead of teaching the silent "e" rule, the linguistics reader would teach the consonant-vowel-consonant-vowel pattern (c-v-c-v), such as *mate, pope, bite*, and contrast it to the consonant-vowel-consonant pattern (c-v-c), such as *mat, pop, bit*. At this point there is no significant research evidence to indicate that either the linguistics program or the phonics program is superior.* There is some evidence to indicate, however, that sound-symbol materials in general enable children to score higher on standardized achievement tests in reading, although this issue has been hotly debated among educators (Chall, 1967).

Phonics Materials

Phonics materials do not employ a single set of phonics rules. Some, like those put out by the Economy Publishing Company, employ a large number of rules. (A brief summary of these materials is found in Appendix B.) Initial activity in that phonics program centers on learning a single sound for each letter of the alphabet.

The phonics program of the Lippincott Publishing Company uses only a few phonics rules. (A summary of this program is found in Appendix B.) The story content of the readers departs from the traditional neighborhood stories and leans heavily toward the folk tale. A much greater vocabulary load is presented in this series than in typical readers. The first grade books, for example, introduce close to 2000 different words—in sharp contrast to some word-frequency

*Linguistics is used here in the manner of Bloomfield and Barnhart, 1961, and Fries, 1962, who focused almost exclusively on phonemics and the structural patterns in English words.

series that introduce approximately 350 words in the first grade. Obviously, the new words cannot be repeated as often in the Lippincott program as they are in series that rely heavily on visual memory techniques.

Linguistics Materials

The linguistics readers are probably more diverse in appearance and construction than any other group of readers. The content varies considerably from a highly repetitive spelling-pattern approach (Charles Merrill Company) to fun-filled stories about frogs and puppies (Harper & Row, Publishers). The Merrill series does not use pictures while in another series an illustration appears on every page. Merrill produces a series that emphasizes spelling patterns and the visual differences, that is, the spelling differences, within the same general pattern, consonant-vowel-consonant (c-v-c). *Bad* represents a different word than *Dad* because the first letter is different. A sample page from Reader 1 says:

> Nat on a Mat
>
> A fat cat sat on a mat.
> The fat cat is Nat.
> Pat the mat, fat cat.
> Is the mat on Nat?
> Nat is on the mat.

The existing linguistics readers differ from the phonics readers in their approach to the sound-symbol relation. Both types of readers are dedicated to giving the student some guidelines for analyzing words, and they both stress the regularity of English words. Phonics materials, however, usually work from a set of rules and isolate individual letter sounds while linguistics materials usually work from a group of words and induce guidelines. They do not try to isolate specific sounds for a given letter but rather encourage the student to listen for sounds in the context of a whole word.

Use of Sound-Symbol Materials

The content of sound-symbol materials should be judged on its environmental and motivational effects, as was suggested for the word-frequency materials. A more important consideration, though, is whether the child needs to be led systematically through a careful sequence of word-analysis techniques in order for him to read independently. These materials lend themselves to group instruction and the teacher's guides that accompany them generally focus on group exercises, as do materials based on frequency of word use. Because of their highly structured exercises, the sound-symbol materials usually are easy to follow, and the child sees his progress almost daily. The teacher, too, may find it easier to assess progress with sound-symbol materials because the tasks are clearly defined and the criteria for evaluation are easily identified, at least in the early stages: Can the child match the symbol and sound (a with /a/)? Can he blend the symbols to produce the complete word sound (*cat* says /kat/)?

For the auditory learner the sound-symbol materials have the obvious advantage of making use of known sounds (speech) to lead him to read visual symbols. For example, the child is asked to note the similarity in the sounds in the middle of the words *bat, mad, ran.* Then he is shown that the middle sound is spelled with "a." This training in relating sound and symbol will help the auditory learner in analyzing words until they become part of his automatic reading vocabulary.

New Alphabet Materials

Though both phonics materials and linguistics materials emphasize the regularity of the English sound-symbol relations, there are some evident exceptions to the rules and the patterns. For that reason a number of new alphabet approaches have been developed to assure greater consistency in the sound-symbol relations and to make it simpler for beginning readers to decode the written symbols.

The initial teaching alphabet (ITA), Words in Color, Unifon, and the diacritical marking system — all attempt to simplify the sound-symbol relation of English so that it more closely resembles a one-to-one relation. New alphabet materials are viewed by their creators as initial means of introducing the child to a fundamental process in conquering the symbols on a page, that is, decoding the symbols into the sounds they represent. Since they are aimed primarily at this initial segment of the reading program, some teachers do not consider them with core materials. When used, however, they are the basic and only materials used to begin training in reading; in the case of ITA the materials extend throughout the entire first grade program and some even into the second grade. Both ITA and Unifon create new symbols so that each of the forty-plus sounds of the English language has its own distinctive symbol. Some of those symbols are the traditional letters of the alphabet, as can be seen in Figure 9.1.

The diacritical marking system uses stories from a traditional reading series and imprints diacritical marks above the vowels and difficult consonants in order to simplify the sound-symbol relation.

Words in Color stands apart from the other materials that we have mentioned in this section. Developed by Caleb Gaeteno, author of the Cuisinaire Color Rods used in teaching mathematics, Words in Color uses only the standard alphabet symbols. Words in Color materials fit with others mentioned in this section in their attempt to get the child to respond initially to a single symbol for each of the sounds of English. Instead of an alphabet symbol, however, initially the child is shown a color that represents a sound. He is told to say /ă/, as in *at*, whenever he sees the white color; /p/, as in *pat*, when he sees the red color; /t/; as in *tap*, when he sees the yellow color; /i/, as in *it*, when he sees the blue color; /k/, as in *cat*, when he sees the fuchsia color, and so on. Charts containing these forty-four columns of color are used to elicit specific sounds. Every time the teacher points to a color the children respond with a sound. On each of the columns of color on the chart are the various letters usually used to spell that sound. For example, the most frequent spelling for /ă/ (at) is the letter "a," But /ă/ is also spelled "au" and "ai"; all of these /a/ spellings therefore appear on the white color strip. The purpose of listing all of these spellings is to get the beginning reader accustomed to the fact that the /ă/ sound has a variety of spellings though at first, he will work only with the "a" spelling, which happens to be the one used most often in words. As he progresses, he is taught to analyze words by trying the other options if the first one does not produce a meaningful word.

As soon as the child has learned to respond to the strips of color with the appropriate sound, he is taught to blend sounds into words and to see the printed symbol on the chalkboard and in little black and white paperback exercise books and readers. The materials carry the learner through the equivalent of approximately one semester of practice to gain automatic response to the various spellings. The charts are placed around the room for reference while the child takes up other materials to learn additional reading skills.

Use of New Alphabet Materials

Research indicates that the new alphabet materials are as successful or more successful than other materials. Bond and Dykstra (1967) suggest that some of the success may be due to the teacher's interest and enthusiasm for what is new.

Because of their emphasis on sound-symbol relation these materials may be used in the same general ways as sound-symbol materials. The new alphabet materials quickly move away from careful vocabulary controls and thus the content of the stories may present problems for some of the slower children. On the other hand, some teachers recommend using ITA and Words in Color for slower learners because initially all the words presented are regular and students are not confronted with confusing spelling irregularities.

Materials for the Language Experience Approach

For the language experience method, as defined in this text, no one set of materials fits the system. In a sense the teacher and the child develop their own reading materials. The teacher has to select materials which foster the development of skills in listening, speaking, and writing, as well as reading, since this system stresses the interdependence of all of the communication skills.

Often, the language experience approach uses an "experience-story" technique to introduce the idea of communication through writing. An experience story is one that is dictated by a child (children) to the teacher. The child then reads back the story while looking at the written copy. The teacher can work entirely from the memory of his students or can use stimulus materials similar to those published by the Chandler Publisher Company. These materials include a series of pictures and a series of readers that use photographs of inner-city scenes. Slides, bikes, and buildings are the subjects of the photographs and brief copy identifies them with appropriate words.

The Encyclopedia Brittanica Corporation publishes a series of guides for teachers and pupils in the development of experiences and stories. These materials are authored by R. Van Allen, whose name is closely associated with the language experience approach as a result of his research and his book on the system (Lee, D., and Allen, R. V., 1963).

The experience story enables the students to build initial reading habits, learn to identify some words, and begin to discuss their experiences as possible subjects for stories. They consider questions as: What are stories? Where do they come from? How are they put together? Having gone through the process of creating stories of his own, the beginning reader soon learns to answer these questions inductively and begins to appreciate how stories in books are organized and prepared for his enjoyment. This technique thus combines listening, discussing, and reading in the child's initial activities.

Once the students see the relation between talk and the creation of a book, the teachers may introduce a phonics or other word-analysis worksheet to continue practice in word analysis and point out the relation between the sound of a word and its spelling.

One teacher used Dr. Seuss books for the listening period because of the author's emphasis on sound and fun (Strickland, 1969). A recent series of readers, *The Sounds of Language* (Holt, Rinehart and Winston, 1967), features stories and poems that make the student conscious of language, words, and the delight he can have with language if he knows some of its music and nuances. This series also contains many activities for speaking and writing about the stories the children have heard or read. The last major activity in the language experience approach is reading a wide variety of selections and

So Many Monkeys

Learning sequence: a) Silent reading,
b) choral reading, and *possibly* c) language analysis.

Monkey Monkey Moo!

Shall we buy a few?

Yellow monkeys,

Purple monkeys,

Monkeys red and blue.

Singular and plural

Contractions and pronouns

Be a monkey, do!

Who's a monkey, who?

He's a monkey,

She's a monkey,

You're a monkey, too!

Invite the children to read this poem to themselves. Then quickly read it aloud together. Have fun with it. And don't be surprised if children go about calling each other monkeys for a while. If you're in the mood, analyze the language. And don't forget the word cards.

by **Marion Edey and Dorothy Grider,**
picture by Kelly Oechsli

79

FIGURE 4-2   Another Basal Reader Page

Reading and language learning can be fun for children and teachers as seen in this page from a basal reader. (From Sounds Around the Clock, *a Sounds of Language Series, edited by Bill Martin, Jr., © copyright 1970. Reprinted by special permission of Holt, Rinehart and Winston, Inc.)*

reacting orally or in writing. Thus the teacher keeps on hand a large supply of books the child can read for enjoyment. Written summaries, reactions, and creative compositions may follow from the individual reading. These compositions, in turn, become materials to be shared, exchanged, read aloud, or posted for students to read at their leisure.

Use of Materials in the Language Experience Approach

Most of the materials designed for the language experience approach can be used in a relatively unstructured classroom setting. The experience story is a fairly personal experience. It must be the child's own story. Pictures and books can be stimulants, but the language and vocabulary on the paper should belong to an individual.

The language experience system has particular applicability for students who need to be stimulated to use language or who need to feel that their language is valuable. For example, the system may motivate the child who seems afraid to speak in class because he comes from a less verbal environment than some of the other children.

In a mountain school in West Virginia, we watched youngsters tell stories with obvious enjoyment and then exchange the written versions of the stories. The children read each others' stories and asked their neighbors for help with the words they did not recognize. The teacher confided that past students in that school had usually been uninterested in reading and had not fared well. But once she enabled children to use their own language and to dictate their favorite stories, they approached reading enthusiastically and their skills improved noticeably. These children put their stories together into a handbound book and were led to read the county newspaper and stories by writers from Appalachia.

Schools or teachers using a language experience system usually set up a series of reading skills they want the children to develop. The ebb and flow of classroom interest, however, often alter the schedule of the program so that the students do not always develop the skills in the exact order in which they were listed. Within the year designated skills are called to the attention of the children and they are practiced. This kind of freedom enables a wider use of creative energy, but places a great burden on the teacher to see that specific skills are learned and appropriate materials used.

For this reason the teacher should acquaint himself with a wide variety of instructional materials that fit into an independent skills program and provide many stimuli to communication. He must also know where to find and how to select books on a variety of topics and written at various levels so that all members of his class can read, discuss, and write on subjects that interest them at a level suited to their ability.

Materials for the Individualized System

The individualized system is probably the most difficult approach for the beginning reading teacher to visualize and undoubtedly the most difficult to administer. As discussed in Chapter 3, one reason that this is true is the large number of books per pupil required to carry on an individualized reading program. What was said about selection of materials for the language experience approach applies equally here. In cooperation with the school and local librarians, the teacher must make a selection of books for the classroom and for the library that will stimulate the children to learn through the interest they have in the books available to them.

Use of Materials in the Individualized System

Finding materials that interest students does not usually pose a problem in the individualized approach. More often, materials are lacking that teach specific reading skills. Some publishers are now producing kits that can be used in an individualized system. The Random House Pacesetters, for example, offer a series of graded, high-interest stories with word exercises and comprehension questions to be answered by the child after he has read the selection on his own. The skills and the exercises proceed in a developmental fashion. Record sheets and check tests give the student and the teacher some indication of progress.

Some teachers find it helpful to build a file of tearsheets from workbooks, filed according to specific skills. As the teacher sees a need for skill development or practice by a particular student, he can pull his file for that skill and have the student work out an appropriate exercise.

In a truly individualized system more materials are needed than in any of the other systems described in this book. In fact, all of the materials mentioned for the other systems should be available for spot use in the individualized approach. A skilled, experienced teacher is required to teach individualized reading, for he must be able to analyze test data, diagnose problems, plan personalized programs, and help students select materials appropriate for them.

Materials for the Programmed Instruction System

The most distinctive-looking materials for teaching reading are those used in the programmed instruction system. The material is written in the form of very short problems, usually boxed off in frames as in the sample shown on page 67

Programmed reading exercises may be given by machine, in

FIGURE 4-3 A Programmed Reader

In programmed texts the student can check his response at once by uncovering the answer column on the left. (Reproduced from Programmed Reading, *Bk 8, by C. D. Buchanan and N. W. Sullivan. Copyright © 1963 by Sullivan Associates with permission of The McGraw-Hill Book Company.)*

which case answers are recorded electronically and some mechanical device enables the learner to proceed or holds him on a frame where he made an incorrect response. More commonly, however, programmed reading exercises are given in a series of paperbound books; each page is divided into frames, and a column at the left-hand side of the page contains the correct responses. A piece of cardboard, a *slide*, covers the column until it is slipped down to reveal the correct answer. The Sullivan programmed reading series is an example of this kind of program. This series moves from teaching the alphabet and the sound-symbol relations into getting facts and main ideas from short paragraphs. (A summary of the program is found in Appendix B.)

Use of Materials in the Programmed System

The reading programs thus far developed under the principles of programmed instruction are not broad enough to be used as the only material. They are usually used as the skills base for individualized reading or for the language experience system. Because of the nature of the materials, programmed readers include only short paragraph-type exercises at the end of their sequence of skills. Programmed reading can often be helpful in a class where there is a wide variety of abilities. After diagnosis of the status of the children the teacher can place each child in the section in which he can develop the skills he needs. The teacher and the child then confer from time to time to evaluate progress. Programmed materials can also be used for dealing with certain reading problems in the classroom. Since programmed material is worked on privately and at an individual pace, the teacher should provide opportunities for the children using the materials to share ideas, stories, and oral reading.

SUPPLEMENTARY MATERIALS

In addition to core materials, the teacher of reading has available to him a variety of supplementary aids, books, and worksheets. These materials are used to give added practice, correct deficiencies, or provide enrichment experiences. They can serve as illustrative devices, means of motivation, and as organizers. They can serve the student by stimulating his interest, giving him additional practice in a needed skill, or providing him with emotional experiences that may not be a part of the core materials.

Related Materials

A teacher's preferences and teaching style determine how many materials related to the basic program he will use. The following pages describe some typical related materials and how they may be used as part of the core materials.

The Big Book

For the first couple of months the first grade teacher may use the big book to introduce each day's lesson. The big book is a chart-size reproduction of one or more of the preprimers. With it the teacher demonstrates how to look at the story and how to read it. The children then turn to their own small books and read the same story as it was demonstrated for the entire group.

Charts

Many kinds of charts are published, for example, picture stories, phonics rules, and vocabulary lists, for different purposes. Word-analysis charts are useful for group drill and can be used as a perm-anent reference if they are placed around the room.

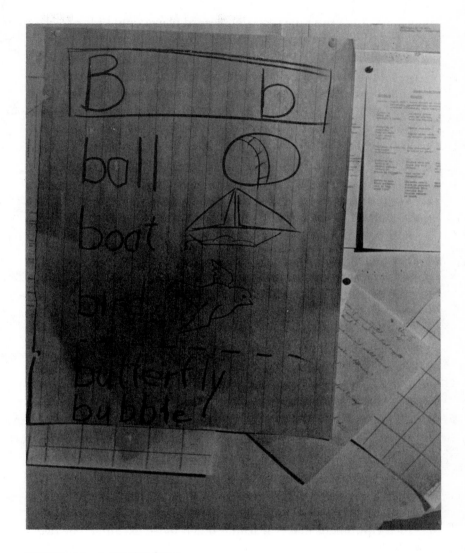

FIGURE 4-4   A Phonics Chart

Phonics charts may be constructed by the teacher for special demonstrations. (Photo by Carl B. Smith)

Audiovisual Devices

Many basic reading programs include records and tapes to provide songs and stories as background for the reading selections. Filmstrips and movies form part of the materials designed to make the lesson attractive and to motivate the child. The modern elementary classroom can easily use a tape recorder, record player, and slide projector as standard equipment. Audiovisual materials are available in quantity and are useful for a change of pace, motivation, reinforcement, and providing repetitive practice exercises.

MATERIALS FOR INDEPENDENT WORK

Core materials in reading instruction are designed to provide a basic structure of skills needed to read efficiently. Materials for independent work differ from the core materials in several ways:

1. They usually are not concerned with introducing all of the essential skills for a mature reader.
2. The materials usually call for short-term activities and do not carry over several years, as is the case with most core materials.
3. The content may be fanciful or different as opposed to the predictable and traditional content of the core materials.
4. The materials are often called supplemental materials as opposed to basic or core materials.

There are many categories of materials for independent work, including audiovisual materials, supplementary books, reading kits, games, workbooks, and teaching machines.

Audiovisual Materials

American schools in the 1970s are taking advantage of the technological age. Teachers work in classrooms that are decidedly different from those in which they were taught as elementary and secondary students. Almost all new schools are equipped with built-in screens, speakers, dimmer switches, and storage areas for valuable machinery and equipment. Teachers are finding that audiovisual equipment can be used to motivate students, and school boards are discovering that such equipment makes learning much more exciting. The overhead projector and tape recorder may soon be in use in every classroom in the country. Filmstrip projectors, movie projectors, and videotapes will be available to any classroom teacher who wants to use them to enhance learning. Many of these devices are specifically designed to teach reading skills.

Sets of overhead projection transparencies, for example, teach the sound-symbol relation, phonics generalizations, and sight vocabulary. Filmstrips can be had for almost any phase of learning to read, including comprehension activities with cartoons and copy that resemble those of a basic reader (Lippincott Publishing Company). Audiotapes for use on a standard tape recorder, like records, can be found for reviewing sounds, building vocabulary, developing experiences, and listening to stories read by professional readers (Imperial Productions, Inc.).

Movies are also available for the reading teacher. Some develop concepts about how to read for facts, how to organize what is read, and how to get the main idea. Others are designed to prepare the child for a teaching system; for example, many publishers have produced movies showing how children use their books and techniques. A recent development in the movie business is the use of filmloops, or cartridges of film, which are usually limited to a single concept. They can be snapped into a small projector without threading the film in the machine and do not require rewinding. When used in a study carrel in an 8mm projector and flashed on the wall of the carrel, the filmloop serves as a handy and interesting device for individual concept building or story preparation.

Use

Audiovisual equipment can be used for group or independent work. More and more schools are setting up audiovisual areas in the classroom. Besides their motivational values, audiovisual devices create strong sensory images, often a valuable technique where strength of impression and repetition are needed to develop language skills, such as vocabulary and automatic recognition of words.

Laboratories and Kits

One of the most popular items for independent study has been the reading kit or the reading laboratory, for example, the SRA Reading Lab. Many publishers produce reading kits made up of a package of reading selections, response sheets, answer sheets, and score cards. The reading selections, which are quite short, are graded from easy to difficult and printed on individual cards or little booklets. Sometimes colored stripes are used to distinguish levels of difficulty within the same kit. A student's reading level is determined by means of a test and he is then told to begin his work in the kit at a place where the selections match his reading level. He reads the short selections one by one, answers the vocabulary and comprehension questions after each selection, and scores his own paper from the answer sheet provided. This exercise provides the learner with practice in reading and in answering certain kinds of questions, usually having to do with finding facts and giving synonyms for words. Each task is relatively short; progress is noted on a personal record chart and by the color of the stripe on the selection. Almost imperceptibly the learner handles more and more difficult reading material. The theory is that his skill is developed through practice by gradually increasing the level of difficulty.

FIGURE 4-5   The Film-Loop Projector

The Film-Loop Projector enables the teacher to snap in a cartridge in a minute and show a movie for concept development. (Photo courtesy of Eastman Kodak Corporation)

Use

Motivation and practice seem to be the major values in the use of these kits. These materials are, of course, designed for independent work and thus are one answer for some teachers who ask, "What practice work can I give the children when there is a wide variety of reading levels in the class?"

Games

A visitor to an elementary school class once asked a youngster what helped him most in learning to read. He said, "I learn my words better when I play the word games."

All kinds of games are available to the teacher of reading, from word cards to manipulative devices aimed at improving perception through coordination activities. The book called *Spice* (1957) lists games and activities for language arts instruction. The name of Edward Dolch has become synonymous with games since he developed a popular series of card games and bingo games to help develop sight words and recognition of sounds (Garrard Publishing Company). Puzzles, tracing materials, and blocks with words on them are other popular devices for the game or activity corner of the classroom.

Use

These items are usually left out for use when the children have finished other work. The teacher explains how each can be used and encourages the students to practice vocabulary sounds, phrases, or sentences by using the games. The sense of competition created by games indicates their motivational force on youngsters, especially boys. Since boys develop reading problems twice as often as girls (Strang, 1969), it is worth encouraging practice by whatever means are available.

Enrichment Materials

Books in the core materials provide skill development and a general content in which vocabulary and meaning can be discussed. From that foundation the child should build his reading repertoire. Reading incentive programs, practice readers, and stories for both girls and boys are available at reading levels from grades one through twelve. Some publishers, such as Garrard, Harr-Wagner, and Steck-Vaughan, specialize in high-interest books written at a variety of reading levels.

Use

Some teachers use book clubs to get books into the hands of their pupils on a regular basis. Scholastic Press, Pflaum Publishing Company, and Grolier, Inc., among others, offer paperback books to children through classroom purchase plans. This arrangement has the advantage of placing books in the children's homes, but it should not be the sole means of providing additional books for the reading program. The teacher and the school librarian working together can form an effective book selection committee for any given group of children. The reading teacher should remind the librarian of the incentive and motivational books that are available and identify the reading levels found in his class.

Supplementary Workbooks

Most of the materials described for a basic system of instruction come with a workbook or a practice book. The textbook publisher's catalog will reveal that many other workbooks are published besides the basic materials. These workbooks may simply contain additional drill exercises on a given skill. Thus, the teacher introduces a skill and the child makes some responses to indicate that he has acquired the concept. Reading skills particularly need to be practiced until they become habitual. For that reason supplementary practice books, used on an individual basis in class or at home, may offer many benefits to the child. Some publishers, such as Continental Press, sell their workbook programs on ditto masters. The teacher can then select the exercise that provides needed drill and duplicate as many copies as are needed.

Some teachers build files of practice exercises and pull out the appropriate skill sheets as a child needs them. Another kind of workbook is a skills text, that is, a limited skills program in workbook format but carrying an explanation of the skill, practice in it, and a check test on it. It is important that supplementary workbooks be chosen to fulfill specific needs and selected on the basis of their design to deliver that skill.

EVALUATING MATERIALS

Books and other instructional aids are used to promote learning. In selecting them, therefore, the purchaser must ask, "Do these materials achieve what is needed in this school?" Some recent materials carry a description of the specific behaviors that their exercises are designed to achieve. A statement of behavioral objectives should help considerably in the evaluation of the materials.

From an instructional point of view materials should be developed by first looking at the educational objective, or the task the child should be able to perform, and working back from that point. In other words, materials should be constructed on the basis of an analysis of the task and its underlying subskills. Programmed reading gives the clearest example of this trend, but it shows up in many of the materials now being developed, from phonics workbooks to practice readers.

Instructional facilities are changing to encourage greater individualization. Classrooms have ceased to be four bare walls enclosing thirty-five chairs. Study carrels, room dividers, learning centers, library centers, and collapsible walls encourage the teacher to break the whole-group instruction habit and plan learning programs that meet individual needs.

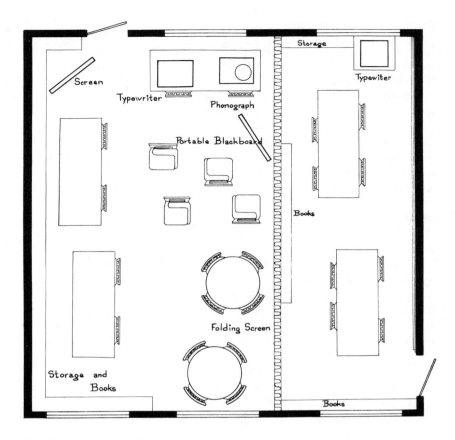

FIGURE 4-6   Sample Classroom Layout

To enable a variety of simultaneous learning activities some teachers partition their rooms with folding screens.

Diagnosis permits the matching of learner and materials. Hopefully, the good teacher makes that match. To do so, though, means becoming well acquainted with reading behavior and with materials.

Keeping abreast of materials can be an overwhelming job unless the teacher uses some selected techniques for updating his knowledge. Reading the monthly columns on new materials in the *Reading Teacher* (International Reading Association) and in *Elementary English* (National Council of Teachers of English), visiting the exhibits at conventions, and getting on publishers' mailing lists are some simple ways of staying current with materials. *The Guide to Instructional Materials in Reading* (Harris, 1968) and *Published Tests in Reading* (Buros, 1968) are two basic references that every teacher should use in searching for and evaluating materials for reading instruction.

Principles for Evaluating Materials

Now that you have read about the great number of books, charts, and machines available for teaching reading, how do you go about picking the right ones for your class? You could turn to research on reading materials. Most of the research on early reading is actually a study of materials and not of systems or teaching strategies. The recent U.S. Office of Education study of first grade reading often pitted one set of materials against another. The materials were found to be quite similar in many respects: in general they used highly structured lessons, a gradual vocabulary stockpile, and stories that show a similar view of home and school. Even the teaching strategies and the internal rewards for students were similar from one set of materials to another. It is not surprising, then, that Bond and Dykstra (1967) concluded that the teacher seems to be the key to differences in performance, not the method or the materials. Do not be misled by this statement, however, for certainly some materials are better than others and some methods are more appropriate than others for specific students. The teacher carries on a continuous search for attractive and efficient materials. Publishers, too, give considerable attention to improving materials and apply research evidence in choosing type size, column width, and number and kinds of illustrations (Tinker, 1965).

How else can you find appropriate books for your classroom? You will undoubtedly want to set some general criteria or principles for judging reading materials.

When selecting books, evaluate these general areas: (1) *instructional techniques*, (2) *content*, (3) *format*, and (4) *classroom effectiveness*. Under each of these areas ask questions similar to the ones listed below and see if the proposed materials seem worthy to be used in your classroom. For the person who has many items to review, a more objective comparison from item to item could be made by making a checklist out of the questions that follow.

Guiding Principle

The first rule in evaluating instructional materials is: *Evaluate materials in terms of your own instructional objectives.* Before you look at materials, you must first determine precisely what the materials are supposed to do. It is unwise to try to select materials for instruction before you have developed a list of specific behaviors a child should exhibit when he has finished the course of instruction. If, for example, you are selecting supplementary independent materials for grade one that give the child practice in using short-vowel words (consonant-vowel-consonant pattern) and give him enjoyment at the same time, three criteria can help you in your search:

1.   Do the materials supplement the first grade book?
2.   Do they provide practice in reading short-vowel words?
3.   Do they emphasize the fun of reading?

With these questions in mind, you may find that some of the Dr. Seuss nonsense books or similar happy books suit your purpose. Once you have identified a body of materials as fitting the learning tasks to be achieved, then you can ask such questions as the following about the instructional psychology, the content, and the format of the materials.*

GENERAL
  1. *Do the materials claim to do what you expect the children to learn to do, for example, get the main idea of a paragraph?*

INSTRUCTIONAL VALUES
  2. *Do the materials fit the population?*
     Is the reading level appropriate? Is the pace of instruction satisfactory (fast, slow)? Do materials appeal to special cultural aspects of the population (setting, illustrations, vocabulary)?
  3. *Do the materials have clearly defined performance objectives?*
     Did the authors know where they were headed?
  4. *Can a child work his way through a series of experiences and arrive at the stated objectives?*
     Do the tasks truly lead him to competency in analyzing short-vowel words?
  5. *Are the instructional tasks arranged in a logical order or organized so that the structure is evident?*
  6. *Can the teacher and the child get clear direction from the student's materials and the teacher's guide?*
  7. *Are the means to evaluate progress indicated for the child and the teacher?*

CONTENT PRINCIPLES
  8. *Does the general story content fit the population?*
     Can the children identify with the action and enjoy the story?
  9. *Does the content provide a variety of reading experiences — in keeping with the objectives of the program?*
 10. *Does the content include motivational and interest factors suitable to the age and culture of the population?*
 11. *Does it lead to appreciation of literature and a lifelong interest in reading?*
 12. *Is it linguistically sound?*
 13. *Is the skills development logical or based on recent research?*

*K. S. Goodman *et al.* discuss the evaluation of materials at length in *Choosing Materials To Teach Reading* (Wayne State University Press, 1966), as does the 1961 Yearbook of the National Society for the Study of Education.

FORMAT PRINCIPLES

14. *Are the materials sufficiently attractive for their purpose?*
    Is the type easily read by the prospective learner? Are the illustrations clear and stimulating? Are there sufficient illustrations?
15. *Are different typographical techniques used to help the reader?*
    Are there a variety of headings, use of italics, and variation of margins?

UTILITY PRINCIPLES

16. *Are the materials durable?*
    How long will they last in the hands of a child?
17. *Are the materials easy to handle?*
    Will they lie flat for reading and writing?
18. *Is the cost commensurate with the instructional value they provide?*
    Will another, less expensive item produce the same effect on the learner?

SUMMARY

Materials for reading instruction were classified into two major categories, core materials and supplementary materials. Core materials are those that carry the major skills and content. Supplementary materials are those that aid the teacher in his presentations or the student in his independent study.

Core materials were described in four major groups, representing examples of books and materials used in each of the four systems of reading instruction: the controlled vocabulary system, the language experience system, the programmed learning system, and the individualized reading system. The controlled vocabulary system has available more materials than the other three systems combined if one includes only those materials specifically published for use in a system.

The large quantity of materials available today, both core and supplementary, makes selection difficult. Guidelines for evaluating reading materials were listed under criteria for (1) instructional techniques, (2) content, (3) format, and (4) classroom effectiveness. All materials must first be judged on whether they can achieve the teacher's instructional objectives.

TERMS

core materials	readability
supplementary materials	new alphabet materials
sound-symbol materials	reading kits
vocabulary load	

Chapter 5

Organizing for Instruction

Previous chapters introduced you to the four systems for teaching reading and the wealth of materials that can be used with each. The next logical step is to consider how you will organize yourself and your students for reading instruction.

Many teachers have faced a room full of empty desks in late August and experienced doubts about their ability to teach twenty-five or thirty children to read. The sheer logistics of assembling groups and scheduling activities for independent work may seem overwhelming. The teacher who wants effectively to individualize his instruction is particularly troubled at such an introspective time. This chapter discusses the matter of organizing for instruction and provides suggestions on how to initiate grouped instruction, plan independent activities, and schedule teacher time when multiple groups are used. The following questions are considered:

If individualized instruction is the goal, why group for instruction?

What kind of grouping is done before the children come into my classroom?

What kind of grouping plan(s) can I use in my classroom?

Is one type of grouping best for teaching reading?

How do I set up my reading groups?

What will I do with the groups after forming them?

How can I profitably engage children not in the group I am teaching?

How many groups should I have?

What can I do to individualize instruction within a group?

GROUPING AS A MEANS TO INDIVIDUALIZATION

Ideally, every youngster should be taught to read by a personal tutor. The adjustment of instruction to individual needs would be complete with such an arrangement. The tutor could observe first-hand the child's every success and failure. The interests of the child could be tapped as a motivational technique and integration of the child's skills and concepts would be a simple matter.

With thirty or more students in most elementary school classrooms, however, a tutorial arrangement is obviously not feasible. On the other hand, the needs and abilities of individual learners are easily overlooked when the class is taught as a whole. Grouping represents a compromise between the two extremes and enables the teacher to work more closely with individual youngsters. *Differentiation of instruction within groups is the key to meeting individual needs.* This chapter presents grouping as a useful if somewhat imperfect technique of organizing for instruction. The advantages and disadvantages of grouping practices will first be discussed. Next, the techniques and instruments used for gathering the information needed in assigning children to groups will be presented. The last section of the chapter describes in detail a plan for meeting with reading groups.

GROUPING PRACTICES

Grouping for instruction has several aspects. Children are often grouped on a special basis for assignment to a permanent classroom. Some grouping practices involve exchange of teachers and classrooms for special subjects. Other grouping procedures are employed within a single classroom. Reading instruction is directly affected by whatever form of grouping is employed.

School-wide Grouping

Often taken for granted by the public and by many teachers is the process of assigning children to classrooms. Much time and thought often go into this seemingly routine operation, however. Depending upon the philosophy of a given school system, children may be grouped into classrooms strictly on the basis of age, ability, achievement, local neighborhood, or at random.

Chronological Age

Children are often assigned to an elementary school classroom on the basis of chronological age. Six-year-olds are usually placed in the first grade, seven-year-olds in the second grade, and so forth.

The expectation for such a practice is that children of the same age will have similar needs and abilities. Thus groups formed on the basis of chronological age are efficient from an administrative standpoint because they are given a common curriculum. A good deal of educational research has demonstrated, however, that this reasoning is poorly founded. A review of the research by Cook and Clymer (1962) indicates that the range of ability in any grade (disregarding the extreme cases at either end of the distribution) is equal to two thirds of the chronological age of the pupils in that grade. For example, in a typical fourth grade the range of achievement is six years (two thirds of the nine years of age a fourth grader has attained). In most cases this means a range of reading achievement from grade one to grade seven for a typical fourth grade (Clymer, 1959).

As a result of such evidence, the practice of grouping by chronological age has been questioned. Many educators believe that children representing such a range of achievement cannot profit from the same instruction. Various alternatives have thus been proposed to create more homogeneous groups. Foremost among these plans is ability grouping.

Ability Grouping

The primary reason for grouping children according to ability is to reduce the range of differences among the learners in a classroom, thereby enabling the teacher to concentrate on one ability level. It has been claimed that the teacher can more adequately provide for the needs of a homogeneous group.

Several factors undermine the apparent logic which supports ability grouping. The work of Hull (1927), Burr (1931), and Balow (1962) clearly demonstrates that learners do not have a single ability but rather many abilities. Furthermore, within a single learner there is a wide range of abilities. Children grouped on one basis, intelligence or reading achievement, for example, exhibit nearly a full range of abilities on practically any other variable such as arithmetic achievement or spelling. This pattern of strengths and weaknesses, called *trait differences*, is familiar to all of us. Some individuals do especially well in writing activities, such as composition, but have considerable trouble with mathematics. The range of abilities for a single person is fully 90 percent of the variability of a normal population (Hull, 1927); that is, a person who stands among the top 10 percent of the population on one ability is likely to be among the bottom 10 percent on some other ability.

The significance of trait differences for grouping is considerable. Grouped on one basis, a class of children will possess nearly a full range of talents in other areas. Balow (1962) grouped ninety-four fifth grade pupils into four classes on the basis of their average scores on eight tests of various reading skills. Before grouping the average scores on the tests ranged from 2.0 to 9.0.* After grouping the four classes appeared to be fairly homogeneous, with the following ranges of scores: class a, 2.0–3.6; class b, 3.6–4.6; class c, 4.6–5.6; and class d, 5.7–9.0. However, further analysis of the scores of individual pupils on the eight tests of reading demonstrated the inadequacy of ability grouping. In class c, for example, where the range of scores was only 4.6–5.6, the ranges of individual pupil scores on four of the tests were: for rate, 1.8–12.7; for comprehension, 2.5–11.1; for word meaning, 1.8–7.9; and for alphabetization, 3.1–12.4 (see Fig. 5.1). Therefore, it can be seen that ability grouping is more of a myth than a legitimate alternative for assigning children to classrooms.

A second factor sometimes overlooked in grouping children is that, once grouped, initial differences between children typically increase. A good instructional program challenges the able and the less able, but serves to separate these extremes rather than bring them closer together. Bright students move ahead of their slower classmates because they learn more readily. Each new experience enables the capable youngster to pull further and further ahead. Clymer (1959) observed that the only way to keep children at the same level is to teach them nothing.

Finally, assignment of children to separate groups on the basis of a given ability is usually dependent upon a single test score or set of test scores. The uncertainty of many educational tests makes this at best a questionable procedure. The difference between scoring at grade level on an achievement test and scoring well above grade level can depend on numerous uncontrolled factors. For example, a difference of only two or three more correct test items can often significantly increase a youngster's standing. Grouping based solely on test evidence fails to take into account the limitations of such instruments. Chapter 6 considers the use and limitations of standardized tests.

A recent study on ability grouping (Goldberg, Passow, and Justman, 1966) requires replication, but provides the most comprehensive evidence yet gathered concerning the effect of ability grouping on achievement. Studying the results of homogeneous grouping on the achievement of over 2000 children in New York City, Goldberg and her associates concluded that, except in several isolated instances, children grouped heterogeneously performed as well in all subjects as those grouped homogeneously. Furthermore, they concluded that an effective teacher was the most important variable in determining the progress of the learners studied.

*Scores of standardized tests are often reported as grade equivalents. Here 2.0 means second year, no months. A score of 5.5 means fifth year, fifth month.

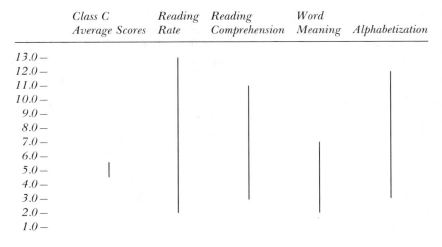

Class C Average Scores	Reading Rate	Reading Comprehension	Word Meaning	Alphabetization

FIGURE 5.1   Range of Scores for Class C When Grouped on Average Score

In view of the factors that limit the effectiveness of grouping and the growing evidence concerning the importance of teacher competency, educators can no longer look to administrative devices to solve instructional problems. Grouping of any kind will never make children alike. However, the range of abilities present in a classroom need not present an insurmountable handicap to the teacher who approaches each learner as an individual. Grouping must be regarded as a means for distributing learners, not as an instructional panacea. Whether youngsters are assigned to classrooms on the basis of age, neighborhood, achievement, ability, or at random, each brings his own unique strengths and needs to the task of learning to read.

Interclass Grouping

Several plans have been developed which involve another type of grouping, interclass grouping or redistribution of pupils. With this administrative technique teachers exchange students during various parts of the school day, usually for selected subjects. For example, two fourth grade teachers, Mrs. Green and Mrs. Brown, might agree to an exchange teaching arrangement. With one plan Mrs. Green is responsible for teaching reading while Mrs. Brown is responsible for teaching mathematics. Students from both classes move from one teacher to the other to be instructed in each subject. In a second procedure both teachers teach reading but divide their students, usually into high- and low-achieving groups. Additional subjects are often handled in the same fashion.

With special features added, all interclass grouping plans follow one of the two fundamental plans described above. *Departmentalization* is the best example of the first procedure. As in the familiar high school pattern, with this plan teachers specialize in subject areas. The *Joplin plan* is an example of the second exchange procedure applied specifically to reading. With this plan youngsters, regardless of grade level, are regrouped for reading instruction. More detailed descriptions of various organizational plans are available elsewhere (Hillson, 1965; Sartain, 1968).

The most noteworthy feature of all interclass grouping plans is that students move from teacher to teacher for part or all of their instruction. Organization plans that fragment the school day and systematically remove the child from his regular classroom may reduce the opportunity for integration of skills. For example, difficulty in other subjects such as social studies can often be traced to a reading problem. Interclass grouping may limit the opportunity to observe such difficulties and plan appropriate corrective instruction (Sartain, 1968).

It is often argued, of course, that exchange teaching enables the teacher to specialize and thereby do a superior job in his own subject area. The Goldberg, Passow, and Justman (1966) study cited earlier supports this view. While instructing a homogeneous group did not seem to increase a teacher's effectiveness according to this study, clear evidence of special teaching skill in one subject was found in case after case. The children in a given classroom often demonstrated unusual growth as a group in one subject. Growth in other subjects was often average, but many teachers were evidently especially skilled in teaching one subject. The authors of the study concluded that, given an opportunity to specialize, teachers can overcome the difficulties created by a large range of student abilities and produce superior growth in their own area of personal strength. It is noteworthy that intermediate grade children were involved in this particular study. Whether similar results would be obtained with younger children is not yet known.

The Self-contained Classroom

The organizational plan most familiar to people educated in U.S. schools is the self-contained classroom. Since a single teacher is responsible for all instruction, with this plan he gets to know each student especially well.

The self-contained classroom has several advantages as a means to individualizing instruction. Its chief value is that the classroom teacher is entirely responsible for instruction and consequently observes the application of reading skills in all areas. For example, the child who has difficulty with the specialized vocabulary in his arithmetic book can be noted by the teacher and given special instruction.

A second advantage of the self-contained classroom is that the teacher can plan his own time schedule and deviate from it if necessary. Exchange teaching requires that all participating teachers carefully observe the time and terminate a reading lesson at the agreed hour. This is not to imply that teachers of self-contained classrooms have no responsibility for planning and following a schedule. The flexibility of scheduling provided by a self-contained classroom is not as easily made with exchange teaching, however.

Admittedly, the self-contained classroom has some limitations as well. In particular, the child who draws a poor teacher is unfortunately stuck with him for the whole school day and school year. Too, the demands of an ever-expanding curriculum place an enormous burden on the teacher in a self-contained classroom. Forced to be adequate in all subjects, he has little opportunity to be superior in any single area. Some teachers may deliberately avoid subjects that make them uncomfortable. Evidence gathered in a national survey indicates that reading is frequently such a subject (Austin and Morrison, 1963).

Intraclass Grouping

Regardless of the school-wide grouping plan employed, teachers are faced with the necessity of grouping for reading instruction. Research cited earlier indicates that even children regrouped on the basis of achievement specifically for reading instruction still represent an enormous range of needs. The following discussion, therefore, applies equally well to interclass grouping or the self-contained classroom.

Once children are assembled for reading instruction, how can they be grouped so that individual needs can be met in the most effective way? There are three basic patterns of intraclass grouping: (1) achievement grouping, (2) interest grouping, and (3) grouping by need. Each has an important function in an effective grouping program.

Achievement grouping is no doubt the most popular form of intraclass grouping. Usually children who are reading at a similar level of difficulty are grouped on a relatively long-term basis for basic reading instruction. The number of groups should fit the apparent need of a class; three groups—high, average, and low—are often formed. While much stagnant and dreary instruction has taken place under the guise of achievement grouping, when properly used the plan can be a major step in differentiating instruction according to individual needs.

A fundamental goal of reading instruction should be to assign reading materials to the learner that are neither too difficult and thereby frustrating to him nor too simple and therefore unchallenging. The label instructional reading level is often used to describe the level of material which meets this midpoint between too difficult and too simple.* Grouping by achievement is a means for assigning children to materials that approximately fit their instructional reading level. If one book meets the requirements of all thirty youngsters in a classroom in this regard, one basic instructional group may be sufficient. Such a situation is highly unlikely, however. Regardless of the number of groups formed, the members of each group are likely to have only one reading trait that is even remotely alike, namely, their instructional level. They still retain very unique needs with regard to skill development. Therefore instruction for the members of a group must still be differentiated. The tools and techniques for diagnosing the needs of each child will be presented in the next chapter.

Interest grouping is highly useful and motivational. Often used in conjunction with a reading unit centering about a theme, interest groups bring together children of varying abilities and achievement levels. Children are grouped strictly on the basis of a common interest. For example, similar or related hobbies might draw together five or six youngsters reading anywhere from first to sixth grade reading level. Each youngster can make a unique contribution to the group based on his personal experiences and individual reading. A group project can be developed which permits each youngster to share a favorite book or present a product of his own making. The opportunity to pursue a topic of genuine interest can be a powerful motivator for even the reluctant reader. The range of interests in a given classroom are likely to be broad and will require a well-stocked library if this plan is to be successful. Most interest groups will be rather short-lived and frequently restructured as interests change and wane. Teachers should plan to form new interest groups often to stimulate reading on a variety of topics.

Another type of grouping is based on *need*. Children with similar deficiencies or limitations in specific skill areas can be grouped for instruction. Such groups are also usually short-lived. As with interest grouping, children reading at any level may need instruction that is directed toward their own special needs. For example, efficient

---

*Betts (1956) defines the instructional reading level as the level at which a child misses only 5 out of 100 running words and comprehends 75 percent of what he reads. A procedure for determining reading levels is described in Chapter 6.

use of an index might constitute the focus of a specially formed group. Children reading well above grade level as well as those struggling with a relatively easy text may have similar misconceptions about the purpose and format of an index. A single brief lesson may suffice for some youngsters, who can quickly be dismissed or given follow-up exercises. Others may require several lessons to overcome their deficiencies. Occasionally the entire class may form a short-term group for review or corrective instruction. More often groups formed on the basis of need will be rather small, perhaps having less than five youngsters.

No single type of intraclass grouping is sufficient for effectively adjusting the reading program to individual needs. Several kinds of grouping should occur in a classroom at the same time. Long-term achievement groups will need to be supplemented with interest groups that draw from all reading levels, for example. Grouping according to need will frequently bring together children with various interests and levels of reading achievement.

Regardless of the basis for its formation, good grouping has several important characteristics. First, groups must be *flexible*. Membership in any group should be based on the child's potential to benefit from instruction. If membership in another group is more likely to tap his potential, immediate action should be taken to move the child. Second, groups, particularly short-term groups, must have *specific objectives*. This means that a specific task or set of tasks must be clearly outlined and activities oriented to the accomplishment of the task. Related to this characteristic of task orientation is a third aspect of good grouping, *termination* of groups that have achieved their purpose. Even long-term groups should be subjected to this criterion. Groups must not be continued in time beyond the limits of their usefulness. Fourth, groups should be kept *small in size* whenever possible to maximize teacher interaction with each pupil. It is not possible or practical to define what is meant by *small* in this case. For some purposes four children comprise a large group; for other purposes ten children can be called a small group. Numbers are not the key; the point is that groups should be small enough to maximize the opportunity for individualizing instruction.

GATHERING INFORMATION FOR GROUPING

Chapter 6, "Assessing Student Needs," will present in detail the techniques and instruments that classroom teachers should use for gathering information about the needs of their students. Grouping must be based on a thorough and continuous evaluation of each child's progress and individual needs. Only with such information can the teacher decide how many groups to create, when to shift a child from one group to another, or when to pull several youngsters from various groups for special instruction.

Each chapter of this book which deals with a specific skill or set of skills also describes procedures for diagnosing individual needs. For the time being it is sufficient to point out that three major sources of information are particularly helpful to the teacher for assigning children to reading groups. First, formal reading tests such as achievement batteries and oral reading tests are useful. Second, informal measures of reading such as daily workbook assignments and checklists provide valuable information. Third, daily observations enable the teacher to note special needs and continuously assess progress.

The teacher who intends to diagnose needs and prescribe appropriate activities for each child stands a good chance of being a successful diagnostician. Knowledge of reading skills and an understanding of how to assess progress prepare an alert classroom teacher for individualizing instruction. Diagnosing individual needs requires both the knowledge of how to proceed and the intent to do so.

A PLAN FOR MEETING WITH GROUPS

Educational textbooks are sometimes criticized, as are methods courses, for an apparent failure to be specific. Prospective teachers badly want for someone to describe *exactly how to* — in this case — *group for instruction*. The standard response to this request is that a recipe cannot be provided because different situations require vastly different solutions. Actually, there is much value if not satisfaction in this stock reply; a textbook or methods instructor cannot anticipate every plausible circumstance and provide a list of surefire remedies.

Nonetheless, at the risk of being misinterpreted, we intend to be specific with regard to grouping for instruction. Only by working effectively with groups can most teachers begin to differentiate instruction and thereby take the first halting step toward individualized instruction. A specific plan incorrectly takes on the appearance of a recipe, a panacea. Herein lies the danger, for no single plan can begin to meet the needs of all teachers in all circumstances. Therefore, it is only prudent and correct that a strong cautionary note be sounded. The plan suggested here is only a starting point. Considerable adaptation and refinement must be part of its application. Despite these limitations, it is a useful and workable approach to the task of grouping for instruction.

Suppose the time of year is mid-August. The workshop prior to school is just getting underway. You have been assigned a third grade class for this, your first year of teaching.* Recognizing that as a beginner you cannot launch a full-blown individualized reading program, yet being unwilling to treat all the youngsters in your class as one, you decide to group for reading instruction. How do you assign children to groups? How many groups should you have? What reading material should each child receive? In answering these questions the use of a controlled vocabulary system will be discussed. Other systems could be chosen, yet beginning teachers especially profit from the careful guidance provided with this approach.

Until the children arrive you are limited to information that can be obtained secondhand. If used properly, the cumulative record file which most schools maintain on each child is an excellent resource. You may have a chance to talk with the teacher or teachers who taught your youngsters the previous year. Old workbooks and other samples of the children's work may be available. You can begin an anecdotal record file by entering the information gathered on each child in a notebook, with a full page or two reserved for each child. Included will be a summary of such data as standardized test scores, unusual attendance figures, results of physical examinations, previous teachers' comments, and the reading level achieved the previous year.

It is best to regard all secondhand information of this sort as tentative. Surprising spurts or setbacks can occur over a summer. Personalities and attitudes can undergo enormous changes. Each child should enter your class with a clean slate insofar as academic and social behavior is concerned. Be cautious about letting the information gathered prior to the beginning of school bias or prejudice your appraisal; instead, let it serve to support or highlight significant information you obtain for yourself during the school year.

A September Reading Program

No reading groups need be formed for at least the first two or perhaps three weeks of the school year. Of course, permanent groups should never be formed, but relatively stable groups can probably be identified after three or four weeks of school. During this initial period of ungrouped activity you should be a diagnostician. At every opportunity children can be taken individually for personal conferences. Brief interviews and informal chats to assess interests, language facility, and attitudes toward reading and school are most valuable. A series of paragraphs graded in terms of reading difficulty, called an informal reading inventory (see Chapter 6), can be con-

*While this description assumes a third grade class, the plan itself is applicable at any grade level with adjustments for the characteristics of different age levels.

ducted with each child. Questionnaires and checklists can be administered.

The school and classroom libraries ought to be fully used during this period. The children should be encouraged to read independently during this time of data gathering. The book selections of each child can be noted and entered in your ever-expanding notebook of pertinent information. These library books can be brought to the personal conference for discussion and for oral reading by the child.

You might take this unstructured period to begin a program for sharing books. A variety of appropriate suggested activities will be presented later. From the standpoint of diagnosis, oral and written book reports provide valuable information for the alert teacher. Comprehension, ability to summarize, skill in noting significant detail, facility with verbal communication, and poise before a group are only a sample of the behaviors that can be observed and noted.

Many school systems administer achievement tests during the fall. The results of the reading and study skills sections of these tests can provide additional information which is valuable for establishing groups. If achievement tests are not given in the fall, other standardized tests can be used to obtain this up-to-date information.

Occasionally a somewhat formal reading activity can be conducted by the teacher. For example, a skill-development lesson might be given with appropriate follow-up exercises. On the basis of participation, alertness, and written work the teacher can begin to get a sample of each child's performance in an instructional setting.

On the basis of all information gathered, trial reading groups can be established during the first month of school. Assignment of children to groups should be based primarily on the child's instructional reading level. The informal reading inventory (IRI) in particular can be used to indicate what level of material is most appropriate for each child. Preferably the material to be used for instruction, usually a basal reading series in the case of first-year teachers, is used in this assessment. Other information gathered during the initial three or four weeks of assessment is especially valuable in supplementing the IRI. Since any single measuring device has limitations, evidence from other sources can be used to confirm the level indicated by the IRI.

We recommend that only two reading groups be formed initially: (1) children able to handle the grade-level text and (2) children not able to handle the text. The main reason for this modest beginning is to protect the teacher. You are probably not ready to administer the details of teaching more than two groups, even though more groups seem necessary. Increased experience and familiarity with your class will gradually enable you to add a third and perhaps fourth group. Two groups will provide you with the experience of planning independent activities for some children and directing a lesson for the remainder of the class.

Trial groups are recommended so that obvious errors in initial placement can be quickly corrected. Furthermore, early in the school year it is a simple matter to move a child into a different group for several days to give him a trial. As the year progresses changes can still be made, indeed should be made, but the initial gap between groups is further widened every day. Therefore, whenever possible, experimentation with group placement should be conducted early in the school year.

Each group should be given reading texts according to its level. Often the same series is used with an entire class, and two different levels of books in the series are chosen to provide material near the instructional level of each group. Or, in some cases, two separate series are used so that each group has a different basal. This latter plan enables each group to read "fresh" stories and avoids the common dilemma of what to do with a child who knows a story because he once heard another group discuss it. The important point is that unless materials appropriate to the reading level of a group are located and used, much of the value of grouping for instruction is lost.

Needless to say, with only two groups a perfect match between the instructional reading level of each child and the reading difficulty of materials is not possible. It is necessary to aim for the middle of a group, choosing materials that are not too far removed from any child's reading level. The extremely high- and low-achieving youngsters are obviously missed with this approach. As your expertness permits, additional grouping and individualization of instruction must be instituted. Suggestions for this expansion of the grouping program will be discussed later in this chapter.

Meeting with Two Groups

A specific plan complete with illustrations of classroom activities cannot be presented unless several assumptions are made. First, a reading period of approximately sixty minutes for basic instruction will be described here. Actual time allotments vary among various states and for each grade level. Again, you are reminded that considerable adaptation of this plan will be necessary before employing it in your own classroom. Second, children grouped in this manner must be capable of working independently. No magic spell can be worked to achieve this requirement. It is essential that clear and concise goals be established for children working independently. The goals or purposes should be readily available to the child on a chalkboard or dittoed sheet for reference.

When dividing your time among groups it is necessary to consider the number of children in each group. Larger groups will require more time, since each child will need and is entitled to an equal proportion of your attention. It frequently happens that the more capable students are deprived of an equal share of direct teacher supervision. In the first place, such youngsters usually work well on their own. Furthermore, most teachers seem to identify with the youngsters who struggle at learning to read, occasionally to the neglect of brighter students. Each child requires direction, even the very capable. Often it is these youngsters who are most retarded in reading if achievement is compared to potential. Therefore, in dividing your instructional time you should consider the size of each reading group and make a genuine effort to work with all youngsters, not just those who obviously have problems.

For this illustration of a plan for meeting with groups we will first discuss a situation having two groups of comparable size. The total sixty minutes of instruction will therefore be divided equally into two periods totaling approximately thirty minutes each. You must schedule yourself with each group for about thirty minutes of activity and also plan thirty minutes of independent activity for each group. The diagram of Figure 5.2 will help you to visualize the assignment of time.

Depending on what has transpired the previous day, various alternatives are possible. Suppose group A has just completed the activities related to a story and is ready to move ahead to a new story. Group B, on the other hand, completed a story the previous day, but has not completed several useful skill-building activities suggested by the teacher's guide and needed by the group. In this case the teacher might get group B started on a worksheet he has prepared which requires the children to find descriptive phrases in the story and rewrite them in their own words. Since this activity will require only ten or so minutes for some youngsters and the entire thirty minutes for a few, the teacher suggests that any spare time be spent on free reading at the reading corner with the purpose of preparing a selection for oral reading.

Under teacher direction group A is given an opportunity to preview its new story and discuss the pictures, title, and general topic. Several new vocabulary words are introduced in sentences on the board and the children are asked to apply their word-attack techniques. When satisfied that the group is reading to understand the story, the teacher directs the children to read for several specific purposes. As the children of group A are reading silently the teacher can circulate in group B to check on progress. Those experiencing difficulty can be aided and a note made on special corrective instruc-

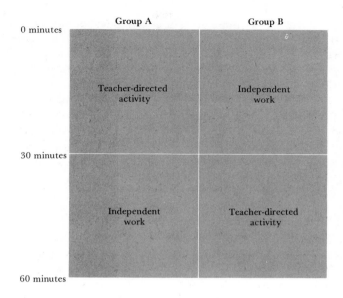

FIGURE 5-2   Meeting with Two Groups

This scheme represents one approach to organizing a reading period with two instructional groups.

tion required by some children. Returning to group A, the teacher has the children discuss the story, checks comprehension, and tests understanding of the new vocabulary. A workbook assignment can be given and group A left to work independently.

Returning to group B, the teacher discusses with the children their descriptive phrases found in their story. Each child gets to share some of his ideas and also personally note the appropriateness of his responses to phrases that other children share. The teacher can then collect the papers for further study and comment and individualize instruction where indicated. Next, the children might share their oral reading selections or immediately be regrouped for corrective instruction relative to the skill just used. Those needing no further instruction could go on to another activity such as a reading game, listening lesson, or creative writing activity. Summarized the teacher spends his time as follows:

1. Starts group B on worksheet.
2. Previews new story with group A.
3. Circulates among group B while group A reads silently.
4. Discusses story with group A; assigns workbook.
5. Discusses and corrects seatwork with group B.
6. Regroups for immediate corrective instruction with group B.

This very stylized plan gives a rough idea of how the teacher moves from group to group and also illustrates the planning that is necessary to carry out such a system. Useful and appropriate activities both for independent and teacher-directed activities must be identified ahead of time. Teacher-developed materials are ready and designed to meet the needs of the particular youngsters in group B. The suggestions in the teacher's guide are studied and appropriate activities used; other suggestions are rejected for the group in question. Special instruction is immediately provided for members of the group who show evidence of confusion; those succeeding with the task are not required to sit through an extra lesson.

Adding Flexibility

Some teachers might wish to adjust the plan for meeting with two groups by dividing the sixty-minute period into three twenty-minute sections (see Fig. 5.3). This arrangement would be especially good for younger children who cannot work independently for long periods of time. As diagrammed in Figure 5.3, group A would receive twice as much instructional time as group B. The allotment of the teacher's time could easily be reversed for the following day's lesson to achieve an approximate balance between groups.

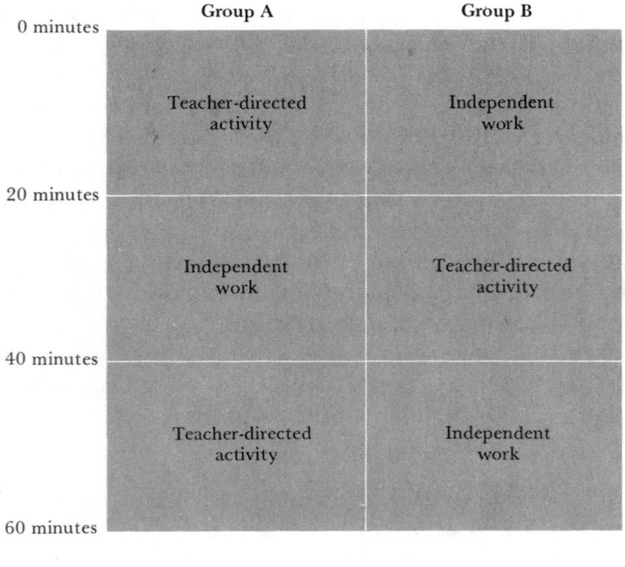

	Group A	Group B
0 minutes		
	Teacher-directed activity	Independent work
20 minutes		
	Independent work	Teacher-directed activity
40 minutes		
	Teacher-directed activity	Independent work
60 minutes		

FIGURE 5-3   Variation of Two-group Plan

If the teacher wishes to have shorter but more frequent instructional periods, this scheme can be useful.

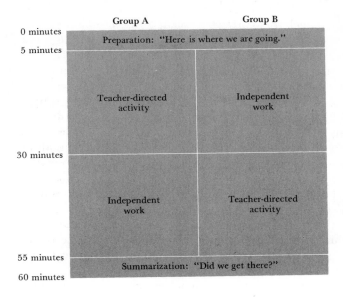

FIGURE 5-4   Adding Preparation and Summarization

A few minutes at the beginning of the reading period should be used to provide young-sters with a sense of direction by clarifying goals. A brief summarization near the end of the period can be helpful in evaluating progress toward stated goals.

Another variation is a brief organizational period prior to reading and a brief summarization period afterward (see Fig. 5.4). Not even a full five minutes is required before dividing into groups to preview what activities are planned for the reading period. Direc-tions can be given and questions answered in order to avoid confusion later. Again, it is important to have available a list of things to do and goals or purposes for easy reference by students. The five-minute summarization at the end of the reading period should be a positive experience. With the help of your students try to highlight the progress that has been made by emphasizing the successes of each group and occasionally of an individual child. You might also dis-cuss why some activities were less than successful and decide with the class how to avoid such problems next time.

Frequently the amount of time allotted to a reading group should be adjusted according to the activity planned. For example, one group might be preparing a dramatization of a favorite story. In this case a twenty- or even thirty-minute period will be inadequate to make real headway. The flexible teacher will simply extend the length of time given to this activity. If this means spending forty or fifty minutes with one group while the second group works independently, do so. By all means occasionally circulate among the independent workers to check their progress and start them on a new activity. You might even allow those who finish their work early to watch the rehearsal of the other group.

Another important policy that is essential to running a smooth, efficient, and flexible reading period is to permit interruptions by members of group A when you are working with group B. Some reasonable limit must be established, of course, but a moratorium on questions from youngsters working independently is shortsighted. Given no opportunity to seek your help, a child having difficulty can soon disrupt a whole group. We suggest that children with questions be encouraged to stand quietly near you until a chance to help them occurs. Then, while one youngster from group B goes to the board or reads orally, you can turn to the child who is waiting and quickly provide the help that is needed. Any serious instructional problems must wait, of course, but only by seeing the nature of a problem can you give the child something else to do and make a note to work with him individually on his problem.

Another possibility is to encourage assistance for a child with a problem by another member of the same group. Again, within limits this procedure is fine. No child should be asked to do the job you are hired to do.

Numerous variations on the two-group plan could be described. Another example will serve further to illustrate its flexibility. Some teachers may want to stagger their reading periods so that their own availability is increased during independent work (see Fig. 5.5). In this arrangement the reading group not working with the teacher can complete other assignments such as creative writing or a science project or do library reading. The teacher is free to circulate during the independent activity to help individual children.

Independent Activities

Grouped instruction is not possible unless the members of a class are capable of working independently. The teacher must be able to leave some children on their own for a period of time if he is to work intensively with a reading group. Most beginning teachers are greatly concerned about worthwhile activities that can be assigned for independent work. How can the children of a group working independently be actively involved? More often teachers ask, "How can I keep the rest of the class busy?"

The teacher who wants only to keep children busy cannot be effective with a grouped approach to instruction. A healthier attitude toward independent work gives real emphasis to these activities. One of the major goals of reading instruction is making each child an independent reader, one who sets purposes for himself, organizes

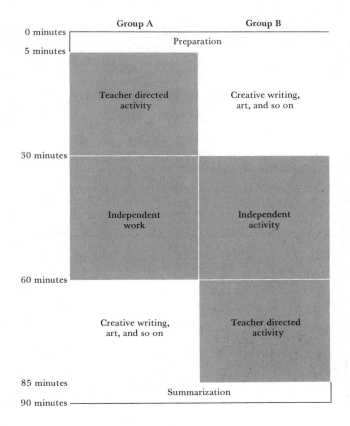

FIGURE 5-5   Staggering the Two-group Plan

Meeting times for instructional groups can be staggered.

his resources, and carries a task through to completion. Only by carefully planning and conducting independent activities as an important aspect of the reading program can this goal be realized.

The first step in building independent work habits is assigning worthwhile activities. A worksheet selected at the last minute and with the sole purpose of occupying children's time stands little chance of capturing interest or enthusiasm. In such a case even the most responsible and mature learner gains nothing from the experience. A worksheet selected because it ties in closely with a newly introduced skill comes much closer to being worthwhile. Children can be helped to see the importance of such a task and are much more likely to put forth real effort in completing it.

A second factor to keep in mind is that frequently all members of a reading group do not need the same assignment for independent work. The worksheet related to a new skill mentioned above is probably more valuable for some than for others. Occasionally the whole group should complete the same assignment. More often different assignments should be given even to children in the same reading group. It is also possible to assign part of a worksheet or similar task to some youngsters who require less drill and plan a different activity for the remainder of their independent work period. Only the teacher who knows the needs and abilities of his students can effectively differentiate assignments in this manner. Diagnostic information obtained by means of the instruments and techniques listed earlier in this chapter and described in detail in Chapter 6 enables the teacher to know student needs and abilities.

Independent activities are not necessarily activities the child completes by himself. Many group projects are excellent for developing independent work habits. Teacher-directed activities are usually not designed to encourage student planning, organization, and execution of a project. Indeed, all independent activities do not necessarily promote these skills either; some independent activities are purely mechanical, practice kinds of experiences. Nonetheless, many independent activities, as will be seen shortly, provide the child with a genuine opportunity to carry out a project alone or in company with his fellow group members.

A variety of possible independent activities will be briefly described here. Later in this text suggested activities for developing specific skills will be given. Chapter 4 contains many suggestions with regard to materials for independent work. Many of the items mentioned can be used as the publishers suggest. The activities suggested below can easily be adapted to fit whatever materials are available, however.

One excellent type of independent activity relates directly to whatever reading selection the child has just completed. For example, the child can select word pictures from the selection or prepare a section for oral reading. A group of children that has read the same selection might prepare a dramatization based on the story. The selection can be studied for evidence proving certain statements true or false or to answer specific questions. Often a workbook or worksheet assignment can be found or developed to further understanding of the selection and promote analysis. Vocabulary items from the story can be used in sentences that alter the meaning of the words. A teacher's guide often contains numerous suggestions for such activities.

Independent activities can also lead the child to make active use of ideas gained from his reading. Individualized and recreational reading in particular ought to draw on these suggestions. An obvious but highly worthwhile activity is to pursue additional reading material on the same or a related topic. The child might construct a model which summarizes or highlights events from a reading selection. Developing an outline of the story or making a comic strip based on its main events can also be valuable activities. A book can be publicized for other members of the class with a pupil-made poster or map based on the story. Other individual projects include making a scrapbook, writing a similar selection, giving the story a different ending, and conducting an experiment.

Group projects such as setting up a special display can be undertaken. A radio broadcast or mural can be developed by a group. Often an appropriate excursion relating to the story can be planned and executed by a group. A quiz program on a selection can be an effective group project also.

Most of these activities may seem to be more appropriate for the intermediate than for the primary grades. However, with adjustment in the amount of teacher direction provided and the length of work periods, many of the same ideas can be effective with younger children as well. Admittedly, independent activities with primary grade children tend to focus specifically on skills and be rather structured. The primary grades are responsible for initiating independent work skills; it is essential that the first experiences be well planned and worthwhile.

Expanding to Three Groups

You will soon want to consider adding another reading group to challenge those youngsters who can handle reading material above grade level. Two factors should determine when a third group will be formed: (1) your ability to plan for and meet with an additional group and (2) specific evidence that certain members of the class need other kinds of attention or activity.

Because each teacher will encounter his own special problems in grouping for instruction, no definite timetable can be given for expanding to more than two groups. Most teachers will want to experiment with a third group on a temporary basis. Appropriate reading materials and the membership of the third group can be decided on the basis of what happens during the trial period. The teacher can also discover how much of a burden is added by forming the third group.

We recommend that the two-group plan be expanded from a two-by-two table to a three-by-three table. Here, as in the earlier plan, the teacher must divide his time among the groups and select useful independent work for the nondirected periods. In the diagram of Figure 5.6 library reading has been suggested as an independent activity. In the primary grades skill-development activities may not permit such liberal use of free reading. However, the importance of

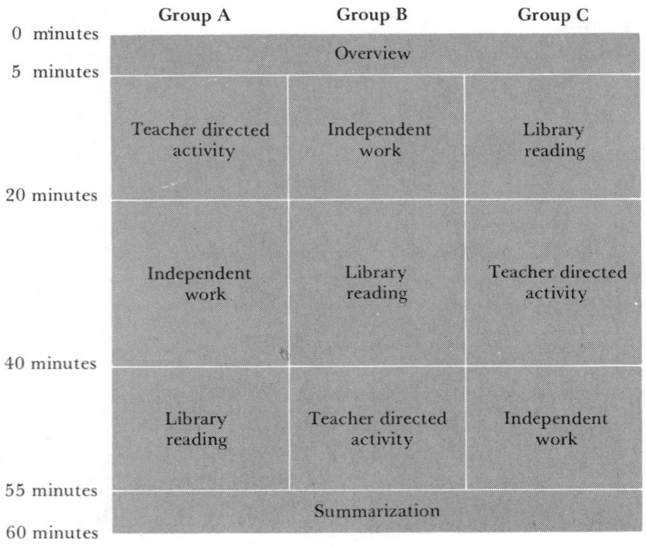

	Group A	Group B	Group C
0 minutes 5 minutes	Overview		
5 minutes 20 minutes	Teacher directed activity	Independent work	Library reading
20 minutes 40 minutes	Independent work	Library reading	Teacher directed activity
40 minutes 55 minutes	Library reading	Teacher directed activity	Independent work
55 minutes 60 minutes	Summarization		

FIGURE 5-6   Meeting with Three Groups

With experience the teacher can expand and refine the basic scheme for meeting with instructional groups.

recreational reading during school hours, particularly during the reading period, cannot be encouraged too much. There is plenty of research evidence to demonstrate that reading is not a popular activity among most adults. A reading program that treats reading for enjoyment as a bad or pointless activity is destined to contribute to this unfortunate situation. A child must be "hooked on books" during his elementary school years or be written off as a defective product of our schools. More will be said about this topic in Chapter 13. It is sufficient to say here that a reading program which fails to encourage reading beyond the basal textbook will not develop lifelong readers.

Dangers of Overgrouping

Most beginning teachers will be doing well if they institute a three-group plan during their first year and run it effectively. Because of special circumstances where one or several youngsters fall considerably beyond the scope of the three groups, complete separation from groups may be required. A child reading material considerably more difficult than his classmates will benefit very little from regular participation in group activities (occasional participation may be quite useful, however). Clearly, special provision must be made for such an exceptional youngster. At the other extreme, a child so severely retarded in reading achievement that participation in a grouped setting would be frustrating should be handled individually. Hopefully, a reading specialist can be asked to work with a youngster of this sort. Expansion of the grouping plan to more than three groups will probably not be helpful in meeting the needs of such atypical learners.

Are more than three groups ever necessary? What is the largest number of groups a teacher can handle? It would be foolish to suggest that three groups will be sufficient to meet the requirements of every classroom. It would be just as foolish to suggest that more and more groups enable the teacher to better meet the needs of each child. Three or four achievement groups should be adequate for most classrooms. Five or more achievement groups require so much preparation and scurrying about that only an exceptional teacher could operate effectively under such conditions. The research reported earlier on the effectiveness of ability grouping should make us cautious about solving our instructional problems with administrative juggling. Instead, a moderate number of groups should be formed and attention then focused on individualizing instruction according to the varied needs of the children within each group. These guidelines for the number of groups do not apply to groups formed on the basis of need or interest. These short-term groups can and should constantly vary in number and size. No guidelines on number are necessary for these specialized groups. Children who cannot benefit from regular membership in an achievement group ought to be handled separately. Occasionally an activity of one group might be helpful to such a child; he could then sit in, of course.

This chapter stated at the outset that most teachers cannot tutor each child, nor do they want to teach only on a whole-class basis. A moderate number of groups can aid the teacher by arranging some mutual experiences for children. Too many groups defeat the purpose of grouping by requiring too much administration on the part of the teacher. An experienced teacher can perhaps handle more groups than an inexperienced one. The suggestion of two to four groups is intended only as a guide. The actual number of reading groups in a classroom is not significant; what matters is the individualization of instruction that occurs.

INDIVIDUALIZING INSTRUCTION WITHIN GROUPS

The point has been made several times in this chapter that grouping can facilitate individualized instruction. Grouping permits the classroom teacher to meet daily on a semipersonal basis with each child. Unless the individual children in a group are given differential treatment, however, grouped instruction is no better than whole-class instruction.

Differentiating Assignments

Earlier a number of techniques and instruments for gathering information on children's reading performance were mentioned. Included were formal reading tests, informal measures of reading, and teacher observation. Evidence for forming reading groups can be gathered with these tools. The same tools are vitally important for individualizing instruction within groups. For example, a basal reader test not only helps the teacher decide a child's reading level but also provides information on needed instruction. An informal reading inventory can be used to assess specific comprehension difficulties which require corrective instruction.

Basically all information the teacher receives through observation, through test performance, or through written assignments is diagnostic data. The alert teacher translates such information into an instructional program based on the child's needs. Whenever an activity is undertaken by a reading group, the teacher then has the information required to differentiate instruction according to need. Youngsters in group A who already possess a given skill, for example, matching sound and symbol, can be excused from a scheduled activity on that skill and given an appropriate alternative exercise. In many cases all youngsters in a group may need the instruction provided by the teacher. Occasionally only one or two youngsters will need assistance. Frequently, selected children from various instructional groups should be brought together for discussion and instruction. The ability to differentiate instruction as suggested here requires knowledge of reading skills, tools for assessing progress, a comprehensive record system that provides easy access to information on each child, and a teacher who is continually diagnosing.

One procedure which incorporates these important elements uses certain principles of programmed instruction. The teacher gathers a set of exercises on a specific skill from old workbooks, commercially prepared worksheets, her own files, the school files, and any other appropriate source. After assembling the exercises the teacher selects useful ones and arranges them in a sequence, beginning with the simple and moving to the complex. The child who can immediately work his way through the exercises can do so independently. His performance is evidence of mastery of the skill. Other youngsters may bog down at various stages in the exercises and require teacher-directed instruction. Children with similar difficulties can easily be grouped for this instruction. Appropriate discussion and follow-up exercises are necessary to make this approach truly differentiated according to individual needs.

This technique can be used to assess progress and provide a systematic record of strengths and weaknesses. It would be a mistake to regard the exercises themselves as the total instructional program. In the case of mechanical skills, actual instruction may be provided by the exercises. Many skills, for example, interpretive reading, may require some interaction with the teacher. A package of materials can be useful in either instance.

A battery of these exercises could be developed for various skills and used as an informal test of mastery. The teacher could then develop a chart which traces each child's progress through the exercises. Figure 5.7 illustrates a set of seven exercises on the long vowel sound. Students who experience difficulty with exercise 2 are given special instruction and several supplementary exercises. Exercise 4 has a similar corrective provision.

Individualizing instruction for children within the same group is primarily a matter of attitude. The teacher who understands that placing children in the same group cannot make them alike stands an excellent chance of meeting individual needs. Recognition of differences is the first step toward individualizing instruction. The second step is differentiating instruction and drill according to the needs identified. The third step is having flexible groups that are changed as developing circumstances dictate. Fourth, the teacher must have different expectations and aspirations for each child according to the abilities and background he brings to a task. The fifth step has not yet been discussed, namely, moving away from grouped instruction as much as possible toward actual individual instruction.

Balancing Group and Individual Instruction

Most teachers cannot hope to tutor regularly every child in their classroom. Grouping has been proposed as an effective alternate, albeit an imperfect solution. The value of one-to-one situations involving student and teacher is undiminished by any grouping plan, even a highly efficient one. Consequently, a balance must be found whereby grouped instruction and individual instruction complement each other. The point of balance is dependent primarily on the ability of the teacher. At first, the new and inexperienced teacher must rely heavily on grouped instruction. Gradually he develops the skill and recognizes the need to free himself for some individualization of instruction. Eventually the bulk of instruction may be handled individually, as with the language experience approach, where grouping serves primarily as a means for developing interests and refining communication skills. Grouping and individual instruction should not become an either-or proposition. Elements of both belong in an effective reading program.

Earlier in this book we placed the four systems for teaching reading along a continuum. The two extreme positions were taken

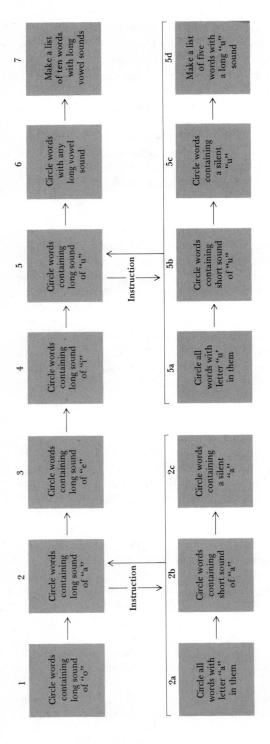

FIGURE 5-7   Exercises on the Long Vowel Sound

A series of written exercises can be used to reinforce skills and provide diagnostic information. The learner progresses through each exercise, 1-7, unless errors indicate that additional practice is needed. Remedial exercises have been added to this illustration for exercises 2 and 5.

by the controlled vocabulary approach and the language experience approach. By combining organizational patterns and instructional systems, it is possible to visualize how the classroom teacher moves away from a highly structured whole-class or grouped approach to reading instruction toward a flexible one-to-one approach emphasizing the integration of communication skills. Seldom will a teacher stand at an extreme position on either the instructional system or type of organizational pattern. Figure 3.3 illustrates how the teacher moves toward his own structure, with less grouping, as he gains experience.

MISUSES OF GROUPING

Grouping is essential to good teaching. The practice is subject to some misuses, however, which must be acknowledged and avoided. Some teachers, for example, use grouping as an excuse for regularly teaching a standard lesson to an entire group. In such a case, membership in a group causes children to lose their individual identity and thereby their individual strengths and weaknesses.

Another serious misuse of reading groups occurs when the teacher mentally assigns each child to the same status in subjects other than reading. Trait differences should caution us as to the dangers of this practice. The lowest-achieving child in a class during the reading period may be an excellent mathematician or speller.

Related to this danger of unfairly giving a child the label low achiever is a long-followed practice of seating children according to reading groups. We strongly recommend that youngsters be thoroughly mixed when seating plans are drawn. Some teachers unconsciously ignore one side of the room during a social studies discussion because the top reading group sits together on the opposite side. It is both unfair and educationally unsound to constantly identify a group of youngsters as a collective body, especially outside of reading class.

Another misuse of grouping occurs when the teacher fails to break up groups occasionally or combine groups for reading activities. Occasionally the whole class ought to participate in an activity. A play or choral reading can offer excellent opportunities for whole-class participation.

Although personal taste dictates actual choice, we are opposed to giving reading groups names which have implied status such as animals. The Robins, Bluebirds, and Crows are labels too frequently used to be humorous examples. Why not use the name of the book being read or the name of a child in the group? While this seems like a small matter, the stigma of group membership weighs heavily on some youngsters. The alert teacher will actively avoid contributing to this circumstance and seek to counteract it whenever possible.

Another misuse of grouping is not giving sufficient time to all groups. While the high-achieving group can and should work independently more often than other groups, this does not mean that teacher direction for this group is not needed. Indeed, with adequate supervision capable youngsters can use their skills of independence to achieve exceptionally well. Left to themselves they are likely to do only what is specifically assigned.

SUMMARY

Children with common instructional needs are frequently grouped together for reading. Grouping is often practiced on a school-wide basis with children assigned to classrooms on the basis of chronological age, ability, achievement, local neighborhood, or at random. Differences among youngsters as well as differences within the same youngster prevent the creation of truly homogeneous groups.

Grouping within a classroom is essential for meeting the needs of the individual. Effective groups are flexible in membership, are formed to accomplish a specific task, are terminated when a task is completed, and are kept small in size. Information needed for forming effective groups must be gathered by a variety of means and on a continuing basis.

The chapter presented a stylized plan for meeting with groups. During the first few weeks of school the teacher should gather evidence on each child and encourage recreational reading. Teachers were urged to begin on a trial basis with two reading groups, splitting their time almost equally between the groups. Gradually a third and perhaps a fourth group can be added as the need arises and teacher ability permits. The importance of planning worthwhile independent activities cannot be overemphasized. Reading groups are not comprised of youngsters with identical needs, and therefore instruction within groups must be differentiated.

Finally, several dangers of grouping are to be avoided in order to employ effectively this approach to reading instruction.

TERMS

trait differences	heterogenous groups
individual differences	Joplin plan
homogenous groups	self-contained classroom

Chapter 6

Assessing Student Needs

The problems of meeting with reading groups and profitably occupying children for independent work are not easily solved, but as you saw in the preceding chapter, neither are they insurmountable. It is apparent that a teacher who constantly gathers information about the progress of his students and regards reading groups only as a means to an end can effectively meet the needs of each learner. The finest grouping plan will be ineffective unless you are able to assess progress and needs accurately. Even the proper matching of learner and materials or choosing an appropriate instructional system are dependent upon accurate diagnosis.

You will find an enormous number and variety of materials available for evaluating reading performance. Your school principal will probably provide you with standardized achievement tests and give you a schedule for administering them to your students. The basal series used by your school district may be accompanied by readiness and achievement tests. The reading specialist in your school system may provide you with an informal reading inventory to be used as you wish with your students. Countless devices of this sort for assessing needs may be available to you. Your ability to organize and use these techniques and instruments in some logical fashion will in large part determine how well you will individualize your reading instruction. The pages that follow present a plan for assessing needs and include an overview of the devices you may wish to employ. The chapter focuses on the following questions:

How can a child's individual needs be identified?

What can be learned from the results of reading tests?

Is teacher observation a source of useful information?

What is an informal reading inventory?

Can a classroom teacher give individual reading tests that are used in a clinic?

Where can critical reviews of reading tests be found?

To be truly effective reading instruction must be differentiated according to the needs of each learner. The classroom teacher is the person who must appraise each child's status, identify his instructional needs, and prescribe the appropriate corrective activities. In order to fulfill the role of diagnostician, the teacher must be armed with techniques and instruments for assessing each child's progress. While the intent to diagnose needs and individualize instruction is essential, a teacher must have, in addition, a strategy for gathering pertinent information and the tools for carrying out his plan. This chapter describes in detail the various tests and procedures that are useful in assessing student needs. You will want to refer back to this chapter at various times while continuing through the remainder of the book.

FORMING READING GROUPS

The assessment of needs in a tutorial situation is relatively simple. With only one pupil to appraise, a teacher can quickly spot difficulties and misconceptions. In such a case remediation is simply a matter of immediate reteaching. Since most teachers must work on a whole-class basis, however, this discussion will focus on how information is gathered on a broader scale. The relation between gathering information and forming reading groups will be emphasized.

Long- and short-term reading groups are formed for instructional purposes on the basis of specific information. How should children be assigned to reading groups? Where does the necessary information come from? What test instruments and classroom procedures can be used to gather information? Three sources of information are especially helpful in providing the evidence required for identifying needs and assigning children to appropriate reading groups: (1) formal reading tests, (2) informal measures of reading, and (3) teacher observation. The classroom teacher needs to employ all of these sources in order to individualize his instruction.

Generally speaking, gathering information begins with the application of gross measures on a whole-class basis. With this approach the teacher screens out learners whose reading achievement and needs are rather apparent and easily identified. Following this general assessment, measures are applied that become increasingly specific and precise for the purpose of further screening. Finally, intensive and detailed analysis is employed with the few cases that cannot be adequately assessed at any previous level.

An inverted pyramid illustrates the successive levels of screening and the decrease in the number of students at each level who require further analysis (see Fig. 6.1).

The approach just described enables the classroom teacher to

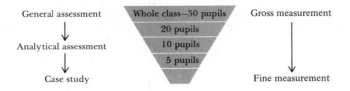

General assessment | Whole class—30 pupils | Gross measurement

20 pupils

Analytical assessment | 10 pupils

5 pupils

Case study | | Fine measurement

FIGURE 6-1   Successive Levels of Screening

At each level more intensive analytic methods are applied to determine the reading problem of the students.

identify one child's specific needs and, at the same time, class-wide reading problems. The instructional program should then be based on the needs identified.

FORMAL READING TESTS

Formal reading tests are of three general types: (1) standardized group tests, (2) basal reader tests, and (3) individual reading tests. The largest category, standardized group tests, is probably the one most familiar to you and the means most frequently used by teachers for evaluating and forming reading groups.

Standardized Group Tests

Standardized group tests are administered under specific conditions following directions given in an examiner's manual. Usually the time period allotted for completing such tests is also standardized. Often the performance of other children on the test is given as norms for the purpose of comparing achievement. Proper use of these instruments can add much to the teacher's understanding of each child's progress and individual needs.

Standardized group tests are helpful to the teacher because they provide information on every child in his class. They correspond to the first level of assessment in Figure 6.1. Achievement batteries such as the *Iowa Test of Basic Skills* (1964) and the *Stanford Achievement Test* (1964) can be used as initial screening devices. These tests usually give an estimate of general reading level and several subscores in such areas as vocabulary, deriving paragraph meaning, and study skills. These tests do not identify specific strengths and weaknesses in reading, however. It is often a good idea to study the errors an individual youngster makes on such tests to obtain some specific information on his performance. Many errors of the same type can alert the teacher to a possible problem. Unfortunately, a teacher seldom has time to do such detailed study for every child in his class.

When used with a good ability measure, achievement batteries can help the teacher decide whether a child is doing as well as might be expected in reading.

While the actual number of items a child must complete varies considerably from test to test and even from section to section in the same test, achievement test batteries typically sample relatively few reading skills and in a rather brief fashion. For example, of the sixty test items a third grader must answer in the reading comprehension section of the *Iowa Test of Basic Skills,* only about five require the child to summarize. Even fewer items require the child to apply critical reading skills. Consequently, the results of such tests must be interpreted in view of this rather important limitation; achievement tests include only a limited number of items on the skills they assess, and even then they do not measure all reading skills. Below are given several items typical of an achievement test.

ACHIEVEMENT TEST ITEMS
Vocabulary

Directions: Choose one of the four words that has most nearly the same meaning as the word in heavy **black** type above them.
1.   A short **tale**
    1.   end
    2.   book
    3.   story
    4.   period

2.   They **seldom** agree
    1.   often
    2.   never
    3.   occasionally
    4.   frequently

The second level of screening in Figure 6.1 might be accomplished with reading tests such as the *Gates-MacGinitie Reading Tests* (1964) or the *California Reading Test* (1963). These instruments are also standardized group tests but focus specifically on reading. Administration of a reading test to youngsters who have unusual results on their achievement battery can provide additional evidence to confirm or refute the earlier scores. In most cases reading survey tests are longer than the reading section of general achievement batteries and thus sample more reading behavior. Because of their greater length, they usually measure more consistently.

Group diagnostic tests such as the *Stanford Diagnostic Reading Test* (1966) and the *Bond-Balow-Hoyt Silent Reading Diagnostic Test* (1955) provide another level of screening. With these tests a profile of scores is obtained for each child (see Fig. 6.2). Patterns of scores may indicate areas needing special attention or point the way to

FORM
W

Stanford Diagnostic Reading Test

LEVEL
II

BJORN KARLSEN • RICHARD MADDEN • ERIC F. GARDNER

NAME _____
                 last   *first*   *initial*

BOY ☐   GIRL ☐   GRADE _____ TEACHER _____

SCHOOL _____ DATE OF TESTING _____
                                                  year   *month*   *day*

CITY OR TOWN _____ DATE OF BIRTH _____
                                                  year   *month*   *day*

STATE _____ AGE _____
                                                  years *months*

T E S T	TEST 1:	Reading	Comprehension	TEST 2	TEST 3	TEST 4	TEST 5	TEST 6
	Literal	Inferential	Total	Vocabulary	Syllabication	Sound Discrimination	Blending	Rate of Reading
RAW SCORE			*					
S	9	9	9	9	9	9	9	9
T	8	8	8	8	8	8	8	8
A	7	7	7	7	7	7	7	7
N	6	6	6	6	6	6	6	6
I	5	5	5	5	5	5	5	5
N	4	4	4	4	4	4	4	4
E	3	3	3	3	3	3	3	3
	2	2	2	2	2	2	2	2
	1	1	1	1	1	1	1	1

*Insert Reading Comprehension Total Grade Score here.

NEW YORK

FIGURE 6-2 The Stanford Diagnostic Reading Test

(Reproduced from Stanford Diagnostic Reading Test, copyright 1966–1969 by Harcourt Brace Jovanovich, Inc. Reproduced by special permission of the publisher)

more detailed analysis with specific skills tests such as the *McCullough Word Analysis Tests* (1962). Because of the time and cost involved in administering, scoring, and interpreting such tests, and the availability of other evidence, not all youngsters need this degree of analysis.

Basal Reader Tests

The second general category of formal measures is basal reader tests. These tests are created by the publishers of basal series to measure the child's readiness for beginning a new book in the series or to provide an appraisal of skills recently introduced. They are therefore more directly tied to the instructional program than the tests previously discussed. For this reason they are especially good for grouping. Basal reader tests may not have accompanying norms and are usually not administered under carefully controlled conditions.

Children often do quite well on basal reader tests, occasionally making perfect scores. Since these tests usually measure mastery of a skill, the focus of the test is the child's grasp of a particular skill or set of skills. The following sample illustrates the number of subtests included in a basal reader test.

SUBTESTS FOR A BASAL READER TEST

Name _____ Age: Years _____ Months _____

School _____ Date _____ Examiner _____

1. Vocabulary:
    a. Word Meaning   _____
    b. Word Recognition   _____

2. Word Analysis
    a. Vowel Sounds   _____
    b. Consonant Blends and Digraphs   _____
    c. Rhyming Words   _____
    d. Attacking New Words   _____

3. Comprehension:
    a. Main Ideas   _____
    b. Sequence   _____
    c. Details   _____
    d. Conclusions   _____
    Comprehension Total   _____

Total: Tests 1, 2, and 3   _____

Summary of Achievement   _____

The use of basal reader tests within the framework of the successive levels of screening is flexible. At times such tests are valuable for whole-class assessment to assist in the identification of instructional groups. At other times children may be regrouped on the basis of need for remedial instruction with such tests since the information provided is immediately useful for planning corrective instruction. Below are several items from a basal reader test.

BASAL READER TEST ITEMS

TEST 1   Vocabulary: Word Meaning

    1.   When you ride in an airplane, you _____.

                          run
                          fly
                          stop

    2.   The last car on a train is a _____.

                    caboose
                    butter
                    cellar

TEST 2   Word Analysis: Vowel Sounds

Select the word having the same vowel sound as the picture.

1. 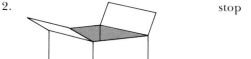   stand   gate   way

2.   stop   pond   roots

TEST 3   Word Analysis: Consonant Blends and Digraphs

Choose the word containing a blend or digraph.
1. dishes   can   chick
2. swim   snow   shoes

TEST 4   Word Analysis: Rhyming Words

Complete the sentence with a word that rhymes.
1.   The big dog ran
      To catch the _____.

                men
                man
                stones

2. I am told
    It is _____.
          cold
          warm
          light

TEST 5   Word Analysis: Attacking New Words

1. A fox lives in a _____.
          den
          men
          pen

TEST 6   Reading Comprehension

Mr. Stone came to Patsy's house.
Patsy liked to watch him work.
First Mr. Stone stirred and stirred the paste.
Next he climbed up and
put the paper on the wall.
The new paper looked pretty.

a. What sentence tells the story best?
    _____ Mr. Stone stirred and stirred.
    _____ Mr. Stone papered the wall.
    _____ Mr. Stone pasted the paper.
    _____ Mr. Stone climbed up.
b. Number in order what Mr. Stone did.
    _____ stirred the paste
    _____ put paste on the paper
    _____ climbed up
    _____ cut the roll

Individual Reading Tests

The third category of formal measures for gathering information is comprised of individual reading tests. Some individual instruments are primarily oral reading tests; others have an oral reading section but contain additional sections that enable the examiner to gather specific diagnostic information.

Tests such as the *Gray Oral Reading Test* (1963) and the *Gilmore Oral Reading Test* (1952) are designed to provide a useful supplement to information gathered by silent reading tests. With these tests the teacher notes the child's ability to read orally paragraphs of increasing difficulty and answer questions concerning the content of what is read. The number of selections that can be read by a child during an administration of these tests limits the amount of reading behavior that can be sampled. Since oral reading tests must be administered individually, they are also rather demanding of teacher time. Furthermore, oral reading requires several skills not necessary in silent reading, thereby increasing the difficulty of assessing only silent reading ability.

Oral reading tests provide, among other things, an estimate of the child's instructional reading level. A great deal of specific information can also be obtained by the skilled teacher who is able to record accurately and interpret reading errors. (Specific suggestions for using oral reading tests diagnostically are given in Chapter 12.) Such tests can also be used to assess silent reading comprehension and listening ability. For silent reading the child is simply asked to read the paragraphs silently and answer the questions. Listening ability can be measured if the teacher reads the paragraphs to the child and then asks him to answer comprehensive questions.

In terms of screening levels, the oral reading test is a type of analytic assessment that can be given to every member of a class. However, teachers often use oral reading tests with children who need more thorough analysis than that which is provided by most group paper and pencil tests.

Some individual reading tests are available in the form of a complete battery. These diagnostic tests can be used to assess the status and needs of those youngsters who require particularly detailed study. The individual diagnostic test focuses intensively on specific reading skills such as knowledge of initial consonants and synthesizing word parts. While relatively few classroom teachers are trained to administer the *Durrell Analysis of Reading Difficulty* (1955) or the *Spache Diagnostic Reading Scales* (1963), knowledge of these tests can be helpful.

The time required to administer a complete individual diagnostic test makes them somewhat impractical for the classroom teacher. The subtests of the *Durrell Analysis of Reading Difficulty* are listed below. One can readily see the degree of detailed analysis possible with this test. It is entirely possible for the teacher to employ profitably parts of this and similar tests.

Subtests of the *Durrell Analysis of Reading Difficulty*

Checklist of Instructional Needs
General History Data
    School Record
    Medical Record
    Psychological Factors — Home History
    Remedial Plans
Oral Reading
    Rate
    Errors
    Comprehension

Silent Reading
    Rate
    Errors
    Comprehension
Listening Comprehension
Word Recognition and Word Analysis
    Flash
    Analysis
Letters
    Letter Naming
    Identifying Letters Named
    Matching Letters
Visual Memory of Words
Sounds
    Hearing Sounds in Words
    Sounds in Letters
Phonic Spelling of Words
Handwriting

The in-depth approach represented by the individual diagnostic test is the logical extension and culmination of a selective screening procedure using standardized tests. With increasing frequency teachers have the services of a reading specialist available to conduct a detailed diagnosis.

Evaluating Formal Reading Tests

For a good many years standardized tests have been the tail that wags the dog in reading instruction. Assessment of student progress has too often been limited to an annual administration of an achievement test. Reading groups have often been formed solely on the basis of grade equivalents obtained from standardized tests. Teachers have too long regarded such tests as sacred measures of their own effectiveness.

Standardized tests have a definite place in a comprehensive evaluation program (Farr, 1970). They can provide gross measures of over-all performance. School districts can use the results of formal tests to make judgments concerning the over-all effectiveness of their reading program. Teachers can use the results of standardized reading tests in conjunction with intelligence tests to determine whether a child is performing up to expectancy. Or children who are reading at approximately the same difficulty level can be identified (this is most often the level a child can attain with maximum concentration, not the level at which instruction should be provided) for purposes of grouping. The time is long overdue for putting standardized tests into proper perspective.

In order to understand fully the limitations of standardized tests, how to use them, and how to interpret them, some special training in educational measurement is desirable. Furthermore, readers should be aware of several valuable sources of information on the evaluation of formal reading measures.

Buros Mental Measurements Yearbook

The *Sixth Mental Measurements Yearbook* (1965), edited by Oscar K. Buros, is a comprehensive source of information on standardized tests. One section deals with tests and a second examines books on measurement. We are primarily concerned here with the section on tests. Entries in the section on tests are classified by type. One major section is devoted to reading tests; subsections include oral reading, reading readiness, special fields, reading speed, study skills, and miscellaneous reading tests.

Each entry provides the following information about a reading test:

1. Title
2. Description of the groups for which the test is intended
3. Date of copyright
4. Part scores (subtests)
5. Whether test is a group test or individual test
6. Whether test is machine scorable
7. Forms, parts, and levels of test
8. Reliability and validity
9. Cost
10. Time required for administration
11. Author
12. Publisher.

A test references section, which lists all known references, published and unpublished, on the construction, validity, use, and limitations of the test, follows each entry. Critical reviews of each test are also included. Some of the reviews are written especially for the *Yearbook;* others are published elsewhere and are only excerpted in the *Yearbook.* In either case the views of experts concerning the value of each test are provided.

One can also find reviews of achievement batteries, intelligence tests, and tests for certain content areas (for example, mathematics, social studies, and science). The entries on character and personality tests may be of special interest to elementary school teachers.

The purpose of the Buros *Yearbook* is to help those who use standardized tests to select the best of what is available and to interpret correctly the results obtained from their use. Unfortunately, many teachers fail to use the *Yearbook*, perhaps because they do not know of its existence or because they do not realize the importance of doing so. It is clear from the reviews in the Buros *Yearbook* that the results of some tests are of practically no value so great are the limitations of the tests, yet they are used and believed. Classroom teachers must assume responsibility for obtaining the information needed for making judgments about the standardized tests they use.

Buros Volume on Reading Tests

Buros has compiled information and reviews on reading tests in *Reading Tests and Reviews* (1969). This volume aids in the task of checking on reading tests; since information has been taken from all six volumes of the *Yearbook*, the necessity is eliminated for following the cross references used in the original yearbooks. A copy of this reference should be available in every school district.

Other References on Reading Tests

The International Reading Association (IRA) and the Educational Resources Information Center/Clearinghouse for the Retrieval of Information and Evaluation on Reading (ERIC/CRIER) have cooperated in the publication of a monograph on measuring reading achievement. *Reading: What Can Be Measured?* by Roger Farr (1970) is a critical examination of standardized reading tests. This publication may be too advanced for most beginning teachers, but it has important implications for the use and interpretation of standardized tests.

Another publication by Farr, written in collaboration with Nicholas Anastasiow (1969), is aimed specifically at the classroom teacher. The authors discuss the use and limitations of achievement and readiness tests and suggest that seven factors be considered in choosing a test: (1) appropriateness of the norms provided by the test published; (2) clarity of directions for administering the test; (3) objectivity of the test; (4) ease of administering and scoring the test; (5) validity of the test; (6) reliability of the test; and (7) completeness of the manual accompanying the test. Readers who lack a fundamental course in educational measurement will find Farr and Anastasiow's discussion of how to use test results especially helpful.

Standardized tests will be used properly and interpreted more accurately when classroom teachers understand the importance of evaluating them or seeking the evaluations of experts.

INFORMAL MEASURES OF READING

Informal measures are teacher-developed instruments and techniques that are designed to assess children's progress in an area of particular interest or concern to the teacher. Such measures are not standardized and, like basal reader tests, are task-oriented.

Five categories of informal measures will be discussed here: (1) workbooks and worksheets, (2) informal reading inventories, (3) cumulative record files, (4) interviews, and (5) checklists and inventories.

Informal measures are particularly useful in providing continuous assessment of a student's performance, thereby providing the information necessary for prescribing immediate corrective instruction. Whereas most group tests measure broad skill areas, informal measures that assess specific skills can be selected and used with individual children. Furthermore, attitudes, tastes, and interests, all of which are difficult to assess by formal means, can be tapped by various informal measures.

Informal measures are useful at various levels in the diagram of successive screening. Information gathered by means of various informal techniques and instruments is especially important when the classroom teacher begins to differentiate instruction by forming groups. In this instance informal measures are regularly used on a whole-class basis. Practically speaking, however, some informal measures are used for intensive diagnosis with only a small percentage of youngsters because of the limited time available to the teacher for such study.

Since informal measures are used at various levels of screening, the following discussion includes a description of the more common functions of each measure. Remember that usage varies with the time and expertness available in a given classroom.

Workbooks and Worksheets

Although not normally regarded as an evaluative device, workbooks and worksheets, when properly used, can be extremely effective means for daily evaluation. Following the introduction of a new skill, the teacher can assign appropriate follow-up exercises in a workbook or provide worksheets on a topic. In addition to providing practice in using the newly learned skill, such a procedure enables the teacher to determine which children might be regrouped for additional instruction and which need individual attention. Teacher-prepared worksheets can be especially effective, since the special needs of individuals within a class are considered as the instructor writes an exercise.

Informal Reading Inventory

The informal reading inventory (IRI) is especially helpful as a means of gathering information for grouping. Essentially the IRI is a series of paragraphs graded in terms of reading difficulty. The selections to be read are often taken from a basal reader series. The IRI is administered by the classroom teacher to individual children. As the child reads the selections aloud errors are recorded and word-attack skill noted by the teacher. Comprehension is usually checked immediately by several questions on the content of the selection. The recreational reading level, the level where instruction can profitably begin, and the level at which the reader is frustrated, can be identified with this instrument. A sample IRI is provided below.

SAMPLE INFORMAL READING INVENTORY

Name _____ Examiner _____

Date _____ Age _____ Grade _____

Directions read to students: I am trying to find out more about your reading ability. I am doing this so that books and other materials which are selected for you are books that you can read. I am going to ask you to read several short selections aloud to me. After each selection, I will ask you a few questions about what you have just read. Do you have any questions? If not, here is the first selection . . .

Directions to examiner: As the student reads orally keep track of his word call errors by marking the accompanying selections.

Errors in each of the following categories during the student's oral reading will be noted in determining functional reading levels (Note: a more detailed scoring system is discussed in Chapter 12):

1. Substitution of a word or phrase
2. Insertion of a word or phrase not appearing in the material
3. Omission of a word
4. Gross or partial mispronunciation of a word

The following criteria will be used in determining the student's functional reading levels:

Levels	Oral Reading Word Call	Comprehension	Behavior
Independent	99%	90% or higher	Freedom from overt signs of tension

SAMPLE INFORMAL READING INVENTORY
continued

Instructional   95%   75% or higher Freedom from overt
                                                   signs of tension
Frustration   Less than 90% Less than 50% Distracting signs of
                                                   tension and nervousness

1. *Independent Level*   This is the level of supplementary and indepen-
    dent reading. A student should be able to read the book at home or
    school without aid. The material should cause no difficulty.
2. *Instructional Level*   This is the teaching level. The reading material
    must be challenging and not too difficult.
3. *Frustration Level*   This level is to be avoided. It is the lowest level
    of readability at which a child is unable to understand. The mate-
    rial is too difficult and frustrates the pupil.

Primer Level* (66 words)

Errors   _____

Comprehension _____

Up the Street and Down

"Oh, hello, Freddie," said Sue.
"Will you please look after my duck?"
Then Sue ran into the school.
    Soon the boys and girls came out.
The boys had airplanes and trains.
The girls had big dolls
and little dolls.
They all had something
for the mothers and fathers to see.
    Freddie look at all the toys.
But he did not look after
the little yellow duck.

Comprehension

1. What is the little boy's name?   (Freddie)
2. Why is Sue talking to Freddie?   (She wants him to do something.)
3. What did Sue ask Freddie to do?   (Care for her duck)
4. What might happen to the duck?   (May get lost)

*In a complete inventory paragraphs would range from the primer to grade 12
level.

Information gained from the administration of an IRI is especially helpful in assigning appropriate instructional materials for each child. Since selections from basal readers are easily included in an IRI, the actual material to be used for the instructional program can be employed. Children can also be assigned to instructional or corrective groups on the basis of an IRI assessment. Because a detailed diagnosis is not easily conducted by means of this informal technique, the IRI is primarily a general assessment tool. A skilled teacher, however, can gather considerable diagnostic information with the IRI.

Cumulative Record File

The cumulative record is a particularly valuable source of information that has been compiled in previous years. The results of formal testing are normally recorded in the cumulative record. More important, the observations of the child's previous teacher are often reported as well as pertinent information concerning health, attendance, and home background. The results of referral for special testing or training are contained in most cumulative records. In grouping for instruction and assignment of appropriate reading material the teacher should take into account such information. Readers were cautioned in the previous chapter about letting the observations of a child's previous teacher prejudice their own appraisal. With the proper precautions the cumulative record file can provide much insight, possibly even showing where one teacher's personal perceptions of a child may have had adverse effects on classroom performance. Successive levels of screening also draw heavily on the information contained in the cumulative record. An in-depth study of one child, for example, often begins with the information contained in the cumulative folder.

Interviews

The classroom teacher should attempt to meet individually with each child in his class on a regular basis. Interaction of this sort permits the teacher to know the child and his needs as no other system can. One-to-one situations involving teacher and student are often difficult to achieve in the modern classroom, yet the information obtained in an interview can be invaluable in forming reading groups and fully individualizing instruction.

The child's attitude toward reading, as well as his reading tastes and interests, can be effectively assessed in a teacher-pupil interview. A quick review of the books a child has recently read and several questions concerning his reaction to them will offer insight no paper and pencil instrument can provide. Samples of oral reading spaced over several weeks and months can highlight progress as well as demonstrate needs and deficiencies. The child's pleasant association between reading and working individually with the teacher in a relaxed setting can be instrumental in building positive attitudes toward reading.

Checklists and Inventories

Checklists and inventories can be developed with many purposes in mind. Information related to a child's home background, travel experiences, interests, hobbies, and personal library can be readily obtained with such devices. These instruments are limited by the ability and willingness of the child to provide accurate responses. An example of a checklist on interest appears below:

INTEREST INVENTORY RECORD

Name_____

What do you like to play best of all? _____
What other games do you like? _____
What do you like to make? _____
Do you have pets? _____
What things do you collect? _____
What are your hobbies? _____
Suppose you could have one wish which might come true, what would it be? _____
What is your favorite TV program? _____
What others do you watch? _____
What is the best book you ever read? _____
What other books have you liked? _____
Do you have any books of your own? How many? _____
Does anyone read to you? How often? _____
Do you go to the library? _____
Do you read comic books? What is your favorite comic book? _____
What magazines or newspapers do you read? _____
What kinds of books do you like best? _____
What kind of work do you want to do when you finish school? _____
What school subject do you like best? _____
What school subject do you like least? _____

Checklists and inventories are valuable on a whole-class basis. Information gathered with these devices enables the teacher to adjust his program in a variety of ways to maximize individualized instruction. Besides being helpful in grouping, knowledge of hobbies may help the teacher guide a youngster's recreational reading or boost his status and self-esteem with the opportunity to present a special report, for example. Examples of checklists and questionnaires as well as other informal measures will be presented throughout this text and their use in special skill areas discussed.

TEACHER OBSERVATION

Teacher observation provides a third means for gathering information for grouping. Some authorities regard teacher observation as the single most important element in an evaluation program (Bond and Wagner, 1966; Smith, 1963). In a single day the classroom teacher has countless opportunities to appraise the progress and needs of each learner. The teacher also has the opportunity to synthesize the diagnostic data gathered from all other sources and adjust his observations to gather missing information. With the press of daily responsibilities, however, teacher observation often fails to provide the information desired.

This gap between the potential and actual value of teacher observation can be overcome by three valuable techniques: (1) systematic observation, (2) anecdotal records, and (3) samples of products.

Systematic Observation

The variety of activities occurring during a reading lesson plus the number of children in a typical classroom combine to form a complex set of interactions for the teacher to observe. Therefore it is essential that specific purposes for observation be outlined ahead of time. The teacher must decide on which child or children he will focus his attention and during which activities. These factors are determined by the need that exists for information. For example, if test data, workbook performance, and interest inventory all point to a specific instructional need for a given child, the teacher may wish to confirm this information with his own observations. By planning, systematic observation can be conducted. Haphazard observation on an incidental basis usually provides little useful information.

An example of systematic observation for a predetermined purpose may be helpful. Suppose that a teacher notices one of his students confusing the prefixes *pre* and *pro* in a workbook assignment. By looking at an achievement test given in the fall, the teacher finds several vocabulary items answered incorrectly when *pre* is used, but several others of the same type are correct. He also recalls a tendency on the part of the same student occasionally to substitute the wrong prefix during oral reading. In view of this incomplete but disturbing information the teacher has a brief session with the child to correct any misconceptions and thereafter pays special attention when the opportunity to observe this skill occurs. Evidence of continued confusion should lead to further instruction.

Systematic observation provides information on specific children and should be used with each child in the room. It is not possible to assign this technique neatly to any given level in the screening diagram. The type of information gathered with this procedure varies with the purposes for which it is used and the expertness of the teacher.

Anecdotal Records

Teacher observations can be further systematized by use of a rather simple anecdotal record-keeping procedure. Pertinent observations concerning an individual child, gathered in either a systematic or incidental manner, are entered in a notebook or noted on file cards. During the press of daily duties a word or phrase can be noted on a slip of paper to aid in recall. Later more explanation and detail can be written into a child's record. Patterns of behavior may emerge in such records, and careful documentation relieves the teacher of trying to recall all significant related incidents. Such records are often useful on a broader scale than reading instruction. A sample anecdotal record appears on the next page.

Samples of Products

Samples of the child's work collected over a period of time can be especially valuable in evaluating the learner. Patterns of errors can be readily identified by this procedure and progress can also be documented. Samples of work should be gathered in specific skill areas or spread across a broad range of skills, depending on the progress of an individual child. The simplest procedure for assembling a collection of products is to develop a folder for each child. Periodically a product from every member of the class can be filed; at other times a particularly revealing or timely product can be filed for individual children.

Information for grouping does not come from a single source nor does it all arrive at one time. The instruments and techniques described in this section are used jointly and continuously to provide the information needed for properly individualizing instruction. As stated earlier, specific application of diagnostic procedures and techniques in specific skill areas will be made throughout the text.

SAMPLE ANECDOTAL RECORD

Ricky Owens
Name

September   2 — Ricky brought a book from home to share with the class. He read orally with excellent expression and phrasing. Title: *Rasmus and the Vagabond.*

September 12 — Especially interested in basal reader story "Hide Rack," story of a dog. Note: Check to see if he has read *Big Red* by James Kjelgaard.

October   14 — Workbook poorly done. Careless errors. Note: Watch Ricky to see if this reading group is too slow for him.

October   18 — Moved Ricky to top group. Seems very pleased and anxious to succeed. His best friend George is in this group. This may be troublesome.

November   7 — Absent today. Missed introduction to Dewey decimal system. Note: Give Ricky individual help and a special worksheet to check his understanding.

November 21 — Very emotional today. Disturbed his reading group during independent work. Check with principal to see if there are any known problems at home.

November 22 — New brother born yesterday. Ricky is proud *and* more normal today.

December   4 — Achievement test results indicate a deficiency in vocabulary. Use listening post and vocabulary-building record to begin corrective program.

SUMMARY

In order to individualize reading instruction effectively the classroom teacher must be capable of assessing each child's personal needs. Various techniques and instruments are helpful in gathering the information required to prescribe appropriate instruction. Formal reading tests, informal measures of reading, and teacher observation were discussed as the most important sources of diagnostic information.

While diagnostic information is essential for planning the instructional program, efficient use of time and resources requires that only necessary information be obtained. A selective screening strategy permits the classroom teacher to identify children who require addi-

Reading

Martha   March 18

Frederick Douglas
    fights for freedom
is about Frederick Douglas
born sometime in Febuary.
He was born as a slave in the
South.

coten feild

FIGURE 6-3   A Child's Daily Work

This sample of a child's daily work reveals a good deal about his comprehension of a story. Children's illustrations are useful sources of diagnostic data.

tional study and at the same time economically discover the needs of every youngster in his class. Diagnostic information should be gathered according to the following guidelines:

1.   Whatever information is gathered should be used to plan instruction that meets the needs of the individual.

2. Comprehensive diagnosis involves more than appraisal of reading skills and abilities.
3. Only pertinent information should be collected and by the most efficient means.
4. Formal and informal procedures are required for complete diagnosis.
5. Decisions with regard to grouping should be based on patterns of scores.
6. Information should be gathered continuously.

TERMS

informal reading inventory	oral reading test
formal reading test	anecdotal record
informal measures	cumulative record file
screening procedure	*Mental Measurement Yearbook*

PART III

INITIAL
READING SKILLS

In order to learn to read, a child needs first to break the alphabet code. To accomplish this he must apply what he knows about language to a system of written symbols. This part of the book contains chapters dealing with perception skills, visual memory skills, and decoding skills. Depending on the child, these skills may be developed at different rates and at different ages. Subsequent growth in reading is built upon these initial reading skills.

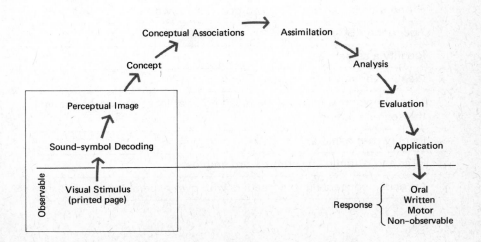

Chapter 7

Visual and Auditory Discrimination and Perception

"Ready or not, here I come!"

This cry from a children's game might apply to a child coming to school. It might fit in two ways: whether or not the teacher is ready to meet him as an individual, he is still coming; whether or not he is ready for the "grade" that he is put in, he is still coming. These are the conditions of a compulsory education system.

How often do teachers wonder where to start when faced with a class of beginning readers, or when confronted with a class of older children, some of whom have not yet learned to read? Should the teacher check the student's vocabulary, give him two dozen words to memorize, teach him the ABC's, or give him a picture book to see if he can "read" pictures?

Since reading is an activity requiring a combination of skills, there must be some that are starter skills. What skills would you choose as initial reading skills? Try to establish an order of priority among the following by numbering from one to nine. The child is able to:

☐ Look at a picture and tell the story of the picture.

☐ Pronounce instantaneously two dozen sight words.

☐ Recite the ABC's.

☐ Identify a sentence.

☐ Identify and name the alphabet letters.

☐ Through pictures indicate the meaning of at least 300 words used in the school reading program.

☐ Identify own name and address in print.

☐ Hear and distinguish various word sounds.

☐ Associate concepts in first readers with own experience.

READY TO LEARN

A child should know that the printed page contains a story or a message using words and phrases similar to those he uses every day; that he can decipher that message by learning to discriminate among the symbols on the page and associating them with the language sounds that he himself makes; that he is to use his own experience to bring meaning to the words on the page. To get ready for reading a child needs these concepts and the skills needed to make the concepts operational. Thus a sense of storytelling, a small working vocabulary, the ability to discriminate among speech sounds, and the ability to discriminate among the letters of the alphabet are crucial skills in the initial stages of learning to read.

This chapter focuses on the initial skills a child needs to approach the printed page. The most obvious ones are related to auditory and visual discrimination. The question of reading readiness is also explored here. In terms of learning to read, the child must acquire perceptions, that is, meaningful images or impressions, based upon what he sees and hears. (See again Figure 1.1 for the place the perceptual image occupies in the reading process.) The role of maturation in the development of perception is treated in this chapter along with the specific visual and auditory skills that are used to discriminate among the written and auditory symbols that enable man to communicate through language. Means of evaluating and of developing visual and auditory discrimination are also described. *Visual discrimination* refers to the ability to note differences through vision, while *auditory discrimination* refers to the ability to note differences through hearing. *Perception* refers to the ability to interpret or give meaning to what is seen or heard. The word *discrimination* should not be confused with *acuity*. Visual acuity and auditory acuity denote the ability of the sense organs to receive impressions, that is, to see and to hear. Evidently, acuity is a prerequisite to discrimination.

At what stage in his development is a child ready to learn to read? This question may seem academic, since most children are introduced to reading in grade one. In many areas, however, education for all children of nursery school age is being seriously considered. Indeed, the federal government has attempted to overcome environmental deficits by early education programs for disadvantaged children, and more and more parents are teaching their children to read before they arrive in grade one. Thus the whole question of reading readiness is pertinent and significant. Teachers and administrators must make decisions concerning when instruction should begin, when and how each child is ready, and which method to use for beginning with specific individuals.

BACKGROUND AND LEARNING

Every human being brings some background experience to a new task. That background assists him in acquiring new knowledge and skill. Whether the learner is a graduate student or a six-year-old, the teacher makes certain assumptions before beginning instruction and adjusts his instruction according to what he discovers about the background of the learner. No one learns well unless he can bring enough knowledge and maturity to the task to grasp it and to see its significance (Ilg and Ames, 1965). In this sense there is a readiness factor in all learning. Through an assessment of readiness emphasis can be placed on the student and learning instead of on the teacher and teaching.

Too often a child's readiness for reading is measured in terms of his physical-motor development and his cognitive development. Tests of hearing, vision, motor coordination, vocabulary, and school-related concepts are administered. Ignored, however, are the child's interests, attitudes, and emotional behavior. It is important in the early stages of reading to determine what interests a child, what his attitudes are toward school and books, and what social-emotional responses he gives to typical events in school. It makes quite a difference in motivating a child to learn to read whether or not he has developed an interest in specific kinds of children's stories, has heard from relatives and friends that school and books are exciting, and learned to listen and to share among members of a group. In order to personalize the initial stages of reading instruction the instructional plan must take these factors into account.

Even though many basal reader series include readiness tests for each grade level, most people think of the readiness program as belonging in kindergarten or the first grade. Typically, there is a readiness period in the kindergarten–first grade years. It has often been looked upon as a period of socialization for the youngster, a time to acquaint him with the behaviors that help him succeed in daily school life. During this period an attempt is made to develop certain common experiences and concepts that the child will be using in his early academic endeavors. Such an experience might be learning what a fireman does and how he helps keep the city safe. Concepts which the children learn may be little versus big, dark versus light, and so on. The identification of certain basic shapes and forms, such as circles and squares, and the names of the numerals and the letters of the alphabet are usually included in the readiness program.

Some educators have questioned the need for the school to offer these kinds of experiences to all children (Ilg and Ames, 1965, p. 5). It is pointed out that watching television and traveling may well provide for many children most of the early readiness experiences once offered in the school. This is an assumption, of course, that the wise teacher will want to test, for the child's environment largely controls the kinds of experiences that he brings to school. There are exceptions, of course. Some very bright children acquire a wide range of valuable perceptions through only a minimum contact with them, for example, while on a visit to the doctor's office. Others may defy the group pattern because a parent reads to them or takes them to library programs. Nonetheless, it is necessary for the teacher to diagnose the very beginnings of learning to read just as he would do at some further point in a sequence of reading skills.

INTEREST IN THE CHILD

Educators sometimes become so concerned with statistical averages that they fail to look at the individual child. Ilg and Ames of the Gesell Institute of Child Development have said, "Education sometimes seems to be interested in everything except the child" (1965, p. 5). This harsh indictment comes from their observation that a compulsory attendance age for first grade often brings with it instruction aimed at the "average child" — a statistical phenomenon and not a real entity. They point out that to be successful the teacher must keep in mind three factors: first, the age and level of maturation of the child; second, the unique individuality of the child; and lastly, the specific environment of the child (Ilg and Ames, 1965, p. 6). The meshing and interrelating of these factors constitutes the learner and the perceptions of the world that he brings to school. The need to accommodate the learning environment to that learner is all the more crucial at the early stages, for it is then that his attitudes and patterns of behavior toward school and learning may be set for years to come.

DEVELOPMENT OF PERCEPTION

Since developmental factors, individual capabilities, and environmental influences all contribute to the child's ability to cope with any learning task, all three should be examined by the teacher who wants to lead the child forward and not ask him to mark time. The developmental aspects are described in other texts, such as Ilg and Ames (1965) and Hildreth (1958). The developmental problem most often discussed in relation to reading is the capability of the child's eyes to accommodate the printed page. There is a divergence of opinion as to the average best age at which to start a child on the visual discrimination tasks associated with reading. As reported in a review of the literature by Silbiger and Woolf (1965), there seems to be as much evidence that the eyes of a two- to three-year-old are able to focus and discriminate print as there is evidence that a child must be six or seven before his eyes are capable of the task of reading. In the light of the research, then, it is feasible, visually, to have a two- to three-year-old read. This statement is neither an endorsement nor an encouragement. If the child wants to learn to read and the parent has the time and resources to guide him, there is little reason to be fearful.

Durkin (1966) conducted studies of children who read early to see what long-term effects such skill produced. She found that the children either led their peers in reading achievement after several years or at least were on a par with their age mates. No ill effects of early reading were reported.

Thus it would seem that the K–1 children generally are able to begin tasks associated with reading. Obviously a number of factors interact to determine readiness for reading—awareness of language, physical ability to hear and see symbols, intellectual and emotional maturation, a vocabulary and body of concepts for social exchange, and a perception of the printed page as a means of communication.

We have already noted that socioemotional and physical factors are concomitant to learning any skill associated with reading. It should follow that the teacher will include those factors in his analysis of the child and will plan activities to promote favorable attitudes toward reading and the development of perceptual skills specifically related to reading. A normal part of teacher thought and planning should be to encourage language growth, to establish interesting ways to explore words, and to make it fascinating to find a new word and to see how it fits into the child's world.

Visual discrimination has an evident relation to reading. The eye must grasp word and sentence units as wholes while simultaneously using internal cues to perceive the sentences as a meaningful utterance prepared by a writer.

Perception relies on accurate discrimination, but a learner perceives from many different vantage points. His perceptions reflect his socioeconomic, emotional, linguistic, and motivational resources. The teacher can use the diversity of perceptual response to show children that reading can be quite personal and yet have some general group meaning as well. When reading, children will use those cues that they need to understand and interpret the printed page. It is the teacher's responsibility to see that the child has the visual discrimination skills needed to focus on and select the cues that enable him to receive the message of the author.

Auditory discrimination too is related to reading, though the connection is not as evident as with visual discrimination. Auditory skills must be refined so that not only whole words and whole utterances are perceived accurately but so that word parts or units of sound may be identified. The ability to grasp small units of sound and attach meaning to them is an important word-analysis skill and is therefore closely related to the development of reading skills.

Maturation and Perception

As the child grows and gains greater control of his body he also develops more accurate and more meaningful perceptions. Most children develop a perception of themselves and objects in the world through exploration and curiosity (Gibson, 1968). Once the differences among other things are perceived, the child strives for additional distinctions to bring order to his world of perceptions. "Objects" that give him food and cuddle him are distinguished from those that do not.

The environment usually aids perceptual development. The child is rewarded for recognizing that things are different. Verbal stimuli are used to encourage perceptual development. *Big* and *little*, *hard* and *soft*, and similar verbal stimuli are used in the environment to assist in the development of language perceptions. Even though the environment aids in this development, maturation seems to account for the child's continuing attempt to organize and stabilize his environment (Gibson, 1963).

Coordination and manipulation play a role in perceptual development, but precisely how important these factors are is not clear. The research does not demonstrate a strong relation between motor coordination skills and reading. Far more important is the need to concentrate on those skills that have an evident and direct relation to the process of reading, such as auditory and visual discrimination skills.

Perceptual Training

A number of factors are typically associated with reading readiness: picture interpretation, a speaking vocabulary that enables the child to be understood in the class, left-to-right orientation, family and neighborhood experiences, desire to read, ability to attend to the task at hand, a sense of sequence, ability to follow directions, ability to discriminate visual forms (letters and words), ability to discriminate similarities and differences in sounds (rhyme sounds and initial consonant sounds), and ability to see spatial relations and other visual-motor perceptions. The teacher provides training in these areas as his review of the children's skills indicates a need. Most of these skills are developed through a variety of social situations, the child hardly realizing that he is learning. The skills associated with visual and auditory discrimination and perception, however, are often given a more formal and direct treatment to ensure their accuracy for reading.

Visual discrimination, because of its obvious connection to reading, receives more emphasis in early reading programs than does auditory discrimination. Children come to school with considerable knowledge about the sound of language. Inductively, they have learned the sounds and the grammatical system. Most of that knowledge is not conscious knowledge, and so the teacher tries to improve the child's knowledge of language by giving him a conscious awareness of its sound system. On the other hand, children usually have very little knowledge and skill in the graphic (visual) system of language. They need basic instruction to develop knowledge, and they need frequent practice to develop visual discrimination and perceptual response patterns that will enable them to read.

In an overly simplified view reading may be considered a series of word perceptions. To distinguish between words, the reader needs letter or grapheme cues. The purpose of distinguishing words, of course, is to relate them to language and communication. That goal must not be lost in exercises or isolated visual and auditory discrimination skills. Thus children must learn automatic responses to the sound and the sight of letters. Accuracy in these skills of auditory and visual perception seems especially important in the early stages. A nation-wide study of first grade reading found that the item most highly correlated with success in reading at the end of the first grade was the child's knowledge of the letters of the alphabet prior to instruction in school (Bond and Dykstra, 1967). To assist the child the teacher should show him how to perceive more accurately the sight and sound of the letters.

The above statements should not be interpreted to mean that a knowledge of the letters of the alphabet results in better reading performance. In reality, knowledge of the alphabet and early success in reading both may be manifestations of some language ability that we have so far not been able to measure.

VISUAL PERCEPTION AND READING

When a reader looks at the printed page he must understand several things in order to get the message. He must understand that the symbols there represent another person's attempt to give him a message. He must know the conventions that are used in printing a message—that in English writing starts on the left and moves to the right; that capital letters and periods are signals for beginning and ending an utterance; that the symbols represent the sound symbols used in speech.

Applying each of the understandings mentioned above involves perceptual habits or skills. Moving the eyes from left to right across the page, using the symbolic cues to recode them into speech patterns, and identifying the punctuation and capitalization cues as indications of juncture and stress are all perceptual skills. All involve processes that take a visual stimulus and turn it into a meaning-bearing internal response. These perceptual skills do not develop automatically. They must be taught as part of the initial reading program if the teacher determines the child did not bring them with him when he came to school.

AUDITORY AND VISUAL INTEGRATION

To start formal reading instruction the child must first perceive that the words he knows from speaking can be represented with visual symbols.

Usually the teacher demonstrates how speech and print are integrated in the reading process by pronouncing a familiar word, such as *ball*, and then writing it on the board. He then uses the word in context and shows a concrete example, where that is possible. He shows them a ball and asks, "Who knows what a ball is? Well, this is the way the word *ball* looks when I write it: *ball*. Now look in this book that I am holding and see if you can find where the word *ball* is written on this page." Thus the sound of the word is isolated; the isolated word is printed in isolation; then the printed form is viewed together with other words on a printed page. The process of relating speech and print has begun.

Using name cards for the children in a class is another effective means of introducing the idea that the sound of each name is different and is represented by different visual symbols. The teacher can have each of the children examine his name card very carefully. "I am going to spread your name cards on the table and see who can find his own card. Remember, every name is different in its sound and so it will be different in the way it is written." Some of the children will already know what their name looks like because they have learned it at home. These children can select their name card quickly and then begin some other activity. The teacher can assist those that have difficulty until some identifying features on their name card will help them find it when they report to class on the following day. Care should be taken that the identifying feature is not a spot of dirt. Letter combinations, m-a-r in *Marla*, for example, should be stressed.

Some teachers prefer to have the children dictate sentences or stories which are then written on a piece of paper or on the board as a means of demonstrating that educated people can represent speech sounds with visual symbols. This technique, known as the experience-story approach, was discussed in detail in Chapter 3. Whatever techniques are used, it is important for an accurate perception of reading for the children to understand that by learning the relation between the spoken word and the printed symbols they will be able to decode the printed page. If the language of the book is close to the language of the child, meaning will be grasped easily.

BEGINNING STAGES OF COMPREHENSION

From the beginning the teacher should emphasize that the printed page carries a message; it is not simply a series of words. It is not enough to respond to the spelling b-a-l-l with the sound /ball/. When *ball* is placed in conjunction with other words, does the child have a visual perception of what is taking place? *The ball bounced into the street.* "When you see the word *ball*, Henrietta, do you have a picture in your mind of what a ball looks like?" "Can you see the ball bounce into the street?" Reminders of this sort by the teacher will assist the children in their attempts to put various words together to form a continuous message.

Initially, of course, the teacher is primarily concerned with making sure that the children have some image, some meaning, that they ascribe to the word they are working with. Evidently the teacher does not have to examine all the words that appear in their exercises to see whether all the children know them or not. It will usually be sufficient for the teacher to ask individuals, "What picture do you have in your mind when you see the word *busy*?" Such a reminder will encourage all the children to strive for meaning in the series of words they see.

Meaningful Units

As quickly as possible written words should be placed in phrases or sentences that are familiar to the students. The sooner they see that written words and their own speech are related, the more likely they will perceive reading as a flow of ideas, as a communication, and not merely as a series of words that sometimes defies comprehension. "I will write something on the board and you tell me what it says." For example, the teacher writes, *Good morning, children. The sun is warm today.* Provided they have already been introduced to each of these words, the children will read what the teacher has written and be pleased that they got the message.

In practice exercises the children must see the isolated words placed in phrases or in complete sentences.

> *Mother.*
> *My mother.*
> *My mother cooks.*

Or the children themselves may be encouraged to provide meaning-ful units. They need not always restrict themselves to the words that have been developed for the entire group. As long as the words under study are put into meaningful context, the children should be able to see the need to think with a series of words instead of just one.

> *Rain.*
> *It's raining cats and dogs.*
> *Cool.*
> *Dig that cool cat, man.*

Whenever possible a concrete demonstration should be included in the learning activities to help in the development of perception for reading.

Once the child begins to read with a certain amount of fluency, he often relies on known sound patterns to identify individual words and the message of the passage. There is often an automatic trigger-ing of known sound patterns by some of the written words that the reader sees. It is easier to see this happening in children with certain dialect patterns than it is with children whose basic speech is similar to that of the text they are reading. For example, certain dialects often omit the "s" in the third person singular verb. *He says, he runs, he fights* turn into *he say, he run, he fight.* In reading aloud the teacher will hear children with those dialect patterns read: "Dan aint (isn't) mean. But when he has trouble, he fight. Then he run to his mother and he say. . . ."

Teachers may feel compelled to correct a child whose dialect shows up in reading aloud, feeling that a reading error is being committed. It is not a reading error; it is a language difference. Consequently, the teacher should *not* say, "You did not read those lines correctly." At an appropriate time when the children are mature enough he may want to discuss the different kinds of dialects and show that reading aloud is one way of learning how to pronounce the dialect that is used in most books. (For further discussion of dialect differences, see Chapter 12.)

Thus it appears that the good reader quickly uses a combination of visual cues and relates them to speech, often triggering known sound patterns from ingrained speech habits (Gibson, 1968; Strang, 1968). He uses as many visual cues as he needs to set the images flowing and to trigger the language habits that previously existed. As he speeds up the process, he is in effect reducing the number of visual cues that he relies on. Initially, however, he may need to examine most words with great care to make sure that the gross and the internal cues are enabling an accurate perception of the words and the images that are intended.

Diagnosing problems concerning the relation of reading to perception involves examining both auditory and visual discrimination abilities as well as auditory and visual perception abilities. It is possible for a person to hear language and perceive it adequately, that is, give it valid meaning, yet not be able to discriminate precisely among the minute sounds of the language. The same relations could occur between visual perception and visual discrimination. A person who looks at a series of words and does not gain an accurate perception of the words may either have insufficient skill in discriminating among the visual cues available or may not have sufficient skill in discriminating among the sounds of words and within words. In either case the relation between sound and symbol is not adequately integrated, and the perception of the word is confused or elicits no meaning.

TEACHING AUDITORY AND VISUAL DISCRIMINATION

In actual teaching, however, auditory discrimination activities precede visual discrimination activities. In the following section on how to teach these skills, auditory skill instruction is described first, then visual discrimination.

Auditory Discrimination in the Classroom

According to Fries (1963), speech sounds are learned through a recognition of the contrasting features of words. Thus a child learns the difference between the sound of *hat* and *bat* not because he is aware of their *at* similarities but because through much practice he has paid attention to the *h* and *b* contrasting sound features. Some linguists believe that the contrasting features in learning speech sounds operate also on a phrasal or an utterance basis (Lefevre, 1964). These linguists are saying, in effect, that the speaker has a built-in system for discriminating among sounds. If the teacher can make the learner conscious of those sounds and the relations among them as they appear in words, then the leaner can move easily and securely into an analysis of printed words by using a sound-symbol pattern to assist him.

Correlation

A number of studies have been conducted over the years to analyze the relation between auditory discrimination skills and reading achievement. Duker (1962) reviewed thirty-two of these studies and concluded that there is a significant correlation between the two factors. It should be remembered, however, that a correlation between two factors does not necessarily indicate a causal relation; that is, one does not necessarily cause the other. There may be a more general factor that accounts for both auditory discrimination skill and reading achievement. Dykstra (1966) did not find a noteworthy correlation between auditory discrimination subtests in first grade readiness tests and reading achievement at the end of the first grade. He did discover that boys learn auditory discrimination abilities less readily than girls and take longer to master the reading process. Since subtests in standardized group tests usually are not highly reliable, the findings of these studies must be interpreted with great caution.

A different kind of relation that adds insight into the value of auditory discrimination skill is that severely disabled readers almost always have a marked inability to discriminate sounds in words (Durrell, 1953). When children were subjected to specific training exercises in recognizing speech sounds there was a marked improvement in their ability to discriminate (Silvaroli, 1966).

As is the case with other language abilities, a child's environment and his level of maturation affect his auditory discrimination. A social environment in which speech sounds are slurred or muffled obviously will not provide as much practice in discrimination as an environment which provides a model for clear enunciation (Deutsch, 1964). The developmental nature of the discriminatory process can be demonstrated from the fact that a decreasing number of children show problems in this area at each higher age level—27 percent with problems in grade one; 19 percent in grade two—according to a study by Wepman (1960). Similar findings were obtained in a longitudinal study by Thompson (1963) who recommended (1) that first grade entrants who show poor scores on an auditory discrimination test be given an extended readiness period in which exercises to develop this ability are presented; (2) that those who develop slowly in the ability also be introduced slowly to phonics instruction; and (3) that those who score high on an auditory discrimination test be introduced to an accelerated program of word study.

Developing Auditory Cues

Since the child comes to school with a built-in sense of the contrasting features of speech sounds (Fries, 1963), he must be taught how to use that knowledge to help him with his reading, including his word-analysis skills. He must learn to think of words as having sound components (phonemes) and be taught to pay attention to certain parts of words so that he can identify beginning sounds, ending sounds, and medial sounds. There are a variety of techniques and exercises that a teacher can use to teach auditory discrimination. Some of them include telling whether words rhyme, matching pictures with word sounds, identifying the similarities and differences in beginning and ending sounds in words, and identifying the limits of phrases and sentences by intonation patterns (the voice usually falls at the end of a sentence). Some samples of these kinds of exercises are given below.

Auditory Discrimination Exercises

The following exercises are designed to develop the student's auditory discrimination:

A. LISTENING FOR RHYME WORDS.
    This very simple exercise is a good one to use with prereaders.
    1. The teacher pronounces two words.
    2. If the words rhyme (*mill-hill*), the students say "yes." If the words do not rhyme, the students say "no."

    Examples:
    drum-hum, boom-bang, cap-mad, bake-cake, small-tall, fan-man, sit-hit, cold-gold

B. LISTENING FOR THE SAME WORD.
    This is a good exercise for prereaders, but it is a little more difficult than listening for rhyme words.

    The teacher says, "I am going to say several words. One word I will say twice. Listen carefully and see if you can tell me which word you hear two times. Raise your hand as soon as you know what the word is."
    Sample lists: *ball*, girl, fork, *ball*
                    tree, fish, *tree*, boy
                    girl, *boy*, run, *boy* ,plan
                    cat, pig, tree, *cat*

C. LISTENING FOR INITIAL SOUNDS.
    The teacher says, "I am going to say several words. Most of the words begin with the same sound as the word *bat* begins with. Raise your hand when you hear a word that does not begin with the same sound as *bat*. The words are: big, boy, *sick*, basket, *camera*, bomb."

    Either single consonants or consonant blends can be used in this exercise.

D. LISTENING FOR MEDIAL SOUNDS.
    The teacher says, "I am going to say several words. Most of the words have the same middle sound as the word *cat* [pronounce very dis-

tinctly]. Raise your hand when you hear a word which does not have the same middle sound as *cat*. The words are: fat, *get*, man, ham, *sit*."

In this exercise most of the middle sounds are vowels.

E.   LISTENING FOR FINAL SOUNDS.
   The teacher says, "I am going to say several words. Most of the words end with the same sound as the word *big* [pronounce very distinctly]. Raise your hand when you hear a word which does not end with the same sound as *big*. The words are: bag, fig, *mad*, sag, *help*, leg, *sick*."

   In the above exercises make sure the children know the meaning of *beginning, middle, end*.

Exercises in workbooks and in basal texts offer similar activities for the teacher to use in helping students develop auditory discrimination skills. All children do not need all of these exercises. They should be applied selectively based upon the specific and identified weaknesses in auditory discrimination. Equipment such as the tape recorder can be used to great advantage because the child can listen to sounds as often as he needs to and can record his own attempts at reproducing sounds.

Evaluating Auditory Discrimination

As we have seen, hearing, or auditory acuity, naturally plays a role in auditory discrimination. If a child has defective hearing, he may not be able to identify certain kinds of sounds. For example, some hearing losses reduce or eliminate the reception of high-frequency sounds. Thus the sounds associated with the consonants f, s, k, and similar sounds would go unnoticed or be effectively obscured. An individual with this kind of hearing deficiency needs reading instruction that emphasizes visual techniques instead of a strong auditory-visual relation (Rosenberg, 1968). The teacher cannot diagnose a specialized hearing loss such as the one just described, but many schools conduct examinations using auditory screening devices called audiometers. If a hearing loss is indicated by the general school screening, the child should be referred to a physician for a complete examination and prescription. The teacher would then use the knowledge of the deficiency and the doctor's recommendations to modify instructions for the child.

   In some instances the teacher may notice symptoms of a hearing deficiency. A child may turn his head as if to listen with one ear or cup his ear or not respond to fairly low-volume instructions. In the light of these symptoms the teacher may want to conduct a rough screening test of his own. This can be done by having two or three children sit with their backs to the teacher, who then whispers their names or their birth dates or other key words. They are to raise their hands when they hear the words that apply to them. If such an exercise adds evidence to what the teacher has previously observed about hearing difficulties, the child should be referred to the school nurse for further testing. Again, instructional techniques should be adjusted to enable the child to function as best he can with his disability, for example, giving him a seat close to the teacher.

Tests of Auditory Discrimination

Assuming that the child has normal auditory acuity, the teacher needs to know how well he can distinguish sounds in words before asking him to make specific sound-symbol connections. Most first grade readiness tests, such as the Metropolitan and the Lee-Clark, contain subsections devoted to exercises in auditory discrimination. As Dykstra (1968) has indicated, however, these short subtest scores are not reliable for an individual diagnosis. They can be looked upon only as very weak indications of the student's skill. As a separate instrument the teacher can use the *Wepman Auditory Discrimination Test*. This test poses a series of paired words (*meal-veal, ball-ball*) and the listener is asked to indicate whether they are exactly alike or whether they are different. The list of words includes comparison and contrasts of all the consonant and vowel sounds in initial, medial, and final positions. A guide indicates which sounds the student is missing and how many errors constitute a serious problem at his age level. Armed with the information that the test reveals, the teacher can set up a series of exercises to teach the specific discriminations that the child needs, or he can proceed with other kinds of instruction if the test shows adequate discrimination in all sounds.

Teacher Test.

The teacher can carry out a procedure similar to the Wepman test using his own list of words, such as the one below. By providing the students with a simple answer sheet such as the following, the teacher could test a group.

> Mark + if words are exactly the same; — if words are different
>
> | | |
> |---|---|
> | 1. _____ | 6. _____ |
> | 2. _____ | 7. _____ |
> | 3. _____ | 8. _____ |
> | 4. _____ | 9. _____ |
> | 5. _____ | 10. _____ |

When the teacher makes his own test he can check on the specific sounds he has taught or he can use it as a pretest for a group of sounds. The students do not have to respond in writing. A list of paired words can be administered to an individual or two who sit with their backs to the teacher. The students raise their hand when the words are different, and the teacher records their correct responses.

The suggestion that teachers construct their own auditory discrimination test needs a caution. Informally constructed tests are always subject to the vagaries of the test-making skill of the person who writes the test. The noise level in the room and the volume, pitch, and articulation of the teacher's voice obviously play a part in the reliability of these informal techniques.

Given below are sample directions and words that could be used in an assessment of auditory discrimination.

General Directions: Try a few samples in each category to make sure the child understands what he is to do. He may respond "yes" if items are the same and "no" if they are different. Then have him face away from the examiner for testing. Be sure not to give any clue, by vocal emphasis or otherwise, to the correct answer. Record responses, as indicated above.

I. AUDITORY DISCRIMINATION

 A. Initial consonant discrimination
     Are these words the same or different? Call one pair at a time.

tip	dip	feel	veal	hill	fill
red	red	boon	moon	leaf	reef
cheap	jeep	bum	dumb	den	ten
pin	bin	yes	yes	peach	beach
shin	chin	sip	ship	fall	fall
pal	pal	fix	fix	cheap	sheep
zip	sip	mold	cold	some	come
goat	coat	yard	lard	feel	feel
coast	toast	thin	fin	yawn	lawn

 B. Final consonant discrimination
     Are these words the same or different?

rack	rag	cup	come	swim	swim
leaf	leave	had	hat	tide	tight
moon	moon	good	good	rub	rum
pit	pill	then	them	seed	seat
razz	rash	sob	sop	wig	wing
rip	rib	ride	ripe	steam	steep
bus	buzz	clay	clay	take	tail
home	hope	Ruth	roof	bat	bad
run	run	much	mush	live	lip

 C. Vowel discrimination

cop	cap	been	bun	hat	hun	beg	big
hit	hat	rod	rod	doll	doll	cut	cut
rub	rib	bug	bug	leg	leg	hit	hut

mat	mat	luck	lock	bit	bet	rip	rap
big	big	had	head	dock	duck	but	bat
odd	add	but	bet	lid	led	ball	ball
man	men	lap	lip	pen	pan	cup	cop

II.   EVALUATION

1. Disregard one error in each category. In kindergarten and first grade expect more than one error in each category. A few errors may occur by chance.
2. Study errors for patterns and clues. Finding error patterns is much more significant than counting the number of errors.
3. List the specific difficulties:
    Beginning position _____
    Ending position _____
    Medial position _____
    Consonant errors _____
    Vowel errors _____

After instruction has been given in specific discriminations the teacher should construct a test or an exercise that will evaluate the child's achievement. The criteria for the test are determined by the elements that have been taught. Success for the child, in other words, should not be measured by his score on some general instruments such as a standardized readiness test but on his ability to discriminate the specific sounds that have been previously identified and taught. Thus if the teacher had taught the sound discriminations between /p/ and /b/, /d/ and /t/, and /ch/ and /sh/, the test should focus on words that enable a child to show his skill in distinguishing these sounds. For example, /p/ and /b/ could be tested with word pairs such as *pear-bear, pate-pate, cop-cob, rob-rob,* and so on.

Visual Discrimination in the Classroom

Visual acuity, the ability to see the fine lines that make up the letters, is only one factor in discrimination, but an important one, as indicated by Strang.

> All but a few exceptional children learn to read by associating the sound of familiar letters and words with their corresponding written symbol. Consequently, both visual and auditory acuity are a basis to success in beginning reading.
>
> To see clearly, eyes must work well together, diverge and converge at will, and integrate two images into one. To achieve this, numerous experiences of integrating sensations are necessary. Normal vision is an important precondition of maximum reading comfort and efficiency; it is basic to perception. Prob-

ably far too many children have been handicapped in beginning reading because of undetected visual impairments, most frequently muscular imbalance and problems of convergence.*

Visual discrimination skill is evidently related to the development of perception as the child attempts to sort out and stabilize his environment. The grosser visual discriminations of early childhood, for example, distinguishing between a happy face and an angry face, must give way to the fine distinctions of identifying letters of the alphabet in kindergarten and first grade in order to learn to read.

The teacher should note any indications of possible visual difficulty and refer potential problems to the school nurse or to an eye doctor. Some symptoms of visual difficulty are:

Cocking the head so as to read with only one eye
Holding the side of one's head when looking at the book or board
Rubbing the eyes during reading
Red eyes, watery eyes
Holding the book too close
Holding the book at arm's length
Complaints of headaches
Squinting or other indications of strain
Complaints of haziness or fading of printed symbols.

The goal of visual discrimination as related to reading is to enable the child to identify accurately the written symbols that an author has used to communicate his message. In order to do this the child must make use of both visual discrimination and visual perception. He has to hold in his mind simultaneously the whole word, its parts, and the sentence with its visual cues, punctuation and capitalization. This means that the reader must pay attention to the wholeness of the word while distinguishing the internal parts that give it characteristic features. Until a child has developed a sense of the patterns of words and sentences and until he has enough practice to develop automatic responses to those general configuration and internal-part cues, he reads rather slowly and laboriously. He has to take the time to see the whole word and then check rather systematically to verify that it is the word he wants to pronounce.

Because reading is a combination of responding to the whole word and to the internal cues, both general-configuration memory techniques and letter-distinction techniques are used in teaching a beginner how to recognize words. It follows that both techniques should be part of initial instruction in word recognition.

*Strang, Ruth, *Reading Diagnosis and Remediation* (Newark, Del.: International Reading Association, 1968).

Research on Visual Discrimination

Success in early reading greatly depends on the child's ability to discriminate among the letters of the alphabet and among basic word forms (Barrett, 1965; Bond and Dykstra, 1967). At least recognition of letters of the alphabet and verbal forms is a better predictor of success than the ability to discriminate nonverbal material, such as circles and triangles. This should not come as a great surprise, for the identification of letters of the alphabet encompasses the ability to identify more gross forms.

A number of research studies help identify the kinds of visual discrimination skills possessed by good and poor readers. Vernon reviewed twenty-two studies relating to perception in reading and found that (1) good readers do not perceive every letter in every word, but focus on a few key words which they appear to perceive as a whole and then infer the meaning of the whole phrase; (2) most readers use the first half of the word as their cue rather than the second half of the word; (3) deleting the lower half of words causes little difficulty in reading them, whereas deleting the upper half makes them almost illegible, for example, baby's crib/baby s crib for baby's crib; (4) children of five years of age are sometimes unable to see the difference between a shape and its mirror image even when it is pointed out. Vernon concluded that

> acquisition of facility in well-integrated perceptual processes requires prolonged practice, much of it in tasks which are singularly difficult for young children. Even when the child has become thoroughly familiar with these processes and can perform them rapidly and easily, he is still at the stage of reading each word separately.*

The instructional consequences of these findings would appear to be a careful examination of visual discrimination skills and perception and a careful programming of instruction in the skills identified as weak.

Disabled readers, those who have had some instruction but have not made satisfactory progress, also give some insight into the need for visual discrimination in reading. Coleman (1953) found that a majority of the thirty-three subjects he examined were markedly retarded in perceptual development; that perceptual development lagged significantly behind the development of general intelligence in a majority of the subjects; and that retardation in perceptual development was cumulative with age. Once again the need for instruction in visual discrimination and visual perception tasks and their carry-over practice in reading was emphasized.

*Vernon, M. D., *Backwardness in Reading: A Study of It's Nature and Origin* (London: Cambridge University Press, 1960).

Environment may often play a hand in perceptual development. Elkind (1965) endorses the Piaget concept that training and maturation contribute significantly to perceptual development. In an environment in which there is little stimulation to make distinctions among various forms in infancy and early childhood, perceptual development may be retarded. For example, if the child does not see samples of circles (balls) and squares (alphabet blocks) and triangles (mobiles) and other objects that babies are usually encouraged to play with, he may not develop the skill of discriminating among forms such as alphabet letters that are essential to reading. The same would hold true for auditory discrimination. It may be retarded as a result of lack of stimulation. Environment may even account for the way a child learns easiest in school. If an auditory presentation alone makes it difficult for the child to learn, then a visual presentation or a combination visual-auditory presentation should be used.

Bateman (1967) found that an auditory-oriented program for first grade children was substantially more effective than a visually oriented program. With a sample of Black boys Katz and Deutsch (1963) found just the opposite — that the visual presentation was the easiest. The kind of language ability possessed by the two groups may be the factor that caused the difference and cautions us against jumping on the bandwagon of any one approach.

Developing Visual Discrimination in the Classroom

Using a diagnostic approach to the teaching of visual discrimination, kindergarten and first grade teachers should first find out which children can identify the letters of the alphabet, both upper and lower case. Children who already can identify the letters as a result of instruction they have received at home need only as much practice with the letters as will make their responses automatic.

The research of Muehl and King (1966) indicates a definite advantage to teaching visual discrimination through the letters of the alphabet. For children who cannot identify letters of the alphabet when they begin kindergarten, the forms of the letters could be shown in large type or in plastic letters. The children can develop discrimination skills and a knowledge of letter forms through tracing, flash card exercises, and seeing and identifying letters in words and in signs. As their visual discrimination and perception ability matures, the size of type can gradually decrease, as in elementary school readers.

The principles for developing visual discrimination and automatic recognition can be used in teaching at all levels, from kindergarten up. The student must see the distinctive differences in the form of the letters or words, and must practice them in isolation and in context; automatic responses should then be developed through such means as flash cards and tachistoscopic instruments. A simple

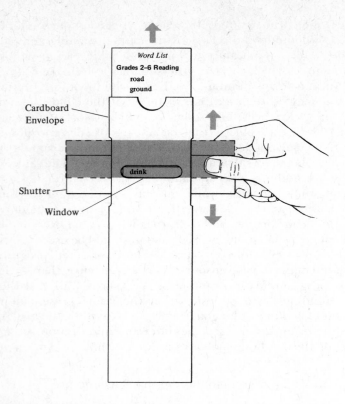

FIGURE 7-1 A Cardboard Tachistoscope

By moving shutter up or down a word is revealed in the window for a brief second. The child responds and the word list is moved so a new word can appear in the window.

tachistoscope can be made by placing a list of letters or words into a cardboard pocket that has a hole cut in the center which will reveal one letter at a time.

Showing the letter on a card, drawing it on the board, and having the children make the letter in the air or write it on a piece of paper are part of an effective sequence in teaching letter recognition. Discrimination activities should include pointing out the distinctive features of the letter that is being demonstrated. Research has shown that the upper half of the letter is especially important in correct discrimination. One study showed that four-year-old children can learn to overcome confusion about letters like "c" and "o" and "u" and "n" (Gibson, Gibson, Pick, and Osser, 1962). It takes emphasis and patience to overcome these confusions, however, because children easily read pictures upside down and are not bothered at first by seeing the symbols "u" and "n," thinking that they are the same symbol. Pointing out the difference in the top part of these and similar pairs of letters ("m" and "w") will assist recognition. The teacher should follow up the discussion with a concrete experience, such as having two children bend over to touch their toes in a head-to-head position: they are the "m"; and having two other children sit on the floor with their raised feet touching: they are the "w."

Various types of worksheets are available to help develop letter identification and discrimination. Initially an exercise that requires tracing the letter will force the youngster to look at and impress on his memory through a visuomotor means the exact lines of the letter. (A sample page of such a workbook is presented here.) A variation on tracing in a book can be achieved by having children work with plastic letters to get the feel of the letter — a kinesthetic reinforcement. Making letters out of clay, cutting them out of paper, drawing them in finger painting and in templates are also useful techniques.

Occasionally a child may not be able to discriminate the letters of the alphabet. Because of a developmental lag or lack of experience, he may have difficulty in making fine discriminations among lower case letters.

If the teacher observes that he has a severe developmental problem in the class, he might refer to a text by Ilg and Ames (1965) which describes typical behaviors and products for different age levels. For example, at age six 58 percent of the boys and 66 percent of the girls in their study were able to print their last names as well as their first names. Ninety-three percent used capitals and small letters correctly, but 22 percent used substitute letters (p. 276). A text of this kind might also be useful in helping a teacher prepare developmental exercises for a child who is significantly retarded in his visual discrimination ability.

EVALUATING VISUAL DISCRIMINATION

Checking the visual acuity of students should be a function of specialized personnel. A visual screening test should be given annually until grade two, the years in which visual changes seem most dramatic, and every other year thereafter. The age of seven appears to be particularly crucial in this respect (Strang, 1968, p. 21). The screening should include a binocular reading test (using an instrument like the telebinocular) to observe the coordinated functioning of both eyes and the functioning of the eyes at far point and near point. Some children's eyes function quite well at far point (20 feet) but do not coordinate at near point (12–18 inches). Reading, of course, occurs at near point. If irregularities are noted, the child should be referred to an eye doctor.

Readiness tests can serve as initial screening instruments for

FIGURE 7-2   Learning the Letters *M* and *W*. (Photo by Suzanne Szasz)

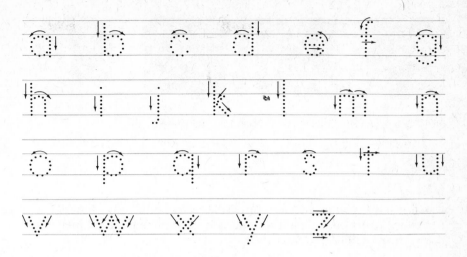

FIGURE 7-3   A Workbook Alphabet

Tracing the outlines of letters of the alphabet forces attention on specific differences; prepares children for writing the alphabet.

identifying children who need discrimination exercises.* Those who score high on the letter-discrimination tests should be given the opportunity to begin immediately to use letters in actual reading activity. Those who do not know the letters must be taught them and then examined again later to see if the teaching has accomplished its objective. Undoubtedly there will be some children who do not know all of the letters. They should be required to practice only those they fail to recognize. It should be a principle of all teaching that the learner not be required to suffer "relearning" what he already knows. His attitude toward school and learning may be damaged by having constantly to cover the knowledge and skill he already has.

Readiness tests (and teacher observations) include other means for evaluating visual discrimination. Typical among these is identifying the one form out of four that is different. When a child does not respond to a direct teaching of the alphabet forms he may need exercises involving grosser forms, such as squares, circles, and triangles. Using cardboard or plastic pieces, he can learn to match forms, placing all the squares together and all the circles together. Some simple children's jigsaw puzzles are happy exercises for working on

*For a more detailed analysis of reading readiness tests, see R. Farr and N. Anastasiow, *Review of Reading Readiness Tests* (Newark, Del.: International Reading Association, 1969).

FIGURE 7-4   An Aid in Evaluating Visual Discrimination

Find the picture that is different. Similar forms are frequently used as tests of visual discrimination ability.

visual discrimination and also on visual perception — the child learns to bring closure to the picture, that is, to complete the total image of the picture by filling in parts.

SUMMARY

Reading demands well-developed perceptual skills. These include not only visual skills but also auditory and general language skills. Since perception develops through a combination of factors having to do with maturation, individual ability, and environment, there is bound to be a range of perceptual abilities in any given group of children. Thus as with any other reading skill, these skills must be evaluated and taught at a variety of levels.

Because of television and the general affluence of modern society, many of the typical readiness skills are being developed in the home and in nursery schools. This fact makes it possible for the school to work sooner with some children on the auditory and visual skills that are directly related to reading instruction, provided it can be demonstrated that the youngsters in the class do indeed have the other skills of language expression and concepts that will carry them through their early experiences in school.

Research indicates that both auditory and visual discrimination skills are correlated to reading achievement, at least in the early stages, and that training in discrimination skills helps children to learn better how to use auditory and visual skills. It has been found that an accurate knowledge of the letters of the alphabet is one of the strongest predictors of success in reading at the end of the first grade. This finding suggests that six- and seven-year-old children are generally able to use letters in their early word-recognition activities.

Schools need to make periodic evaluations of hearing and vision to discover possible deficits in acuity, and teachers should evaluate perceptual skills through criterion tests to assist pupils in seeing progress in learning to read. A caution was given in regard to discussing isolated skills: no matter how many separate skills are identified, reading seems to be greater than the sum of its parts.

TERMS

perception	correlation studies
readiness	*Wepman Auditory Discrimination Test*
perceptual development	audiometers
auditory discrimination	binocular
visual discrimination	telebinocular
tachistoscope	auditory perception
closure	visual perception
picture reading	

Chapter 8

Visual Memory of Words

A kindergarten teacher once claimed that in a very simple way she could teach her children to read. She used highway signs. All around her room were a variety of actual road signs, and any visitor who wished to test the children would find that they all knew what each sign said.

Can you think of a way to teach kindergarten children to read these signs?

By the time children reach kindergarten most of them are accustomed to using different-shaped signs as marks of identification. From television and the labels on breakfast cereal boxes they soon learn that a certain kind of script means Coca Cola; that the name of their favorite toy company appears in a figure eight; that in their race car game landing on a circle means they get another turn while landing on a square means they must stop. Some will also know that the octagonal sign on their street corner means "Stop."

Because children already have some orientation for using different basic shapes as a means of identification, it does not take a special magic—unless imagination is magic—to get kindergarten children to remember what six or eight road signs mean. After all, adults respond to the shape of the road sign before they read the message on the sign. They may not realize it, but they do not read "Stop" every time they approach a stop sign. The octagonal shape at the intersection means "Stop"!

In actual driving the driver must read carefully what some road signs say. It makes a big difference, for example, whether the triangle indicates a curve to the left or a curve to the right. So, too, the child needs more than a response to the general shape to say that he knows how to read. Nonetheless, the general shape of road signs can be an effective start to remind the child that these geometric forms represent an idea they can respond to.

As you read this chapter see if you can find the answers to these questions:

Do competent readers decode the words they meet or do they respond to the general shape of the words?

What is meant by a visual memory of words?

What words are likely prospects for learning through a visual memory approach?

How can difficulty in learning words through a visual memory approach be overcome?

DEVELOPING AUTOMATIC RESPONSES

Most of the effort that goes into teaching children to read words is aimed at developing instantaneous or automatic responses to as many words as possible. The more words a person can respond to automatically, the easier it is for him to read a message quickly with a minimum of effort. He can concentrate on analyzing and evaluating the message instead of wasting effort on deciphering words. It is not feasible, of course, to train most readers to respond instantly to all the words they will meet in their reading. That is why every reader continues to need and to use a wide variety of word-analysis skills. The more a person reads, the less frequently he will see a word that causes him to stop and analyze it; because of frequent practice he will have an instant reaction to it.

The competent adult reader may be described as a whole-word reader. He responds instantly to the whole word, perhaps to an entire phrase. He goes through no evident analytic process as his eye sweeps across each word. He stops for analysis only when he does not have an automatic perception from the visual stimulus. Much like the kindergarten children who responded automatically to the road signs, the competent reader is using his visual memory of the shape of the word to assist him with that instant response. But unlike the kindergarten children who would not be able to tell the precise difference between two square signs which contained different directions, the competent reader is also able to use simultaneously internal cues that enable him to distinguish *horse* from *house*, though the gross shapes of the words are identical. His repertoire of skills and response patterns enables him to respond instantly to either *horse* or *house*, making use of both the general shape or configuration of the word as well as other cues without being conscious of any analysis taking place.

Children too learn to respond instantly to shapes and forms. No matter how crude the art, most children at three or four can instantly respond to the silhouette of a camel, an elephant, and an alligator. These are distinctive animal forms they have seen in pictures, in television cartoons, and in the drawings of their friends. But they do not respond automatically at an early age to a tiger versus a mountain lion versus a leopard versus an alley cat. These animals have very similar shapes; one has to read the spots and the stripes in order to tell one cat from the other. Once the child learns the internal cue system, however, he soon knows the difference between the tiger and the leopard.

By using such examples, the teacher can make the child aware that the goal of reading instruction is to get him to react instantly to words but that the shape of the word is only the first of many cues he will have. One of the objectives of initial skill instruction, therefore, is to make the child conscious of the wholeness of words. This statement does not contradict a previous one, that a student must be taught the relation between the sound and symbol of language systematically and sequentially. Sound-symbol–analysis skills are used to achieve the eventual goal, the instant recognition of words as whole units.

USING A VARIETY OF WORD-RECOGNITION TECHNIQUES

Word recognition as used here means the ability to recognize the sound and the meaning of words in print. Word recognition refers not only to the identification of words that a reader already knows by sight but also to the reader's ability to "unlock" words that are not familiar in their printed form. The teacher helps the child develop various techniques for unlocking and recognizing words independently. Such methods include sight words (those that are a part of the visual memory mechanism), context clues, phonic analysis, structural analysis, and linguistic analysis. No one learns all of these techniques at once, and so the school and the teacher must decide which skills to introduce first.

The first grader about to begin formal reading instruction already has some familiarity with sounds, words, and communication. In his daily conversations he uses thousands of words in complex sentence patterns and has little or no difficulty in listening to others talk. Seashore and Eckerson (1940) estimated that the typical six-year-old has a listening vocabulary of approximately 25,000 words.

Most of the words in the reading material prepared for the first grade child, therefore, are almost entirely from the child's listening vocabulary. The words are usually unfamiliar in written symbols only, not in sound or in meaning. This is an assumption the teacher will want to evaluate with each group of children he teaches, however.

An initial task of beginning reading instruction is to have the child understand that the printed word is a symbol for the spoken word; that books are talk written down. Picture stories, experience stories, and charts can be utilized to demonstrate for the child what words in print mean. Simple experience stories are especially helpful to show the child that symbol units stand for a flow of speech.

One of the first steps that most children take in learning to read is to identify several words by remembering their total form or shape. Probably their name is one of these words. Others might include *the*, *is, girl*. Thus they can immediately "read," *The girl is Madonna.*

Out of curiosity and pride beginning readers strive to memorize more and more words so they can prove that they can read. This does not mean that the letters within the words should be ignored. On the contrary, the children should see from their initial instruction that their ability to discriminate among the letters of the alphabet will aid them in learning to recognize individual words. In other words, in describing the distinctive features or shapes of the word, the teacher should demonstrate how letters of the alphabet contribute to these distinctive features. The name *Tony* has a tall "t" at the beginning, whereas the name *Marla* has a tall "m" at the beginning and a tall "l" near the end of the word (Muehl and King, 1966).

ASSOCIATIVE LEARNING

Visual memory techniques for learning whole words fit into the category of associative learning activities. Basically, the learner attempts to associate a written symbol with an image, or a perception, that he has of an object or person. Common means for making an association are associating pictures with their names, labeling objects in a room, and relating an individual's own word patterns to the way the words are printed, for example, through an experience chart.

Labeling pictures constitutes a frequently used technique for teaching children to visually associate the printed word with the image of the object it stands for. Pictures with labels on the back can be purchased from publishers, or teachers and students can make their own file of words and pictures to match. The picture should be fairly simple in composition so the child will easily and immediately recognize the content. The teacher asks the class, "What is this picture?"

"A horse."

"That's right. And here I have written the word *horse*. It begins

FIGURE 8-1   Labeling Classroom Objects. (Photo by Suzanne Szasz)

with a tall letter, h. Do you think you will remember what the word looks like the next time you see it? What other letters are there in the word *horse*?"

Reinforcement of this learning is provided by having the children later identify the word *horse* in a group of two or three other words; or they can match the picture with the word. The word and the matching picture should remain on display for at least one day so the children have ample opportunity to see the associated pair.

A matching procedure does not have to be limited to pictures and posters. Many objects in the classroom can be labeled. The door, wall, desk, closet, pencil case, and bookshelf can serve as object lessons of the relation between speech and print. All the teacher has to do is tell the children why objects in the room have labels and let their curiosity and powers of observation motivate them to retain the words for future reading use.

Children's names can be used effectively in teaching that words have distinctive shapes and cues. Children in nursery school and kindergarten can use a visual memory approach to identify their own names.

Experience stories and charts provide another effective technique to indicate the relation between speech and writing and to develop the visual memory skill. Through the experience-story approach the teacher leads the child to proceed from the known, his oral language,

FIGURE 8-2   Word Recognition Teaching.

This teacher uses sentences made of word and picture cards to teach word recognition skills. As the boy finds the correct word in the stack of word cards on his desk, the teacher replaces the picture card with the word card. (Photo by Carl B. Smith)

to the unknown, the graphic representation of that language. The teacher helps the child conceptualize that what he can say can be written, and what can be written he can read.

Most early primary pupils want to share their experiences. It is relatively easy, therefore, to elicit "stories" from an individual or from a small group. Experiences that occur during the school day can be discussed by the children and incorporated into charts. The teacher guides the discussion and motivates the children to follow the development of their story on the chart. One value of the experience chart is that it can be used to develop several sight words for the entire group.

Experience stories can be developed around anything that interests the children. One class acquired a pet hamster. When the initial excitement had subsided the teacher mentioned the possibility of having the class write a report for the local newspaper. Even if the newspaper did not print their story, the children could put the story on the bulletin board. Then everyone who came into the room could read about their pet hamster.

The teacher led the children in the discussion, having them note significant items that should be included in the report, such as the name of the hamster, where he lived, and how they felt about him. The children then dictated sentences which the teacher wrote on the board. As each sentence was written, the teacher reread it immediately. Several children were also asked to reread the sentence. Since their reading was primarily a recall of what was said, the teacher asked others in the group to make any corrections when a child failed to say the words exactly in the order they had originally been dictated. The students then determined which sentences best described the hamster. The final product that the class put on a chart was the following:

Our Hamster

We have a hamster in our room.
Her name is Miss Lori Blackberry.
She lives in a cage.
She likes to roam around the room.
We like our hamster.

On the hamster's cage the teacher had printed a label that said, "Miss Lori Blackberry." The label was a major clue for the children to use in identifying the words on their experience chart. After the chart was completed the teacher reread the entire story for the class; two children were assigned to illustrate the chart so everyone would know what Miss Lori Blackberry looked like. The teacher made a second chart with the same story on it. She cut out each sentence from the story so that each was on a separate strip of paper. First as a group exercise and then individually the children were asked to put the sentences in order. They had the entire story hanging on the bulletin board and so they could match the sentence strips with its counterpart on the bulletin board. Matching their arrangement with the one on the board was a way of checking to see whether they got the sentences in the correct order.

Next, the teacher cut up each sentence into individual words. Sentence by sentence the children put the story back together again, checking with the model on the board to see if they had the words in the proper order. This time the matching process called upon their knowledge of the letters of the alphabet; at first, however, the process relied primarily on the children's sense of form and shape to identify and remember the words in the story.

Because of its high motivational value, the experience story offers many opportunities to have children engage in sentence- and word-matching activities. Some classes make up a bulletin board newspaper. Children in the first grade can prepare at home or with a teacher

FIGURE 8-3   Pets Can Help Guide Beginning Readers

Animals often provide a warm, common experience wherein children develop vocabulary and experience stories. (Photo by Suzanne Szasz)

assistant daily reports about the weather, holidays, birthdays, and personal items about children in the class. Through experience chart techniques a wide sight vocabulary can be built, all based upon the language the children themselves use.

The experience-story technique can be used effectively as a spontaneous writing activity. Broadly interpreted, writing an experience story can begin in kindergarten. For example, a child draws a picture on one side of an open notebook ($8\frac{1}{2}$ by 11 sheets). He dictates a story about the picture to an aide or to the teacher. The story is then printed on the facing page of the notebook. Ample space should be left between lines of print to enable the child to trace over the letters or to copy them directly below the line on which they are written. Of course, no marks are placed on the booklet to correct or grade the child's writing. Nothing should be done at this point that might inhibit or kill the child's desire to express himself in writing. The child will usually build his own story booklet so that he can read it to himself and to others. It can become a source of great pride for the child and provides excellent one-to-one contact.

One first grader's notebook contained a drawing of a blue car accompanied by this story: "We have a new car. It is a 1972 Chevie."

The child was able to take his picture and story home, not only to show his drawing but to show his family that he could read the words that accompanied the drawing. A short note from the teacher suggested to the parents that they could help the child by writing each word from the story on a separate slip of paper and flashing the words to help him recall them. If he could not recall a word, the child was asked to match the word with its counterpart on the experience chart.

CONFIGURATION

The major emphasis of making experience charts or labeling pictures and objects is to develop the realization that sounds and symbols are related. Along the way the child forms definite visual perceptions of what specific words look like; often he gains these perceptions by remembering the configuration, or shape, of words. This does not mean that he does not use other cues, such as the first letter of the word. Initially, however, visual memory techniques are used to develop a few sight words, that is, words recognized instantly from visual memory as opposed to any systematic decoding technique.

Many words have individuality in their general contour or word form. The individual configuration is apparent only when the words appear in lower case letters, for example,

stop   help   apple   grandfather   grasshopper

When they are printed with capital letters, the individuality of form is lost, except for length.

STOP   HELP   APPLE   GRANDFATHER   GRASSHOPPER

In teaching children to use configuration as a device for remembering certain words, the teacher points to certain striking characteristics. The word is long or short and it has some tall or high letters or has some letters with tails that hang below the line. The name *Tony*, for example, begins with a tall letter and ends with a tail letter, and it is a short word. That is why it looks like this: Tony

The utility of configuration as a word-recognition device is quite limited. The teacher should restrict its use to words that have rather evident or unique characteristics, such as *alligator*, or to words that have a high emotional value to the child, such as his own name or that of his pet.

More than one word should be used to show the children what configuration cues are. An effective practice is to use words they have already seen in some manner. Take the story about the hamster, Miss Lori Blackberry. Some cues that might be indicated are the length of *Blackberry*, the two tall letters in *hamster*, and the two "o's" in *room.* The teacher might list five such words on the chalkboard. Then together she and the children would note the characteristics of each word, such as length, double letters, ascending (b) and descending letters (y). As the analysis proceeds the teacher could box the word [stop] to further show the class the differences in word form.

SPECIAL WORDS FOR VISUAL MEMORY

Though it was recommended earlier that visual memory techniques should be used only on a few initial words in the child's reading vocabulary, some words are learned best and easiest through a visual memory technique. For example, many short words with a high frequency of use and often having an irregular spelling pattern are prime candidates for learning through a visual memory technique. Words such as *the, there, when, was,* and *would* must quickly become sight words for the child. Many words which linguists call function words are also probably best learned by a visual memory approach (LeFevre, 1964). One way of teaching these words is to use them in context as captions for pictures, for example, Mary *and* Tom *are* running.

The words listed below are samples of many of the high-frequency words that need to be learned early and without undue emphasis on decoding.

85 HIGH-FREQUENCY SHORT WORDS

about	do	is	over	this
after	don't			those
all	down	many	please	though
along		may		to
also	each	might	second	two
another	eight	most	seven	
any	every	much	shall	very
are		must	should	
around	first	my	some	was
as	for	myself	such	were
	four			what
because	from	near	than	when
both		not	that	where
but	goes		the	which
by		of	their	while
	have	off	them	who
come	his	one	then	why
could	how	other	there	
		our	these	yes
didn't	into	out	they	you
			third	your

Another category of words that lends itself to learning by visual memory contains words that have high emotional content for the child. *Mother, Father, thunder, laugh,* and *house* are examples of words that elicit strong feelings of happiness, sadness, and security. Various cultures give an assigned emotional value to specific words (Ashton-Warner, 1963). As with their own names, the children will want to learn those words quickly and will apply extra energy to retaining them through visual memory techniques (Braun, 1968).

Extensive studies have been devoted to the cues children can and do use in order to recognize words. A short list of some of these studies is provided at the end of this chapter.

WORD MEANING

To a degree, word meaning or vocabulary is taken for granted in many of the word-recognition exercises in beginning reading instruction. At the same time, vocabulary development forms an integral part of the reading program. At first the child needs a constant expansion of vocabulary and must be shown how to use his background to learn new words and concepts. In the middle and upper grades vocabulary must become more precise, and technical words in science and mathematics must be learned in addition to a general use vocabulary.

To learn a word with ease and enthusiasm the reader must have in his mind a clearly defined concept that is associated with the word. Trying to get a child to learn a word for which he has no concept or only a vague concept is akin to wheel-spinning; there may be movement and noise, but no progress.

Several means can be used to check on a student's knowledge of the words being used and to encourage the development of a basic vocabulary. Ask the child to describe a picture in his mind when he hears a word — *bargain.* Have someone use the word in a sentence. Encourage the children to ask about a word when they do not have an image or perception in their minds or find that they do not know how to use the word in a sentence. Question individuals in the class about the meaning of special words that appear in an individual's experience chart. The children can exchange their experience stories and help one another to read them. They too can be made conscious of the need to explain to others some of the words they have used. The boy who dictated an experience story about his pet dog "leaping off the basement stairs and bumping into the steam pipe" has two possible vocabulary problems for other members of the first grade class — *basement* and *steam pipe.* Many of the children may have no perception of these words. Both the teacher and the pupils should be alert to such situations and make use of them to expand the vocabulary of the entire group.

TEACHING A SIGHT WORD VOCABULARY

The preceding pages described teaching sight words through making experience charts and labeling and matching pictures and objects. Other ways of building a sight vocabulary through visual memory approaches follow.

Standard Technique

The following procedure is typically used to introduce a new word by the sight method. The teacher shows the written symbol to the child and then writes the symbol on the chalkboard or on a card. The teacher says the word and asks the child to repeat it. Then the teacher and child discuss ways to remember the word—by configuration, striking characteristics, picture clues, concrete demonstration. Through some practice exercise the child then learns to recognize the word. In the early stages of learning the teacher usually introduces the written symbol and assures the child that he can proceed securely in matching a word sound with the written symbols for it.

Words may be introduced in isolation, as they are when associated with a picture or with an object, or they may be introduced in a complete statement, as they are in an experience story. Either way, at one point the word is isolated so that the child must respond to the word as a separate entity; then at another point the word should be placed in context to see if the child can recognize it in actual reading. Both procedures are essential to learning to read. In context, the child has the opportunity to test himself on his recognition accuracy. If the word that he calls does not seem to make sense in context, then the chances are he has not correctly identified the word.

The very nature of a sight word means that it is overlearned. It is practiced until the learner can respond automatically, without any conscious effort to recall or to associate the word with configuration or picture clues or other analyses. To reach this overlearned status the teacher must provide children with frequent practice activities similar to those described below.

EXERCISES FOR ACQUIRING SIGHT WORDS

Clap Your Hands

The child is told to clap once when the teacher displays the word card containing a word he names. For example, he may say "three" and begin to flash the word cards. The child claps his hands when the word *three* appears. If the child fails to identify several of the words, the teacher must provide additional instruction on those words.

Word Hunt

The teacher writes a vertical row of words on the chalkboard and then writes the same words but arranged differently in another row. Two children have a contest to find each word in their respective rows as the teacher or an assistant reads one word after another. The rest of the students serve as judges and keep score on who identified the words first.

Word Bingo

Each child has a card marked with squares. Words to be practiced have been written in the squares. The teacher says a word. If the child has the word on his card, he places a marker on it, as in "Bingo."

Train Game

The children are divided into two groups, each group representing a train. The cards are flashed to the engine (first child) and then to the rest of the cars in order. Any child who does not know the word which is flashed is given the card to hold. The train with the lightest load (the fewest number of held cards) wins the train race.

Captions and Pictures

Pictures are displayed. Appropriate titles using the sight words that are to be practiced are prepared on cardboard strips. The child must match the written caption with the correct picture. Sample titles would be *School Bus, Two Fishermen.*

Picture Dictionary

When a child learns a new sight word he writes it in a notebook. He then either draws a picture of the word or finds one in an old magazine that he can paste next to the word.

Word Pairs

Words that are often confused by the child are written on the chalkboard or on a worksheet in pairs:

when	where
house	horse
there	then

The teacher says one of the words. The child is to draw a line under that word.

Others

These are only a few of the practice activities that a teacher can develop to promote the visual memory of words. Numerous other activities can be found in books like *Reading Aids Through the Grades* by Russell, 1951, *Spice* by Platts, 1960, and the laboratory manual associated with this text.

WORD-FLASHING DEVICES

Technology has made large strides in helping youngsters learn mechanical tasks. The visual memory approach to learning words is particularly suited to the use of mechanical devices to relieve the teacher of time-consuming responsibilities. For example, instruments which resemble film projectors enable the learner to respond to a symbol (or a word or phrase) flashed on the screen at a controlled speed. The general term for these instruments is tachistoscope, though they are sold under various trade names by different companies, such as Educational Development Laboratory and Keystone Corporation. A word list on a filmstrip is inserted into the machine and each word is flashed at a set speed; after the learner responds the word is returned to the screen so he can check the accuracy of his response.

During the late 1960s, dozens of companies marketed machines that had as one of their functions to show a word for an instant as a practice technique in recognizing words. Some of those devices are simply manually operated shutters. They add a semblance of technology to a drill that teachers often accomplished by means of 3 by 5 flash cards. Other, computer-type machines tell the pupil whether he is right or wrong and then provide him with a new problem to solve (a new word or phrase) in keeping with the kind of response that he made on the previous problem.

Some audiotape machines are also programmed to develop a sight vocabulary. Typically, the student looks at a sheet of paper or a card on which is written the word or word list he is to learn. The tape pronounces the word while the student looks at it on the card or on the worksheet. The student may be asked to write the word on paper or in the air as a means of reinforcing the image. While these machines do not provide a flashed image, they make it possible to have a student repeat an exercise as often as is necessary for him to fix the image of the word in his memory while listening to the sound of the word. The Bell and Howell Language Master is an example of a specialized tape recorder that can be used for these purposes.

The advent of federal funds for the development of innovative programs pushed forward many years the use of mechanical devices in the classroom. Most schools try these aids on a pilot basis before working them into the teaching system. Even though there are problems in training personnel to use machines and in designing the curriculum and the classrooms to take full advantage of technology, these mechanical aids to reading instruction will substantially increase the freedom of the teacher to act as a diagnostician instead of a drill master. Certainly machines provide no panacea. They are only one more factor that is making it feasible for diagnostic teaching to grow in the schools.

One weakness of most machine programs is that the word lists and the other exercises that are used may not fit the needs of the children in the class. The teacher must examine these programs carefully to match them with the needs of his students lest he trap the students in a stereotyped machine program under the guise of using it to give him more time for diagnosing and treating specific needs.

ASSESSING PROGRESS IN SIGHT WORDS

As with any other skill, progress in learning sight words is measured in terms of the specific objectives the program set as its goal. What objectives were set up for the children in learning words through visual memory techniques? If the objective was to get a group of children to recognize the Stone and Bartschi (1963) basic word list, then test words ought to be selected from that list and administered to the children through a flash-type procedure so that success in instant recognition can be determined. If the objective was to have the child learn a number of words that he himself proposed through experience stories, then each child should be tested with words selected from his own experience stories—or from the group stories, if these were used.

In grades two, three, and higher the Stone and Bartschi word list (Appendix D) may be an appropriate criterion, for at these points most children would have gained instant recognition of these high-frequency words. The development of a sight vocabulary continues throughout the grades. Though the student gains more independence in reading because he acquires a variety of word-analysis skills, he needs reminders and assistance in systematically enlarging his sight vocabulary.

At the beginning of a new year a teacher should check on his students' knowledge of visual memory techniques. A checklist like the one below would enable the teacher to see which students need additional guidance.

SIGHT VOCABULARY CHECK LIST

1. Has the child been exposed to the following methods of spontaneously discriminating among words by similarities and differences?

   a. Unusual length (for example, *grandmother*). yes__no__
   b. Configuration (for example, *fudge* ⌐‾⌐). yes__no__
   c. Root words (for example, *play* in *played*). yes__no__
   d. Compound words (for example, *mailbox*). yes__no__
   e. Initial letters or sounds (for example, *hat, bat, cat*). yes__no__
   f. Double letters (for example, *butter, took*). yes__no__

2. Is the child capable of building a word bank of words that have been identified originally by some other method but through repeated encounter have become sight words? yes__no__

3. What is the child's reading level on the Stone and Bartschi word list?

The child's reading level can also be determined grossly by testing him on the number of words he knows on the Dolch Basic Sight Vocabulary List (Dolch, 1942).

Number of Words Correctly Identified	Reading Level
75	preprimer level
120	primer level
170	first reader level
210	second reader level
220	third reader level

For individual use of the list (Dolch, 1942) have the child read aloud all the words, line by line. At the same time, record on another copy just what the child does. If he cannot call a word, cross it out. If he substitutes another word, write in that word over the one on the list. If he mispronounces a word, indicate what he said.

Such an individual record is valuable in showing, first, which words the child knows and, second, what kinds of mistakes he makes when he does not know a word. The kinds of mistakes a child makes indicate what kind of reteaching he needs.

Since we are concerned here primarily with the skills needed to get the learner started in reading, we would not anticipate that long lists of words such as those constructed by Stone and Bartischi (1963), Stone (1956), Fry (1957), and Dolch (1942) would be used as criteria of success. A much more limited group of words should probably be the criterion for the initial weeks of reading instruction. The teacher's list of two dozen emotion-packed words, for example, or twenty words from the experience charts, or randomly selected words from the basal reading word list are more appropriate criteria.

In addition to checking the child's skill in recognizing two dozen flashed words, the teacher should determine whether the child recognizes those words in context. Testing word recognition in context emphasizes for the student that the only purpose of word exercises is to enable him to read better. Meaning, therefore, is stressed from the beginning and the child never fools himself into saying that he is reading when he pronounces a single word in isolation.

If the teacher finds that a student does not respond with a high percentage of correct answers on the sight word criterion test, he can proceed with several alternatives. It is entirely possible that the student's poor performance has its cause in some vision problem. These possibilities were discussed in Chapter 7. It is possible, too, that the student learns slowly through the visual modality, in which case the teacher may find an auditory approach more successful. It is also possible that the child has poor memory habits and will have difficulty building sight words no matter what instructional techniques are used. He must first receive help in building habits of memory.

BUILDING MEMORY HABITS

Memory habits may have a great deal to do with the child's success in the initial stages of reading. Unless a child can compare word forms, noting essential likenesses and differences, he will have difficulty in using effectively either phonic analysis or structural analysis. The following suggestions for building memory habits may assist later in the memory of words:

A. List a series of numbers on several cards.
    175
    2389
    78906
    098673
    Show a card to the child for half a second and then ask him to repeat the numbers on the card. As soon as he is able to make several correct responses with four digits, move him to cards with five digits, and so on. The concentration and the use of left-to-right progression will be extremely helpful habits for use with words. A similar procedure is used in the Wechsler Intelligence Scale for Children for auditory memory. The examiner calls out numbers which the child tries to repeat.

B. Use a group of related objects, such as a pencil, a pen, an eraser, and a notebook. Children observe carefully for a second and then hide their eyes. The teacher adds a ruler or some other related item. The children try to identify what has been added (or removed). Or the arrangement of the items may be changed and the children are to duplicate the original arrangement.

C. In order to test a child's skill at recognizing words in context, the teacher can give the child a passage in which several of the criterion words are found and listen while he reads aloud. With a check sheet he can then identify the words that the child recognizes without hesitation and those that he does not. If the test involves a group, the teacher can construct multiple choice test items similar to the ones below:

Indians _____ in Florida.

      like
      live
      give

The ball _____ into the street.

      bounded
      bubbled
      robbed

Tony _____ with Father.

      will
      want
      went

To answer these items the child has to use both meaning clues as well as word-form clues.

LIMITATIONS OF VISUAL MEMORY TECHNIQUES

The goal of all reading instruction is to move the child from being a dependent reader to being an independent one. Since the visual memory technique requires the presence of another person to supply unfamiliar words, it has a limited potential. The cues used in sight word recognition also contain limitations. Confusion may arise when the beginning reader sees a new word with a configuration similar to one he already knows. *Blueberry* may be confused with *blackberry; grandfather* with *grandmother; book* with *look.*

When words of similar configuration confront the child (*went* and *want*) he has no distinctive cues to help him identify the word except its meaning in the sentence. In other words, the word must always be checked against the context of the words around it.

Some children will find it difficult to remember large numbers of words. Even for those who find it easy, visual memory techniques are inefficient in trying to develop a large reading vocabulary. It makes good sense to use the visual memory approach initially because it puts the child into reading on the very first day of instruction. The techniques exemplify immediately that there is a relation between words in speech and words in print. The child also needs word-analysis techniques that will give him a greater sense of independence and will enable him to proceed at the pace that his skill in analysis permits him to. He needs to know not only that words in speech are represented by written symbols but that sound units within words have graphic counterparts that make a sound-symbol analysis for the native speaker a fruitful way of deciphering the printed page and of becoming an independent reader.

SUMMARY

Configuration and the striking characteristics of words provide cues for the recognition of whole words by visual memory. Starting word recognition through visual memory techniques aids the child in associating written symbols with words that are already in his listening and speaking vocabulary. Use of visual memory learning techniques for word recognition is known as the sight word or the whole-word approach to reading. In this approach a whole word is presented to the child, first by saying it and then by relating it to pictures or concrete experiences or constructing experience charts. The child then establishes an association between the pronunciation of the word and its printed form. Through a variety of practice activities these words are overlearned and become sight words, that is, they are recognized instantly without analysis.

The goal of reading instruction is to create a vast reservoir of words the reader recognizes instantly. This enables the reader to concentrate on the message and not worry about the mechanics of analyzing words. The use of flash cards, tachistoscopic devices, and experience stories are some of the means used to establish the initial group of words to be learned by visual memory techniques. For purposes of practice, some words are isolated. All the sight words need to be practiced in context, however, so the student knows from the beginning that words are for meaning.

Some words, such as high-frequency short words and emotion-packed words, are probably learned best by the visual memory approach. The teacher should be cognizant of local environmental words that have high emotional value and use them as part of the sight word group.

The assessment of sight words is directed to a small group of words that formed the objective for the first few weeks of instruction. They should be tested both in a flash-word test and in context. Failure may indicate a nonvisual learner or a lack of instruction and practice.

Though visual memory of words may be stressed during the first weeks of reading instruction, a child should be taught from the beginning that there are internal cues for distinguishing words with similar shapes (*dog, dig*). Therefore he needs decoding skills to form the basis for his independence in reading.

TERMS

sight word	context clues
configuration	visual modality
visual memory techniques	cue reduction
tachistoscope	flash cards
experience chart	decoding skills

Chapter 9

Decoding
Word Symbols

Suppose your instructor printed the following symbols on the chalkboard:

ΔΗΚΩΔΙΝΓ ΘΙΣ ΜΕΣΕΓ ΙΖ ΛΙΗΚ ΛΕΡΝΙΝΓ ΤΥ ΡΗΔ.
ΡΙΗΤΙΝΓ ΙΖ Α ΚΩΔ ΦΟΡ ΣΠΗΧ.

Then he said: "What I have written on the board is a message in English, but I have used capital Greek letters instead of the ABC's to write it. How would you go about knowing what the message says?"

You could then discuss what one has to know and what skills he must have to decipher the message and get its meaning. A beginning reader is in a similar situation. Things the adult reader takes for granted have to be explained to the beginner. He needs to know that the symbols stand for a message; that there are ways of identifying the beginning and ending of individual utterances (punctuation and capitalization); that there is a relation between the sound of speech and the symbols; that he has to know which sound or sounds each symbol stands for; that the pattern or arrangement of the symbols gives some hints as to how they will be pronounced, for example, the trigraph consonant-vowel-consonant (c-a-t) in English usually stands for a short sound of the vowel.

The decoding operation is thus not a simple process. It requires a great deal of background knowledge in addition to the ability to translate individual visual symbols into speech sounds.

Now decipher the message using the symbol code given below, where the symbols are matched to letters of the English alphabet.

Code symbols

Α	Β	Γ	Δ	Ε	Η	Θ	Ι	Κ	Λ	Μ	Ν	Ο	Π	Ρ	Σ	Τ	Υ	Φ	Χ	Ψ	Ω	Ζ
A	B	G	D	Ĕ	Ē	TH	I	K	L	M	N	Ŏ	P	R	S	T	U	PH	CH	PS	Ō	Z

Alphabet symbols

As you can see, the code is not too different from the regular English alphabet, yet it looks quite confusing. Can you decode the message? Do you agree with the message?

The present chapter will help you to answer the following questions:

How long have phonic methods and whole-word methods been used in U.S. schools?

How do modern reading authorities view the whole-word (visual memory) approach to teaching word recognition? the use of decoding techniques?

What is the difference between phonics and linguistics?

How does one teach sound-symbol relations functionally?

How does one teach sound-symbol relations synthetically?

What role does word meaning play in a decoding approach to word recognition?

A reader needs many means for identifying words if he is to become independent. A group of skills sometimes called decoding skills is one important means. Everyone who has read children's mystery stories or has deciphered coded messages on the back of cereal boxes knows that decoding means translating visual symbols into ideas, usually into word sounds that represent ideas. For that reason, *phonics* is the term that most people think of when they hear the word *decoding* in relation to reading instruction. No one will question the value of using the sound-symbol relation in translating the visual symbols back into the word sounds for which they stand. There is more to the notion of decoding, however, than knowing that the letter "c" represents the sound at the beginning of the word *cat* or that "ph" usually represents the /f/ sound.

DECODING

The use of the term *decoding* in the teaching of reading can be used in a very narrow sense to mean identifying the relation between the letters of the alphabet and the sounds in words. Thus pronouncing a list of words or pronouncing nonsense words, such as *cac*, is decoding in the narrow sense. A broader definition of *decoding* includes making the sound-symbol relation plus using many other visual cues that enable a reader to take a printed page and relate it to communication through language. Inflection, dialect patterns, idioms, punctuation, and other cues that would place the passage in a total language setting are included. In this view of decoding the reader assimilates the written code when he is able to make the sound-symbol relation as well as use these other cues to bring meaning to the printed page. Many linguists encourage educators to implement this broader view of decoding. Linguists such as Bloomfield and Fries have also offered prescriptions to teach children the letter-sound relations.

Thus both phonic analysis and linguistic analysis may be included in the definition of *decoding*. Professionals in the field of reading have not adopted a universally accepted definition for the term. We prefer the broader definition and use *decoding* to mean deciphering the entire communication, that is, decoding language, as opposed to decoding that focuses on letters and spelling patterns.

Since this chapter is concerned with initial reading skills, the decoding skills presented here are limited to those a child might acquire in the early stages. These would include understanding the letter-sound relations, some spelling patterns (phonic generalizations), and certain writing conventions (periods, commas, capital letters, and so on).

Obviously written symbols cannot communicate as fully as oral language. Gestures, inflections, and voice volume are three aspects of oral language that are not easily cued into written language. The wise teacher will encourage learners to try to pick up as many cues as they can that will reveal these aspects of oral language, thus using the action and emotion in the words and in the incidents to suggest how a passage would be spoken.

It is recommended that instruction in symbol decoding be given along with instruction in visual memory techniques. Simultaneous instruction in these two areas will enable a child to read words and sentences from the very beginning while learning other techniques to decipher unfamiliar words.

This chapter briefly reviews the beginnings of phonic and whole-word instruction in the United States, discusses the importance of decoding skills for the beginning reader, summarizes what research says about decoding systems, gives examples of how to teach decoding, and treats means for assessing decoding skills.

TEACHING WORD RECOGNITION
IN THE UNITED STATES

Until the middle of the nineteenth century the teaching of reading in the United States was a rather placid, uncomplicated affair for the teacher. Even though teachers had devised different techniques of presentation, the teaching of reading was accomplished primarily through an alphabetic method. The teacher taught the student that each letter of the alphabet has a sound and asked him to identify words by sounding out the letters. Through much drill and practice the student gradually became familiar with the vagaries of spelling and sound in the English language and thus learned to read.

In 1837, however, Horace Mann became disturbed by the drill required by the alphabetic method in the Massachusetts schools he supervised. He believed that students were being taught to identify words but that they did not always know the meaning of the words they sounded out. Mann said that the children were making empty "sounds of vocal organs on the air" (Walcutt, 1961, p. 33). In defense of the children, however, it should be pointed out that they were reading sentences such as: "The multiplicity of considerations subsumed under the intransigeant prognostications of enthusiasm is formidable" (Walcutt, 1961, p. 35). The children were not being tested on an ability to read; their knowledge of language and vocabulary was being challenged.

Nonetheless, Mann believed that the method of teaching reading was at fault. He called for an entirely new approach. Mann's method, which came to be called the *whole-word method,* did not become popular immediately because no commercial material was available to propagate it.

In the 1840s John Russell Webb, a teacher in a one-room school, made an independent discovery that was similar to Mann's. Webb was reading a newspaper in a farmhouse when a little girl came up to ask what he was doing. He told her he was reading. "This is the word for *cow,*" he said, and pointed out the window to a cow in the barnyard. It was not long before the little girl ran excitely to her mother and showed her the word *cow.* She could read.

From that incident Webb theorized that all reading could be taught simply by the whole-word method. He set about writing reading exercises using a basic vocabulary as the foundation for the exercises. His book of exercises, which he called *A New Method of Teaching Children To Read,* became a standard reader of the time (Flesch, 1955, p. 46).

From that time to this there have been two quite different approaches to the teaching of word recognition — the sight word or whole-word approach (see Chapter 8) and the phonics approach. Variations in each method were developed over the years, but the primary distinction remained. The phonics people said that word recognition should be taught through associating the letter symbols with the sounds of the spoken word; the advocates of the whole-word method said that word recognition should be taught by focusing attention on the over-all appearance of a word and that no attempt should be made to teach the alphabet and the letter sounds — at least, not in the beginning stages of reading. This dichotomy between phonics proponents and whole-word advocates does not exist today. Most modern authorities encourage the use of both whole-word teaching and decoding as complementary skills (Russell, 1961; Tinker and McCullough, 1962). There remains, however, a disagreement over precisely how to start these skills for the beginning reader.

Today *word attack* implies several kinds of activities, including word identification by visual memory techniques such as configuration and word form (Chapter 8); part-of-the-whole and structural analysis (Chapter 10); and phonics and linguistics (Chapter 9). Readers need competency in all of these skills.

The Great Debate

The issue today is whether reading instruction should be gradual and analytic, based upon a comparison of words the student already knows by sight, or intensive and synthetic, based upon a concentration on sound-symbol relations and spelling patterns.

Eventually instructional techniques are turned into commercial materials, and it is usually the commercial materials that are used to conduct studies of the effectiveness of instructional techniques and methods. In a nation-wide first grade study (Bond and Dykstra, 1967) most of the twenty-seven research projects used (synthetic) phonics or linguistics materials. Comparison between methods showed generally that children taught by a synthetic phonics system achieved higher scores in word recognition and in deriving paragraph meaning at the end of first grade than children taught by a gradual phonics approach. A second grade followup (Dykstra, 1968) on those children showed similar advantages on word recognition tests for those who received early and intensive teaching of sound-symbol correspondences. They did not, as a general rule, demonstrate superiority in reading comprehension.

In 1967 Chall's *Learning To Read: The Great Debate* focused critical attention on the teaching of reading. Following her review of research from 1912 to 1965, Chall concluded that a code-emphasis method, using intensive decoding, produces better results than a meaning-emphasis method using gradual decoding. She cited correlational studies that showed a significant relation between the ability to recognize letters and the sounds they represent and reading achievement. She noted that this knowledge appears to be more essential for success in the early stages of reading than other factors such as intelligence and oral language ability. Chall pointed to the need for a systematic method of introducing decoding skills to the child rather than leaving the acquisition of those skills to chance or haphazard practice.

Heated controversy between educators who agreed and disagreed with Chall's methods of analysis and her conclusions brought about renewed interest in decoding methods in the early stages of reading instruction.

The research evidence is not strong enough to convince every reading authority that intensive decoding is the way to begin instruction in reading. There have, however, been demonstrable changes in the early reading materials that are being published. The number of intensive phonics and linguistics materials appearing on the market is constantly increasing; in addition, the revised editions of the traditional basal readers are introducing more phonics earlier and sometimes providing supplementary phonics workbooks. The latter give a synthetic, intensive, presentation, working beside the gradual analytic approach of the basal readers.

TEACHING INITIAL DECODING SKILLS

The relation of symbol to sound can be demonstrated for students either analytically or synthetically. Initially a teacher usually uses one method or the other to keep the learning technique fairly simple, but both techniques are used as the situation indicates later in the development of word-analysis skills. Both initial approaches have proved effective in achieving their goals, as is attested by the many mature readers today who once learned decoding skills by one of these means.

The gradual, analytic method initially presents the student with a list of words that become part of his sight vocabulary through visual memory techniques. Subsequently he is taught to analyze these words to identify certain common sounds that appear in the words. For example, the sight words *milk, man,* and *mother* are shown to the child, who is asked if he sees anything about these three words that is the same. Having identified the letter "m," which is common to the words, he reads them. The teacher cautions him to listen to the sound he hears at the beginning of each word. "Whenever we see this letter (m) in a word we will hear the sound that we hear at the beginning of *milk* and *man*. Can you think of some other words that begin like *milk* and *mother*?"

The proponents of the analytic method contend that it keeps decoding part of the reading act, since the sounds are never isolated but are always taught within the context of the word.

In contrast, the synthetic method advocates the teaching of letters and their sounds first and in an intensive manner. These sounds are then combined, or synthesized, into words. For example, the pupil has learned the sounds of the letters "c," "a" and "t." The teacher writes the word *cat* on the chalkboard. The child synthesizes these known sounds into a word. This could be done as follows: "What is the sound of the letter 'c'? That's correct, 'kuh.'" The same procedure of eliciting the sounds is done with the other letters. The three separate sounds are then combined (kuh-aa-tuh) into the word *cat*.

The synthetic approach is utilized by strict phonics materials and some of the linguistics materials which stress sound-symbol relations. Included here would be materials like the Economy Phonics Program and Words in Color. Both teach the sounds in isolation and synthesize the sounds into words. Some linguists, such as Fries (1963) and Hall (1960), deplore the total isolation of letter sounds because they say total isolation tends to distort the sounds. Some children, however, fail to discriminate the sound within a word and may be able to learn it in isolation, as experience with remedial reading cases has shown. The teacher adjusts the procedure to fit each child's needs.

Since English spelling does not provide a one-to-one correspondence between distinctive word sounds (phonemes) and the letters of the alphabet (graphemes), a system for analyzing the spelling patterns that correspond to sounds in words must be carefully developed and systematically taught. It is not sufficient, for example, to condition the children to respond with one sound to each letter of the alphabet. There are only twenty-six letters of the alphabet, but there are a minimum of forty-three or forty-four distinctive sounds (phonemes) in the English language. Most instructional systems for teaching initial decoding skills use English spelling as it is found, but some use specially devised tools to set up a one-to-one correspondence between sound and symbol. The ITA and Words in Color charts are two devices that have been developed for helping the beginning reader simplify his decoding problem.

ITA

If English orthography had one symbol for each of the forty-three to forty-seven phonemes (opinions vary on the number), the decoding problem in reading instruction would be quite simple. A teacher could condition the children to respond with a specific sound each time he saw a letter symbol. By blending sounds the words could be decoded or, more precisely, recoded from writing into sound. Sir James Pitman's initial teaching alphabet, ITA, attempts to simplify the initial decoding problem by creating a symbol for each phoneme. The forty-four symbols that ITA uses and some examples of the way the symbols look when put together in words are shown in Figure 9.1.

The ITA is being used on an experimental basis by many schools in the United States and Great Britain. Its proponents claim it elim-

girls and bois lern

tω reed wiŧh i|t|a

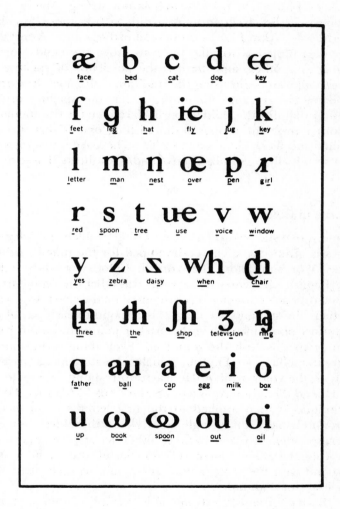

FIGURE 9-1 The Initial Teaching Alphabet

The sound-symbol correspondences shown here demonstrate the similarity of ITA to the traditional alphabet. (From the story of ita. copyright © 1965. initial teaching alphabet publication, inc. Reprinted by permission of the publisher) inates many of the failures usually associated with beginning reading and point proudly to the creative writing that many first grade children produce because the ITA medium enables them to disregard the spelling hazards of traditional orthography (Downing, 1967). The opponents of the ITA claim that the comparative research studies are inconclusive and do not warrant assuming the problems of ITA when the research is not strong (Marsh, 1968). The problems most frequently referred to are those associated with the transfer from ITA to traditional orthography. A certain amount of unlearning has to take place to move the child from one system into another, and there is the possibility of spelling problems when children begin using the traditional alphabet. Research studies to date, however, do not indicate that the spelling problems are greater than for the child who was started on the traditional alphabet. Another problem, though a diminishing one, is that there are only limited supplies of books in the ITA. The learner is somewhat bound to use initially only those books and worksheets that are printed in ITA.

Words in Color

A more realistic picture of the decoding problem a reader of English faces is given in the charts developed for the initial reading system called Words in Color. The Words in Color system lists under each of the English phonemes the various ways that the phoneme is spelled in words. Each phoneme is represented on the charts by a bar of color. Initially the students are taught to respond to each bar of color with a distinct phoneme. When the teacher points to the red bar, the student responds with the sound /ă/. Even though the sound /ă/ has several spellings in English, initially the student learns to respond only to the color symbol. He learns to respond rapidly to the colors and blend them into complete word sounds (/k/-/a/-/t/). The blending technique is then applied to the first letter symbol in each color bar, and usually it is a single letter. /k-a-t/ therefore has a one-to-one correspondence to *cat*. Because other letters are superimposed on the color bar, the student realizes that eventually he must learn to respond with the same sound (phoneme) to each of those possible spellings for that sound.

Both ITA and Words in Color exemplify attempted solutions to the irregularities of the English spelling system. They also indicate the kinds of problems associated with establishing a new means for overcoming these difficulties—indeed it becomes clear why most educators and publishers prefer to develop solutions within the framework of traditional orthography.

ſhe ræn

ſhe ræn is ræniŋ aull
around.
it faulls on feeld and tree.
it ræns on ſhe umbrellas
heer
and on ſhe ſhips at see.

robert looi steevenson

FIGURE 9-2   A Storybook Using the ITA

A variety of poems and stories are available in the ITA repertoire. (From poems, *Albert J. Mazurkiewicz and Harold J. Tanyzer, consultants. © copyright 1965 initial teaching alphabet publication, inc. Reprinted by permission of the publisher)*

PHONIC AND LINGUISTIC TECHNIQUES

Most methods for teaching initial decoding skills work within the regular English spelling system. Whether the techniques are phonic or linguistics oriented, they try to give the student some generalizations about the spelling system and its relation to word sounds. The student then sees that there is considerable regularity within English spelling patterns which can assist him greatly in applying sound and symbol patterns as part of the decoding process.

To avoid confusion the teacher should ordinarily limit his first lesson on the sound-symbol relation to words that have a fairly consistent one-to-one correspondence. Trigraphs, such as *man, bet, pit, pop,* and *cup,* in the consonant-vowel-consonant pattern often have a one-to-one correspondence between phoneme and grapheme and are therefore good examples to use in the early lessons. Thus after providing instruction on the sounds related to the symbols /t/, /p/, /c/, and /a/ and the sound of "a" in the c-v-c pattern, the teacher can present the words *at, cat, tap, cap,* and *pat* and expect the student to pronounce the words. Each letter represents a single sound.

After establishing the phoneme-grapheme relation for several letters of the alphabet the teacher should begin to introduce the child to the patterns in which the phonemes and graphemes occur. Initially the patterns should be simple ones. Many of the phonic and

linguistic reading programs begin with the consonent-vowel-con-
sonant pattern, which usually stands for a short sound of the vowel:
bat, bet, bit, bop, but. Phonic programs often teach these patterns
through rules or generalizations which may be learned deductively
or inductively.

Phonics

Modern phonic programs give the learner certain rules or generalizations to help in analyzing words. Several researchers have questioned the utility of some of these generalizations (Clymer, 1963;
Emans, 1966; Bailey, 1967). Of the forty-five phonic generalizations examined in these studies, some seemed to have high utility for
the elementary school child while others appeared to be quite useless.
Clymer examined materials from the primary grades; Emans, materials above the primary grades; and Bailey took samples from the six
most popular basal readers of the 1960s for grades one through six.
These reseachers asked first of all whether the phonic generalization
seemed to apply to at least 20 words out of 2000. They then applied
the generalization to see whether it gave the reader an accurate pronunciation of those words. The percentage of utility for the forty-five
generalizations is summarized in Table 9.1.

If the generalization applied to only 30–50 percent of the words
that fit the definition of the generalization, the student would have at
least that much assistance in deciphering the words. This does not
mean that a student should memorize all the rules; most of them
should become operational through practice with words in context.

Emans wrote eighteen generalizations that had a high percentage
of utility in the middle grades. They are reproduced in Table 9.2. A
phonics approach is not without problems if used strictly without
regard to meaning in context. If a child is taught to identify words
only by means of a pronunciation guide, his daily lessons could degen-
erate into the word-calling mechanics that bothered Horace Mann.
There is a wide variety of spelling patterns or graphemes for the same
sounds or phonemes in the English language. This variety encourages
teachers to guide students in finding generalizations and applying
them. Some words, of course, defy phonic analysis. Though Hay and
Wingo (1960, p. 13), and Fries (1963) estimate the percentage of
such words at less than 8, that 8 percent must be learned by the whole-
word method through visual memory techniques.

Linguistics

In the early forties the Yale-based linguist Leonard Bloomfield
proposed that word recognition be taught according to sound patterns (1961). He argued that there is a direct correspondence be-

TABLE 9.1   Forty-five Phonic Generalizations

	Percentage of utility	Clymer	Bailey	Emans
1. When there are two vowels side by side, the long sound of the first vowel is heard and the second vowel is usually silent. (*leader*)		45	34	18
2. When a vowel is in the middle of a one-syllable word the vowel is short. (*bed*)		62	71	73
3. If the only vowel letter is at the end of a word, the letter usually stands for a long sound. (*go*)		74	76	33
4. When there are two vowels, one of which is final *e*, the first vowel is long and the *e* is silent. (*cradle*)		63	57	63
5. The *r* gives the preceding vowel a sound that is neither long nor short. (*part*)		78	86	82
6. The first vowel is usually long and the second silent in the digraphs *ai, ea, oa,* and *ui.* (*claim, bean, roam, suit*)		66	60	58
	ai		71	
	ea		56	
	oa		95	
	ee		87	
	ui		10	
7. In the phonogram *ie*, the *i* is silent and the *e* is long. (*grieve*)		17	31	23
8. Words having double *e* usually have the long *e* sound (*meet*)		98	87	100
9. When words end with silent *e* the preceding *a* or *i* is long. (*amaze*)		60	50	48
10. In *ay* the *y* is silent and gives *a* its long sound. (*spray*)		78	88	100
11. When the letter *i* is followed by the letters *gh*, the *i* usually stands for its long sound and the *gh* is silent. (*light*)		71	71	100
12. When *a* follows *w* in a word it usually has the sound *a* as in *was*. (*wand*)		32	22	28
13. When *e* is followed by *w* the vowel sound is the same as represented by *oo*. (*shrewd*)		35	40	14

Table 9.1 Continued

Percentage of utility	Clymer	Bailey	Emans
14. The two letters *ow* make the long *o* sound. (*row*)	59	55	50
15. *W* is sometimes a vowel and follows the vowel digraph rule. (*arrow*)	40	33	31
16. When *y* is the final letter in a word it usually has a vowel sound. (*lady*)	84	89	98
17. When *y* is used as a vowel in words it sometimes has the sound of long *i*. (*ally*)	15	11	4
18. The letter *a* has the same sound (*o*) when followed by *l*, *w*, and *u*. (*raw*)	48	34	24
19. When *a* is followed by *r* and final *e* we expect to hear the sound heard in *care*. (*flare*)	90	96	100
20. When *c* and *h* are next to each other they make only one sound. (*charge*)	100	100	100
21. *Ch* is usually pronounced as it is in *kitchen*, *catch*, and *chair*, not like *ah*. (*pitch*)	95	87	67
22. When *c* is followed by *e* or *i* the sound of *s* is likely to be heard. (*glance*)	96	92	90
23. When the letter *c* is followed by *o* or *a* the sound of *k* is likely to be heard. (*canal*)	100	100	100
24. The letter *g* is often sounded similar to the *j* in *jump* when it precedes the letters *i* or *e*. (*gem*)	64	78	80
25. When *ght* is seen in a word *gh* is silent. (*tight*)	100	100	100
26. When the word begins *kn* the *k* is silent. (*knit*)	100	100	100
27. When a word begins with *wr*, the *w* is silent. (*wrap*)	100	100	100
28. When two of the same consonants are side by side only one is heard. (*dollar*)	100	100	100
29. When a word ends in *ck* it has the same last sound as in *look*. (*neck*)	100	100	100

Table 9.1 Continued

	Percentage of utility	Clymer	Bailey	Emans
30.	In most two-syllable words the first syllable is accented. (*bottom*)	85	81	75
31.	If *a, in, re, ex, de,* or *be* is the first syllable in a word it is usually unaccented. (*reply*)	87	84	83
32.	In most two-syllable words that end in a consonant followed by *y,* the first syllable is accented and the last is unaccented.	96	97	100
33.	One vowel letter in an accented syllable has its short sound. (*banish*)	61	65	64
34.	When *y* or *ey* is seen in the last syllable that is not accented, the long sound of *e* is heard. (*turkey*)	0	0	1
35.	When *ture* is the final syllable in a word it is unaccented. (*future*)	100	100	100
36.	When *tion* is the final syllable in a word it is unaccented. (*notion*)	100	100	100
37.	In many two- and three-syllable words the final *e* lengthens the vowel in the last syllable. (*costume*)	46	46	42
38.	If the first vowel sound in a word is followed by two consonants, the first syllable usually ends with the first of the two consonants. (*dinner*)	72	78	80
39.	If the first vowel sound in a word is followed by a single consonant, that consonant usually begins the second syllable. (*china*)	44	50	47
40.	If the last syllable of a word ends in *le,* the consonant preceding the *le* usually begins the last syllable. (*gable*)	97	93	78
41.	When the first vowel element in a word is followed by *th, ch,* or *sh,* these symbols are not broken when the word is divided into syllables and may go with either the first or second syllable. (*fashion*)	100	100	100

Table 9.1 Continued

	Percentage of utility	Clymer	Bailey	Emans
42. In a word of more than one syllable the letter *v* usually goes with the preceding vowel to form a syllable. (*travel*)		73	65	40
43. When a word has only one vowel letter the vowel sound is likely to be short. (*crib*)		57	69	70
44. When there is one *e* in a word that ends in a consonant the *e* usually has a short sound. (*held*)		76	92	83
45. When the last syllable is the sound *r*, it is unaccented. (*ever*)		95	79	96

SOURCES: Theodore Clymer, "The Utility of Phonic Generalizations in the Primary Grades," *The Reading Teacher*, Vol. 16 (January 1963), pp. 252–258. Mildred Hart Bailey, "The Utility of Phonic Generalizations in Grades One through Six," *The Reading Teacher*, Vol. 20 (February 1967), pp. 413–418. Robert Emans, "The Usefulness of Phonic Generalizations above the Primary Grades," *The Reading Teacher*, Vol. 20 (February 1967), pp. 419–425.

TABLE 9.2   Modifications of the Original Forty-five Generalizations

Generalization	Percentage of Utility
1. The letters *io* usually represent a short *u* sound as in *nation*.	86
2. The letters *oo* usually have the long double *o* sound as in *food* or the short double *o* sound as in *good*. They are more likely to have the double *o* sound as in *food*.	100
3. When a vowel is in the middle of a one-syllable word, the vowel is short except that it may be modified in words in which the vowel is followed by an *r*.	80
4. When the vowel is the middle letter of a one-syllable word, the vowel is short.	80
5. When the first vowel in a word is *a* and the second is *i*, the *a* is usually long and the *i* silent.	83
6. When the first vowel is *o* and the second is *a*, the *o* is usually long and the *a* is silent.	86
7. The vowel combination *ui* has a short *i* sound.	79

Table 9.2 Continued

Generalization	Percentage of Utility
8. The two letters *ow* make the long *o* sound or the *ou* sound as in *out*.	100
9. When *y* is used as a vowel, it most often has the sound of long *e*.	92
10. The letter *a* has the same sound (ô) when followed by *w* and *u*.	84
11. One vowel letter in an accented syllable has its short sound if it comes before the end of the syllable and its long sound if it comes at the end of the syllable.	78
12. One vowel letter in an accented syllable has its short sound if it comes before the end of the syllable and its long sound if it comes at the end of the syllable except when it is followed by an *r*.	97
13. When *y* of *ey* is seen in the last syllable that is not accented, the short sound of *i* is heard.	97
14. A *-tion* at the end of a four-syllable word indicates a secondary accent on the first syllable with a primary accent on the syllable preceding the *-tion*.	95
15. Taking into account the original rules 5, 28, 29, 31, and 41, one sees that if the first vowel sound in a word is followed by two consonants, the first syllable usually ends with the first of the two consonants.	96
16. Except in some words with a prefix, if the first vowel sound in a word is followed by a single consonant, that consonant begins the second syllable and the vowel sound in the first syllable will be long, *or* if the consonant ends the first syllable the vowel sound will be short.	84
17. A beginning syllable ending with a consonant and containing a short vowel sound is likely to be accented.	95
18. When a word has only one vowel letter, the vowel sound is likely to be short unless the vowel letter is followed by an *r*.	78

SOURCE: Robert Emans, "The Usefulness of Phonics Generalizations above the Primary Grades," *The Reading Teacher*, February, 1967, pp. 419–425.

tween the sound of a word in the spoken language and the way it is written.

Bloomfield pointed out that linguists have devised frequency tables to identify the most frequently used vowel and consonant sounds. Thus, in his suggested exercises he starts with words and phonic elements that will be simple and useful to the beginning reader. These elements, he says, are the short vowel sounds followed by the long vowel sounds. After the graphic symbols for these sounds have been mastered, the irregular sounds and symbols can be introduced.

By arranging regular words in consistent, sequential patterns, Bloomfield teaches the child to identify the phoneme-grapheme relation and to build on previously mastered sound knowledge.

Bloomfield starts with words that have a one-to-one sound-to-letter relation. He first uses words that have the short sound of "*a*" and then proceeds with the short sound of *e, i, o,* and *u.* The student is taught a large number of three-letter words, all having a short sound of the vowel. Thus Bloomfield produces practice sentences like, *Dan can fan a man.* He then presents his second pattern, the long sound of the vowel. In this pattern, too, consonants remain in a single, uncomplicated form. Each element is introduced in the order of its frequency of use in oral language.

Another linguist, Charles Fries (1963), advocates the teaching of reading according to spelling patterns. Like Bloomfield, he insists that the beginning reader should not be asked to identify irregular words before he has mastered the regular patterns. He insists also that the simplest spelling pattern be stated first — not only because it is simple but because it represents the most frequently encountered spelling pattern in the English language. Fries identifies two major spelling patterns:

I.   consonant-vowel-consonant, for example, *m-a-d.*
II. consonant-vowel-consonant-vowel, for example, *m-a-d-e.*

According to the Fries method, the child should not be asked to identify words in pattern II until he has mastered all the regular forms of pattern I. No irregular words should be introduced until all the regular spelling-patterns have been mastered. In pattern I, for example, *b-a-d* can be distinguished from another word of the same shape by noting the difference or the contrast in either first, second, or third position: *p-a-d, b-e-d,* or *b-a-t* indicate the changes that can take place by altering one letter only. Table 9.3 gives comparative data on the decoding programs suggested by Bloomfield and Fries.

Fries's method of teaching word recognition rests on his theory

TABLE 9.3 Linguists' Methods of Teaching Reading

	Bloomfield	Fries
Basic principle	Alphabetic principle	Words are identified through visual or perceptual contrasts
	Phoneme-grapheme relation	
		Develop recognition responses to graphemic contrasts
	Phoneme orientation, that is, start with sound	
		Grapheme orientation, that is, start with spelling
	SOUND-SPELLING PATTERNS	SPELLING PATTERNS
Reading readiness	Visual discrimination	Oral language responses to familiar situations (pictures)
	Left-to-right progression	
	Auditory discrimination through rhymes	Alphabet
	Visual recognition of alphabet	Letter names Visual recognition with 100 percent accuracy on upper and lower case
	Auditory recognition of alphabet	
General procedure	Teach the children to respond to all the regular sound-spelling patterns; then teach them systematically to respond to the irregular sound-spelling patterns.	Develop automatic recognition responses to words by identifying graphic contrasts within a pattern and graphic contrasts between patterns.

Regular	Irregular	c-v-c	c-v-c-v	c-vv-c
kid	knit	mad	made	maid
kin	knife	met	mete	meat
kit	knee	bit	bite	tied
		hop	hope	boat
		cut	cute	dues

Overpractice the regular patterns. Once the base of regularity is formed, the deviations will not cause trouble.

about how a person learns to read. He says that learners develop high-speed recognition responses to the written word by noting the contrastive features of words (*mad* versus *made*). These high-speed responses are developed through much practice, and they are not achieved without frequent practice. The contrastive features are shown by the difference in spelling, that is, the arrangement of the letters. It follows, therefore, that the alphabet is a basis for high-speed recognition responses to words.

Both Fries's method and Bloomfield's resemble the whole-word approach to word recognition. Both stress the need to develop high-speed recognition responses to words automatically through considerable practice with regular patterns. At the same time, the two methods are very different from the original whole-word approach. The latter relies primarily on visual memory without reference to spelling patterns or to the alphabet. The linguists, on the other hand, insist that the phoneme-grapheme system is fairly regular and can therefore be more easily taught through its regular forms first. The words to be identified are set up according to scientific principles of regularity, simplicity, and frequency.

Multiskills Attitude

It is not physically or psychologically possible to develop all reading skills at once, simultaneously. No one expects competency after one week in school. But there is psychological and instructional value in letting the child know that reading requires more than one skill, though these various skills will be developed over a period of years.

The teacher attempts to teach as many of the reading skills as are feasible. While the children are learning that their own talk can be written down and read, they are also learning to recognize words through visual memory techniques and are being taught the rudiments of decoding. With these three elements interwoven in the initial teaching stages, the child realizes that reading is communication. He wants to build a large storehouse of instant words, but he knows that for those he does not recognize instantly he can use the letters of the alphabet and the spelling patterns (phonic and linguistic generalizations) to assist him in identification. It is a reasonable success story: "Reading makes sense, and I have a system for deciphering the words, which, in turn, will enable me to get the message."

TEACHING DECODING SKILLS

For diagnostic purposes all teachers should be able to identify the more commonly used patterns or generalizations. You might try the brief phonic test that follows and discuss the answers with others.

EXERCISE FORMAT
Teacher's Knowledge of Phonics

Circle the one that doesn't belong with the others. Give a brief reason for your choice.
1. pr, gl, tw, sh, spr
2. l, r, o, t, z
3. gh, ch, ph, th, tr
4. gnat, wrap, pneumatic, knee, press
5. a, e, m, i, y
6. can, red, pill, boat, rug
7. sh, sp, ch, th, ph
8. ci, ai, ea, oa, ee
9. cot, road, doe, soul, beau
10. thin, thing, thick, this, path
11. pro, re, ness, in, ab
12. can, crust, sup, come, cent
13. able, ly, ship, age, mis

A study by Emans (1967) identified eighteen phonic generalizations with a high percentage of utility. They were presented earlier in Table 9.2 and may assist the reader in making decisions about correct answers for the test just given.*

Phonic Generalizations

A teacher will recognize many of the generalizations even if he is not able to consciously formulate them. Certain generalizations should be committed to memory by teachers. Those that have a high usage potential should be memorized to assist students who have difficulty. Given below are generalizations that every teacher should know Given below are generalizations that every teacher should know well in order to guide students through their initial decoding experiences.

1. *Short vowel rule:* When there is only one vowel in a word or syllable that vowel usually has a short sound if the vowel stands at the beginning or in the middle of the word; for example, *at, but.*
2. *Long vowel rule:* When a two-vowel word or syllable has a silent "e" at the end, the first vowel in the word usually has a long sound; for example, *made, side.*
3. *Long vowel rule 2:* When there is a double vowel in a word or syllable the first vowel usually has a long sound and the second vowel is silent; for example, *maid, beat.*
4. *Murmur rule:* When a vowel is followed by an "r" it has a modified sound that is neither characteristically long nor short; for example, *car, hurt.*

*Answers to teacher's test. 1. sh, 2. O, 3. tr, 4. press, 5. m, 6. boat, 7. sp, 8. ci 9. cot, 10. this, 11. ness, 12. come, 13. mis.

5. *Diphthong rule:* Certain double vowels have linked sounds that make use of both vowels; for example, the double vowel "ou" in *house,* "ow" in *now,* "oi" in *oil,* and "oy" in *boy* (C. Smith, 1967, p. 21).

Beyond a knowledge of the more common phonic generalizations, the teacher should have in mind a sequence for teaching phonic skills and should be acquainted with materials and techniques to give practice in decoding (phonic) skills. With that knowledge the teacher can observe and test students to determine what skills they have and how well they are learning the ones being taught.

Sequence of Decoding Skills

Assuming that the child has the prerequisite background, auditory and visual discrimination skills, and vocabulary to make himself understood in school and knows the names of the letters of the alphabet in order to talk about them in class, the following sequence of decoding skills may be used:

1. Match rhyming words, such as *cat* and *mat.*
2. Identify the sound of beginning consonants and their letter symbols. Initially the consonants should be presented so there is a sufficient contrast between one and the next. A teacher might start with b, s, t, c, p, w, h, and so on. These sounds and their symbols should be developed through whole words and not in isolation—"You can hear the sound of 'b' at the beginning of the word *bat.*"
3. Identify the sounds of consonants at the end of words. Demonstrate with whole words—"You can hear the sound 'b' at the end of the word *tab.*"
4. Identify short vowel sounds in trigraphs—*cap, bet, pit, cot, but.* One of the phonic generalizations and the consonant-vowel-consonant pattern apply to short sounds in trigraphs.
5. Identify consonant blends at the beginning of words, then at the end of words. BR in *bread,* ND in *sand.*
6. Identify long vowels in words that have a silent "e" or that fit the consonant-vowel-consonant-vowel pattern. *make, bite, rope, cute.*
7. Identify consonant digraphs at the beginning of words; at the end of words. CH in *church,* SH in *show,* PH in *digraph.*
8. Identify the long vowels in words that have a double vowel or that fit the consonant-vowel-vowel-consonant pattern: *maid, seat, boat.*

That sequence would take at least the first year of instruction for the average child. For a longer list and more technical information about phonic and linguistic skills there are short texts devoted specifically to that subject (Lamb, 1968; Cordts, 1956; Heilman, 1967).

The sequence itself indicates very little about strategy and instructional techniques. Obviously various combinations could be made within the sequence to make the instruction clearer and more interesting. There is no reason, for example, why all of the consonants have to be learned before a vowel can be introduced. For the sake of getting the child into the decoding of an entire word, the teacher would be wise to introduce a short vowel after the child has learned enough consonants to pronounce a few words using those consonants and the vowel he has learned. "b," "t," and "s" plus short "a" give the child enough sounds and their symbols to analyze words such as *bat, sat, tab, at*. This assumes that the child also knows that the trigraph consonant-vowel-consonant pattern often indicates the short sound of the vowel.

For those who use the gradual analytic approach to teaching decoding skills, the sequence listed above has only a minimum value as far as instructional strategy is concerned. A teacher might use the sequence as a means of knowing which elements to test and emphasize as opportunities arise. It could likewise serve as a general schema for diagnosing decoding problems and prescribing instruction to help a student who has failed to keep up with the skills he needs. Thus, if a child cannot blend the trigraph *cat,* he may need instruction in the effect of the c-v-c pattern on the sound of the vowel, or he may need instruction in identifying the sounds of the consonants in the initial and final positions.

Teachers who use the gradual, analytic approach, for example, in the language experience method, need many ready answers and instructional directions about decoding words. They need to be thoroughly acquainted with phonic generalizations and the sound-spelling patterns of English. Some of the basic information that a teacher needs follows.

The English alphabet is divided into consonants and vowels, the vowels being "a," "e," "i," "o," "u," and sometimes "w" and "y." The vowels are the most important sound elements in the language because they carry the open or unobstructed sound of the words, and they can be easily pronounced when they are isolated from words. The consonants act as interrupters and modifiers of the vowel sounds.

Vowel sounds are said to be long or short. They are long when they say their own name. The vowel "a," for example, is long in the word *made* and short in the word *mad*. Because of certain letter combinations the vowel may be modified so that it is different from the short sound and the long sound. The "a" in *car* is modified by the "r" which follows it. The vowels "o" and "i" in *boil* are also modified.

Their separate sounds cannot be heard clearly. Only closely linked modified sounds can be heard. Phonic generalizations attempt to organize the sounds of the vowels and consonants into usable patterns. One way to get children to practice a generalization once it has been introduced or discovered through class work is to have them search the daily newspaper for words in headlines or in the copy and to mark the words that fit the rule or rules they have just learned. Beginners will be restricted mostly to one-syllable words.

Teachers who use one of the linguistic approaches might employ various strategies, perhaps depending upon the materials being used. Bloomfield formulated his teaching around these points:

1. Children should learn the alphabet before reading instruction is begun.
2. A one-sound–one-symbol correspondence is employed initially.
3. Regularly spelled words are taught first (for example, *rat, hat, bed*) before irregular words are introduced.
4. Words are always read as wholes. Sounds are never isolated.
5. Oral reading is stressed in the beginning stages of instruction (Bloomfield, Barnhart, 1961).

With these principles Bloomfield believed a child could be led to independence with words that fit the patterns introduced.

If a teacher wanted to construct an exercise based upon the regular words that have been introduced, he might write a simple story like the following as an exercise based upon the regular words that have been introduced:

A Cat and a Rat

Can a cat bat a rat?
A cat can bat a rat.
Bam! Bam! Bam!
Bad cat.
Sad rat.

A child could read the story aloud, applying the c-v-c sound pattern. The teacher should observe his attack of each word and supply guidance on individual sounds or upon the pattern, as indicated. Questions can be asked to check on meaning. "What did the cat do?" With a story like this, however, the subject is exhausted with one or two questions.

The irregular words which do not follow a pattern, for example, *the, there* and *is*, are learned by visual memory techniques; they are developed as sight words and should be taught in context. Tony *is* a tiger.

Learning Decoding Skills

Some ways to induce beginning readers to learn the decoding skills listed in the sequence earlier are presented in the following paragraphs. These examples are given so that in diagnosing a need the teacher can construct an appropriate training exercise or will know what to look for in the materials he has available in the classroom.

Alphabet Sequence

Have the children match plastic letters with those written on paper. Then scramble the plastic letters and have the children put them in alphabetical order.

They can learn the lower case letters by tracing over a set of printed letters. Then they should write the letters in sequence (if they have been taught to write them while they are learning what they are) or use cut-out letters to place them in sequence.

Rhyme Sounds

First ask the child to tell which word rhymes with "Joe."

> I know a boy named Joe
> Who froze his little toe.

Later, when rhyming seems easy for the child, ask him to supply the rhyme word:

> There's a big black bunny
> That looks very _____ (funny).

Associating Sound and Symbol

At first, each letter of the alphabet should be given a regular sound value ("z" as in *zipper*). The exceptions and combinations can be developed after the regular values are learned. Teach the letter sounds as they are heard in words. Do *not* try to isolate the letter sounds, for example, saying "tuh" for "t." Rather, say, "You can hear the sound of 't' at the beginning of the word *top*. I am writing 't' on the board. You write it in the air." The examples below indicate the regular sound values for the consonants and vowels. The cue words should be concrete and familiar to the children.

One way to develop a sense of beginning consonant sounds is to have the children cut pictures from magazines and newspapers to

TABLE 9.4   Regular Sound Values for Letters of Alphabet

CONSONANTS		(short)	VOWELS	(long)
b—bed	p—pop	mad	a	made
c—cat	q—quart	pet	e	Pete
d—dog	r—rob	bit	i	bite
f—fish	s—sun	hop	o	hope
g—goat	t—top	cut	u	cute
h—hem	v—vat		w	know
j—jump	w—wish			now
k—kite	x—x-ray	baby	y	cry
l—lip	y—young			
m—mud	z—zip			
n—nose				

indicate things that begin with those sounds. They should find pictures of things other than those used as cue words, such as the cue words in the list just given.

Vowel Generalizations

The teacher and the pupils can make lists that demonstrate the patterns or the generalizations that are being introduced. The children should be encouraged to make up as many words as they can think of to fit a given pattern.

	Pattern I	Pattern II
Teacher Chart:	mad	made
	pet	Pete
	bit	bite
	hop	hope
	cut	cute
Student Chart:	bad	
	cap	cape
	had	
	can	cane
	ham	

The newspaper continuously serves as a valuable source for word-identification work. When a pattern has been introduced in class have the children take one section of the paper and mark all headline words that fit the pattern.

Blending Sounds

Blending sounds in order to achieve recognition of the word is a difficult and crucial skill. Sometimes it is helpful to play a tapping game with the children as an introduction to the blending of letter sounds. "Tap after me." The teacher taps a pattern and the child taps in imitation:

I   I   I
II   II   II
III   III   III
I   III   III   II

Then transfer the finger tapping to vocal tapping. "Repeat after me."

s-s-s-at-at-at
s-s-s-s-at-at-at
s-s-at-at
s-at
sat

Use a similar technique to test blending but use nonsense words so visual memory will not interfere with your check of the children's skill in blending. For example, "Here are some nonsense words— they are not words at all, but I'd like to see if you can read them anyway."

fis	bute	lort	keat	faim	vin
tope	gud	kim	muts	hin	hife

ASSESSING DECODING SKILLS

The use of nonsense words is a way of checking on an individual's skill in decoding. It eliminates the possibility of the student using visual memory for correctly answering some of the test words.

The teacher of beginning reading should make up a check sheet with a sequence of skills on it that he has set up for a semester's program. Through a combination of tests and observations the teacher can note for each student the skills that he has and therefore the point in the sequence where instruction should take place.

To assist in ‚the collection of information about the student's performance, several sample test exercises on decoding skills are provided below. All can be administered to groups and provide criteria by which the teacher can judge a student's competence with that specific decoding skill. Also available are formal, standardized group tests, such as the *McCullough Word Analysis Tests* and the *Botel Reading Inventory.*

SAMPLE TEST ITEMS OF INITIAL CONSONANTS

Give a copy of the test to each child. The teacher pronounces the two words in each row, asking the pupil to listen to the beginning sound of each word. The pupil is to find the letter that represents the sound and circle it on the pupil answer sheet.

Look at row 1. The words are *wagon* and *window*. The pupils should circle the letter "w" on the pupil answer sheet.

1.	wagon	window		4.	tail	tent
2.	girl	gate		5.	carts	car
3.	lion	leaf		6.	met	map

Pupil Answer Sheet   Name_____

                                  Grade_____Date_____

1.	r	w	l	m	4.	d	h	f	t
2.	c	j	p	g	5.	g	n	r	c
3.	r	w	l	f	6.	n	h	m	w

SAMPLE TEST ITEMS OF VOWELS, VOWEL DIGRAPHS, AND DIPHTHONGS

The teacher pronounces each pair of words; the pupil listens carefully and then circles on the pupil answer sheet one of the four vowels or vowel combinations which represents the vowel sound heard in the word.

1.	cake	tail		7.	for	more
2.	bad	cat		8.	up	just
3.	hot	top		9.	play	day
4.	fur	turn		10.	wait	tail
5.	tie	kite		11.	sound	about
6.	farm	barn		12.	boy	toy

Pupil Answer Sheet   Name_____

                                  Grade_____Date_____

1.	e	a	i	o	7.	ir	or	ar	
2.	u	o	i	a	8.	u	o	e	a
3.	e	u	i	o	9.	ay	ea	ew	oy
4.	ar	er	or		10.	ea	ou	oi	ai
5.	e	o	i	u	11.	oi	aw	ew	ou
6.	ar	ur	ir		12.	ay	ou	oy	aw

TEST OF INITIAL CONSONANT BLENDS AND DIGRAPHS

Review, if necessary, the principle that consonant blends represent more than one sound whereas consonant digraphs represent only one speech sound. Pronounce the two words that begin with the same consonant sound. Ask the pupils to circle the letters that make that sound.

1. cherry chicken
2. grass green
3. step stairs

4. truck train
5. crowd crow
6. flag floor

Pupil Answer Sheet   Name _____

                                   Grade_____ Date _____

1. cl   ch   sh   th
2. cr   gr   ch   bl
3. sl   fr   cl   st

4. th   dr   tr   fr
5. cr   dr   ch   wr
6. ph   fr   gr   fl

SAMPLE TEST ITEMS FOR CONSONANT BLEND AND DIGRAPH PHONOGRAMS

Have pupils look at the three phonograms that follow the first two letters. One of these phonograms added to the first two letters forms a word that the child knows. Direct the pupil to circle the phonogram that forms the word and then write the word in the blank.

1. bl   ame   ate   ay   _____
2. bl   urch ock   im   _____
3. br   ud   ool   ing   _____
4. br   ick   ank   out   _____
5. cl   ab   ock   ine   _____
6. cl   ack   ace   ight _____

Any word-analysis skill must, of course, be assessed in terms of the student's ability to derive the meaning of a complete sentence. Within the context of a sentence, is the student able to use decoding skills and gain an accurate concept of the meaning of the sentence? Once he has pronounced the word, does he know what it means in context? "Tell me in your own words what that sentence means. Tell me what that word means that you figured out (sounded out)."

SUMMARY

The whole-word approach to reading represents an attempt to overcome meaningless word pronouncing through a letter-by-letter phonic approach. Although authorities disagree about when to start decoding and how it should be taught, all believe that it should be taught with other skills and that it is an extremely important tool in analyzing words.

Some educators believe that decoding should be taught gradually and analytically from meaningful context, that is, as the opportunities for using a skill arise while reading. Others believe that an intensive and synthetic approach ought to be used in the beginning stages of reading. Both phonic and linguistic material have been published that fit the intensive, synthetic definition. Research on these materials, though beleaguered by weaknesses in design, indicates that intensive, synthetic materials produce superior results at the end of the first grade on word-recognition sections of standardized reading tests.

We recommend combining both analysis in context and synthetic practice material. In order to teach children teachers must themselves know what the generalizations and the patterns are that help in decoding English spelling. They should likewise have in mind a sequence of decoding skills that will guide them in diagnosing the skills of their students and in planning instruction that will make them more independent readers. Some group test samples were provided on specific decoding skills.

TERMS

functional phonics	digraphs
synthetic phonics	diphthongs
linguistics	spelling patterns
phoneme	letter-by-letter phonics
grapheme	

PART IV

PRIMARY
READING SKILLS

After a child learns the initial code-breaking skills he concentrates on word-recognition and comprehension skills necessary for functional literacy, for example, reading the daily newspaper. A variety of word-recognition and word-analysis skills are described in the chapters that follow, as are various kinds of comprehension skills. Oral reading skills, techniques for developing interest, and standards for choosing books complete this part of the book.

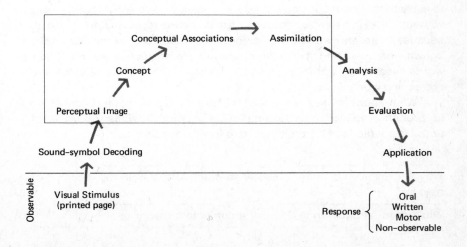

Chapter 10

Word Recognition and Competent Reading

Everyone who reads extensively occasionally finds himself faced with a word he has not seen before or at least has not seen often enough to recognize instantly. For the adult it may be a new technical term such as *multivariate analysis*; for the elementary school child it may be a word as common as *schoolbus*. Both the adult and the child foresee that they will meet the word again, and the next time they would prefer to respond automatically to the word instead of having to analyze it. How does one go about analyzing a word and then fixing it in his memory so that the word becomes a part of his reading vocabulary? How does one teach a child to do this?

All kinds of cues are available for the reader who knows how to make use of them. The more the reader knows about word cues and the techniques for identifying and getting the meaning of words, the more likely he will enjoy reading and spend less time on the mechanics of reading. The child who has been trained to sweep his eyes over an unknown word to see what kinds of cues he can use will quickly solve *schoolbus*. Almost without thinking he knows that there are two parts (syllables) to the word, because there are two vowel positions, "oo" and "u." He then looks for known words and finds two, *school* and *bus*. He has learned each of these words separately in previous reading. Blending the two words yields the compound word *schoolbus*.

What about *multivariate analysis*? How would the adult reader solve its pronunciation and its meaning? This chapter provides a number of possible solutions as it considers the following questions:

Why does word recognition receive so much attention in the teaching of reading?

What word-recognition skills does a competent reader use?

How do word analysis and automatic word recognition differ?

What is meant by context clues, structural analysis, and association skills?

In what order should word-recognition skills be taught?

What means does the classroom teacher have for assessing the word-recognition skills of his students?

In what ways are word-recognition skills and meaning skills related?

No area of reading education receives more attention than how readers analyze and recognize words. A system for teaching children to recognize words seems so central to learning to read that most of the controversies of recent years have focused on different word-recognition techniques. As we stated early in this book, reading involves many skills other than word recognition, but the learner has to start with words because they are the units that make up the message he wants to understand. Thus even though word-recognition skills are only one part of the many skills a competent reader uses, they are thought of first when reading skills are discussed.

Word-recognition skills are a variety of decoding and perception skills that enable the reader to decipher, pronounce, and form a basic understanding of the words he sees on the printed page. In terms of the model of the reading process of Figure 1.1, word-recognition skills follow immediately after the visual stimulus and come before the development of a concept. By looking again at the model one can see that a major interference in decoding and perception prevents concepts from being formed and therefore prevents the message from being comprehended. Facility in these skills, therefore, stands as a crucial launching point for the entire reading process. That accounts for the great concern and the large emphasis placed on word-recognition techniques.

The competent reader employs a variety of perception skills and decoding skills in identifying or analyzing words. He either recognizes a word instantly or he applies analyses that will enable him to identify the meaning of the writer. By definition the competent reader rapidly, almost concurrently, employs all the techniques he needs to solve problem words—context clues, phonics, syllabication, sound-spelling patterns, structural analysis, association, and picture clues. During the years that he was learning these skills he developed his own routine for applying them and now does so in whatever order seems to work best for him.

Most mature readers probably use context clues as their initial skill for word identification. If that does not give a clear identification, they apply other techniques depending on the evident cues available in the word. Perhaps using the beginning and ending consonants along with context will reveal the correct word. If that fails, syllabicating the word, analyzing the meaningful parts, or trying to associate it with other words or objects may be devices used to bring forth the correct response.

Though the competent reader may first use context, the beginning reader cannot start comfortably with that skill because he must first learn what a printed word is and how it is formed. Thus the initial stages of learning word identification are concerned with analyzing the letter patterns and other structural parts of the word for clues to its pronunciation and meaning.

It is not feasible for a person to turn to the dictionary every time he comes upon a word that he does not recognize. Usually the dictionary is a last resort or a means of verifying the solution the reader's analytic skills have predicted. Dictionaries certainly should not be overlooked as a means for solving unknown words, but use of the dictionary typically is not discussed as a word-analysis technique.

WORD-SKILL CATEGORIES

One way of grouping the various word-recognition techniques so they can be seen in perspective is to group them as follows:

1. *Synthetic skills.* These word skills are concerned almost entirely with relating the printed word with one that is in the child's listening and speaking vocabulary.
2. *Analytic skills.* These word skills are concerned with finding letter patterns, dividing the word into parts, and using context to suggest the appropriate word.
3. *Syntactic skills.* These skills are concerned with what is expected on the basis of the language pattern, the position of the word in the sentence, other punctuation, and linguistic cues.

These categories are not mutually exclusive and should not be considered entirely discreet. They are presented here as a means of organizing and remembering the various skills and as a means of creating a framework for teaching them.

Synthetic skills include knowledge of sound-symbol phonics and memory of a word according to its configuration or shape. Sounding out a word letter by letter or memorizing a word by a distinctive feature, such as the camel shape for the word *modular*, are artificial or synthetic means for introducing the beginner to the written form of certain simple words that he already knows from listening and speaking.

Analytic skills include knowledge of spelling patterns, syllabication, structural analysis (for example, roots and affixes), and context clues. In these cases more than a conditioned response is used to work out the pronunciation and the meaning of the word. Though the process may be rapid and there may be a crossing over of some synthetic skills with the analytic, still the reader categorizes the word and responds on the basis of his analysis.

Syntactic skills include context clues, punctuation cues, and identification of the position and the function of the word in the structure of the sentence. The reader has certain internalized responses to the kinds of words that are underlined in the following sentence: "Justus was <u>warned</u> against swimming in the <u>lagoon</u>." Assuming he did not recognize instantly those underlined words, their positions and their functions indicate a past participle verb for 1 and a word for water in 2. The auxiliary verb <u>was</u> and the prepositional phrase <u>in the</u> create those expectations in the native speaker of the language. It is believed that most syntactic skills result primarily from the internalized language habits of the reader and not from a teaching scheme.

Time Allotment for Word Skills

As the child moves through his reading program he learns a variety of word-recognition skills. From grade to grade or from level to level the amount of time or the emphasis given to these skills shifts. Figure 10.1 represents in a general way how the emphasis shifts from synthetic skills in the very beginning to analytic and syntactic skills later in the elementary school program.

During the early weeks of instruction most of the time is spent on the visual memory of words and a sound-symbol decoding of them. As the months and years pass, however, less and less time is devoted proportionately to configuration and phonics. More time is devoted to syllabication, structural analysis, and the use of context. Many recent reading series also include syntactic pattern skills in their exercises. Many publishers have made a linguist part of their editorial team to advise them on what linguistics reveals about the structure and regularity of words in a sentence.

ADDITIONAL WORD-RECOGNITION SKILLS

In previous chapters decoding (phonics) and visual memory (sight words) were discussed as techniques often used very early in teaching a young child to read. But soon after the child understands the significance of the printed page and the relation between speech and print, he needs to be taught a number of other word-recognition techniques.

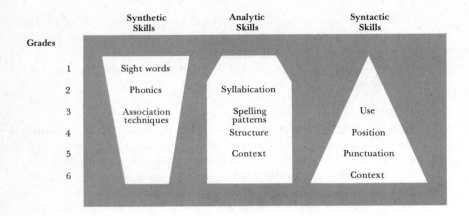

FIGURE 10-1 Time Spent Teaching Word-Recognition Skills

Time spent on synthetic word skills usually decreases with each year in school. Time for analytic skills remains fairly constant. Syntactic skills assume more teaching time later in the elementary years.

All of the techniques discussed in this chapter can be taught to some extent in the first grade. Depending on the development of the child, some may be delayed until later. At least the rudiments of these word-recognition techniques may ordinarily be introduced in the first year: context clues, structural analysis, syllabication and syllable phonics, and association, along with the previously discussed sight word skills and decoding skills. Most reading curricula introduce a variety of word-recognition techniques in the first year and then expand, refine, and reinforce those techniques in succeeding years. A teacher, therefore, has a variety of ways available to help a child so that he can find his own best road. These techniques are discussed here after the order of skills presented in the reading-process model of Figure 1.1. Ways of diagnosing word-recognition problems are also related to the model.

Association Techniques

Association techniques are means of relating an unknown word to another stimulus, whether visual, tactile, and/or auditory. This association between the word and a stimulus aids the reader in recognizing the word when he meets it in subsequent reading.

Good teachers often use association techniques to teach children word symbols, and reading tests use association techniques to evaluate reading vocabulary. Words denoting concrete objects (truck) and sensory impressions (fire) lend themselves well to associative learning techniques. The senses of touch, smell, hearing, sight, and taste can be exploited to impress a word on a reader's memory; for example, *garlic—The smell of garlic filled the Italian restaurant.* Braun (1969) found that children learn more readily words that are associated with things in which they are interested. A popular book, *Teacher* (Ashton-Warner, 1963), reported similar success with words that were associated with deep emotion, for example, *mother* and *shark*.

The association process is often used cooperatively with another word-analysis technique. Where one technique ends and the other begins is difficult to determine, however.

The associations made by one person can differ greatly from those made by another. The connection that is formed is a highly individual one. The value inherent in this technique is the unique and personal image that the association process enables each individual to make. The teacher's task is to develop the child's observational powers so he can utilize these personal examples and associate them with the written word.

Below are several examples of the personal images some individuals have associated with words in their reading lessons:

> Sarah associates "whistle" with the noon factory whistle she hears every day during recess. (hearing)
>
> Rhoda remembers the word *chocolate* because she visited a candy factory and tasted samples of the chocolate. (taste)
>
> Tony's reading lesson contains the word *pony*. He recalls pictures of Indian ponies that his father showed him. (sight)

The teacher can foster and encourage the use of association as an aid to remembering words by providing materials and experiences in the classroom. One teacher presented new words through a filmstrip about a farmer. The picture of the barnyard was projected on the chalkboard. She then labeled the various objects in the picture (barn, tractor, silo, fence, and so on), writing the words on the chalkboard and pronouncing them. With that the children could associate the word with the pictured object. When the teacher switched off the projector the words remained alone on the chalkboard, but the memory residue would continue to help the children identify the words. Their position on the chalkboard was related to the location of objects on the projection. If some children exhibit difficulty with specific words, the projection can be shown again to reteach and reinforce the association.

Further development of associative processes can be encouraged through the use of matching games and exercises which put the written word and the associated stimulus together:

1. The child can match words with the pictures on a bulletin or flannel board. (visual)
2. The child can match colored squares of paper with the names of the colors. (visual)
3. Pieces of cloth, for example, velvet, corduroy, or wool, can be matched to their written symbol. (visual and tactile)

The teacher's role is similar to that of a guide. While he is ready to point out the association that can be derived or used to remember the word, he is also ready to stand back and allow the child to bring his own interpretation and association to the written symbol.

Structural Analysis

Many basic words undergo change in meaning and pronunciation because of prefixes, suffixes, inflections, and compounding. Making use of these word parts to arrive at the meaning or the pronunciation of words is the skill of structural analysis. For example, the above sentences have a number of words containing structural parts — *means*, *subjected*, *under/go*, *meaning*, *reader*, *pre/fix/es*, and so on. The utilization of this technique by the mature reader is a result of instruction and practice. Children must be taught to use it too. The visual learner should find it particularly helpful, for the reader is searching primarily for visual cues in looking for meaningful word parts, though auditory skills are certainly operating, especially with regard to inflectional endings.

The teacher must lead the children to analyze the word into meaningful units and thereby derive a recognition and understanding of the word. This is not an easy task, for the cues that are a part of structural analysis are many and varied. Some of the cues children must learn are:

Root word — A word base that is not compounded or modified by a prefix, suffix, or inflectional ending and that remains unchanged through such modification. (*bound, bounded*)
Compound word — Two or more root words are combined to form one word. Sometimes the compound word keeps the meaning of the original two words (for example, *classroom*), but frequently the meaning of the compound is completely new (for example, *broadcast*).
Inflectional endings — These are endings that change root words grammatically, such as case, gender, number, tense, person, mood, or voice. (*girl, girls*)
Prefix — A unit of meaning attached to the beginning of a word thereby changing that word's meaning (*re* in *report*).

Suffix — A unit of meaning attached to the end of a word thereby changing that word's meaning (<u>ful</u> in <u>wonderful</u>).

Contraction — A shortened form of two words that have been combined into one word. In this process one or more letters has been omitted. Such missing elements are indicated by the addition of an apostrophe (') (*can't*). (Smith, 1963, p. 216)

Instruction in the recognition and use of structural analysis cues can begin as soon as words containing prefixes, suffixes, inflectional endings, compounds, or contractions begin to appear in the child's reading material. When that occurs, the child has a supply of sight words which the teacher can use as a basis for teaching structural analysis. Suppose these sentences appeared in the children's text: *They got on a bus. They go to school.* An exercise for introducing structural analysis might use the compound *schoolbus*, thus using two familiar parts to make up the new form. Identifying the two parts of the compound and labeling a picture of a schoolbus would be one way of introducing children to the concept that words change by combining and adding parts.

By using words from the child's supply of sight words the teacher develops an understanding of what a root word is. This understanding must be taught early because it is the basic word unit — the root word — which then is modified or changed. If the child can identify the root word unit in a modified word, he has mastered a basic concept in the use of structural analysis.

An explanation of the root word generally is not given to the child until the reading text shows a root that has been modified by a prefix of an inflectional ending. For example, *David went walking down the street.* Suppose the reader had previously learned the word *walk*, but stumbled and was unsure of this new form *walking*. The teacher could write *walking* on the chalkboard, covering the inflectional ending "ing" with his hand. "What word do you see here? That's correct — *walk*. *Walk* is a root word or a base word to which we can add parts. We have added '-i-n-g'" (The teacher removes his hand and continues instruction in the root-plus-ending explanation.)

A similar process is effective when leading the child to identify the root in other modified words, for example, *report, raincoat, wonderful*. Of course, instruction should not stop with mere identification of the root word. Each of the various additions and changes that take place must be demonstrated and the student needs opportunity to practice them. Of course, this demonstration is not accomplished in one short lesson. Different kinds of word changes are discussed at different places in the sequence of the reading skills program. A lesson on compounds and one on inflectional endings often will be taught in the first grade while a unit on prefixes and suffixes may not be developed until the second or third grade.

Sequence

As with other kinds of reading skills, structural analysis should not be tied to a specific grade level but rather ought to be taught as the child develops and can assimilate (or needs) a new skill. Given below is a sequence of structural-analysis skills that may guide the teacher who is working in a nongraded or an individualized curriculum.

Meaning-Structure Sequence

1. Basic words, for example, *boy, run*
2. Inflectional endings, for example, *s, es, ed, ing*
3. Compounds, for example, *sailboat, capgun*
4. Identify root words, for example, *loading, loaded, loader*
5. Introduce prefix, for example, *mismatch*
6. Introduce suffix, for example, *artful*
7. The effect of certain form words on the structure of the word that follows, for example, *a man, the men,* or *the man, these men.*

Compound Words

Early in his reading program the child meets words that are made up of two or more simple words. Such words are compounds.

Identifying compounds is usually not difficult for the student. Generally, the compound words the child meets are composed of shorter words he already knows. However, the instructor should not conclude that just because the child knows the parts of the compound in isolation he will be able to transfer this knowledge and recognize the parts when compounded. This conclusion may be erroneous. To the child the compound is a new word regardless of the fact that it is made up of two or three words with which he is familiar. He has never met them in this form. His visual perception mechanism has not been prepared for the combined form. Therefore it is advisable at first to help the child see the separate word units in the compound word, if he cannot do it alone.

The following kinds of activities will help to illustrate compounds to a child, thereby making him adept at identifying them:

1. Auditory perception of the two or three words within a compound word may be developed by having children listen to the teacher say a new compound word, *schoolbus.* They must tell what two words they hear. The compound may be written on the chalkboard and each word identified visually.
2. The teacher writes the compound word on the chalkboard. Using her hand, she covers up one of the words. A child must identify the uncovered unit. The teacher then proceeds to cover

the other word and a child identifies the uncovered unit. This leads the child to see the two word units in the compound word.

3. As the teacher points to compound words on the chalkboard she tells the children that the words are made up of two words. They must find these two words. "Search for the two words in *sailboat.*"

4. The children can be given two columns of words. The column on the left contains the first part of the compound words; the one on the right, the second part. The children must draw lines connecting the words in the two columns which together form one word.

grand   basket
worth   room
waiting   mother
waste   while

Inflectional Endings

Inflectional endings occur frequently in all reading material. In fact, the addition of the simple endings "-s," "-es," "-ed," and "-ing" to known words may often be the first use a child makes of structural analysis. Instruction in inflectional endings is relatively simple. The teacher can use the same technique whenever the child confronts words having these endings. "What happens to the meaning of the word *walk* when we add '-s,' '-ed,' or 'ing'? Read the new word."

The child already knows and uses inflectional endings in his speech. Relating speech sounds to the written symbol may be quite helpful in teaching the concept of inflectional endings. The goal of instruction is to lead the child to *read* the endings that he automatically uses when *speaking.* Here are sample exercises and procedures for developing an understanding of inflectional endings.

1. The teacher can write an uninflected word on the chalkboard, for example, *hat.* He then explains: "I will add an ending to this word to show that there is more than one hat." After "-s" is added, the children or the teacher will pronounce the new word. This word is then used in a sentence. "Do you have two hats?"

2. The words "want" and "kick" can be written on the chalkboard. The children pronounce the words after which the teacher adds the endings "-s," "-ed," and "-ing." The children frame the root word in each instance. want s, kick ing

3. Written exercises similar to these can be provided.
   a. Circle the root in these words:

   plays   playing   played
   walked   walks   walking
   planting   plants   planted

b. Draw one line under the root word and two lines under the part that has been added to it.

raining   throws   played   asking

c. Write the correct word in the blank.

John is _____ for his hat.

    looked
    looking
    looks

He _____ ball yesterday.

   plays
  playing
  played

As the child becomes familiar with inflectional endings he can begin to make some generalizations concerning their spelling and therefore their pronunciation.

1. Very often inflectional endings are added with no change necessary in the root word (*walking, matches, called, girls, going*).
2. If the root word ends in a final "e," the "e" is usually dropped when adding an inflectional ending that begins with a vowel (*hoping, taking, baked*).
3. When a root word ends in a single consonant following a single vowel the final consonant is usually doubled when an ending is added (*running, dropped*).
4. When the word ends in "y" preceded by a consonant the "y" is usually changed to "i" before adding the ending (*cried, ponies, cries*).
5. If the final "y" is preceded by a vowel, the ending is added with no change in the root word (*buys, monkeys*).
6. If the word ends in "f," the "f" is usually changed to "v" before adding an ending (*calves, wolves*).

Prefixes and Suffixes

A similar technique is used to identify words with affixes (prefixes and suffixes) as was used to recognize words with inflectional endings. The root word is first identified; then the affix is isolated.

Probably the best way to develop an understanding of prefixes and suffixes is to have the child draw a line around the affix and tell how it changed the meaning of the root word. A knowledge of the meanings of some of the more common prefixes and suffixes will therefore aid the pupil in recognizing the derived word and attaching the proper meaning to it. The tables list some of the most common prefixes and suffixes the child will meet.

TABLE 10.1   Common Prefixes

Prefix	Meaning	Example
ab-	off from, away	absent
ad-	to, toward	admit
co-, con-, com-, col-, cor-	together, with	contest
de-	away, down, out of	depart
dis-	not, opposite	dislike
ex-	out of, formerly	extend
in-, im-, il-, ir-	in, not	immoral
pre-	before	precede
pro-	forward	proceed
re-	back, again	review
un-	not, opposite	unhappy

TABLE 10.2   Common Suffixes

Suffix	Meaning	Example
-able	capable of, worthy	lovable
-ance, -ence, -ancy, -ency	act or fact of doing, state, quality, condition	allowance
-er, -or	person or thing connected with, agent	teacher
-ful	full of, abounding in	helpful
-less	without, free from	helpless
-ly	like, characteristic of	kingly, queenly
-ment	state of, quality of	amazement
-tion, -sion, -xion	action, state, result	election, tension

Development of the meaning of prefixes and suffixes is not a simple task because some have more than one meaning. However, by first presenting those affixes that are fairly consistent in meaning, the problem will be diminished.

The following illustration shows the procedure one teacher used to present the prefix "un-." She wrote the sentence *His shoes were not tied.* on the chalkboard. The children then read the sentence. She rewrote the sentence, this time using the prefix "un-" in place of the word *not: His shoes were untied.* The explanation was given that the two sentences said the same thing because "un-" often means not. Further practice was given to reinforce the learning of this prefix by writing other root words on the chalkboard such as *happy, kind, dress.* The prefix "un-" was added to each of these in turn. The children read the new words and discussed their new meaning. The words were then used in sentences.

In other words, children must know what a prefix and suffix are in order to use them in recognizing words accurately and efficiently. Using prefixes and suffixes to dismantle words to discover their meaning is an important skill (Dawson and Bamman, 1959).

Exercises such as the following will enable the child to practice analysis of words containing prefixes and suffixes.

1. When the child comes to a word such as *unlike*, if he has had the word *like*, the teacher can draw a line under *like* and ask what that part of the word is. The child should then give the prefix and combine the prefix with the root of the word.

2. Have children make a list of common prefixes, for example, "mis-," "im-," and "-ir" along with words in which these prefixes appear, for example, *mislike, impossible, irresponsible.* Do the same with suffixes.

3. Written exercises.
    a. Add the suffixes in column 1 to the words in column 2. Write the new word.

        ness (state of being)   1. cold
                                   2. happy
                                   3. kind
        er (one who or more)   1. labor
                                   2. long
                                   3. wish

    b. Draw a line through the word in each row that does *not* have a prefix or suffix.

1.	dislike	will	react
2.	knee	enclose	unlock
3.	boundless	wonderful	book
4.	recount	real	return

    c.   Draw a line from the letters on the left to the word which uses that that prefix or suffix.

ly	wiser
er	careless
con	proceed
less	connect
pro	lovely

    d.   Underline the root word and write the prefix or suffix (or both) in the correct column.

	Prefix	Suffix
indirect	in	
regardless	re	less

    e.   Read the following sentences and supply the missing word.

A laborer is a man or woman who _____.

A farmer is a man who _____.

A helper is a person who _____.

What suffix is added to all of the above words? _____

    f.   Draw a line under the prefix in these words and tell how it changes the meaning of the root word.

unhappy	dislike
displease	retake
unknown	mistreat

As often as possible these exercises should be carried out in conjunction with the reading of sentences and paragraphs. Without application in more meaningful context the practice activities may be sterile.

Contractions

Contractions appear frequently as a part of everyone's speech. Rarely does a person say, "I do not want that." Instead, he generally abbreviates, saying, "I don't want that." In fact, it may even sound like "Idonwannat." The contraction is a shorter way of saying two separate words. Since these words are generally contracted in everyday speech, reading and writing them in a shortened form is a logical step.

Explaining this logic to the child may help him with a sometimes troublesome analysis, for contractions may not always sound like either of the words they stand for, such as *don't* for *do not*.

The teacher can write the words *let us* on the chalkboard, after which the contraction *let's* is also written. It is explained that *let's* is a shorter way of saying *let us*. The teacher will further say, "This mark [pointing to the apostrophe] shows that we have left some letters out. We call this mark an apostrophe. In *let's* the apostrophe tells us that one letter has been left out. What letter is it?"

As with other instruction in word-analysis skills, the instructional sequence should proceed from simple to complex. Therefore, words in which single letters are left out (*is not, isn't*) should be first. Later, the words in which two or more letters are missing (*he would, he'd*) should be presented.

The following exercises allow the child to work with contractions:

1. Draw a line from the words in the first column to the correct contraction in the second column:

    does not   can't
    it is   doesn't
    cannot   isn't

2. Rewrite the sentences using the contraction for the words in italics.
    He will go to the house.
    I *do not* want to go.
    You will have to do it.

3. Write the words that each contraction stands for.
    I'll   _____   you've _____
    we've _____   can't _____
    we'll _____   it's   _____

In all exercises involving structural analysis the reader should be encouraged to search for the largest possible unit that he can recognize and then figure out how the other part(s) of the word change the pronunciation and the meaning of the basic unit. In other words, the reader should not feel compelled to look first for the root and then the affixes of *reconstruction* when he recognized instantly the entire first part, *reconstruct,* and knew that it meant "to build again." Structural analysis is not a mental gymnastic but a tool to assist the reader in figuring out the pronunciation and the meaning of a word not recognized at first glance.

Syllabication

Syllabication and syllable phonics may be considered an extension of the phonics skills presented in the previous chapter. It involves the separation of longer words into pronounceable units (syllables). As the syllables are recognized and pronounced, they are synthesized to yield the pronunciation of the entire unknown word. Accent in words is an intrinsic part of this skill.

Prior to instruction in syllabication the child must have mastered the vowel and consonant sounds (including the schwa). For that reason the teaching of syllabication usually comes relatively late in the sequence of word-recognition techniques.

Instruction in syllabication is usually started with ear training, which is designed to help the child hear the syllables within words. As a word-analysis technique it may be especially useful to those who learn best through the auditory modality. An understanding of syllables can be given to children in the following procedure: "The word *sun* has one syllable or part. The word *sunny* has two syllables. What do you think a syllable is?" The children's responses may include the notion that a vowel sound is needed for a syllable or that you can tell the number of syllables by the number of "beats" (rhythmic beats) in a word. In this way the teacher moves the children toward a definition of syllables.

Further practice is necessary before children will recognize the number of syllables in words. Exercises such as these will provide this practice:

1. Using their own names, have the children say their names in unison, clapping the syllables as they do so. A chantlike effect will result: "Ted-dy, Sar-a, John, James, Tho-da, An-dre-a . . ."

2. The teacher can pronounce words having one or two syllables. The children will respond when they hear a word having two syllables. Responses could be by clapping, raising hands, and so on.

Eventually the children should be led to the awareness that a word has as many syllables as it has sounded vowels. Very often, in fact, a vowel alone constitutes a syllable. However, a child must also recognize that a syllable may contain more than one vowel but that those vowels are pronounced as one (for example, *boat*).

To develop an understanding of the vowel-syllable relation the teacher can provide the children with a list of words. They must identify (1) the number of vowels; (2) the number of vowel sounds; and (3) the number of syllables. For example:

	Vowels	Vowel Sounds	Syllables
fact	1	1	1
summer	2	2	2
float	2	1	1

Accent

Another part of the syllabication technique is recognizing accents in words. In words of two or more syllables one syllable is usually pronounced more forcibly than the rest.

To develop syllable accent the teacher can tell the children: "Listen carefully while I say this word—*básket*. Now listen to me say it

again." This time he puts the accent on the second syllable—*basket!*
The children must identify which pronunciation was the correct
one. They should also discuss why *básket* was the correct pronunciation. They may reply that *básket* just sounded right, while *basket'*
sounded odd because the second part was too loud. The teacher can
then explain accent, saying, "In words that have more than one syllable we usually say one syllable more forcibly, or loudly, than the
others. This loudness or stress is called accent."

A feeling for accent can be developed further when children are
instructed to tap or beat the accent with their fingers or pencils as
they pronounce lists of words. They will tap harder with the accented
syllable.

Knowledge and awareness of accent in words is helpful because
accent affects vowel sounds. For example, "the vowel 'a' has the long
sound when accented in *able*, but a different sound when unaccented
in *apart*. The vowel principles apply to accented syllables, but they
usually do not apply to unaccented syllables" (Smith, N. B., 1963, p.
235). The child should be aware of accent so he can use it to apply the
correct vowel sound to each syllable.

One of the troublesome aspects of applying vowel-sound rules is
that unaccented syllables generally have a muted sound known as
the schwa sound. No matter what letter is used to spell it, the unaccented syllable sounds something like the short ŭ sound (*hut*). In
acceptability, for example, both the "a" and the "i" are used in syllables with the schwa sound. Experience indicates, however, that
pupils do not need to understand the effect of the unaccented syllable
on the relation between the spelling of that syllable and its actual
sound.

When the child has mastered auditory recognition of syllables
and accent he is ready for formal instruction in dividing written words
into syllables. This will enable him to analyze unfamiliar polysyllabic
words in context.

His ability to divide written words into syllables is greatly facilitated if he has generalizations to follow. The teaching of these principles should be done inductively. That is, the child should analyze
many words that fit under one principle. Then, with teacher guidance, he will generalize the process or principle that can be applied
when dividing these words into their component parts.

Syllabication Generalizations

The following six generalizations are helpful for syllabicating words:

1. When two consonants fall between two vowels the division of
   syllables is usually between the two consonants. (*rab-bit, sis-ter*)
2. When a vowel is followed by a single consonant the consonant
   usually begins the second syllable. (*be-fore*)

3. When a word ends in "le" and a consonant precedes the "le" then that consonant goes with the "le" syllable. (*ta-ble*)
4. If the word contains a prefix, the division comes between the prefix and the root word. (*re-view*)
5. If the word has a suffix, the division comes between the suffix and the root word. (*like-ly*)
6. Consonant digraphs and blends are never divided. (*rock-et*)

The recognition of a word's pronunciation does not entirely stand or fall upon the child's being able to know exactly where the breaks between syllables occur. For example, knowing whether the division of syllables in the word *amble* comes before or after the "b" does not assure accurate pronunciation of that word. For this reason, and because these principles of syllabication do not apply to all words, they are recognized as being generalizations, not rules. They are helpful clues that the child usually can rely on to aid him in dividing a word into syllables which can then be subjected to phonic or structural analysis to arrive at pronunciation or identification.

Correct division of a word into its syllables will, however, greatly facilitate the child in determining the pronunciation because of the effect that open and closed syllables have on the vowel sound. A syllable ending with a consonant is termed a closed syllable. The vowel sound in a closed syllable is short. If the syllable ends with a vowel, however, it is called an open syllable. The vowel sound in this case will be long, for example, *Bantu.* Therefore, correctly dividing a word into syllables yields clues for determining that word's pronunciation.

Context Clues

Place yourself in the following situation. While you are reading an article in the library you come to a place where the page has been torn. When you place the two edges back together you discover that a word has been obliterated from the selection in the process. The illustration on the next page illustrates such a dilemma.

What will you do? Abandon the article? Probably not. More likely you will provide a word that will fit into the meaningful pattern of the sentence. Maybe you did this while reading the above selection. Perhaps you inserted *patient* or *subject.* Either word is suitable in meaning to complete the text.

Studying the setting of the unknown word for clues to help in identifying the word is what is meant by context clues. Use of context as an aid is not limited to such an occurrence as a torn page with a deleted word. Context is also effective as an aid to word recognition when the word is available in print but unknown by the reader.

Utilization of context to aid in word recognition is a necessary

BLAIBERG DIES

Borrowed time ends

The world's longest-surviving heart transplant died at 7:40 p.m., Sunday, Aug. 17, at Groote Schuur Hospital in Capetown, South Africa. Chronic rejection was the cause of death. Rejection problems have led to a decline in the number of heart transplant operations (SN: 6/21, p. 598).

Dr. Philip Blaiberg, the dentist whose own heart's failure would have cut off his life at the age of 58, lived to be 60 —19 and a half months after Dr. Christiaan Barnard transplanted the heart of 24-year-old Clive Haupt, who died of a brain hemorrhage. Dr. Blaiberg received his new heart on Jan. 2, 1968. He had pneumonia as well as kidney and liver failure when he died.

As of Aug. 18, 143 heart transplants had been performed; 38 survive.   ◇

23, 1969/vol. 96/science news/147

and valuable technique whether one is a beginning reader or a mature reader. Any unknown word must fit into the thought pattern. Use of context clues forces the reader to think while he reads. Too, of course, context always provides a check for the other word-recognition techniques that the reader uses. Most reading authorities agree with Tinker and McCullough (1962), who cite context clues as being "one of the more important aids to word recognition" (p. 150).

In the example of the torn page you used context to decide on an appropriate word. As a mature reader you use the same skill frequently to "guess" at the meaning of new words. Perhaps you learned to use context clues on your own. Some persons do. However, successful acquisition of a skill is questionable when left to chance. All children will benefit from direct, well-planned, and sequential instruction geared toward developing awareness and use of contextual aids.

The teacher can promote the use of meaning clues. For example, during story time, he can stop momentarily at an appropriate place and ask, "What word do you think will come next?" The children will provide words that they think make sense. The words they contribute will then be checked by inserting them into the actual sentence. The children themselves can decide if their words fit.

"Perhaps the best way to develop contextual sensitivity and ability is to make the most of each functional opportunity while the children are reading" (Smith, N. B., 1963, p. 184). Thus, the teacher will give help in identifying an unfamiliar word using contextual clues whenever opportunity arises.

Instruction should not rely on the teacher's beguiling encouragement, "Guess the word." Such guidance can actually become *mis*guidance. Instead of leading the children to think, it may lead them to make wild guesses. Therefore, the teacher should ask, "What word do you think would make sense?" Such questions as these will guide the child to use his cognitive skills on the text.

Another suitable instructional technique is to take children's language experience stories and write them on the chalkboard with some words left out as in the following example:

We have a hamster in our _____.
Her _____ is Lori Blackberry.
She lives in a _____.
She likes to _____ the place.
We like our _____.

Cloze Method

The teacher does not have to rely upon experience stories for material to construct exercises such as this. He can make use of paragraphs that he has written or that he has selected from books.

Mother planned a birthday _____ for Mary.
Mary invited all her _____ from school.
She planned _____ for her friends to play.
Her friends gave Mary _____.

Exercises like this are incorporating a technique known as the *cloze method*. Based on the gestalt idea of closure, which is the impulse to complete a structured whole by supplying a missing element, the reader provides closure of the sentence by filling in the missing words. When using the cloze method the teacher can ask, "What word do you think should go into that blank to finish the sentence?" The word or words that are volunteered are checked by inserting them in the sentences; several may be correct.

Further practice to develop the child's ability to use contextual clues can be given with isolated sentences that require the addition of one word to complete the meaning. Pupils are asked to supply words that fit the blanks and thereby complete the sentence. Often in exercises using isolated sentences the number of options that the children can give will be larger. Take, for example, the sentence "Dick _____ home after school." Any of the following words could conceivably be used: *came, ran, walked, went, skipped, called.* Now, if he wishes, the teacher can utilize other word-recognition techniques to narrow the choice to one word. He may say, "All of these words could be used, couldn't they? But now I want you to tell me what the word is if it begins with the letter 'r.'"

Practice to strengthen contextual hints likewise can be provided by having the pupils choose from a group of words the one that fits the meaning:

Jeff played _____. (*boy, bit, bat, ball, work*)

For beginning readers it may be helpful to supply several possible choices. Once they have the idea though, the cloze method makes them more conscious of a variety of cues.

These and similar exercises should develop the child's ability to utilize context clues to aid in word identification. Frequently a teacher provides informal guidance in context clues when he tells the children to read the rest of the sentence and then come back to the unrecognized word.

The cloze technique can also be used to estimate the appropriatness of a book for a child. Bormuth (1962) deleted every fifth word in passages from elementary school texts and found that the accuracy with which children could supply the exact words in the blanks was significantly related to their scores on comprehension tests. He found, for example, the following equivalents:

Percent of cloze items passed	Percent of comprehension items passed
50	95
40	80
30	65

The percentage points on the comprehension items are often used in making judgments about success in comprehension and sometimes in determining how difficult the book is for the student. A teacher can get comparable data from a cloze text. By deleting every fifth word from classroom books a teacher can test a child's capability to read them.

What should a teacher do if 50 percent of the cloze items are passed? If 30 percent of the cloze items are passed?

There are no simple answers to those questions, but an adjustment in the difficulty of the books seems appropriate where tested materials seem too easy or too difficult for an instructional level.

Types of Context Clues

As a child moves through the grades and masters reading skills he should be taught seven types of context clues:

1. Definition type. The definition of an unknown word is provided by the sentence in which that word appears. "Jane and Susan live next door, so they are my *neighbors.*"
2. Experience type. The child must rely upon his own experiential background to predict the unknown word. "The mouse *gnawed* a hole in the box with his sharp teeth."
3. Comparison type. Words in the sentence that contrast or compare with the unknown word give the clue. "You do not have to go around the mountains; go *through* them."
4. Synonym type. A synonym for the unknown word is included. "The *twins*, Tom and Don, moved next door."
5. Familiar expression type. A knowledge of everyday expressions is necessary for clues to be received from this type of context. "The tired old bunny thought the grass felt soft as *cotton.*"
6. Summary type. The unknown word provides a summary of the ideas that precede it. "They marched all in line, just like a *parade.*"*

Often the context alone will indicate the appropriate word, although sometimes context clues do not work. Therefore other word-analysis skills are necessary to check the accuracy of the word chosen or to identify it in the first place.

The identification of an unfamiliar word through contextual clues is not a matter of chance. The reader must carefully consider the meaning implied in a sentence or paragraph as a whole and in the light of this meaning deduce what the unrecognized word might be.

The context clue is widely used by mature readers. This does not imply that it is used to the exclusion of the other word-recognition techniques. Instead, the context clue is most successful when it is used in conjunction with the other techniques, and children should be directed to use it that way.

Vocabulary Expansion

Most children are interested in words. They hear new ones and try them out. They have an intuition that words are power; an increased vocabulary is a sign of maturity. For that reason a teacher may find that he can gain practice in word-recognition skills by capitalizing on children's desire to expand their listening and speaking vocabulary.

*McCullough, Constance, "Recognition of Context Clues in Reading," *Elementary English Review*, Vol. 22, January 1945, pp. 1–5.

By establishing a "word-for-today" routine the teacher can encourage groups or individuals to learn one new word each day. "Gertrude, it is your turn to provide a new word. . . ."

"*Astronomy*. Astronomy is the study of the stars."

"Now who can write it on the board for us? Can someone use it in a sentence?"

With such an approach the teacher leads the students to look at a word and to use all their word-analysis techniques to fix the word in their memories. "How many syllables? How is each syllable pronounced? What other word has a similar beginning? (*astronaut*)." Thus the vocabulary exercise helps the child recognize the word for reading, and the motivation stems from the child's own internal drive for self-improvement and growth.

Some classes may enjoy keeping a vocabulary notebook. Or the notebook idea can be expanded to include a vocabulary bulletin board. Reserve bulletin board space for new words for a week. Every day the children display a new word they have discussed. The word, its definition, and a sentence using the word are then displayed. At the end of the week the children can enter the words from the bulletin board into their notebooks for purposes of review and motivation. The bulletin board can be stripped for a fresh supply of words next week.

Continuous Development of Vocabulary

Vocabulary expansion and the related word-analysis exercises are not limited to the early grades in school. In fact, they are more important in the upper grades as the subject work becomes more complicated. From the primary grades through the secondary school teachers and students should consider word power an important part of their instruction and conceptual growth.

In the early years of school more emphasis is placed on building concepts though firsthand experiences than on gaining them through vicarious means. Teachers want to involve the student as directly as possible so that the words and the concepts of stories and composition activities in the class have a clearer and more vivid meaning. As trips to factories, museums, libraries, and zoos become slightly less important to children, teachers begin to involve them more in projects, experiments, and exhibits, such as building scale models of towns, collecting sea shells, and so on. A teacher who guided an experiment in the speed and direction of the wind added the following words to his student's reading vocabulary:

direction	measure	intensity
pressure	anemometer	instrument

It is not always feasible for the teacher to provide the child with real experience. Happily, much worthwhile experience, and vocabulary can be gained vicariously. Secondhand experiences are obtained from films, pictures, maps, radio and television presentations, recordings, stories, and so on.

Providing children with experiences alone will not expand their vocabularies. A child can conceivably go to the zoo and not learn a single new word. There must be conversation; he must hear the words. He must then be encouraged to use the words over and over until he integrates them and their meanings. The teacher's task is to present the words visually for analysis and storage in the reading vocabulary bank.

One of the most effective means of enriching the child's vocabulary is to encourage him to read widely. In this way he meets many new words in different fields and also becomes familiar with their different meanings in a variety of contexts.

Vocabulary can also be enriched by giving children experiences with figurative language. For example, they can study sentences using figurative patterns of speech to determine the meaning of the sentences:

His face fell.
Don't throw your money away on that.
He threw himself into his job.

Having the child find synonyms, antonyms, and homonyms of words he already knows provides another means of vocabulary enrichment.

Synonyms. Words that have similar meanings (*often, frequently*)
Antonyms. Words that are opposite in meaning (*warm, cool*)
Homonyms. Words that are pronounced alike but are unlike in both spelling and meaning (*wait, weight*).

Direct, structured instruction in these types of words is a necessary and meaningful development in the vocabulary of the elementary school child. Exercises such as the following may be helpful:

Underline the word in each row that has the opposite meaning.

run	walk	race
good	go	bad
big	large	small

Which word in each line means the same as the first word? Which word means the opposite?

merry	gay	was	sad	time
soft	green	hard	sack	pliable

What words are pronounced the same in the following two sentences?
Do they have the same meaning?
Jack wore a blue tie.
The wind blew.

The other techniques described in this chapter are concerned primarily with words the reader already has in his listening or comprehending vocabulary. An often neglected means of getting children to learn to remember words for reading is to teach them words that are new to their vocabulary. At the same time the word is pronounced and defined it should be spelled and written on the board or on a piece of paper so it can be analyzed and discussed as a word to be recognized and read. The technique the child uses to commit this word to memory may be a single method or a combination of word-recognition methods, but the motivation for learning is provided by the fact that he is noticeably expanding his vocabulary.

The normal child has an interest in expanding his vocabulary and the teacher can use that interest to relate a general-meaning vocabulary to an analysis of a word for purposes of reading. Once the child's interest is focused on a word only the teacher's imagination limits the ways the word can be presented for a visual analysis.

APPRAISING WORD SKILLS

Word-analysis skills, like other skills, should be assessed immediately after they are taught. Since word-analysis skills are developed gradually over five, six, or more years, and since it is generally assumed that the skills build on one another, it is important to identify success or failure in a skill before trying to push the child on to some new area. As we say in Chapter 6, the teacher has four general means for diagnosing reading: informal testing, observation, introspection, and formal testing. Depending on the situation, he will use one or all of these general means for appraisal. Table 10.3 indicates typical classroom situations and the four means for assessing word recognition. Several examples of how word-recognition skills fit into the matrix are provided. Using the examples given as guides, what word-analysis skills would you put in each box in Table 10.1? Provide your own estimate of the skills that can be tested easily and efficiently using the activities, and the means of appraisal that are indicated.

After teaching a specific word-analysis skill the teacher may ask individual children to read a word list aloud. As the child pronounces the words the teacher notes whether he is applying the skills that have just been taught. The teacher also looks at the child's practice exercises, whether on worksheets or on the chalkboard. If he observes several repeated errors, he will want to schedule additional instructional time for that child.

As the child reads aloud from a book the teacher can note whether he analyzes words using recently taught skills and can also ask the child to explain what he is doing as he meets a word that requires analysis. At times, the child's own description of his word-attack techniques will guide the teacher in planning instruction for that student. For example, a student reads *combine* for *consider,* saying he saw *com* and *combine* made sense. The teacher must show him how to look closely at the internal elements of an unknown word.

Workbooks and reading texts often contain tests to determine mastery of a given skill. Teacher-made tests and the tests provided by the publishers for specific achievements in reading should be used as diagnostic instruments as much as possible. Their purpose is to isolate a specific skill, such as using initial consonants and final consonants as a clue to word identity. Since the tests are constructed to examine specific tasks, the teacher should examine them to see whether or not the child can perform the tasks. The score is not as important as the pattern or the regularity with which the child applies the skill or fails to use it.

TABLE 10.3   Means for Assessing Word-Recognition Skills

Classroom activities	General Means			
	Informal testing	Observation	Introspection	Formal testing
Oral reading	Oral reading can be used as an activity for all of these general means and for an analysis of performance in phonics, structural analysis, syllabication, and content clues.			
Word lists	Phonics, Structural analysis			
Workbook exercises			Sight words using context	
Tests (written)		Not generally compatible		

In the case of each of the word skills discussed in this chapter, the teacher wants to know two things:

1.   Does the child know the generalization that will assist him in analyzing words?
2.   Can he apply the generalization in a variety of situations — reading aloud, doing a workbook exercise, taking an achievement test?

Context Clues

Because of the nature of context clues, a simple word list does not provide an adequate testing device. A connected communication must be used. Suppose that you want to determine whether or not a child understands that he has to think while he reads in order to use the context clue technique.

Probably the most direct means for determining a child's knowledge is to ask him how he proceeds. Ask him to suggest what skill he uses when he has no dictionary available and does not see how phonics or structural analysis will help him identify the word. He may respond that he *thinks* while he is reading and gets a good idea of the word by the context.

To appraise his ability to apply context clues he needs some reading exercises that will try to answer the following questions:

1.   Can the child supply a reasonable substitute for the blank in the sentence?

     Henry dropped the egg and it _____ all over the floor.

2.   Can he use internal word cues in addition to context to help him find the correct word?

     The drowning man gr--p-d for the log.

3.   Can he infer meanings of words from context?

     Being fired from his job was Henry's *Waterloo*, for it was a defeat from which he never recovered.

A similar series of evaluation questions can be asked about the other word-analysis skills discussed in this chapter. It is not absolutely necessary for the child to be able to articulate the generalization behind the skills, but it reassures the teacher if the child remembers the generalization. The important determination, of course, is whether or not the child can apply the skills and thus answer questions like those that follow.

APPRAISING STRUCTURAL ANALYSIS

1. Can the child recognize root words in derived words? (information)
2. Can he recognize compound words? (cupcake)
3. Can he analyze and define words made up of familiar roots, prefixes, suffixes, and inflectional endings? (predated)
4. Can he add necessary prefixes, suffixes, and inflectional endings to words to give these words the appropriate meaning and form necessary in the sentence? ("Can't stand it!" un+bear+able)

APPRAISING SYLLABICATION

5. Can the child identify the number of syllables he hears in a word?
6. Does he know that the number of sounded vowels in a word indicates the number of syllables?
7. Can he apply the syllabication generalizations to words when dividing them into syllables?
8. Is he aware of the effect of accent in words of more than one syllable?
9. Can he apply common accent generalizations?

APPRAISING ASSOCIATION SKILLS

10. Can the child match the printed word with the visual, auditory, or tactile stimulus symbol used in instruction?
11. Does he recognize the word in subsequent meetings?

APPRAISING VOCABULARY ACQUISITION

12. Can the child write, give, or find the correct word when the definition is given?
13. Can he give the meaning of a new word?
14. Can he use the new vocabulary words in writing sentences and in conversation?

Any evaluation of pupil performance in these skills should have the direct effect of indicating to the teacher which skills should be treated in subsequent instruction and which children need that additional help. Therefore, if the child has grasped the skill, the teacher can continue to present other skills in the sequential program. If evaluation indicates that the child is not able to utilize the skill in question, the teacher should then schedule further teaching and practice.

WORDS HAVE A MEANING

The various word-recognition techniques that have been presented in this and the preceding chapters are designed to help identify words. They are also aimed at giving the child methods of acquiring meaning from what he reads. The whole point of reading is getting a message from the printed page. No one reads merely to pronounce words. The reading teacher, therefore, must guard against giving too much emphasis to word identification and pronunciation to the neglect of meaning. The teacher's responsibility is to demonstrate how to get meaning through a variety of word-perception skills. He creates an attitude about the centricity of meaning while building perception skills that enable the student to achieve meaning.

In beginning reading exercises most words are meaningful as soon as the child recognizes their sound. Thus when the word is pronounced it is also understood. This occurs naturally because the textbook writer uses words that are a part of the average child's listening and speaking vocabularies. Evidence of the child's listening and speaking vocabularies is seen in his ability to participate actively in conversations with his teacher, parents, and classmates. Participation calls for a grasp of words and their meanings. If a child can gain meaning from the words he hears and speaks, he should have little difficulty in transferring his knowledge of these words when he meets them in print. As the reader advances into more difficult selections the vocabulary and the concept load become heavier. Acquiring meaning, therefore, demands an increase in instructional time and energy.

To keep the acquisition of meaning a prime goal of reading, both instructional and practice reading materials must coincide with the background and performance skill of the child. Disregard of that prescription will not only provide the child with extremely frustrating and unenjoyable reading experiences but it will also result in his focusing his attention upon the pronunciation rather than the meaning. For this reason modern reading authorities frequently stress the use of selections with an appropriate readability level.

The provision of graded reading materials will not, however, guarantee that the child is reading for meaning. The importance of reading for meaning can be illustrated to the child when the word-analysis techniques are taught and practiced in context frequently and systematically. Combining recognition skills with meaning was suggested earlier as a reliable method of checking the word that has been analyzed.

The relation between pronouncing (identifying) the word and understanding the word (meaning) can be shown during any reading lesson. For example, prior to reading, words that are new or that consistently cause difficulty for children can be pulled out of the reading selection for purposes of analysis. Following identification of the words through use of appropriate word-analysis techniques, the process can be reversed by replacing the words in context to show their function in developing the meaning of the passage. In addition to this procedure exercises similar to those discussed earlier in this chapter in the section on context clues are appropriate for demonstrating the relation between word recognition and meaning.

Linguistics and Word Meaning

Linguistics is also concerned with words and their meanings, as was discussed earlier under "Syntactic Clues to Word Recognition." (A broader discussion of linguistics and meaning appears in Chapter 11.)

Linguists maintain that the larger utterances, for example, phrases and sentences, of which isolated words are a part, provide keys to word meanings and determine word use. Thus the meaning of a given word depends upon the other words with which it forms a sentence as well as upon the position it has in the sentence.

A word does not act independently of the other words in a sentence but joins with them and interacts with them. This interaction determines the exact meaning of a word. In one sentence a word may have one meaning while in another sentence it has a different meaning. The range of possible meanings a word can have is reflected in the definitions found in a dictionary.

Take, for example, the word *nut*. Webster's New Collegiate Dictionary lists six distinct meanings for *nut:*

1. A dry fruit or seed having separate rind or shell and interior kernel or meat; also, the kernel or meat itself.
2. Something likened to a nut (sense 1) in the difficulty it presents.
3. A perforated block (usually of metal) with an internal, or female, screw thread used on a bolt or screw for tightening or holding something.
4. *Slang.* (a) The head
    (b) Fellow — used disparagingly
    (c) One whose thinking or conduct is eccentric
    (d) A crank
5. *Bot.* An indehiscent, polycarpellary, one-seeded fruit, with a woody pericarp, as an acorn, hazelnut, chestnut, etc.
6. *Music.* In stringed instruments, the ridge on the upper end of the finger board over which the strings pass.

A very real problem is now apparent. If someone hears the word *nut* in isolation, how will he know which meaning to apply to it? He cannot. Ascribing the appropriate meaning to the word *nut* is possible only when the word is used in a larger unit such as a phrase or sentence. This concept is illustrated in the following sentences:

1.   That math problem is a hard *nut* to crack.
2.   She dropped her violin and broke the *nut.*
3.   They went to the hardware store to buy some *nuts* and bolts.
4.   You're a *nut*, you clown!
5.   We're going to the woods to gather *nuts.*

When the word can be used for more than one sentence function it is even more apparent that the larger utterance vitally affects the meaning of the word. For example, here is a word first used to denote an object (noun) and then used to show action (verb).

1.   He sat on a *chair*.
2.   Harry will *chair* the class meeting.

Demonstrations of this type, that is, using words in a variety of ways in different sentences, can be understood by second graders, and even by many first graders. As early as possible the teacher should make children aware of these variations to emphasize the need to use a variety of skills in understanding the printed page.

You may be saying to yourself at this point, "Wasn't that discussion simply another plea for the use of context clues in reading?" In a sense it was. The linguists are not concerned with the cues a reader uses, however, but rather with the situations and the rules that generate the similarities and the varieties that exist in the English language. If the insights of the linguists can make reading specialists aware of how word meaning develops, perhaps teachers will discover clearer and more efficient ways of understanding, explaining and illustrating techniques for identifying and comprehending written words.

SUMMARY

The chapter discussed word-recognition and word-analysis skills beyond the initial skills of visual memory (sight words) and sound-symbol decoding. A variety of word-perception skills are needed for a reader to cope with the printed page efficiently and competently. In addition to the visual memory and decoding skills discussed in previous chapters, a reader needs to be able to analyze words on the basis of syllables (sound structure), on the basis of meaningful structures such as roots and affixes (meaning structure), and on the basis of context clues (thought and syntactic structure).

Even though the competent reader probably uses context clues most often in his attempts to identify and define new words, ordinarily context analysis is not the first skill taught in a sequence of word-recognition skills. After visual memory and phonic techniques, syllabication and structural analysis techniques are usually taught. At first the child needs to understand the symbolic code and to decipher the parts and the patterns that words exhibit. Once he has developed several semiautomatic techniques for analyzing and responding to words, he can pay more attention to the running message that words carry in context, which in turn helps him with individual words.

Linguists have recently reinforced a dictum long honored in the field of reading education—that word-recognition exercises should always terminate in a meaningful utterance, in a sentence or paragraph. For words are rather hollow sounds and hollow shells when standing alone. It is the whole utterance that gives them meaning, especially connotative meaning.

TERMS

word recognition	picture clues
word analysis	context clues
structural analysis	synthetic skills
syllabication skills	analytic skills
association skills	syntactic skills
phonics skills	syllable phonics

Chapter 11

Reading Comprehension

One of the most frustrating cases you will encounter as a teacher of reading is the child who "reads" beautifully but does not seem to understand or remember a thing. He recognizes the words but does not grasp the message they transmit. With most children this problem is a matter of degree; they understand some of what they read but they should understand more.

The time-honored approach to this difficulty is admonishing the child to *think* as he reads. "Don't just say the words, think about them," the teacher scolds. Or the admonition to *try harder* may be offered to a frustrated child.

We recognize that reading without meaning is not acceptable. How then do we teach a child to comprehend as he reads? This chapter focuses on the following questions:

How is reading comprehension related to thinking skills?

What are the prerequisites for reading comprehension to occur?

How can comprehension problems be identified?

Is there more than one type of reading comprehension?

Is low IQ responsible for comprehension problems?

Is it possible to teach a child to think?

What effect do poor language skills have on comprehension?

How can comprehension abilities be measured?

What is a guided reading lesson?

Children learn at a very early age that people read to gain understanding, that the printed page contains a message, and that the
reason for reading is to derive a message. Big brother laughs aloud
as he reads a comic book. Dad gets angry when the newspaper reports a tax hike. In a humorous bit of mimicry, two- and three-year-
olds may page through a book making up their own story. At times
they use pictures for clues; at other times their "story" bears no
resemblance to the contents of the book. But unlike the three-year-
old who is free to make up his own message, older children and adults
must learn to obtain accurately the meaning of what they read.
Comprehension is the label usually applied to acquiring meaning from
reading.

The term *reading comprehension* is analogous to the cigarette filter
that is "recessed in." How, other than in, can something be recessed?
How can reading occur without comprehension? Decoding word
symbols without attaching meaning is not reading but merely word
calling. Nonetheless, the term *reading comprehension* has been useful
from the time it was coined in the 1920s by William S. Gray. Gray
used the term largely in reaction to what he considered to be an
undue emphasis upon oral reading in U.S. schools (Cleland, 1965).
Up to Gray's time the primary goal of reading instruction had been
the proper pronunciation of words, with heavy emphasis given to
oral eloquence and dramatic interpretation. As educators came to
understand the importance of comprehension, oral reading became
less emphasized as an end in itself (see Chapter 12 for a discussion
of oral reading).

Few people today would question the statement that gaining
meaning is the foremost goal of reading and therefore should be
the major focus of reading instruction. The term *comprehension*, however, has become a blanket term that no longer carries the meaning
it did in the early twenties. In fact, considerable confusion is generated by the present indiscriminate use of the term. Kerfoot (1965)
points out that research on reading comprehension is confused
by a welter of inconsistent definitions and personal attempts at
classification. Teachers are misled by tests that give them a "reading comprehension score." They sometimes conclude that comprehension is the same as intellectual capacity and not subject to improvement through instruction. Some order must be brought to
this confusion.

Our first task is to consider more specifically the components of
reading comprehension. Next, we will examine the prerequisites
necessary before comprehension can take place. Finally, we will present means for the classroom teacher to facilitate the development
of comprehension.

THE READING MODEL

A visitor from outer space would be curious and a bit amused to come upon an avid reader bending over a printed page in deep concentration. Imagine the reaction of such a newcomer at the sight of our earthling engrossed in tiny marks on a page.

The spaceman could only witness the reader's reaction because the internal processes that occur between the time a reader looks at a visual stimulus (word symbol) and reacts to its message are impossible to observe. We know or can surmise with some accuracy how a word symbol is decoded. Various experiments have established fairly well what happens during the recognition of a word. Chapter 10 explained this process in some detail. However, the steps that evidently occur between recognition of a word symbol and the observable response to that symbol are difficult to assess. The process is especially complex and difficult to describe when the stimulus is a large number of words arranged in sentences, paragraphs, and pages of print.

Let us consider what takes place when the reader attacks a single word. At the simplest level he gains a perceptual image from the symbol he decodes. (The model of the reading process presented in Figure 1.1 will help to clarify the sequence of steps discussed here.) For example, the symbol *tree* probably causes the reader to think of a large green plant. His mental picture is perhaps of a tree in his own backyard, probably the one his swing is on or the one he and his friends use as a goal line for football games. The word *tree* has meaning for the reader only when it evokes for him an image of the object it represents. Usually a word the reader understands in spoken communication has meaning when he decodes it. Without meaning, decoding is only a game of word calling and not reading.

At the next stage in the reading process the reader generalizes his perceptual image of a word symbol to form a concept. In the previous example the word *tree* in a story may not have referred to the specific plant in the reader's own backyard. Another specific tree, one on the school playground, may have been the correct referent. Or the referent may have been trees in general — in other words, no specific tree that the reader could actually picture mentally or touch. The name and symbol — *tree* — must come to represent "treeness" — in all sizes, shapes, and types. Unless the reader has a full and accurate concept for the symbol *tree,* his understanding, his comprehension, can go astray. Suppose the tree in question is a giant redwood. Being unaware that the concept *tree* includes such mammoth examples as well as the particular one in his own backyard can interfere with the reader's correct understanding. "The building was as tall as a redwood tree" tells the reader one thing if he pictures the correct referent and quite another if his concept of *tree* is limited to his own backyard.

In addition to having a correct perceptual image and a full and accurate concept for a word, the reader must be able to make *conceptual associations* in order to comprehend a sentence. The last example involved an association of several concepts. The symbol *building* represents a concept. The reader must be able to draw on his understanding to lend meaning to this word. *Building* includes the school he attends, the house he lives in, and the stores downtown. The generalized term *building* must be conceptualized by the reader and associated with the concept *tree*. The author of the sentence has chosen to illustrate his idea by means of a comparison — the height of a large building with a huge tree. Comprehension depends upon the reader's (1) vivid perceptual images, (2) full and accurate concepts, and (3) ability to associate concepts correctly.

Finally, to comprehend the sentence, "The building was as tall as a redwood tree," the reader must be able to assimilate the separate concepts and place them in proper relation in order to gain full understanding of the author's message. Linguistic skill and intelligence are required to take this step. Through determining the proper relation he understands the author's message and thus comprehends what he reads.

This description has simplified some highly complex tasks and assumed several important abilities on the part of the reader. The intricacies involved in gaining meaning from the printed page will now be considered in more detail.

FACTORS AFFECTING COMPREHENSION

We have frequently heard teachers remark that Mindy or Juan or Willie has a comprehension problem. When asked to specify what kind of comprehension problem, these same teachers can seldom pinpoint the nature of the difficulty. "He doesn't understand what he reads" is a frequent attempt at clarification. Because reading comprehension is so complex, there is an understandable hesitancy on the part of teachers and reading authorities to be explicit in defining it. We too are concerned about the inaccuracy that may be involved in attempting to account for all of the variables that affect reading comprehension. But diagnosing difficulties and planning instructional activities for overcoming problems requires that some definitive description be provided.

Figure 11.1 depicts the major factors that affect reading comprehension. It is an oversimplification of a highly complex process and consequently contains some error. Nonetheless, it enables teachers to

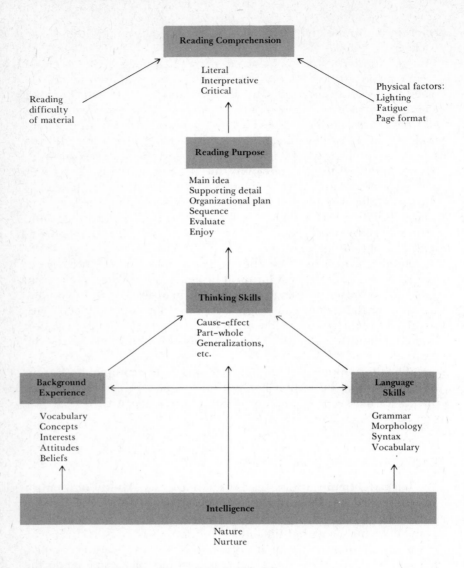

FIGURE 11-1 A Reading Comprehension Model

This model represents one way to organize the major components of reading comprehension.

become specific in discussing comprehension problems. By employing techniques and instruments that assess a child's status in each of the areas cited it's possible to determine the nature and extent of his instructional needs.

In Figure 11.1, four factors are listed as the primary determi-

nants of reading comprehension: thinking skills, background experience, language skills, and intelligence. The reader must possess these attributes in order to comprehend. Purposes for reading
act as controlling agents to direct the reader's application of the skills
and abilities necessary for comprehension to take place. External
factors such as the reader's physical well-being and the difficulty of the
reading material also affect comprehension. Each of these factors is
discussed in the following sections. Where appropriate we will also
present means for assessing the reader's status with regard to these
factors as well as suggestions on how the teacher can overcome limitations.

Thinking Skills

Reading does not take place without comprehension, and comprehension cannot occur without thinking. Evidently the reading process is
intimately linked to thinking. A classical study by Thorndike (1917)
supports this conclusion.

Background experience is a necessary component for thinking
since it provides an individual with the raw material he manipulates
during the thinking process. Broadly defined, background experience
includes books previously read, lectures attended, discussions held,
trips taken, and so forth. Without getting into the nature-nurture
argument over whether heredity or environment is more important
in determining intelligence, it is clear that thinking cannot occur without some basis in real-life experience.

A second factor, ability to use language, is also important for
thinking to occur. Some authorities believe that thinking cannot take
place without language — that an infant does not truly think until he
has a label for objects (Osgood, 1963). Others believe that thinking
can occur without formulized language but readily admit that most
thinking of a conscious nature is based on internal manipulation of
concepts and ideas by means of language (Laird, 1953).

For our purposes it is not important to dwell on the subtleties of
such philosophical arguments. Background experience and language
skill are fundamental components of the thinking process. Teachers
must consider the importance of both in their planning. A third factor important to thinking is intelligence. Intelligence may be defined
in many ways; here we refer to intelligence as the *innate mental ability*
of an individual, his potential for manipulating thoughts. To be sure,
one's ability to utilize this potential is greatly influenced by the first
two factors; in fact, efforts to measure intelligence are quite dependent
upon a child's background of experience and his language skill. Typical IQ tests ask the child to identify an object and specify its uses, give
synonyms for words, solve problems of logic, and follow directions

step by step. Evidently measures of intelligence are largely measures of other factors as well (Bond and Fay, 1950; Clymer, 1952). Nonetheless, when discussing children's thinking intelligence is a third factor to be considered in addition to background experience and language skill. Figure 11.2 illustrates the interdependence of these factors.

Definitive works in children's thinking have been undertaken by Russell (1956), Piaget (1959), Guilford (1959), and others. Central to these works is the notion that children's thinking develops in an orderly and sequential fashion. Some youngsters progress through the various stages more rapidly than others, but all follow much the same pattern. Furthermore, instruction can speed the process of reaching the more mature levels of thought, but only when the child is intellectually ready to move on. For example, the period during which children do not understand the concept of the conservation of matter may be shortened by demonstration and illustration. The principles underlying the constancy of matter may be taught *if the child is ready to benefit from structured experiences*. Thus, a piece of clay may be cut into many smaller pieces. That the same amount of matter still exists can be demonstrated to a child by lumping the small bits together again. Another child, equally "ready," might not develop as fast without an opportunity to observe a demonstration such as this.

The implication of these principles for reading instruction is clear: Teachers must demonstrate how to apply certain thinking processes to the act of reading. For example, when a child is ready to understand cause and effect relations the teacher must plan reading lessons that point up these relations. A story with a simple but illustrative cause and effect principle can be selected. Carefully planned questions and discussion can be used to clarify the relation. For example, in the familiar nursery rhyme Humpty Dumpty has a great fall from a wall (cause); the result is that he gets broken into pieces (effect). Gradually other less obvious examples of cause and effect can be provided as the child grows in ability.

What other thinking processes must the teacher emphasize in this manner? What guidelines are available for the teacher? The complexity of the thinking process has prevented researchers from coming to grips with it. Another complicating factor is that no direct assessment of thinking can be made since it occurs internally. Russell states that "American psychologists in general have been wary of studies of mental life" (Russell, 1965, p. 370). Some definitive works are available on the subject, however. Irving Lorge (1960) attempted to define thinking by listing as many verbs about it as he could. He grouped forty-nine verbs according to common elements. Next, he arranged the groups into sequence for two types of thought: list A represents the behaviors exhibited in learning for mastery; list B includes the behaviors involved in problem solving.

Many of the verbs in Lorge's list are descriptive of the processes

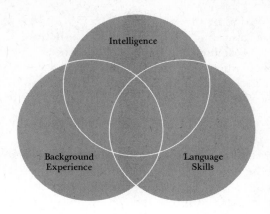

FIGURE 11-2   Interdependence of Skills

The interdependence of these three variables makes it difficult to separate them for analysis.

LIST A	LIST B
attend, orient	concentrate
observe, regard	seek, search
relate, recall, associate	ascertain analyze
abstract, conceive, conceptualize	deliberate, contemplate, ponder, mediate
generalize	speculate, consider, guess, imagine
comprehend, understand	judge, reason, surmise, infer, hypothesize, deduce
review, reorganize	restructure, plan
know, believe	solve, discover
evaluate, appreciate	verify, decide, conclude, confirm, act, resolve*

involved in gaining meaning from the printed page. The classroom teacher is apt to be a bit overwhelmed at the prospect of developing and applying all of these skills in reading, however. The task can seem more reasonable if some organization can be brought to Lorge's lists.

*Irving Lorge, "The Teacher's Task in the Development of Thinking," *The Reading Teacher*, XIII, Feb. 1960, 170–175.

Bloom's taxonomy of educational objectives (Bloom, 1956), with some slight modification (Sanders, 1966), is helpful in organizing Lorge's lists and delineating the thinking process. The stages presented here provide an organizational framework for studying the thinking process. The appropriate pupil behavior is also described to illustrate what is required at each level or stage,

ADAPTATION OF BLOOM'S TAXONOMY TO THE THINKING PROCESS

1. Memory: The pupil recalls or recognizes information.
2. Translation: The pupil changes information into a different form or language.
3. Interpretation: The pupil discovers relations among facts, generalizations, definitions, values, and skills.
4. Application: The pupil solves a lifelike problem that requires the identification of the issue and the selection and use of appropriate generalizations and skills.
5. Analysis: The pupil solves a problem through his conscious knowledge of the parts of thinking.
6. Synthesis: The pupil solves a problem that requires original, creative thinking.
7. Evaluation: The pupil makes a judgment of good or bad, or right or wrong, according to designated standards.

These general guidelines help the teacher recognize all that is involved in children's thinking and to plan classroom activities that encourage various levels of thought. It is helpful to see the relation of levels of thinking to reading comprehension. Table 11.1 gives Smith's (1967) translation of Bloom's thinking stages into four categories of reading comprehension: (1) literal comprehension, (2) interpretation, (3) critical reading, and (4) creative reading.

Children must be given opportunities to apply each level of thought described by Bloom to the reading process. Teachers are

TABLE 11.1   Comparison of Bloom's Taxonomy and Smith's Reading Levels

Bloom's Cognitive Levels	Smith's Reading Levels
Memory Translation	Literal comprehension
Interpretation Application	Interpretation
Analysis Synthesis Evaluation	Critical reading and creative reading

largely responsible for determining the level of thought children will engage in by the type of questions they ask (Guszak, 1968). In practice, teachers' questions tend to fall into Bloom's first or second level, *memory* and *translation*. Thus pupils are asked to answer questions about their stories that ask *who, when,* or *where.* This level of thought is important, since higher-level thinking must build on factual information. This level of comprehension, often called literal comprehension, usually answers the question, "What did the author say?" (Cutter, 1966).

Shaw (1968) points out that literal comprehension is not a simple matter. Initially a first grade child has little trouble comprehending the literal sense of what he reads because the messages that he can decode are so simple. Little meaning is present in simple declarative sentences such as, "See the ball," or "Jump, Dick." But later, in grades two and three, getting literal sense from a sentence becomes more demanding. The reader must be able to follow a sequence of thoughts, relate details to the main idea, vary his rate of reading, note divisions and subdivisions of a selection, and understand the author's plan of organization.

Children who have difficulty with literal comprehension must be given help that enables them to find and remember the answers to *who, when,* and *where* questions. Suggestions for providing this kind of help are given later in this chapter.

Many reading comprehension problems arise when children are expected to engage in thinking that goes beyond the literal level. The third level of Bloom's taxonomy, *interpretation,* along with level four, *application,* frequently cause a difficulty for young readers. At these levels the child is asked to discover relations among facts, not just remember them; he must generalize and begin to make inferences about what he reads. Again, the teacher's questions are crucial in determining whether the child will engage in this type of thought. Here questions that ask *why* and *how* are important.

Bloom's *interpretation* and *application* stages correspond to Smith's second level of comprehension, interpretation. Smith states that "interpretation probes for greater depth than literal comprehension. It is concerned with supplying meanings not stated in the text" (Smith, 1967, p. 12). Several different kinds of thinking are required for interpretation: (1) making generalizations, (2) reasoning cause and effect, (3) anticipating endings, (4) making comparisons, (5) sensing motives, and (6) discovering relations. In addition, all of the fundamental skills required for literal comprehension are also required for interpretation. The reader must find implied meanings in a selection and extend them to new situations. Cutter (1966) suggests that interpretation answers the question, "What did the author mean?" Shaw (1968) describes this level as one requiring the ability to recognize implied meanings. The right connotation for a word must be supplied. The reader must understand figures of speech, irony, and sarcasm. If literal comprehension is *reading the lines,* interpretation is *reading between the lines.*

Several examples can be drawn from McCloskey's *Homer Price* (1951). One story, "The Doughnuts," requires the reader to provide his own interpretation in several cases. When Uncle Ulysses leaves Homer in charge of the automatic doughnut maker in his lunch room he says, "There won't be much business here until the double feature is over and I'll be back before then." The reader must infer that Uncle Ulysses is referring to the local movie to understand the statement about the double feature. Later a stranger tells Homer about his mode of travel: "Yeah, I ride the rods between jobs, on freight trains, ya know what I mean?" In both examples some interpretation is required; literal translation fails to provide sufficient meaning. Later in this chapter activities will be suggested for developing skills of interpretation.

The third comprehension level described by Smith is critical reading; this corresponds to Bloom's *analysis, synthesis,* and *evaluation* stages. At this level of comprehension the reader must analyze, synthesize, and evaluate the quality, value, accuracy, and truthfulness of what he reads. Critical reading involves comparing what is read with some criterion. To operate at this level the reader must be able to make critical judgments about the information his lower-order thought processes gather for him. In effect, at this level he is reading *beyond the lines.*

To comprehend the basic aspects of the story *Charlotte's Web,* for example, the reader must gain a literal understanding—an understanding that enables him to answer questions such as, "Who was Charlotte?" "What did Charlotte do to save Wilbur's life?" To comprehend the deeper meaning of the story certain inferences must be made. The answers to such questions as, "Why did Charlotte save Wilbur's life?" and "Do you think Wilbur understood the sacrifice Charlotte made for him?" reveal a reader's ability to interpret the implied meaning of *Charlotte's Web.* The test of a reader's critical reading skills is whether he can go beyond the answers to these previous questions and answer questions that involve making judgments— "Was the story believable?" "Did the ending seem appropriate?" "Tell why you think Charlotte was a true friend to Wilbur."

Smith's fourth and highest level of reading, creative reading, has no corresponding level in the Bloom taxonomy. It too is a "beyond the lines" type of reading that requires the reader to make some original or unusual use of what he reads. In this sense creative reading builds on all the other levels but is not necessarily the outgrowth of all reading activity. Critical and creative reading are discussed more completely in a later chapter.

It should be clear that the teacher directs children's thinking through the types of questions he asks. To ask useful questions teachers must be aware of the various levels of thinking that take place in the classroom. The plan suggested here is only one way of classifying questions. Each reading lesson should include questions that fall into more than one category. The higher levels should be emphasized in particular. Others can also be used (Guszak, 1968; Santos, 1968). The scheme described in Table 11.2 was developed by Meehan

TABLE 11.2 Classifying Reading Questions Using Key Words and Tasks

Mind set	Reading behavior	Thinking level		Type of task
Grasp ideas	Read the lines	Knowledge (Can you . . . ?) (When did . . . ?)	1.00	State . . . Name . . . Recall . . . Notice . . .
		Comprehension (What . . . ?) (Is . . . ?) (How many . . . ?) (Did . . . ?)	2.00	Observe . . . Recognize . . . . . . saw happen . . .
React to ideas	Read between the lines	Interpretation (Based on information given.)	3.00	Interpret . . . Implicate . . . Explain . . . Describe . . .
		Application (Use of a principle.)	4.00	Compare . . . Conceive of . . . Relate . . .
	Read beyond the lines	Analysis (Why . . . ?) (Would you . . . ?) (What way . . . ?)	5.00	Anticipate. . .
Produce ideas	Read beyond the lines	Synthesis (What ways might . . . ?) (Summarize . . .)	6.00	Infer . . . Originate . . . Hypothesize . . . Predict . . .
Produce ideas	Read beyond the lines	Evaluate (Do you agree . . . ?) (How many kinds are . . . ?) (In your opinion . . . ?)	7.00	Judge . . . Think . . . Order . . .

SOURCE: Adapted from Meehan, Trinita, *The Effects of Instruction Based on Elements of Critical Reading Upon the Questioning Patterns of Pre-Service Teachers.* Unpublished doctoral dissertation, Indiana University, 1970.

(1970) to probe higher-level thought processes. The value of the schema is that it enables a teacher to analyze the questions he is using to develop comprehension. Meehan has indicated the relation between the questions teachers ask and the kinds of comprehension skills that children develop. Teachers ought to examine their questions, therefore, to determine the level at which they are directing their students' thinking.

The Meehan scheme is used by analyzing the questions asked by applying the key words in the third column, "Thinking Level."

Promoting Thinking

We have seen how different kinds of thinking are related to reading comprehension. Evidently one way of promoting children's thinking is through asking questions. However, the problem of promoting thinking is too complex to be so easily resolved. Because thinking is a mental function not subject to direct assessment, we are almost forced into a process of elimination to determine whether poor thinking or some other factor is causing a child's comprehension difficulties. If a child's language skill, background experience, and intelligence are adequate for a reading task, poor thinking may well be causing his problem. In addition to asking good questions, what other alternatives are open to the teacher?

One is simply to wait for the child to mature. Some thinking processes apparently are not hastened by instruction. In practical terms this means that the child should not be asked to comprehend material that requires thinking processes he does not yet possess. An accurate sense of chronology is an example of a thought process that requires some time for development. Thus, most second graders cannot study historical fiction with any true understanding of dated events occurring within fixed periods of time. The best alternative may be to wait for the process of maturation to overcome this limitation.

A second alternative is to give direct instruction on the thinking processes. Authorities on children's thinking agree that instruction will not hasten maturity, but it can maximize learning once the child is intellectually ready. Demonstrations on the constancy of matter, for example, can help a child who is ready to understand the concept. Experiments with liquids, clay, and beads can be conducted to illustrate that a quart of matter in a tall, thin beaker is exactly equal to a quart of matter in a short, squat beaker. Other concepts such as cause and effect can also be demonstrated for the purpose of maximizing growth.

A third alternative is for the teacher to read aloud and discuss with his class the thought processes implicit in a selection. Occasionally a good lesson can be learned by listening to one who is more experienced explain an idea or illustrate a relation. For example, the teacher might write a complex sentence on the board and then show the class how to analyze and relate the various elements in order to arrive at the intended meaning.

Probably all three of the above alternatives have a place in the classroom. Above all, the teacher must *expect* comprehension. Sometimes it seems easier to accept a child's garbled explanation or half-answer. *How Children Fail* by John Holt (1964) documents the danger of this approach. When understanding falters the teacher must lead the child back to a selection and discover why a problem has developed. Through his own example the teacher can promote reading that demands understanding and effectively related background experience, language skill, and thinking ability.

BACKGROUND EXPERIENCE

Assuming that a reader has no difficulty decoding a word, to comprehend he must associate some meaning with the symbol. He must find in his background of experience a perceptual image for the word. For example, most intermediate grade children can decode the word *truncate,* yet the act of pronunciation alone provides no clue to the meaning of the word.

Background experience is therefore important to reading comprehension in a number of ways. Background experiences build vocabulary, help to develop concepts, create interests, and influence attitudes and beliefs.

Background Experiences Build Vocabulary

Earlier in this chapter the word *tree* was used to illustrate how a child develops a perceptual image of a written symbol. The obvious association for a child to make between a word and its image is an object from his own experience. In the example cited, a tree in the child's own backyard was used as a referent. But what about a child who has no backyard, let alone a tree with a swing? What meaning does the word *tree* or a story that uses the word have for such a child? Many inner-city youngsters grow up in an environment largely devoid of trees. The only tree some may have seen was a skimpy tree growing from a large concrete box in the business district. With such limited experiences association with the word *tree* is limited and extremely narrow.

Limited background is not unique to deprived children, however. City children, whether from the inner city or the suburbs, may have no vocabularly for events and objects on a farm. Their experiences frequently have not exposed them to a tractor, a hayloft, a litter of pigs, or an apple orchard. *Tractor*, for example, may cause some children from suburbia to think of the ten horsepower miniature their dad uses to mow the lawn and plow snow. When Farmer Jones gets on his tractor in their story and pulls a wagon loaded with many bales of hay, their experience may not square with the description. Dad's tractor can pull a toy wagon and one bale of hay but not many bales at once. Comprehension is unlikely to occur when unfamiliar vocabulary fails to draw on the reader's background of experience.

Background Experiences Build Concepts

A second aspect of comprehension closely related to vocabulary is the matter of concepts. Normally concepts develop along with vocabulary as the result of stimulating experiences. The child who has a narrow or inaccurate concept of *tree* lacks a more complete understanding because of inadequate background. On the other hand, a youngster raised in a small town in the Midwest is almost certain to have a thorough familiarity with trees of all types and consequently a rich association for the concept of *tree*.

Most youngsters regardless of their background have a wide variety of concepts and the vocabulary associated with their own experiences. Unfortunately, until recently schools often failed to recognize the need to adapt reading materials to the special backgrounds of various populations. Thus ghetto children struggle to understand the vocabulary and unfamiliar ideas presented in a typical basal reader. Their experiences prepare them to bring meaning to stories about playing stickball in the street and cooling their bodies under an open fire hydrant.

Reading materials are now beginning to reflect the unique backgrounds of inner-city children (Bank Street Readers, Skyline Series), Indian children (Modern Curriculum Press), and Oriental children (Scott-Foresman and Company). Comprehension difficulties are not eliminated by these new materials, but the problem of inadequate background is reduced. Experience stories that draw directly on the child's background are especially helpful in overcoming limited background.

Another factor to be considered is that seldom is a concept completely formed. Even adults learn daily and broaden already rich concepts. One's concept of *river* is constantly growing as new experiences provide new information. For example, understanding the role of waterways in the development and settlement of our nation is a subtlety not easily grasped. Man's concept of space is another, more dynamic example of an ever-growing understanding. Except for very simple writings, it is safe to say that complete understanding of a selection is seldom accomplished. As the appropriate concepts deepen and expand, greater comprehension of a selection previously read is increased. The point is then that no matter how advantaged the child, he can expand his concepts to increase his understanding of what he reads.

Background Experiences Create Interests

Stimulating background experiences provide a child with the vocabulary and concepts necessary to understand as he reads. At the same time, such experiences contribute another important factor that increases comprehension, namely, interest. Research evidence abounds to support the notion that interest is important to success in reading. (Chapter 13 explores this topic in some detail.) Even in the absence of research evidence, personal experience convinces us that a dull or uninteresting reading selection is often poorly understood simply for lack of reader involvement.

Background Experiences Influence Attitudes and Beliefs

Most people have experienced the pleasant feeling of loving a character in a book or wanting desperately to help a character out of trouble. We read, especially recreationally, probably as much for the feelings we experience as we do for the information we obtain. Unfortunately, personal feelings and reactions often get left out of the classroom reading program. Perhaps one reason we often fail to develop lifelong readers in our schools is that we spend little time discussing how we feel about a story and much time digging out the facts.

Teachers need a plan for helping them deal with the attitudes, beliefs, values, feelings, and other personal aspects of responding to what is read. Just as the cognitive processes have been organized into a taxonomy by Bloom, so has the affective domain been organized by Krathwohl (1964). Like Bloom, Krathwohl developed his taxonomy with the expectation that educational outcomes or objectives could be more readily achieved if some scheme for classifying them were available. Krathwohl's work is useful to us here in the same capacity that we used Bloom earlier. A condensation of Krathwohl's *Taxonomy of Educational Objectives, Affective Domain*, follows.

KRATHWOHL'S TAXONOMY

1:00 Receiving—the learner is sensitized to the existence of certain phenomena and stimuli
2:00 Responding—the student is actively attending
3:00 Valuing—the student regards a thing, phenomenon, or behavior as having worth
4:00 Organization—more than one value is relevant
5:00 Characterization—the individual acts consistently in accordance with his values

The Krathwohl Taxonomy appears to have particular usefulness in the area of reading comprehension. Just as Bloom's taxonomy is useful in classifying teachers' questions in the cognitive domain, Krathwohl's taxonomy can be used to classify questions that probe children's *feelings about what they read*. Through skillful handling of a discussion, with careful attention given to the affective as well as the cognitive aspects of a selection, children's comprehension can be deepened considerably. The example used earlier of a child who read *Charlotte's Web* is also helpful here. At the lowest level of feeling (receiving) the child can be helped to see the friendship develop between Charlotte and Wilbur. At the second level, responding, the child can be asked to discuss the friendship, how it developed, and why it continued throughout the story. Next, the child can study and discuss the value of the friendship to the end that he either accepts or rejects the phenomenon as worthwhile. At the fourth level, organization, other feelings such as loyalty or jealousy might be brought into the discussion. Finally, the child internalizes the value, in this case friendship, and acts consistently with the value in his own life.

In some respects the Krathwohl taxonomy only formalizes an approach that some teachers have practiced for many years. Some might call this approach looking for the human aspects of a story and discussing them along with the "hard information." Nonetheless, the fact that Krathwohl's taxonomy provides a strategy for dealing with the affective domain makes it especially valuable. Without such a strategy the personal feelings that children experience as they read can easily be overlooked.

In view of the important role that background experiences play in reading comprehension, the teacher must know how to assess this variable. The next section will discuss several means for accomplishing this.

Identifying Limited Background Experiences

The classroom teacher must rely on informal diagnostic techniques to identify specific background limitations. Standardized tests and other formal instruments can only generally indicate that a youngster has difficulty with comprehension. To determine whether limited background is particularly responsible for comprehension difficulties the teacher has several means at his disposal.

Questionnaires

One of the primary advantages of teacher-constructed questionnaires, as we stated in Chapter 6, is that special concerns can easily be in-

corporated in their design. In other words, the teacher can write
certain items to obtain information of great relevancy to a special
topic or theme. For example, suppose a group of second grade children is about to begin a unit in their developmental reading program on pets. Recognizing that understanding and interest are
greatly dependent on familiarity with concepts and vocabulary, the
teacher could construct a questionnaire like the one that follows to
assess his students' backgrounds.

INTEREST QUESTIONNAIRE

Name _____

1. Do you have a pet? _____
*2. What kind of pet do you have? (Or what kind of pet would you
     like to have?) _____
3. What other pets have you had before? _____
4. Where does you pet sleep? _____
5. How do you care for your pet? _____
6. Does your pet get a bath? _____ How? _____
     When? _____
7. What does your pet like to eat? _____

*Note: Children who indicate in item 1 that they do not have a
pet can answer subsequent questions for a former pet or the pet
they would like to have. Their answers still provide the teacher with
a knowledge of the child's background and understanding.

Questionnaires can be adapted so that even younger children
can provide the information a teacher needs. In this case a first grade
teacher might read the questions to his students and ask them to draw
a picture for their answer. A questionnaire can also be used individually with a child in a conference, the teacher jotting down the
child's responses.

Questionnaires can be designed to gather more general information on a child's travel experiences, hobbies, interests (see Chapter
13), play activities, or other topics relevant to classroom activities.

Observations

Classroom discussions provide the teacher with an excellent opportunity to note a youngster's background and understanding. Contributions that show misunderstanding or general ignorance should alert the teacher to the possibility of a poor background. For example, a first grade child who does not know the difference between a helicopter and a jet airplane may never have been to an airport nor seen a helicopter hovering overhead. This lack of understanding could be troublesome if the child were going to read *Helicopters and Gingerbread* from the Ginn 360 Series.

At the same time, a child's unwillingness to contribute to a group discussion might also indicate a lack of background. A teacher would have to deliberately include the child with a direct question or talk individually with him to assess his background. Boredom can explain silence just as easily as ignorance, so additional evidence must be obtained.

A teacher can also collect valuable information by observing a child's behavior during independent reading, by noting work errors, and by listening to his oral reading. Certain groups of children with limited backgrounds in one area tend to be generally restricted in their experiences. In time the teacher will learn which students require further background experiences on most school-related activities. It would be dangerous to categorically label a child good or poor in terms of background; constant diagnosis is necessary. Nevertheless, the teacher's observations can be guided to a degree by past experience with his class.

Conferences

One of the best means for assessing background experience is through personal conversation with a child. Whether a pupil-teacher conference is structured by the completion of a questionnaire or is simply an informal chat, the alert teacher can gather valuable information about a child's experiences. Particularly valuable is a technique recommended by Strang (1969), introspection by the child. Strang suggests that the child be invited to describe his thinking process in reading a selection. The teacher may ask the child how he managed to pronounce an unfamiliar word or know the meaning of a word he had not been taught or arrive at the meaning of a sentence or paragraph. The child may be asked to explain a specific difficulty as he sees it. Given the opportunity, even young children may be able to explain where their comprehension begins to falter. Breakdowns in understanding due to lack of background should become evident with this approach.

Overcoming Limited Background

Once a teacher has assessed background experiences it becomes essential that limitations be overcome.

Numerous suggestions for overcoming limited background experiences were given in Chapter 7. Many of these activities are useful even with children in grades two, three, and above. For example, the daily sharing period offers an excellent opportunity for youngsters to learn from each other. One child's hobby may spark the interest of another child. A description accompanied by postcards, snapshots, souvenirs, and personal memories of a trip to Yellowstone Park or a NASA space center enriches the background of the whole class and provides the speaker with a chance to improve his oral communication.

Field trips are especially good ways to build background experiences. Even visits to common sites can be valuable when the teacher directs the child's attention to previously overlooked objects and events. For example, a hike through an open meadow near the school enables a teacher to alert his class to foliage, rocks, and animal and insect life. The children may have seen some of these things before but never appreciated them. Of course, trips to unusual places not visited by the members of a class on their own are also good builders of background. A visit to a museum, art gallery, fire station, supermarket, restaurant, or print shop can greatly enrich children's backgrounds.

Other suggestions will be given in a later section of this chapter on the guided reading lesson. Readers are urged to consult various language arts textbooks such as Strickland (1969), May (1967), Tiedt and Tiedt (1967), and Burns and Lowe (1966) for additional suggestions on building background experience.

LANGUAGE SKILLS

A basic knowledge of the English language is essential for reading comprehension. The reader must understand that in a simple sentence such as "The dog ran away" a subject is identified and some information about the subject is provided (predicate). Fortunately, children learn the structure of their language intuitively from their first utterance. Whether they can specify *the dog* as the subject of the sentence or not, children's knowledge of their language leads them to conclude that it was indeed the dog that ran away and not the *away* that *dogged*. In other words, past experience tells children how to interpret the information communicated by the sentence they read once they decode the individual words.

Children who do not understand the basic structure of their language can neither listen to nor read English with understanding. For example, Marcus (1968) reported the following examples of faulty communication:

Question: "If a car ran over your pet, how would you feel?"
Child's answer: "Good."

Question: "If you could be a policeman or a fireman what would you choose?"
Child's answer: "Gum."

How can these bizarre answers be explained? Research at Louisiana State University indicates that the children were responding only to that part of the message they understood. They seemed to tune in to key words only, mentally rearranging them to "make sense." Thus in the first question the key words . . . *how, you,* and *feel* were probably understood. "Good" is a reasonable response. In the second question *what, you,* and *choose* may have been interpreted, "what you chews." "Gum" is a reasonable answer to this query. Marie Marcus, the researcher who gathered these and numerous other examples of "miscomprehension," contends that the disadvantaged children in her sample heard each word of the question but did not understand the sentence structure nor the hypothesis of the question. This explanation is logical; further research must establish its validity. Meanwhile, it is unlikely that children with a language deficiency like those who responded "good" and "gum" to the questions stated earlier are prepared to interpret correctly the printed page.

Pratt (1966) states that the reader needs two fundamental linguistic skills in order to comprehend. First, he needs to know what a word symbol refers to. We have seen that background experience is the key to this information. Second, the reader needs an understanding of the grammatical relations inherent in the message he reads. Grammar in this instance is not limited to the formal study of "correct" English. Rather, it implies an adequate enough understanding of the morphology (word formation) and syntax (word arrangement) of English to comprehend what one reads.

To illustrate the importance of morphology and syntax to understanding, consider the following sentence: *The jurd sumped dooly to the rem.* Most of the words in this example do not have lexical (or dictionary) meaning. They do have structural meaning, however. Persons who are familiar with English can readily determine that the subject of the sentence is *jurd.* Furthermore, the structure of the sentence indicates that the jurd *sumped.* How did it *sump*? It *sumped dooly.* And we also note that its destination is known, for the *jurd sumped dooly to the rem.*

Structural meaning is signaled in English in three ways:

1. By inflectional endings
2. By patterns of word order
3. By function words with little or no ending of their own (Goodman, 1963).

In the above example the inflectional ending *ed* on *sumped* tells us that (1) sump is a verb and (2) whatever action occurred took place in the past. In the same way *dooly* is evidently an adverb telling how the *jurd sumped*. We also know that only one *jurd* was involved in the action; the inflectional ending *s* would be used to indicate more than one *jurd*. In addition, the words in this nonsense sentence follow a common pattern for American English: the subject-verb-object pattern. *Jurd* is the subject of the sentence but not because of any inherent quality indicating that it is the recipient of the action (Goodman, 1963). Finally, *the* serves as a function word in the nonsense sentence, marking *jurd* and *rem* as nouns. Examples of other function words are *very, not, there, when, yes, no,* and *well*.

There is general consensus among reading experts that reading comprehension is dependent upon understanding how sentence structures deliver meaning. The International Reading Association included an entire section on the linguistics aspects of understanding the printed page in a recent book of readings on comprehension (Dawson, 1968). An introduction to this section succinctly states the current point of view regarding the implications of linguistics for reading comprehension:

> The nature of the language we use is a factor in comprehension. American English is characterized by the relative infrequency of inflectional endings of words, by the importance of word order — or "the flow of thought through a sentence" — and the word groupings within sentences in terms of clustering of words around key words. In other terms, linguistics is an important consideration in teaching children and youth to handle language as they seek to understand fully and well what they are reading. (Dawson, 1968, p. 65).

Many linguists have turned their attention to reading instruction, and some have been concerned with comprehension in particular (Goodman, 1965; Ives, 1964; Allen, 1964; Deighton, 1966). Unfortunately, they have not yet agreed on any comprehensive program for incorporating principles of linguistics into instructional programs. Some linguists have participated in the development of basal programs. Presumably their materials reflect sound linguistics principles insofar as suggestions for teaching comprehension are concerned. It appears to us, however, that as consultants to basal programs linguists have focused their attention primarily on the issue of decoding. A few prominent linguists have dismissed comprehension on the grounds that once word symbols have been decoded, the child's oral language skills enable him to understand what he reads (Fries, Bloomfield). Others regard the study of language factors in reading comprehension as a most fruitful area for exploration. The work of some authorities in this area is reviewed in the following section.

Implications of Linguistics for Comprehension

Ives (1964) states that any method of reading instruction that stops with recognition of words is relying on the child to reconstruct the relations and understand the contribution each part makes to the whole. To understand a sentence the reader must comprehend its linguistic ingredients. According to Ives, each sentence has a structure comprised of various levels. Meaning is carried by the separate elements of that structure and the interrelation of the elements. Ives believes that reading instruction must include an analysis of the linguistic elements and an understanding of how they transmit meaning.

For example, Ives recommends that word form (morphology) be studied through careful attention to inflectional endings. The importance of syntax must also be taught. The teacher can illustrate this fact by using a word such as *run* in various positions: *dogs run fast* and *scored a run*. The word *run* takes on different meanings in the context of different sentences.

Without spelling out any detailed instructional program Ives urges incorporation of linguistics principles into the developmental reading program. Some linguists have begun to explore the feasibility of Ives's recommendations. Unfortunately, most of this work is being done on a piecemeal basis by individuals who have an intense interest in some specific area of linguistics. Many helpful teaching procedures are being generated by this work, but no over-all organization has yet been brought to the implications of linguistics for reading comprehension.

As a case in point, a study by Robertson (1968) has direct and rather specific implications for instructional programs that seek to overcome comprehension difficulties. Based on the idea that the structure of language provides clues to meaning, Robertson's study focuses specifically on the ability of intermediate grade youngsters to understand *connectives* in reading, that is, the linguistic forms that connect a clause to another clause or to some word in the clause. For example, *but* is a common connective. In the following sentence *but* joins the two clauses and also expresses the nature of the connection:

"John likes strawberries, but usually gets a rash from eating them."
But tells the reader that the first phrase is qualified by the second
subordinate phrase.

Robertson states that although children use connectives in their
speech, some time elapses before youngsters can understand the same
relations when expressed in written form. Her findings indicated
that the basal readers used in her study employed connectives freely,
often forming rather complex links that expressed cause and effect,
and comparisons. Sentences containing certain connectives resulted
in low reading comprehension for children in grades four, five, and
six. These were *however, thus, although, which, and,* and *yet.*

These findings indicate that teachers can plan specific lessons to
overcome comprehension difficulties due to students' lack of familiarity with connectives.

Deighton (1966) has directed his attention to the flow of thought
through an English sentence. He states that meaning in the English
language is conveyed through groups of words *working together,* not
by words *added together.* He cites the following phrases as examples of
how meaning cannot be established until the word *house* is reached:

the . . .
the little . . .
the little white . . .
the little white house. [Deighton, 1966, p. 322]

Deighton's point is simply that the reader must hold meaning of a
unit—a sentence or a phrase—in abeyance until he has reached the
end of the unit. Because of multiple meanings words take on different
relations in various sentence constructions. Only at the end of a
sentence can the relations be established and meaning derived.

A second factor requiring the reader to hold meaning in abeyance is the variety of English sentence structures. Deighton cites
four separate ways that words can be related to each other:

1. Subject-predicate relation
2. Coordinate relation
3. Complement relation
4. Modifier relation

The complexities involved in sorting out a sentence so that words
are correctly related to one another prompts Deighton to recommend
that reading instruction include the study of how sentence structures
deliver meaning. As a first step in this direction he suggests that it
is helpful to note the direction of word flow in a sentence. The flow is
not, as we might suppose, consistently from left to right—it is not always additive. While some sentences are additive, for example, *Tom hit
the ball,* in a great many English sentences the flow of words is circular:

Tom is the president. The verb is a form of *be* and is called a linking verb. The words following the verb refer to the word preceding the verb. Thus the flow of thought is from left to right and back to the beginning, or circular. To comprehend the sentence the reader must hold meaning in abeyance. Deighton states that all linking verbs such as *look, remain, stay, sound,* and *get* and *keep* in certain constructions deliver meaning by identification, characterization, or description. They attribute specific features to the subject of the sentence and therefore transmit information in a circular pattern.

The pattern of delivering meaning from left to right (*Tom hit the ball*) is characteristic of action sentences and occurs in a relatively small number of cases the reader encounters. More often the meaning is attributive and therefore circular in terms of flow. Deighton concludes that teachers should help children analyze the flow of thought in a sentence but that this is just one of the linguistic tools the reader needs to gain meaning from the printed page. Additional tools have not yet been adequately identified but remain for further study by those who regard principles of linguistics as means to developing comprehension skills.

In the same vein Robert L. Allen (1964) has developed an approach to grammar, called *sector analysis,* that he believes will help children understand the sentence as a unit and the relations among sentences in a passage. He points out that children have almost no trouble understanding the meaning of a simple sentence such as "See the bird fly." Even if the sentence must be read word by word, the message is simple and can be understood as long as the child knows the individual words. Longer, more complex sentences are not so difficult for the child to understand when they are *heard* because the additional clues of pitch, stress, and juncture serve to identify the subject and predicate (Allen, 1964). These clues are not present on the printed page. Allen's solution is to teach the child to recognize the boundaries between syntactic units.

Basically the technique has the child rearrange the elements of a sentence to ask a yes-no question and then change the question to an emphatic (or negative) sentence. The elements of the sentence that consistently perform a function can be identified as the subject and predicate.* Since the interpretation of a sentence is dependent upon the reader's ability to identify and properly relate its fundamental elements, this technique seems to have some merit, particularly for complex sentences. The example below illustrates Allen's approach with the sentence "That funny old man who lives in the house across the street likes cats."

*A more detailed explanation may be found in Robert L. Allen, *English Grammars and English Grammar* (New York: The Macmillan Company, 1967).

^xThe man who lives in the house^x
across the street   likes cats

Does the man who lives in the
house across the street   like cats

The man who lives in the house
across the street   does like cats

Subject
^xThe man who lives in the house^x
across the street   likes cats

Ruddell (1965) sought to determine whether reading comprehension could be improved by providing children with written materials that were highly similar to their oral language in terms of sentence structure. His findings indicated that for the sample of fourth graders in his study reading comprehension was significantly greater when materials that utilize high-frequency patterns of oral language structure were used.

Stevenson (1965) also discusses the importance of reading materials that resemble children's spoken English. He urges that special attention be given to intonation as a means for increasing reading comprehension. To this end he suggests using reading materials that provide intonation clues by means of diacritical markings. Since the greatest stress is placed on the subject of a sentence, Stevenson recommends that an accent mark be placed above it. Arrows indicate where voice inflection should rise ($\uparrow$) and fall ($\downarrow$). Junctures or pauses are indicated with a space marker (#). Thus a story would appear as follows:

"I see the póstman, $\uparrow$" (said Tom.)
"I will go and get the létters. $\downarrow$ #"
"Here, Tom $\uparrow$" (said the postman.)
"Here is a letter for your mother and a little letter for Betty. $\downarrow$ #"

Stevenson supports his approach by pointing out that the average six-year-old knows all the essential structural patterns of his language. The task of teaching him to read is one of showing him how those patterns are represented in writing.

The cloze procedure, that is, deleting every fifth, eighth, or tenth word from the children's stories, was described in detail earlier. Cloze tests have been successfully used to measure both the readability of selections and the comprehension abilities of students. It is evident from the nature of the cloze procedure that an understanding of the relations among ideas and vocabulary in a passage are necessary in order for a reader to supply a deleted word. Without understanding, incorrect words will not be supplied by the reader. Bormuth

(1969) states that cloze tests can be designed to measure comprehension of the following skills: vocabulary, explicitly stated facts, sequences of events, stated causal relations, main ideas of the passages, inference, and author's purpose.

Some investigators have demonstrated that the cloze procedure can also be used to increase children's comprehension (Schneyer, 1965; Bloomer, 1962; Bormuth, 1962; Jenkinson, 1957). The act of studying a passage to determine the identity of a missing word forces the reader to note, among other things, the structure of the language surrounding a blank. This active process entails noting the part of speech of a missing word; looking for patterns of words; noting relations such as cause and effect statements, analogies, or opposites; and generally attending to grammatical and syntactical clues to meaning. The practice of noting the relation among words in a cloze passage evidently transfers fairly well to normal reading situations. Students in Bloomer's (1962) study, for example, made significant improvement on a standardized reading comprehension test after completing a graded series of cloze exercises.

Schneyer's (1965) findings do not agree with Bloomer's, but he suggests each response by students might prove beneficial. An overt response such as discussing a word chosen for a blank with the teacher or other members of a reading group would provide the opportunity to learn why some alternatives are more appropriate than others. Considerably more research evidence is needed on the best technique for using the cloze procedure in an instructional setting. Meanwhile this approach can be used experimentally by classroom teachers as a means for focusing students' attention on meaning.

This sampling of linguistics research directly related to reading comprehension is difficult to synthesize. Much of potential value is being done by these and other individuals. At this point, however, it is necessary to apply ideas on a patchwork basis. As additional research and study are completed, the implications of linguistics for instructional practices will be better organized and clarified. Clearly teachers can improve the reading comprehension of their students by specifically calling attention to the manner in which meaning is delivered by the English language. Analyzing with the class the relation between clauses in sentences which demonstrate that meaning must be held in abeyance until an entire sentence has been read or discussing how word form affects meaning are two activities the teacher will find useful.

Assessing Language Skills

By its very nature the cloze procedure is an excellent measure of the child's understanding of linguistic principles. Therefore teachers can profitably employ the cloze technique as a means for assessing a child's language skills. When asked to produce a word deleted from a passage the reader must study the surrounding context and make his judgment based upon his understanding of the author's message. Clues are gained from the grammar of the sentence. Thus an understanding of syntax enables the reader to supply a word of a certain class. Noun markers such as *a, an, the,* and *their* are used as aids to supplying the correct deleted word. Other markers provide clues to other parts of speech (for example, verb markers: *am, are, is, was*; phrase markers: *up, down, in, out*; clause markers: *if, because, although, even*).

Morphology likewise supplies important clues to the identity of a deleted word. For example, "The boy _____" can be completed by the word *sings* but not *sing*. The subject and predicate must agree, so an inflectional ending *s* is required.

The cloze procedure can be adjusted to delete every fifth word, every tenth word, indeed, every *n*th word or only words of a certain class. By deleting only adjectives, for example, the teacher can measure the child's understanding of modifiers. Or connectives may be deleted to assess the child's understanding of the relation between clauses. The lower the percentage of correct responses, the poorer the child's understanding of that type of word.

A more detailed discussion of assessing language skill is beyond the scope of this text. The work of Bormuth (1969) promises to be particularly valuable in this respect. Language arts texts such as Strickland (1969), Tiedt and Tiedt (1967), and Lamb (1967) are also excellent resources.

Overcoming Limited Language Skill

Activities that encourage children to use language stand the best chance of overcoming language deficiencies. We noted earlier in this chapter that experiences which broaden backgrounds also stimulate vocabulary and language growth.

The research of Robertson, described earlier, offers some direction for planning classroom activities that promote facility with language. Children evidently need help in understanding how connectives serve to link clauses. Experience stories composed by the children themselves are an excellent starting point since they include such connectives as *but, and, then,* and *where.* A sentence such as "I will go to the store, then to the playground" contains two clauses linked by a connective (*then*). By noting the meaning of this message in one of their own experience stories children see the function of the connective. The next step would be for them to analyze other selections such as their basal readers or library books for additional instances of the word's use. Gradually an understanding is gained of how each word functions.

Another approach would be to construct sentences that contain blanks where connectives might appear:

The boy jumped, _____ the girl did not.
I want to go to the party, _____ I cannot.
She went to the store _____ I went with her.
There is the boy _____ hit me.
I will wait _____ you get dressed.

From the sense of the sentence children can supply an appropriate word.

The teacher can suggest other possibilities to provide experience with words not frequently used in children's speech such as *however, thus,* and *although.*

It did not rain _____ the sky was gray.
    although
    where
    when
    however
He scored the last basket _____ winning the game.
    thus
    although
    however
    yet

A modification of this approach would be to use a number of connectives in the same sentence to see how the meaning is or is not changed by the substitution of various words.

I like strawberry *and* blueberry is my favorite.
I like strawberry, *but* blueberry is my favorite.
I like strawberry, *however,* blueberry is my favorite.
I like strawberry; *therefore,* blueberry is my favorite.

Another activity can be used to focus attention on the function of certain types of words. One approach is to give children a list of sentences such as the following and instruct them to underline the words that tell about time:

1. The week seemed to pass slowly.
2. In one year the rosebush had grown a great deal.
3. Every day I find something new and interesting.
4. I will be there in ten minutes.
5. He will come while you are here.

After completing a story the children can be instructed to go through and find all the words referring to time. Naturally, other types of words such as size, sequence, number, or color can be treated in a similar lesson.

The purpose of these activities is to involve children firsthand in the process of studying how words deliver meaning. The teacher can gain insight into each child's understanding and possible confusion by studying his responses. Corrective activities can be planned immediately if evidence of misunderstanding is found.

PURPOSES FOR READING

Reading comprehension often suffers because no specific purpose for reading has been established ahead of time. With no goal in mind the reader usually forms only a general impression of a selection and cannot recall specific facts, the main idea, or the author's organizational pattern. This approach may be satisfactory for some recreational reading in which general impressions are all that a reader desires; however, most reading, including a good deal of recreational reading, requires more than a general impression to be clearly understood. Even a relatively simple children's story such as *Homer Price* loses much of its humor and significance if the reader is unable to follow a sequence of ideas or to perceive part-whole relations. Reading for a general impression will often not provide this information.

Purposes for reading are important for comprehension because they direct the reader's attention to specific aspects of a selection. The mature reader varies his approach as his purpose for reading changes. This ability to adjust reading behavior according to different purposes takes on special importance in view of the wide variety of reasons for which people read. Consider the difference between reading a newspaper report of a football game and following a recipe for making fudge. The newspaper story may present a considerable amount of detail, but we usually read such material for the main ideas—the final score, who scored the touchdowns, the team's record, and so on. Of course, occasions arise when main ideas are not enough and a more thorough reading is desirable even of a football story. On the other hand, one normally reads a recipe for quite another purpose—to follow it step by step in preparing a dish. Nothing less than a careful word-by-word reading will enable us to achieve the purpose of correctly following the recipe.

Since there are so many purposes for reading, it is more accurate to speak of comprehending for a specific purpose than simply comprehending. The teacher's task is to help children understand when different purposes are most appropriate and how to adjust reading behavior according to different purposes.

Five Common Purposes for Reading

Purposes for reading are similar for the beginner and the mature reader. The level of thought that is required to achieve the same reading purpose varies with the difficulty of a selection and the skill of the reader. Different authorities suggest a variety of purposes for reading. We believe that most of these can be organized into five categories: (1) finding main ideas, (2) finding supporting detail, (3) grasping the author's plan of organization, (4) following a sequence of events or thoughts, and (5) critically appraising the author's work. (A discussion of critical appraisal appears in Chapter 14.)

Finding Main Ideas

Probably the most fundamental reading purpose is finding main ideas. Initially the child reads materials that contain only one main idea. In the story "Mr. Pine's Signs" (Clymer, 1969), for example, the main character, Mr. Pine, is asked to make new signs for Little Town because the old signs are badly faded. No complexities enter the story to confound this main idea. In later grades more complex stories are encountered and several main ideas must be identified for adequate comprehension to occur.

The teacher helps focus a child's attention on main ideas by asking questions such as, "What is the story about?" and, "What would you tell a friend about this story?"

Finding Supporting Detail

The main ideas of a passage or a selection are communicated by specific facts and events. The young child often confuses main ideas and supporting detail, as is evidenced by the amount of information the child typically includes when telling someone about a story. Sorting out main ideas and supporting detail requires an understanding of the relation between the two. For example, in a well-known tale Chicken Little rushed to spread the news after deciding that the sky was falling. The details of each conversation with animals she meets are important in explaining the actions of these characters but have little meaning without an understanding of how they support the main idea. On the other hand, the facts concerning Chicken Little's first episode with a falling object do not support her belief that the sky *was* falling. Unless the reader recognizes this incongruity between detail and main idea, the whole story of "Chicken Little" is meaningless.

Again, the teacher's task is to ask questions which help young readers find supporting details and in some cases relate them to the main ideas of a story. Questions such as, "What tells us that Mary was happy?" or, "Who was at the party?" can be asked to focus attention on detail.

Grasping the Plan of Organization

A more complex purpose for reading is to grasp the author's plan of organizing his work. He may, for example, make his point by contrasting two sides of an argument or by providing similar events from the past. Subheadings and special type faces may provide clues as to the author's arrangement of key points.

The teacher's task is to discuss the author's plan and direct the attention of the reader with questions such as, "How does the author divide the story into sections?" or, "How do we learn that something bad may happen in the cave?"

Following a Sequence of Events

Closely related to the organizational plan of a selection is following a sequence of events or ideas. An author may, for example, organize his writing into sections that progress in *chronological sequence.* Following the sequence of events or ideas in a selection is a most important purpose in reading. Whether in a recipe or a mystery story, real understanding requires that the reader grasp the correct order. "Cinderella" is a rather meaningless story if the reader fails to understand the order in which the royal ball, midnight, and Cinderella's return to normalcy occurred.

Through asking questions such as, "What happened to Mary first?" or, "What did the dog do next?" the teacher focuses attention on sequence.

Setting Purposes

The teacher needs, of course, to study a selection to determine what purpose or purposes can best be pursued by his youngsters when they read the story. Some stories may offer an excellent opportunity to follow sequence; others may lend themselves to studying several important main ideas. The teacher should vary the assigned purpose in order to provide practice in all types of reading. He must also give some consideration to the complexity of reading purposes, emphasizing more fundamental tasks with younger readers. For example, finding main ideas is usually more straightforward than finding the author's organizational pattern. Beginning readers require practice in reading for both purposes, but they should devote more time to the former activity, which is more basic and usually easier.

Obviously, purposes for reading must be established before a selection is read. Only through this procedure can the reader properly direct his attention during reading. Afterward the stated purpose can be used as a basis for discussion to determine whether the reader has achieved the goal.

Purposes for reading should be as real and interesting to children as possible. A question regarding sequence of events may get little response if always phrased, "What happened next?" With a little imagination the same question can generate real interest and still focus reader attention on sequence. For example, "If Goldilocks isn't careful someone may find her in their house. What do you think will happen? Let's read to find out if you are right." Teachers' guides for basal readers often give helpful suggestions for reading purposes. The teacher will want to select carefully from these suggestions and frequently add his own.

Children should participate in establishing their own reading purposes as early as possible. Ultimately they will be entirely responsible for this task, so practice under the teacher's direction is desirable. At first, *rereading* a selection for a purpose arrived at by group discussion may be valuable. Later, a preview of the title, pictures, and general content of a story by a group can be used to set purposes for an initial reading.

Many specialized purposes can be created within the five major purposes for reading cited earlier. Reading for main ideas includes reading to summarize a story; sequence of events includes specialized purposes such as following directions and putting events into a time line; supporting detail and main ideas can be related by having children develop an outline of a reading selection. Countless variations are possible on the five major purposes. The needs of the students and the unique content of the reading selection will determine which ones are most appropriate. The teacher need only be creative and flexible enough to adjust to the opportunities he will discover.

ADJUSTING READING RATE TO PURPOSE

Just as the reader must adapt his reading to meet various purposes, he must also adjust his reading rate. The answer to a specific question concerning supporting detail will require the reader to skim for the right section and then read that section carefully for the correct answer. Following directions calls for slow, careful reading, as does reading an account of a scientific experiment. On the other hand, recreational reading and reading the newspaper usually call for a rapid rate of reading, but usually not as fast as skimming.

Generally the reader should read as fast as he can and still achieve his purpose. It is generally accepted and often demonstrated in practice that good readers usually read faster than poor ones. In some respects rapid reading accounts for good comprehension, since thoughts and phrases are more easily gathered into wholes. Slower readers sometimes miss the point of a sentence or paragraph because they concentrate so intensively on individual words that synthesis of thought becomes difficult.

The teacher has two primary tasks with regard to reading rate. He must (1) demonstrate the need to adjust reading speed according to purpose and (2) encourage maximum speed for all reading. (A more complete discussion of improving reading rate is given in Chapter 16.)

THE GUIDED READING LESSON

Evidently no single answer can be expected to solve the problem of reading comprehension difficulties. Numerous factors alone or in combination can stand in the way of understanding. Nonetheless, it is the teacher's responsibility to remove as many of the potential stumbling blocks as possible. One practical solution that can minimize comprehension difficulties by anticipating students' needs is the guided reading lesson. This technique is useful for teaching reading as well as social studies, mathematics, science, and language arts. Essentially the guided reading lesson is a teaching procedure for guiding children through a selection.

Made familiar by the ever-present basal reader, the guided reading lesson consists of five steps:

1. Building background
2. Setting purposes
3. Independent reading
4. Follow-up discussion
5. Development of related skills.

Building Background

The section on background experience demonstrated the importance of the reader's having some familiarity with a topic before reading about it. In the reading-process model (Fig. 1.1) we saw that perception is dependent upon the reader's personal experiences for the development of meaningful associations. Vocabulary, concepts, and, to some degree, interests, attitudes, and beliefs are founded on background experience. Thus the teacher's first task is to build and broaden the child's background prior to reading a selection.

Suppose a reading group in a second grade class is about to read "The Airport" (Sheldon and Austin, 1968), a story about two boys who take their first plane ride. It would be surprising if a broad range of background experiences were not present among the members of a reading group on this general topic. One child's father may be an airline pilot while the child sitting next to him may have only a vague notion of what an airport is. Other children may have been inside a jet, eaten lunch at an airport, or met a visiting relative who arrived by plane. On the other hand, lack of familiarity with the air industry may be characteristic of the entire group.

Understanding "The Airport" will be especially difficult for children who lack basic background experience on which to draw for meaning. This particular story is included in a basal reader that uses a controlled vocabulary and that limits the number of concepts that are introduced. These controls help to reduce the difficulties children will encounter but do not guarantee comprehension. It becomes the teacher's job to assess background experience and build sufficient understanding to profit from reading "The Airport."

Well in advance of the day his reading group will tackle the story the teacher can begin to assess background experience and gather resources for overcoming limited backgrounds. The teacher can prepare a questionnaire that explores each child's familiarity with airports and airplanes. He may have noticed youngsters with a special interest in airplanes whom he can ask to be ready to share a book or models they have built with the group. If the school district has an instructional materials center that stores or obtains films and other teaching aids on various topics, the teacher can request materials on airports and airplanes. In some instances it might even be profitable to arrange for a trip to an airport as a means for building the necessary background. The extent to which the teacher should go in gathering materials and arranging background experiences depends on the readiness of the youngsters to proceed without this special preparation and the amount of time the teacher can devote to such activities. A balance must be struck between giving adequate time to building background and making an unjustified production out of such activities.

On the day the reading group is ready to begin "The Airport" the teacher can introduce the topic and make use of the resources he has gathered. In addition, the children should have an opportunity to discuss the story. The teacher can initiate such a discussion by asking questions and relating personal experiences. For example:

> Boys and girls, today we are going to read about Ben and Matt's trip back to their own home.
> How do you suppose they will travel? (*Children give suggestions.*)

You will see that they are flying by jet airplane.
Have any of you ridden in a jet? Tell us about it. (*Sharing takes place.*)
What was the airport like? What interesting or unusual things did you see there? (*Comments by children.*)
What happens to your luggage at the airport? (*Suggestions are given; the teacher tells about losing his luggage on a recent trip.*)

The discussion should be guided to cover topics that are important in the story (the handling of luggage, for example). As the discussion proceeds, the teacher should introduce vocabulary items orally and sometimes on the chalkboard to be sure they have meaning for the children when they are encountered in the story. A model airplane might be shown and a predesignated child asked to tell about his hobby of flying models with his father.

These activities are designed to create interest in reading the story as well as to build vocabulary and related concepts. The goal is not to guarantee that every child knows the same amount about airplanes but rather to provide sufficient information for every child to understand the story. Because of past experience the pilot's son will find much more personal meaning in the story than George, a deprived child. Nonetheless, George will be better prepared to comprehend the story, having heard and seen the planned activities before reading.

Setting Purposes

Once the teacher is satisfied that adequate background has been built, he must provide a purpose or purposes for reading the story. The teacher's guide may suggest several alternatives that seem appropriate for the group, or the teacher may decide that special practice is needed on a certain skill. Suppose that sequence of events is causing some comprehension difficulties. The children could be directed to read for the purpose of determining what steps were involved in getting to the airport and on board the airplane. Or they could be asked to take the five main ideas of the story (written on the board by the teacher) and arrange them in correct order.

The purposes for reading must be keyed to the content of a story as well to the needs of the children. Imposing on a story a purpose that is ill-suited to its content does not improve comprehension or provide useful practice.

As the child sets about his task of reading he should have easy access to whatever purpose(s) have been established. He can write them down on a piece of paper, or the teacher can put them on the chalkboard. This point of reference helps him to remember why he is reading.

Independent Reading

The teacher's task during independent reading is to be available to answer questions. Beginners can read only short sections at a time and may need a new purpose for each page of their book. By grade two children can usually be sent to their seats to read an entire selection silently, but the teacher should be ready to provide assistance when needed. One procedure is to have students who need help go to the teacher and stand quietly until an opportunity to help them occurs. In this way, even while working with another group, the teacher can see that the child's progress is not unduly delayed.

Follow-up Discussion

Schedules do not always permit the ideal, but whenever possible the discussion of a story should immediately follow independent reading. The story is fresh in the children's minds at this time and confusion or misunderstanding can be cleared up while a problem is still fresh.

The discussion should not be a time for testing whether each child remembers every detail of the story. Instead, it should focus on the purposes established ahead of time and permit the children to share their reactions to the story. The need may occur to return to certain passages of the story for clarification. Different interpretations of incidents are natural and should be taken as an opportunity to study the author's wording or plan of organization.

At times the story may be reread with a different purpose in mind. Oral reading is quite appropriate during the follow-up session. A dramatization could be undertaken, for example.

The teacher's role during the follow-up discussion is that of a diagnostician. Evidence of misunderstanding can be obtained from the children's comments. The teacher can design his questions to explore understanding of new vocabulary and concepts. Children's responses can provide the insight for planning additional instruction.

Written responses to questions can occasionally be gathered so that evidence of each child's understanding is available. Discussions sometimes limit the number of responses that can be heard, and the ideas of some quiet children may go unnoticed.

Below are listed a few additional follow-up activities for checking a child's comprehension. Some of these suggestions are described as written activities but can easily be adapted for discussion purposes. For the story just read:

1. Match pictures and sentences.
2. Write answers to definite questions.
3. Finish incomplete sentences.

4. Draw illustrations of characters, actions, or scenes.
5. Collect main points to be written on the chalkboard and discussed.
6. Find key words.
7. Prove or disprove a statement.
8. Classify words that describe a given object, person, or time.
9. Select the part of the story liked best.
10. Discuss an important character in the story.
11. Make outlines.
12. Select the sentence that tells the story best.
13. Select the best title for the story or paragraph.
14. Tell in what way two characters are alike and in what way they are different.
15. Discriminate between crucial and incidental facts.
    a. The most important part of the story is ____.
    b. Some incidents I liked are ____.

Skill Development

One of the most important aspects of teaching comprehension begins once a reading group has completed a selection and discussed it. The language and thinking skills that are necessary for comprehension must be applied directly to the act of reading. For example, cause and effect reasoning during a discussion becomes comprehending for cause and effect during the reading act.

Skill instruction can be based on the story a reading group has just completed. By returning to a passage that caused some pupils difficulty the teacher can demonstrate the application of a principle. For example, comprehension may have faltered because a figurative statement, for example, "Jack was up a tree," was taken literally by the children. To overcome this problem several other figures of speech might be cited by the teacher and discussed by the group. A practice exercise could then be assigned on interpreting figurative phrases.

This example illustrates the important role of the teacher in actually providing instruction. Resource material such as the teacher's manual can be highly useful, but the teacher is still responsible for guiding a learning experience. If sequence of ideas is the skill causing difficulty, a demonstration of following sequence might be given by the teacher. Or he may guide the group in identifying a sequence of events. The actual teaching technique used will vary from teacher to teacher and group to group. What must be avoided is the notion that children learn to overcome difficulties simply by being given a workbook assignment or similar written activity.

When used selectively, the workbook that accompanies the basal reader can provide practice on comprehension skills such as finding main ideas and locating specific facts. It is a mistake, however, to regard the workbook itself as a teaching device. Most exercises make no provision for instruction but merely provide drill for the learner.

Occasionally the teacher can help a reading group complete a workbook page, perhaps discussing the reason for choosing one answer over another. Used in this fashion, the workbook exercise does provide some instruction.

SUGGESTED ACTIVITIES FOR DEVELOPING COMPREHENSION SKILLS

It is not possible here to suggest an activity for developing every comprehension skill needed, but the following ideas are useful for practice and may easily be adapted to reinforce different skills.

1. THE FIVE W'S

   The children write *What, Who, When, Where, Why* to head columns at the top of their papers. They look through the story to find the answers. This may be done as a class project or the children may do it individually. This same idea may be used by having the children find all the words in the lesson that could be classified under these five headings.

2. QUESTIONS AND ANSWERS

   Two sets of cards are used. One set contains questions that pertain to the reading assignment, social studies, or science. The second gives the answers to the questions. Two or four children can play the game, or the teacher may use the question cards and have the child who has the right answer read it.

   Example:

Set 1	
Who sells sugar?	The grocer
Who digs coal?	The postman
Who sells postage stamps?	The miner
Who carries mail?	The postmaster

   These packs of cards may be placed in envelopes or boxes and used over and over again. The number of questions to prepare will depend upon the number of children using the game at one time.

3. MATCHING PARAGRAPHS AND TITLES

   Paragraphs from old readers or science books may be pasted on $2\frac{1}{2}$ by 5 inch cards. Titles that fit these paragraphs are typed on another set of cards with numbers for use in preparing a key. Children may work individually or in pairs, reading the paragraphs and deciding upon the best title for each paragraph. They may write their own paragraphs and titles.

4. MULTIPLE CHOICE QUESTIONS
    The teacher duplicates this exercise. She uses sentences taken from the lesson and gives three or four choices for completing the sentence correctly.

    Example:
    Draw a line under the correct answer.
    a. The man had a _____
                        tame bear.
                        wild bear.
                        white bear.
    b. The bear could _____
                        march and sing.
                        dance and hop.
                        walk and jump.

5. GUESSING RIDDLES
    The teacher or the pupils make up riddles about animals or people in the story. One child reads the riddle and the others guess the answer. The teacher may duplicate the riddles and the children write the answers. For first grade, the child may draw a picture of the object described.

    Example:
    I have a long neck.
    I have a big bill.
    I have webbed feet.
    I am _____.

6. MATCHING SENTENCES
    The exercise using sentences or words from the reading lesson may be duplicated, written on the chalkboard, or printed on strips or cards for individual activities.

    Example:

A.	B.
a. We write_____	1. in the air.
b. Bread is baked_____	2. on a tree.
c. Birds fly_____	3. with a pencil.
d. Snow falls_____	4. in an oven.

7. SENTENCE COMPLETION
    Sentences from other assignments may be used. All necessary words may be given for the lower grades, but older pupils should be able to complete the sentences from their recall of the materials read. The exercises are either duplicated or written on the chalkboard.

Example:
Provide the correct endings.

a. My dog   c. Jack and Jill
b. Miss Muffet   d. Little Jack Horner

8. TRUE OR FALSE STATEMENTS
Some true and some false statements which refer to the reading assignment may be used. For lower grades the children write *yes* or *no* after
the sentences. The material may be duplicated or written on the chalkboard.

Example:
Write YES after the sentences that are true and NO after those that
are not true.

a. Elephants are larger than tigers ____.
b. The little boy can run as fast as a horse ____.
c. The crow could talk as well as the boy ____.

After the children have learned and practiced a comprehension
skill in a reading lesson an opportunity is needed to apply it in a
second reading lesson. In establishing the purposes for reading one
of the next stories the teacher can provide for application of the skill
by stating it as a purpose to be pursued. Independent reading occurs
and the skill is applied. Follow-up discussion should then focus
specifically on the new skill so that an appraisal of progress can be
made. Evidence of confusion permits the teacher to immediately
provide corrective instruction. This *teach, practice, reteach* procedure
is depicted in Figure 11.3.

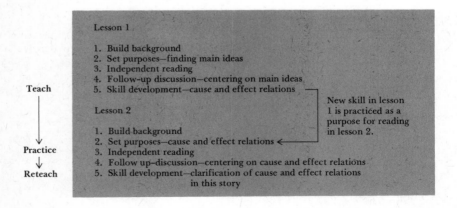

FIGURE 11-3   Teaching New Skills
*New skills introduced in one lesson should be applied in a subsequent lesson. This
provides practice and enables the teacher to assess progress.*

SUMMARY

Reading comprehension was defined as the process of deriving meaning from reading. Four components of reading comprehension were discussed: thinking skills, background experience, language skills, and purposes for reading.

Thinking skills are dependent upon the child's native intelligence, environmental influences, and his facility with language. Specific thought processes are learned as the child matures and has the opportunity to observe their underlying principles in operation. The teacher's primary task is to see that thinking skills are applied to the act of reading.

Background experience provides the child with the vocabulary and concepts he manipulates during thinking. Interests, attitudes, and beliefs are also largely determined by a child's experiences. Without the appropriate background reading becomes mere word-calling, since the child brings no meaning to the symbols he decodes.

Language skills permit the child to relate correctly the vocabulary and concepts used by an author. His knowledge of grammar enables him to understand what action occurs and who or what is involved in the action. Linguists are just beginning to explore the implications of their field for techniques to improve reading comprehension. It seems certain that classroom activities of the future will focus the child's attention more specifically on the way his language delivers meaning in its written form.

Purposes for reading are necessary for directing the reader's attention to specific aspects of a selection. The danger in reading for no specified purpose is that no goal will be achieved. Reading behavior, including reading rate, must be adjusted according to various purposes. Practice is needed in knowing when a specific purpose is appropriate and how to adjust accordingly.

The complexity of reading comprehension guarantees that no teacher can eliminate all obstacles to his children's success. However, the guided reading lesson makes allowances for minimizing difficulties and is recommended for use with all instructional systems and all subject areas.

The guided reading lesson is comprised of five steps:

1. building background,
2. setting purposes,
3. independent reading,
4. follow-up discussion, and
5. development of related skills.

TERMS

cloze procedure	Piaget
syntax	Thorndike
morphology	Nila B. Smith
guided reading lesson	Bloom
grammar	John Holt
connective	Robertson
introspection	Deighton
vector analysis	

Chapter 12

Oral
Reading

You can probably recall your elementary school days when each member of your reading group dutifully took his turn reading aloud while your classmates followed along in their books. While some of your friends struggled to pronounce each word, your eyes may have raced ahead to discover for yourself the meaning of the story being read. But just in case your turn came next, part of your awareness remained with your friend, holding your place, urging him on.

You may have given some thought to the "old days' and wondered what place oral reading has in today's schools. You may have resolved to avoid in your own classroom this tiresome round-the-circle oral reading. Your experiences as an adult tell you that skill in oral reading is used infrequently, yet occasions do occur when reading aloud is of great importance. Therefore, some attention to oral reading seems appropriate; the thorny questions are how much and when.

This chapter will describe several kinds of oral reading and suggest methods for teaching children to become effective oral readers. Oral reading by the teacher will also be discussed. Look for answers to the following questions as you read this chapter.

Should children read orally every day?

How can oral reading errors be corrected?

Should a child's oral reading mistakes be corrected immediately or later when others are not listening?

If a child cannot read a word, should he be helped or left to struggle with it?

How are errors in oral reading related to silent reading errors?

Should the teacher read orally to his class?

What oral reading tests are available?

When one child reads aloud should others follow along in their books?

We have demonstrated in earlier chapters that practically all of the reading process goes on internally. Except for movement of the eyes and facial reactions that show such emotions as tension, frustration, or mirth, the reader seems to proceed mysteriously and silently across a line of print and down the page. One cannot observe his thought processes, his questions, or his confusions. The model of the reading presented in Chapter 1 suggests that not until the final step, the reader's response, do we have the opportunity to observe a reaction.

One of the possible overt responses that can be observed is reading aloud, usually called oral reading. (It is important to remember that various other responses are possible, including nonobservable ones.) The oral response enables an observer to share the reading process with a reader. The reader's mispronunciations or lack of correct phrasing tell the observer a reading error has occurred and that understanding may be going astray. Smooth oral reading with correct intonation of the voice *seems* to indicate that all is going well. (It will be seen later in this chapter that difficulties may exist despite fluent oral reading.)

For a good many years oral reading was regarded as the best method for assessing reading skill. Consequently, undue stress was placed on correct pronunciation and phrasing. The result was a misguided program of reading instruction.

This chapter will take a brief historical look at how oral reading came to be so heavily emphasized in our schools. The recommendations of current authorities concerning oral reading in the classroom will be presented along with a look at present classroom practices. The various types of oral reading will then be discussed. Classroom techniques for evaluating and improving oral reading will be presented. Next, the use of oral reading for diagnostic purposes is described in some detail. In particular, the importance of patterns of oral reading miscues will be presented along with suggested corrective activities. Finally, a section on oral reading by the teacher is included in this chapter.

THE HISTORY OF ORAL READING

According to Smith (1965), the origins of oral reading in this country date back as far as reading instruction itself. The ability to read was intimately linked with religion during the Colonial period when English institutions and customs were predominant. At that time the American colonies felt the influence of the Church of England, which was moving from Catholicism to Protestantism. Following the Reformation each individual was believed to be directly responsible to God for his own salvation; reading the Bible was central to the achievement of this goal. The Bible was the center of family religious life and was read aloud on numerous occasions.

A dearth of reading materials during Colonial days helped to place an emphasis on oral reading. In order to share a book it was necessary for one to read and for many to listen. Frequently illiterates, who were many, relied on the oral reading of others for the Scriptures. Thus reading instruction rested heavily on religious writings and the reading act was practically synonymous with oral reading.

Smith (1965) describes a second major period in American reading instruction as one of nationalistic-moralistic emphasis. After the break with England and until about 1840, great stress was placed on patriotism. The goals of the state were building national strength and making good citizens. Among other things, reading instruction was expected to purify and standardize the American language. The correct pronunciation and enunciation of the language was achieved in part through oral reading. Consequently, the public schools, established to prepare good citizens, stressed oral reading. Smith (1965, p. 40) states that the paramount aim of reading instruction of that day was "developing eloquent oral reading." A quotation from a book of the time is particularly revealing: "Try to read as if you were telling a story to your mother or talking to some of your playmates. Reading is talking from a book" (Smith, 1965, p. 41).

It is not difficult to visualize a reading lesson during those times. Given the goals a young nation had set for its schools, a curriculum featuring plenty of oral reading was quite natural. The quality of a child's education was frequently judged by his ability to translate print into flowing oratory and recall specific facts about his government and nation (Mathews, 1966).

Oral reading continued to be a fundamental aspect of reading instruction throughout the remainder of the nineteenth century. It was not until the period 1918–1925 that any basic change took place with regard to oral reading. The explanation for this change is lodged in a movement in education that began to develop in 1840. Gradually more emphasis came to be placed on meaning in education. Radical educators of the day such as Pestalozzi, Mann, and Herbart questioned practices that required children to memorize and recite without attention to understanding.

The work of Parker and Huey was particularly significant in applying the concept of meaningfulness to reading instruction. Reading was regarded by these and other advanced thinkers as a thought-getting process rather than as one primarily concerned with pronunciation of words (Smith, 1965). Research evidence gathered about this time (1918) demonstrated the superiority of silent reading over oral reading both in speed and in comprehension.

Educational research was often accepted without criticism in the early twentieth century. Thus the findings of rather poorly designed studies were often given undue attention and sometimes influenced instructional practices without sufficient verification through additional study. As a case in point, the immediate and drastic reaction to evidence concerning the superiority of silent reading was the complete abandonment of oral reading by some educators. The research evidence had not related directly to the role or importance of oral reading; nonetheless, some now taught silent reading almost to the exclusion of oral reading. Numerous standardized silent reading tests were published. Professional texts contained procedures for teaching silent reading. Exercises were written that required children to read and respond silently to various skill activities.

Not all educators jumped on the silent reading bandwagon. Buswell (1923), for example, cautioned in his writings against an extreme reaction against oral reading. In general, the reaction was moderate and quite healthy; oral reading assumed a place in the curriculum but was largely regarded as a supplement to silent reading by most reading experts.

THE CURRENT SCENE

The present attitude of reading experts is remarkably similar to that of their counterparts in 1925. Heilman (1967), for example, suggests, much as Buswell, that oral reading be taught as a useful skill, but in proper balance with silent reading. Bond and Wagner (1966), Smith (1963), and Strang (1969) take similar positions.

Despite the recommendations of authorities, oral reading practices today come surprisingly close to the practices of 1870. Austin and Morrison (1963) comment in their national survey of reading programs: "A number of years ago the indiscriminate use of 'barbershop' or 'taking turns' style of oral reading was denounced by reading authorities as being unsound. Yet, while the present study was being conducted, this was by far the oral reading activity most frequently observed" (Austin and Morrison, 1963, pp. 44–45).

Based on personal visits to literally hundreds of elementary school classrooms throughout the United States, we likewise have observed that a disparity exists between the recommendations of experts concerning oral reading and its actual use. Many teachers seem to have the incorrect idea that each child must be "heard" reading every day. Consequently, the age-old reading circle and the "barbershop oral reading" method carry on.

In the light of this brief historical look at oral reading, prospective teachers must critically consider the role oral reading will have in their instructional program. Clearly some oral reading is necessary. The following sections of this chapter will help in deciding how much oral reading is desirable and what activities can be planned to provide the necessary practice.

TYPES OF ORAL READING

Oral reading has a definite place in today's reading curriculum. While we are presently aware of the rather limited use of oral reading outside the classroom, occasions for reading aloud do occur, and such occasions are important to the reader. Sharing an interesting or amusing incident from the evening newspaper with a member of the family requires proper enunciation, phrasing, intonation, and generally effective speech patterns in order to communicate well. Thus skill in oral reading is desirable even today. The classroom teacher therefore has a responsibility for instructing students in the fundamentals of reading aloud. A broadly based reading program provides children with the opportunity to read orally in a variety of situations. Two major categories of oral reading are especially important: (1) audience oral reading and (2) oral reading for diagnosis.

Audience Oral Reading

The apparent reason for any oral reading is to share information with an audience. The label audience oral reading may therefore seem redundant. However, some forms of oral reading that will be discussed later in this chapter have as their primary purpose the evaluation of a child's reading skills; the audience in this case is limited to the teacher. True audience oral reading implies a broader set of listeners — fellow classmates, parents, friends, children from other classrooms, a church congregation, television viewers, and so forth.

Audience oral reading requires, first, *an audience*. The audience is a person or persons who must listen to the one who reads aloud in order to understand what is being shared. A mother who listens to her son read an interesting item from the newspaper is an audience. She understands what is communicated only through the words that are spoken, the pauses that are inserted, the intonation of her son's voice, and the enunciation he gives each syllable. In the same sense the children of a reading group who follow along in their books as one child reads aloud are *not* an audience. The purpose for listening has been eliminated in the latter case; the speaker-listener communication chain has been broken. Since most children can read faster silently than orally by the beginning of grade three, "barbershop" oral reading lacks one necessary component for audience oral reading — an audience.

Since audience oral reading is intended to be a form of communication between one person sending the message and others who are listening, the message must flow smoothly and accurately in order to be understood. It follows that an opportunity to prepare, rehearse, or practice a selection helps to avoid faulty communication that snags on word-recognition difficulties, poor phrasing, or improper use of punctuation. Suggestions for overcoming these problems will be made later.

A child who shares an interesting library book with his peers by reading aloud an exciting incident has much at stake. He is the speaker and his audience depends on him for understanding. Preparation increases the probability of good communication. Furthermore, the teacher should quickly supply a difficult or troublesome word when the need occurs to facilitate the sharing process. Such a highly emotional setting is no time to embarrass the oral reader or frustrate his audience with a side trip for a review of word-attack skills. Instruction of this sort can be conducted later in a personal manner once the time for sharing has passed.

Two fundamental points are important to remember with regard to audience oral reading of any kind: (1) a genuine audience is required and (2) the opportunity to prepare ahead of time is desirable. Three specific types of audience oral reading will be discussed in this chapter: (1) sharing a selection with others, (2) dramatics, and (3) choral reading.

Sharing a Selection

Regardless of the instructional system employed for teaching reading, or the grade level, many opportunities arise for sharing a selection. The material to be shared can vary from a single paragraph discovered in a children's magazine to an entire chapter of a favorite book. The language experience approach to reading provides an excellent source of oral reading material through the experience story. A youngster will practice long and hard at polishing his delivery of a story he has authored himself. The individualized approach facilitates sharing parts of a library book that a child has completed and wishes to read aloud to his peers.

These examples illustrate the first real value of sharing a selection — the child's self-concept and personal ego are enhanced by the chance to be a contributor or star. Regardless of the materials read, each youngster can be the center of attention and find success at his task. Even poor readers can practice a selection sufficiently to make an acceptable presentation. The motivational aspects of such an opportunity are also a powerful factor in favor of a genuine effort by the child.

A second value of sharing a selection is the practice it provides for the child in using good speech habits. With the proper setting a child who reads aloud is *the* communicator. Others must listen to understand, and consequently a premium is placed on proper enunciation, articulation, phrasing, attention to punctuation, volume, posture, expression, and breath control. Evidently such skills are not automatically employed because a child decides to read orally. Thus an instructional program for improving the various aspects of oral reading is undertaken, but with real interest on the part of the child who wants to be an effective sharer. Again, the motivational aspects of a sound oral reading program are underscored.

Oral reading can also provide the child with an opportunity to share ideas, engage in a discussion, and think on his feet. For example, when asked to prepare for reading aloud the part in his basal reader story that explains how John, the main character, escaped from a forest fire, the child may encounter disagreement from his classmates. Others may regard a different part of the story as more revealing. By reading each section aloud a discussion can ensue during which ideas are exchanged and real thinking takes place. Another example at the intermediate grade level might involve the sharing of newspaper items and a follow-up discussion of the meaning or significance of various events. The youngster who shares an item would be expected to present his point of view and perhaps defend it. Thus, the value of sharing a selection can be extended to include stimulation of language skills and the exchange of ideas through discussion.

Sharing a selection orally also serves to increase the child's understanding and retention of words. Preparing a selection to be read provides a good opportunity for word study. Word-analysis techniques can be applied and the dictionary consulted. Rereading to smooth phrasing and expression provide additional exposure to new words, thus increasing their familiarity and expanding the child's sight vocabulary. Finally, reading the selection requires the child to concentrate on interpretation and in the process further deepens his understanding of the words he reads.

Sharing a selection with others is especially valuable in helping children understand reading as a communication process. The transmission of a message is emphasized by oral reading. An activity that makes this point is the preparation of a radio script by children. A broadcasting studio can be created in the classroom. Those children who read the script orally are asked to be genuine communicators in this situation. Their "audience" must listen to them as they read the message—news script, commercial, soap opera, or whatever—thus reinforcing for them with real force the concept of reading as communication. Interpretation and understanding are intimately linked for the child by such an experience.

Finally, sharing a selection with others is the type of oral reading a child will later employ outside the classroom. He will want to share interesting information with others. For this reason alone instruction and practice are required to help the child achieve skill in oral reading. Reading the secretary's minutes at a business meeting is an example of an infrequent task, but one requiring some skill and therefore some instruction and practice.

Dramatic Oral Reading

The term "dramatics" causes many of us to remember our high school days and the senior class play. Certainly dramatics of this sort, probably on a less grand scale, are occasionally appropriate at the elementary school level. More often, however, dramatics does not involve elaborate scenery, careful rehearsal, and the memorization of lines. Considerable value can be gained from simple dramatics that amount to little more than reading and acting out the parts of a story in a book, a children's magazine, or a reader. With only limited practice the lines or dialogue can be read orally for a very satisfactory creative experience and will not require a large investment of class time.

Every child in a classroom should have the opportunity to participate in dramatic oral reading. While only a limited number of major parts may be available, some children can supply sound effects while others can alternate at reading nonspeaking narration. Repetitious parts may even be read by a chorus, or the same story may be read by two separate casts. While one group performs the remainder of the class listens, and vice versa. Participation may be limited to being part of the audience so long as the same child is not always a member of the listeners group.

The advantages of dramatic oral reading are several. A message must be communicated by dramatics; a story must be told. Consequently, interpretation becomes an extremely important element in the presentation. The dialogue of the meek little man in the "Brave Little Tailor" must be read with special feeling and understanding. The challenge of playing this part will test the skill of a child assigned the task. The dialogue of the angry giant places an entirely different demand on the child selected to read this part. Feelings of shyness or embarrassment are readily overcome when the child can slip into the relative security of being somebody else. The result of a genuine effort to interpret a story is to encourage deep appreciation and understanding of the characters and events. As with reading a selection to others, good speech skills are practiced and reinforced during a dramatic oral reading.

A variation of the plan suggested above, often found to be especially effective with younger children, is the use of hand puppets for characters in a story. Again, the retiring child may find it easier to be free with his voice and language when permitted to lose himself in the personality of a story character.

Reading poetry aloud falls into the realm of dramatic oral reading. As with dramatics, poetry is intended to be read aloud. The sound and rhythm of language are nowhere more apparent than in a poem effectively interpreted aloud. Children can profit from hearing each other read poetry orally as well as listening to the teacher. Again, the language and speech skills emphasized in other oral reading activities are present in the oral reading of poetry. The importance of interpretation through the pacing of phrases is also highlighted.

A fundamental goal of language instruction is to help children enjoy words and express their thoughts to others. Poetry in particular can be useful in helping children have fun with words with little necessity for analysis of stanza and verse. Oral reading of poetry places additional emphasis on reading as communication.

Choral Reading

Classroom choral reading consists of having children read a selection aloud in unison much as a chorus would sing a song. Occasionally solo voices are heard; the pitch of high and low voices is employed for special effect and to aid in communication. Frequently poetry or prose with a special rhythm and beat are presented orally by readers in unison.

Choral reading makes several unique contributions to the reading program and probably ought to be used more often than it seems to be. In particular, the steady rhythmic reading of a choral presentation is an effective device for smoothing the speech habits of participating youngsters who lack facility with language. Special emphasis is placed on reading by phrases in choral reading. This, too, can be good practice for a child who tends to call each word individually or fails to follow the punctuation guideposts in reading aloud.

Choral reading also removes the pressure of being the only reader by enlisting the child in a group undertaking. The mistakes of one child are not easily noticed and the pace of the group carries even the poor reader along at a steady clip. Furthermore, every child can participate in choral reading and be the equal of his classmates in this activity.

Not every poem or reading selection is appropriate for choral presentation. Teachers' magazines such as *Instructor* and *Grade Teacher* frequently carry excellent choral reading material. The rhythm and sound of words included in candidate materials are of special importance. Special opportunities for voices of various pitch and quality are especially good. The best test is probably trial reading aloud by the teacher with attention to the features just mentioned.

Combining dramatic oral reading and choral reading may easily be accomplished. For example, as suggested in an earlier section, repetitive parts of a dramatic play can be read by a choral group. Sound effects might be provided for a dramatic play in much the same manner.

As with the other types of audience oral reading, choral reading places a premium on good speech habits and encourages the child to regard reading as a communication act requiring interpretation.

Evaluating Audience Oral Reading

Evaluation of any kind should be keyed to whatever objectives are established for an activity. Only by having a predetermined standard against which to assess performance can meaningful evaluation occur. In the case of audience oral reading, the primary objective is communicating with others through the oral interpretation of written symbols. Oral reading must therefore be evaluated against the criterion of effective communication.

Linguists make a science of studying the nature of man's verbal behavior. They report that a number of variables are important in man's spoken communication. Words alone do not comprise the sum of oral language. Syntax, or the arrangement of words in some order, is an important variable. Stress, pitch, and pauses or junctures also play an important role in communication. It follows that oral reading as a form of spoken communication is dependent on these same factors. Evaluation of oral reading must take these variables into account. The flexibility of the reader's voice is an example of a specific application of pitch and stress. A monotonous voice that drones on at one level without variation does not communicate effectively. Other variables include proper phrasing, expression, volume, breath control, and use of punctuation. Articulation and enunciation are also factors to be considered. One final item that can aid and promote the variables mentioned above is proper posture. In summary, good speech habits are important to good oral reading. Whatever is likely to facilitate effective speech is essential in oral reading as well.

Good oral reading by children can be encouraged by developing a set of specific guidelines to serve as goals. It is especially important to have children participate in the development of their own criteria, since standards imposed by the teacher are likely to seem more like rules than actual goals. One possible means for encouraging children to help create guidelines is to play samples of oral reading on tape. Several samples that demonstrate a marked difference in performance can be used to contrast poor communication with good communication. Focusing attention on what one reader does that makes his presentation better can lead inductively to a beginning set of standards. As oral reading activities proceed, the original criteria can be expanded and refined. The samples of oral reading for this approach can be prepared by the teacher, or better yet, by a good oral reader in the group who deliberately varies his skill from selection to selection. A sample checklist is shown here.

CHECKLIST FOR EVALUATING AUDIENCE ORAL READING

	Never	Infre- quently	Often	Always
1. Does the reader maintain comfortable and pleasing posture as he reads aloud?				
2. Is he able to look up from the reading to maintain eye contact with the class?				
3. Is there adequate volume so that he is easily heard?				
4. Does he enunciate words clearly?				
5. Does he articulate words, clearly distinguishing sounds?				
6. Does he utilize voice flexibility so that interest is aroused?				
7. Does his eye move ahead of his voice so that meaningful thought units are interpreted clearly?				
8. Does he observe punctuation in order to preserve intended author meaning?				
9. Does he have good breath control?				

Once standards for audience oral reading are established, the second step is to provide each youngster with feedback about his performance. Again, a tape recorder can be especially useful. Most children can spot difficulties in their own oral reading by hearing a recording of their work. Self-identification of problems is especially good for stimulating improvement. Natural defensive reactions are less likely with this approach. Caution should be taken to see that some children are not totally discouraged by their lack of skill. The best plan is to focus on one specific skill at a time. As progress is made in phrasing, for example, a new skill can be undertaken.

Valuable feedback on oral reading performance can also be provided for a youngster by his teacher and his peers. Using the guidelines developed by the class, the child can obtain specific suggestions for improvement. Naturally, special attention must be given to the human relations involved in peer evaluation, but this experience can be good for both reader and listener.

Improving Audience Oral Reading

While it is probably true that practice in reading aloud to an audience is in itself a worthwhile activity, efficient improvement in oral reading depends upon a carefully defined skills program. Activities should be planned to promote these specific skills. Evaluation procedures become necessary in order to note evidence of oral reading improvement as well as to pinpoint those skills still needing attention.

A number of meaningful practice activities have already been suggested in this chapter:

1. sharing a favorite part of an interesting library book
2. reading a language-experience story
3. giving a report on current events
4. creating a mock radio broadcast
5. dramatizing a story
6. giving a puppet show
7. sharing a poem
8. participating in choral reading.

This list by no means exhausts the myriad of useful and interesting activities possible. Durrell (1956) describes a divided-story approach to oral reading in which a story is cut into sections and mounted on cards for easy manipulation by the child. The cards are numbered sequentially and then distributed to the members of a class or small group. Each child is permitted to preview his card or cards before joining in an oral reading session, sharing his part of the story in proper order.

Creative writing activities provide an excellent opportunity for oral reading. Whether stories are centered on a given theme or are products of incidental, individual experiences, reading to an audience reinforces the author while providing him with a valuable oral reading experience.

Other meaningful oral reading situations can be created that require narration. For example, children may draw a series of pictures highlighting main events in a story and then prepare a script to accompany their picture presentation. As the pictures are shown in proper sequence several children can read the script. Similarly, a shadow play or puppet show provides opportunity for appropriate narration.

Types of oral reading activities are endless. Only the imagination of the teacher places a limit on what can be effectively done. In all instances, however, activities must have a specific purpose, one that is understood by the teacher and the child. If, for example, James experiences difficulty in achieving enough volume as he reads, an activity designed to meet his specific need is planned. Ideally, the activity is suited to his special interests as well as his need. In this way James will more likely be motivated to improve. If one of his interests is baseball, he may wish to do a sports broadcast where increased voice volume is a prerequisite in helping an audience enjoy the show.

A tape recorder is an invaluable aid in improving oral reading skill. Being able to hear one's own voice is perhaps the best motivator and the most accurate record available. By using the recorder James can discover for himself that his volume was too low during his performance despite the fact that it seemed adequate to him. He can subsequently evaluate each variation of his performance.

Important to remember is that each technique, activity, or corrective practice put into effect will meet a variety of needs in oral reading skill development. Conversely, each area of need can be met by a variety of activities. The teacher needs to discover specific weaknesses and plan within the total framework of oral reading activities those that most completely fulfill a child's needs.

ORAL READING FOR DIAGNOSIS

Numerous opportunities occur every day for a classroom teacher to gather diagnostic information about his students. A child's errors in completing a workbook page or incorrectly outlining the major events in a story give the alert teacher important information concerning possible instructional needs. The same is true of oral reading. The teacher who regards oral reading as an opportunity to gather diagnostic information and knows how to classify the information obtained can greatly increase the effectiveness of his instructional program. With the information gained from oral reading performance, a child's strengths and weaknesses can be better understood and appropriate skill development undertaken.

Oral Reading as a Check of Comprehension

Whereas the main purpose of audience oral reading is interpreting information for others, oral reading can also be used as a check of the reader's comprehension in the daily instructional program. For example, a reading group may be given the task of determining which of two events occurred first in a story. By reading aloud the section of the story that provides a clue to the correct sequence, a check of comprehension is provided. Interpretation and proper phrasing are important even in this type of oral reading but are secondary to the assessment of basic reading skills. When a child reads aloud the answer to the earlier question about sequence of events, the appropriateness of his response is more crucial than his oral performance. Has he found the evidence needed to support or refute an idea? Has he correctly followed the author's logic? Did he skim the selection and find the section containing the information required?

In this sense, as an instructional technique oral reading is probably used most frequently and most effectively after a group of youngsters has a common reading experience. During the discussion that frequently follows the completion of a story numerous opportunities are provided to check comprehension through oral reading. As stated earlier, the answers to specific questions can be located and read aloud. Questions can vary along the cognitive domain from *who, when,* and *where* to *how* and *why.* Special emphasis needs to be placed on questions that probe the higher thought processes. Further discussion of this point appears in Chapter 14. It is sufficient to observe here that questions requiring only specific recall and literal understanding neglect the more difficult but essential skills of critical reading.

Children may be asked to skim their story to find where the author describes the discovery of a new mineral. Or they may be directed to read the section they believe provides a clue to the mood of a gathering crowd. They can be asked to speculate as to what factors might have lead a character to become a bully and then to find evidence for their ideas in the story. Countless illustrations could be given of the variety of tasks that can be assigned.

Related to the task of reading aloud to answer a question is oral reading to prove a point. Indeed, when the answers of several children to a specific question differ, proving a point becomes the natural next step. In the broader context of a good discussion oral reading to prove a point need not be limited to questions raised by the teacher. Especially in the areas of social studies, language arts, science, and mathematics excellent opportunities arise for employing the technique of oral reading to prove a point. In the upper grades reporting current events naturally leads to class discussion, which in turn may require supportive evidence to prove a point. What political leader proposed a bill being discussed? What did he expect to achieve with a new law? What have critics said about the bill? Are there facts to support their criticisms? In such a setting reading becomes a necessary tool and reading aloud the means for using the tool.

From the teacher's standpoint valuable information can be gained from the performance of children in oral reading to answer a question or to prove a point. The child who misunderstands what he has read because he literally interprets the figurative phrase "pushed the panic button" apparently has a deficiency the teacher must help him to overcome. Or a child who does not find evidence to support his views, clinging instead to personal bias, has a definite need for critical reading and research skills.

Every reading program ought to provide opportunities for oral reading in both audience and instructional situations. Many classroom activities can be developed to combine the two. For example, when a child is permitted to present an oral report on a trade book recently completed he has the opportunity for audience oral reading. His favorite part of the book may be shared. In addition, the class or teacher may have questions about the topic, thereby tapping the child's grasp of the story as he attempts to give answers. Detailed discussion of this sort should probably be handled in a personal conference between student and teacher. Nonetheless, even a group discussion offers some evidence concerning the youngster's comprehension.

Another oral reading activity that has considerable value from both an audience and an instructional standpoint is sharing language-experience stories. The high motivational aspects of reading one's own story to an audience are obvious. In addition, specific audience questions concerning his experience story can require the child to find the answer with the context or perhaps lead him to refine and expand his story if he finds he has omitted relevant information.

In Beginning Reading

Earlier in this chapter the limitations of "barbershop" oral reading were presented. In particular, the practice of requiring children to read along silently as a peer reads orally was questioned. One reason for discouraging this practice should be reexamined at this time.

Children in grades three and above are usually capable of reading more rapidly silently than orally. Consequently, requiring all children to follow along word by word and phrase by phrase is unnatural for most readers after grade two. While silent readers are slowed down by this requirement, oral readers feel the pressure of being too slow for their peers. In this respect, however, the practice of reading aloud while others follow along may not be entirely indefensible with beginning readers.

Let us explore the rationale for this recommendation. Linguists remind us that the child's normal mode of communication at age six is oral. He *speaks* his own thoughts and *listens* to the thoughts of others. Strickland (1962), Loban (1963), Labov (1967), and Templin (1957) have found from their research on children's language development that by the age of three or four most children have gained an intuitive understanding of their language. They transform sentences from "John hit Mary" to "Mary was hit by John" without formal training. They create regular—though incorrect—forms of verbs, thereby demonstrating their grasp of our basic language structure. For example, "I gived my dog a bath" is substituted for "I gave my dog a bath," or *buyed* is substituted for *bought*.

These examples illustrate that children possess a facility with their spoken language by age six. The job of learning to read is a new task, however. Whereas all previous communication has been oral-aural, reading is visual; whereas children have heard and spoken an astonishing number of words, they can decode few if any printed symbols.

Many experts on children's language development are beginning to urge a closer association between the child's oral communication and the reading task. Keislar and McNeil (1968) demonstrated this principle in an investigation with beginning readers. They concluded that an oral method is more effective than a nonoral method and suggested that the overt response of saying a word helps the child tie the word symbol to its oral counterpart for the word. Lefevre (1964) makes much the same point in stating that the preschool child is ready to learn to convert the sound system into the graphic system, and vice versa. Like Keislar and McNeil, Lefevre stresses the importance of linking the child's concept and spoken label with the written symbol. For example, the learner must associate his experiences with the family pet and the symbol *d-o-g*.

The application of this theory to actual classroom practice would have the teacher encourage and require oral reading in the beginning stages of instruction. Special emphasis should be placed on relating the child's spoken language to word symbols. The experience chart is especially valuable in this regard. Children are occasionally heard to remark with surprise and revelation at reading their own experience story, "Gosh, reading is just talk wrote down."

Perhaps even more fundamental from the standpoint of this chapter is the opportunity afforded the teacher to assess progress when the beginning reader "talks" his way through a story. Faulty habits of word attack can be noted immediately, difficulties with unknown words observed, and confusions easily corrected. In short, the teacher is better able to provide assistance immediately when the beginner makes reading errors aloud.

Since silent reading is as slow or slower than oral reading among beginning readers, having other children follow along is acceptable. Indeed, the reinforcement of seeing a word and hearing it pronounced has distinct advantages. A word of caution is appropriate at this point, however. Even in grade one all reading must not be oral. Practice at reading silently is necessary if this skill is to develop and shortly take its place as the primary form of reading. Furthermore, since the teacher cannot *hear* every child every day, some independent reading is necessary.

To avoid making the task of listening to others read a laborious one, some grouping of children is desirable. Those who take to the reading act quite readily certainly do not belong in an instructional group with those who must struggle with every word. While following along in a book can be good practice for some youngsters, for others it merely slows them down. The key is flexibility and sensitivity to individual needs in resolving this matter.

The Use of Oral Reading in a Conference

When used as an instructional technique oral reading provides some feedback for the teacher on reading difficulties a child may be experiencing. It is unlikely, however, that sufficient information can be gathered with this procedure to take the place of an individual diagnosis.

Prepared and Unprepared Oral Reading

Information on miscues in oral reading is needed to help a child overcome faulty reading habits. In addition, some indication of silent problems can be gained through an analysis of miscues in oral reading. When a child makes an error in oral reading he may not necessarily make the same error in silent reading. That is, a mispronunciation of the word *liver* may indicate faulty word-attack skills and thus represent a silent reading problem. Or it may not only be symptomatic of faulty speech habits and interfere in no way with effective silent reading. More will be said about this issue later, but the most reasonable view appears to be that oral reading miscues may be a clue to silent reading errors. In particular, consistent oral miscues are subject for concern and are likely to represent a difficulty worth pursuing.

These preparatory remarks are helpful in understanding the alternatives of having a child read aloud with or without preparation. For purposes of diagnosing errors that may indicate reading difficulties, unprepared oral reading is usually recommended. In this way the child's first encounter with a word and a total passage is oral and enables the teacher to observe attempts at word attack, the breadth of sight vocabulary, and ability to comprehend. By "sitting" through the first exposure to a passage while the child reads aloud, the teacher learns what reading skills he employs well and what skills need attention. By asking questions about what the child has read the teacher obtains a quick check of comprehension.

Most oral reading for purposes of diagnosis will therefore be unrehearsed by the child. Close interaction between teacher and child is preferable for diagnostic sessions, which should be held in a quiet place free from interruptions. Only the teacher and child should be included. Many teachers will have to be satisfied with a corner of their classroom away from the other children who work independently during this time. This arrangement is not ideal but should be satisfactory.

Oral Reading Tests

Oral reading diagnosis is frequently conducted by having the child read a series of paragraphs that increase in length and difficulty. The teacher usually has a copy of the passages so that errors can be noted and recorded while the child reads from his copy. A stopwatch is useful for providing a measure of the child's reading rate. Finally, comprehension questions are desirable to check for understanding of what is being read. Several oral reading tests, *The Gray Oral Reading Test* (1963), *The Gilmore Oral Reading Test* (1968), *Classroom Reading Inventory* (1969), and the informal reading inventory (IRI), are of this type.

The *Gray* consists of four different forms, each containing thirteen different passages ranging in reading difficulty from pre-primer to adult. The *Gilmore* has two forms and is comprised of ten paragraphs ranging from grade one to grade eight in terms of reading levels. Exact directions for administering these instruments are provided in the examiner's manuals which accompany each test. Both the *Gray* and *Gilmore* tests are designed to assess oral reading errors. The test authors are careful not to create the expectation that silent reading errors can be determined by these instruments. However, because of the close relation between silent and oral reading, valuable clues to possible silent reading difficulties can be obtained with these tests.

The *Gray* test provides for recording eight types of oral reading miscues, including (1) aid given to child, (2) gross mispronunciation, (3) partial mispronunciation, (4) omission, (5) insertion, (6) substitution, (7) repetition, and (8) inversion (reversing a word). The examiner marks his own copy of the passages whenever a miscue of the type listed above is made. A special scoring system is given in the manual. The examiner also times the reading of each selection and assigns a passage score based on the number of miscues recorded and the time required to complete the passage. Four questions designed to test specific recall of information are also provided for each passage. The manual for the *Gray* gives grade equivalents for the child's total passage scores. Boys and girls are treated separately when converting the total passage scores to grade equivalents.

The manual for the *Gray* also provides some assistance in interpreting the child's performance. The results are useful along with supplementary information in assigning children to reading groups. Careful analysis of a child's performance may enable the teacher to gather specific diagnostic information. For example, a reader may have a pronounced tendency to omit words when he reads aloud. In a case where connecting words such as *the* and *and* are omitted, it is likely that the child is simply trying to read too fast. Corrective activities can focus on slowing down and reading more accurately. If whole phrases are omitted, a perception difficulty may be the contributing cause. Special help from a person trained to handle such problems is called for in this case. Another example might be an instance in which a child mispronounces many words by failing to read the proper ending. Initial consonant sounds may be attempted correctly, but the rest of the word is incorrect. In this case some instruction in word recognition that forces the child to notice differences in word endings is indicated. Finding rhyming words provides such practice. Other examples of various oral reading miscues and their possible origin are presented in Table 12.1. Readers are cautioned that the examples cited here are only for illustrative purposes. More detailed discussion of the interpretation of the Gray may be found in the Examiner's Manual.

The *Gilmore* test is similar to the *Gray* except that the various passages are related to one another to form a story about the same characters. The *Gilmore* also provides for eight types of reading errors, including (1) substitutions, (2) mispronunciations, (3) words pronounced by the examiner, (4) disregard of punctuation, (5) insertions, (6) hesitations, (7) repetitions, and (8) omissions. Three

TABLE 12.1 Common Oral Reading Miscues and Their Possible Causes

Deficiencies	Possible Causes	Illustrative Corrective Measures[a]
Substitutions or insertions with no significant change in meaning	Depends too much on content. Too much oral reading. Eye travels so much faster than voice that substitutions of equivalent words or phrases are made.	Not so much oral reading. Ask questions which demand the exact words.
Omissions of portions	Visual defects. Nervousness. Irregular habits of perception. Timidity. Embarrassment. Excessive ambition. Inattention. Trying to read too fast.	Study before reading aloud. Do not stress speed. Relieve self-consciousness as far as possible. Flash card work. Written and printed directions to be carried out. Correct physical and emotional difficulties.
Inability to break up sentences into proper phrases	Defective beginning methods. Speech defects. Inability to recognize thought units. Short eyespan. Unable to profit by punctuation marks.	Overcome speech defects as far as possible. Flash card work. Written and printed directions to be carried out. Correct physical and emotional difficulties.
Wrong accents	Poor hearing. Bad teeth. Nervousness. Adenoids. Tonsils. Low mentality. Insufficient word drill.	Correct physical defects. Phonics drills, word drills. Drill in pronouncing words he has most difficulty with.
Mispronunciations	Impediment in speech. Eye defect. Defective beginning methods. Too little phonics. Carelessness. Overdependence on context clues. Material too difficult.	Word analysis. Phonics drill. Apply phonics and word-attack methods. Supply material which requires accurate recognition. Build up a large vocabulary.

[a]The corrective measures are only illustrative and not uniformally appropriate. Certain activities are useful only with specific deficiencies.

TABLE 12.1 Continued

Deficiencies	Possible Causes	Illustrative Corrective Measures[a]
Reading word by word	Short eye-voice span. Unable to get words through context. Material too difficult. Insufficient phrase drill. Too much oral reading. Defective beginning methods. Poor vision.	Much eyespan work. Less oral reading. Much easy, attractive reading material read under pressure. Correct visual defects.
Unable to answer fact questions based on material read	Failure to direct attention to meaning. Reading without a purpose. Material too difficult. Background inadequate for understanding what was read. Poor assignment.	Use material within pupil's ability to understand. Give questions for pupil to find answers. Have him read a paragraph and answer fact questions on it; gradually increase amount read before asking questions until whole selection can be read. Make good assignments which will prevent this deficiency. Let pupils know that questions about the selection will be asked.
Repetitions	Visual defects. Nervousness. Insufficient phrase drill. Material too difficult. Poor comprehension of what precedes. Poor reading vocabulary. Low mentality.	Correct physical defects. Eyespan work suited to ability of child. Much attractive reading material suited to ability of child. Develop good sight vocabulary.
Substitutions or insertions that change meaning of content	Limited vocabulary. Lack of thoughtful attitude while reading.	Adjust the material to pupil's vocabulary. Give material that demands accurate interpretation. Give printed and written directions to carry out.

TABLE 12.1 Continued

Deficiencies	Possible Causes	Illustrative Corrective Measures[a]
Depends upon others to pronounce words	Teachers and parents have pronounced words for him too often Has insufficient training.	Lead him to see his dependence on others. Create in him a desire to pronounce words independently. Give training in methods of word recognition.
Pointing with the finger	Materials too difficult. Used as a crutch to aid in holding place. Visual defects. Nervousness.	Lead pupil to see that it retards his speed. Set standard before reading that finger or other pointer will not be used. Read under time pressure. Use easy, attractive reading material.
Reversals in reading. Confuses "p" and "q". Reads "was" for "saw" and "cat" and and "dog" for "dog" and "cat"	Left eye dominance. Unable to attack new words. Improper initial instruction.	Use a pointer and run along the word or line from left to right. Trace the letters in the words which have been written in large letters.

scores are obtained for each performance on the *Gilmore:* (1) an accuracy score based on reading errors, (2) a comprehension score based on the five questions that accompany each passage, and (3) a reading rate based on the number of words read per minute. Norms are provided to facilitate conversion of errors in accuracy and comprehension into grade equivalents. Like the *Gray,* performance on the *Gilmore* is timed and the number of words read per minute computed. The manual gives some attention to uses of the test results and suggests that an in-depth analysis of an individual's performance be undertaken to ascertain patterns of errors and possible reading difficulties.

The informal reading inventory is essentially the same as the *Gray* and *Gilmore* tests except that it is usually developed by the classroom teacher and consequently lacks normative data. Passages selected from a basal series are especially good for the *IRI* (see Chapter 6). Not only are the passages graded in terms of reading difficulty when selected from basal texts but the reading material used for testing is similar or identical to the material used in the instructional program. Determining the child's best level for instructional placement becomes a straightforward matter when the actual reading text is used. Whichever book the child can comfortably handle becomes his instructional text. The teacher must create his own comprehension questions for an IRI. This is often an advantage, since various types of understanding can be tested in addition to the recall of facts and the literal comprehension normally assessed with standardized oral reading tests.

Deciding What Constitutes a Genuine Error

Some disagreement over what should be counted as an oral reading error is apparent in the directions for scoring the *Gray* and *Gilmore* tests. Table 12.2 contrasts the categories of errors for these two tests. General agreement is found for five types of errors: aid, omission, insertion, substitution, and repetition. Mispronunciation is an error according to either scheme; however, the *Gray* system differentiates between partial and gross mispronunciation. The *Gray* also calls an inversion a specific type of error; the *Gilmore* shows an inversion as a mispronunciation only. The *Gilmore* has special categories for disregard of punctuation and hesitation.

Disagreement over what constitutes an oral reading error are not limited to the *Gray* and *Gilmore* tests. Other oral reading tests such as subtests of the *Durrell Analysis of Reading Difficulty* (1955) and the Spache *Diagnostic Reading Scales* (1963) contain their own definitions of what constitutes an error. For example, the *Durrell* instructs the

---

TABLE 12.2   Comparison of Errors Recorded on *Gray* and *Gilmore* Tests

Errors Recorded in the *Gray Oral Reading Test*	Errors Recorded in the *Gilmore Oral Reading Test*
1. Aid	1. Word pronounced by examiner
2. Gross mispronunciation	2. Mispronunciation
3. Partial mispronunciation	3. Omission
4. Omission	4. Insertion
5. Insertion	5. Substitution
6. Substitution	6. Disregard of punctuation
7. Repetition	7. Repetition
8. Inversion	8. Hesitation

examiner to count as errors all words that are repeated. The *Spache* counts repetitions as errors only when two or more words are repeated. The *Durrell* counts any hesitation as an error; the *Spache* does not.

What order can be brought to this apparent confusion? When is an oral reading "error" really worth counting and when is it only a momentary stumble, a speech pattern, or some miscue related to the stress of reading orally? This question can best be answered in terms of the purpose for identifying miscues, namely, to provide a basis for improving reading performance. Consequently, an oral reading miscue that interferes with the message or indicates an inability to attack an unknown word should be counted as a genuine error. Thus omitting *not* from a sentence changes considerably the meaning of a message and constitutes a serious error. On the other hand, adding *and* to a sentence is unlikely to interfere with the message and can probably be ignored as an indicator of any serious reading problem.

Another example can be provided to demonstrate a difficulty with word attack. The word *protest* in the following sentence might easily be misread *protect:* "The students formed a circle around the statue to protest its dedication." The meaning of the message is certainly altered by substituting *protect* for *protest*; however, the two words can easily be confused if the context of a sentence does not make one obviously incorrect (as in the above example, neither is obviously incorrect). A serious word-attack problem would be indicated if a student read the word *protest* as *drive.* Here the initial consonant is completely wrong; the word does not fit into the context of the sentence, and the child is evidently guessing blindly at an unknown word. Both examples given here would be regarded as errors serious enough to be recorded. One is obviously more serious for indicating a fundamental reading problem.

This rather flexible approach to diagnosing oral reading errors is consistent with the recommendations of Harris (1961), who states:

> The important questions to answer are: 1. To what extent, and how successfully, does the child make use of the context? 2. How does he attempt to attack new words, and with what degree of success can he employ various methods of attack? And 3. What specific kinds of errors does he make that may require specific remedial attention? Finding the answers to these questions is not an automatic result of counting different kinds of errors, but involves an attempt to understand what the child is trying to do as he reads, as well as noting what he does. It is a qualitative rather than a quantitative method of analysis that is most helpful.*

Kenneth S. Goodman (1969) of Wayne State University has

---

*Harris, Albert J., *How to Increase Reading Ability* (New York: Longsman, 1961), p. 203.

undertaken a more detailed analysis of oral reading miscues. Goodman is interested in the nature of unexpected responses in oral
reading from a psycholinguistic perspective. Like Harris, his view is
based on the idea that all miscues are not of equal importance. In fact,
some miscues may provide positive proof of a child's reading skill. For
example, some substitutions may fit into the syntax of a sentence and
not affect meaning. Miscues of this type can indicate that the child is
making heavy use of context and comprehending the message as he
reads. Additional evidence to support this view is obtained when other
substitutions that alter the meaning of a sentence, or fail to fit into the
syntax of the sentence, are corrected by the child. Goodman's approach (Goodman, 1969) is yet in the developmental stages and
appears at this time to be too time consuming for regular classroom
use, but promises to place oral reading miscues into clearer perspective once it is complete.

Naturally the norms and grade equivalents accompanying any
commercial test cannot be used when a revised scoring procedure of
the type Harris and Goodman recommend is used. When the goal is
diagnosis of a child's specific reading problems grade scores are relatively unimportant anyhow. The identification of patterns of errors
on a test reveals much more insofar as remedial instruction is concerned than arbitrary comparisons with the performance of the
youngsters in the norming population.

A special word is needed concerning the assessment of oral reading miscues of children with regional or subcultural dialects. Some
teachers unwittingly record and score as reading errors pronunciations that "sound wrong" to them. For example, *that* pronounced *dat*
is sometimes scored as a mispronunciation. In view of the earlier
recommendation concerning what to regard as a genuine reading
error, pronunciations learned in a particular region of the country or
in a particular cultural group should not be regarded as reading
errors.

The translation of graphic symbols into their oral counterpart
depends largely on the reader's background of experience and resulting language patterns. For example, Kasdon (1968) reports that
Negro subjects in a study of oral reading consistently read *was* for
were and sometimes pronounced *with* as *wif*. Latin Americans frequently substituted "b" for "p" as in *bet* for *pet*, "v" for "b", as in *vril-
liant* for *brilliant*. There can be no doubt that these subjects were reading, if reading is defined as gaining meaning from the printed page.
Regarding the above "mispronunciations" as *reading errors* is indefensible.

The question as to which language pattern is "correct" is currently undergoing a needed reappraisal. In many ways some southern

Negro youths learn standard English much as a Mexican or French child learns English — as a second language. A more complete discussion of this issue is left to language arts textbooks. It is important to remember that oral reading miscues must be identified and interpreted in the light of peculiar speech patterns that may appear at first glance to be mispronunciations.

Scoring Systems for Oral Reading Tests

No two oral reading tests have exactly the same system for recording errors. Indeed, we have seen that few oral reading tests are even in agreement on what constitutes an error. Let us now consider the matter of a scoring system.

The *Gray* test requires that a line be drawn under any word not read by the child within ten seconds; the examiner then provides the word. The *Gilmore* requires that a check be made above a word not recognized by the child within five seconds and that two checks be made if the examiner then provides the word after five more seconds. Is one system better than the other? Probably not. What is important is that a scoring system be simple. It must be easily memorized and quickly used. Elaborate marks cannot be made by a teacher as the child races along a line of print. Consequently, checks, circles, underlining, and similar marks are best. We recommend the following system for use with an IRI and any commercial test that lends itself to this scheme:

Reversal	(saw) ✓
Hesitation (prolonged)	John ꞌgalloped. . .
Omission	He had written, (but) I ignored him.
Addition	He ^*had* wrote to Henry.
Substitution or mispronunciation	She was a ~~lovely~~ *pretty* girl.
Awkward phrasing	I saw/ a cat in/ the window.
Word supplied	Give me a field of <u>daffodils</u> for bed.

Note what word-attack skills the child tries to use when faced with an unfamiliar word.

The use of this scoring system is demonstrated below. No serious reading difficulties are evident in this sample. In two instances (*quickly* and *jockey*) the reader did not attempt to pronounce a word. Other words with the same beginning consonants might be presented to this child to determine whether he is able to associate any sound with these symbols.

ORAL READING SAMPLE

The bay horse moved <u>quickly</u> to the inside of the track. Mud flew

up from his ˅hooves as he hit the soft, wet ground. ~~Several~~ *Some* other horses

raced alongside the big bay∧*horse* forcing him to run near the rail. Slowly the

<u>jockey</u> moved his horse away from the soft ground (and) back to the firm

~~part~~ *place* of the race track.

As the/crowd cheered the/bay caught and passed the/leaders.

Ahead the finish line waited.˅Victory looked certain.

CAUTIONS CONCERNING ORAL READING

In addition to the cautions sprinkled throughout previous sections, several general comments concerning the limitations of oral reading are in order.

First, oral reading tends to be a highly emotional experience for some youngsters. All of us have experienced stagefright to some degree at one time or another. The prospect of standing before a group as a performer is forbidding to many children, particularly those who have difficulty with reading. It is important that an atmosphere of support and acceptance be created for oral reading activities. A healthy attitude toward improvement is necessary, but not to the extent that mistakes are feared. The importance of preparation for oral reading by the child is underscored. Furthermore, any words not recognized immediately should be supplied by the teacher when a child is reading aloud to an audience.

Among beginning readers oral reading undoubtedly encourages vocalization, or the tendency to mouth words during silent reading. Undue stress on oral reading may encourage vocalization to continue beyond the point where it is helpful or necessary. This habit is common and not particularly alarming among beginning readers and perhaps even into grade two for some youngsters. However, vocalizing slows down the mature reader and probably interferes with comprehension. Most children outgrow vocalization in a natural transition from the hesitant word-by-word reading of the beginner to the rapid phrase-by-phrase reading of the maturing child. An overemphasis on oral reading may interfere with this transition.

Oral reading is also limited by the fact that only one child can be engaged in reading at a time. Small groups can offset this limitation to a degree; nonetheless, it should be remembered that silent reading permits each child to participate and therefore is preferable to oral reading for most activities.

Finally, oral reading is more difficult than silent reading. All silent reading skills are used during oral reading plus the skills necessary for effective speech. Thus the reader must concentrate on pronouncing each word in addition to recognizing it. If comprehending a message is the purpose of reading, it follows that saying the words aloud is unnecessary except when it aids the reader or a listener to understand. The point is simply that unless a good reason exists for reading aloud, silent reading is easier and therefore preferable for most children.

ORAL READING BY THE TEACHER

As a starting point, we make the blanket recommendation that every teacher should read orally to his students each day of the school year. While this goal may be difficult to achieve during some extremely busy periods such as parent-teacher conference time or when the annual music festival is being prepared, the value and importance of daily oral reading by the teacher are undiminished.

Oral reading by the teacher contributes in many ways to an effective reading program. First, it forms an integral part of the total literature appreciation program. Huck and Kuhn (1968) state that some children's literature is best discovered by a child in the company of an adult. So-called children's classics in particular are often beyond the grasp of a child reading individually. The vocabulary and concepts may be tough going, especially for children with reading difficulties; but more important, the characters, theme, setting, and even the plot are often more meaningful when shared with an adult. Discussion centering about various aspects of a story can increase the child's understanding and appreciation of subtleties he might otherwise miss.

Oral reading by the teacher need not be limited to the classics. In fact, a wide selection of books should be presented to broaden the reading interests of children and build their background in unfamiliar areas. In other words, the teacher can actually stimulate children's reading by the type and breadth of reading he shares. Children frequently read silently a book their teacher has shared, or find another book by the same author. This is another excellent reason for oral reading by the teacher.

Oral reading by the teacher may stimulate the child's language development. His vocabulary is expanded and enriched through hearing the use various authors make of words. Through encountering words in various contexts the child gains a broader understanding of their meanings. Moreover, the polished language found in many published stories provides a good model for the child to emulate in both his oral and written communication. Jointly hearing a story is an excellent stimulus to children's language development. Group discussions can center on characters and events met through this approach.

The opportunity to develop effective listening skills is provided by oral reading, particularly when the teacher chooses and presents the selection. With some thought and planning the teacher can select an appropriate book and prepare his class to listen for any number of specific purposes. For example, a story involving special attention to sequence of events might be read to provide practice in this listening skill. Or the use of descriptive phrases might be given special emphasis in a story containing many such passages. General ability in attending to the spoken word is encouraged by any oral reading; however, lessons prepared with special attention to fostering specific listening skills are more likely to yield results.

Oral reading by the teacher can also be an effective tool for building rapport with a group of children. The act of sharing a pleasant experience each day is bound to bring teacher and student closer together. Furthermore, the teacher can express his personal likes and dislikes in a very human way while sharing a story aloud. The understanding that a teacher is human often comes hard to children; sharing a story provides some insight for youngsters along this line.

Oral reading can be used as a means for settling a group or breaking the routine of a school day. Many teachers find that immediately after physical education or lunch is a good time to read orally from the standpoint of classroom management. The quieting effect of listening to a story is a technique teachers can substitute for more punitive approaches. After an intensive period of concentration on mathematics or reading, a few minutes of relaxation while listening to the teacher read aloud will make the transition to another subject less tedious for the child.

Not to be overlooked is the bibliotherapeutic value of teacher oral reading. Books with a special theme can be selected to suit the needs of a group or the events of the day. *Ladycake Farm* (Hunt, 1952), a story of racial prejudice, may provide the opportunity for some youngsters to face individually their personal biases. Or group discussions can be stimulated where exchange of ideas encourages reflection and self-analysis.

The skill of many teachers at oral reading can serve as an excellent model for their students to emulate. The effectiveness of proper phrasing, clear articulation and enunciation, and dramatic interpretation are very apparent to children when demonstrated by their teacher. Special attention can be called to these factors and the students helped to concentrate on each element in turn while the teacher reads orally.

Since not all teachers are effective oral readers, and because of the need for a variety of models, records and tapes of others reading aloud may be used. Leonard Bernstein sharing *Peter and the Wolf* with your students can be a valuable listening experience. Boys especially will benefit from the opportunity to hear male voices reading aloud.

SUMMARY

Oral reading appears to be a subject about which there is general accord among reading experts. Some skill in reading aloud is necessary to meet the demands of everyday life. Because of its rather infrequent use, however, oral reading is second in importance to silent reading. Various historical reasons for special emphasis on oral reading are no longer valid. Nevertheless, misuse of oral reading is still common in many elementary school classrooms today.

Two types of oral reading by the child are discussed in this chapter, audience oral reading and oral reading for diagnosis. Audience oral reading makes the reader a source of information; his audience must listen in order to grasp the message. Good speech habits are necessary for effective audience oral reading; those variables important to good speech are also important to good audience oral reading.

Oral reading for diagnosis provides the teacher with an opportunity to discover possible reading difficulties. The alert teacher can employ oral reading to determine comprehension problems during instructional sessions. Individual conferences can be held to administer special oral reading tests. Patterns of errors made by the child are helpful to the teacher in locating individual needs. Caution must be used in deciding what constitutes a genuine oral reading error. Only miscues that indicate a word-attack difficulty or seem to impede comprehension are genuine errors.

Oral reading by the teacher is an excellent practice and should be a frequent occurrence. Children can be exposed to a broad range of excellent literature with this technique. The model provided by a good oral reader is helpful in improving the child's performance.

TERMS

aid	choral reading
substitution	informal reading inventory
"barber-shop" reading	*Gray Oral Reading Test*
audience oral reading	*Gilmore Oral Reading Test*

Chapter 13

Selecting Books

Most people who decide to pursue a teaching career have been fairly successful in their school experiences. They usually associate pleasure with school and wish to continue that happy relation by becoming a teacher. Not too surprisingly, such people also are often avid readers. They probably found in their youth that learning to read was an interesting challenge they could meet successfully.

You probably fit this description to some degree. Given your choice, you would no doubt spend more time reading for pleasure than your busy college schedule permits. Reading is an enjoyable as well as functional skill for you.

Not all youngsters are so inclined toward reading, however. Reading is a last choice as a recreational activity for some children. As a teacher you must try to "turn on" these alienated and uninterested children. Your own experience tells you that great joy can be found between the covers of a book. Your commitment is to interest every child in reading. Enthusiasm is essential, but in and of itself inadequate for the job. This chapter provides additional help as you find answers to these questions:

What is known about children's reading interests at different age levels?

Should book reports be required?

What can the teacher do to encourage the habit of reading?

How can parents encourage their child to read?

Why do some teachers have a reading corner in their classrooms?

How can a child who refuses to read be encouraged to try a book?

Is it wise to teach the principles of literary analysis to elementary school children?

Should children be expected to read the classics?

The teaching of reading in our schools focuses primarily on the development of basic reading skills. The importance of a large sight vocabulary and effective word-recognition techniques is usually understood by teachers and emphasized by the various instructional systems. Comprehension is central to the purpose of reading and thus also receives a great deal of attention. Yet too often in an effort to teach these fundamentals of reading another requirement is overlooked or given only passing attention. This essential component is a genuine *interest in reading*—a lifelong commitment to acquiring information and enjoyment through the act of reading.

There is little point in teaching children to read if this skill is not used in later life. Recent studies indicate that the average adult in the United States does not read as much as a single book in the course of a year (Hackett, 1967). Few educators, however, would seriously suggest that we stop teaching reading because of such findings. Rather, such statistics demonstrate that greater emphasis must be placed on the use of reading in the daily lives of students. Hopefully students who learn the joy and value of habitual reading will carry a disposition to read into their adult years.

The first major section of this chapter discusses the home as the origin of interest in reading and describes what the parent can do to encourage his child to read. Next, the role of the school in developing reading interests is considered, with special attention being given to the importance of a classroom atmosphere that encourages reading. Some research on children's interests is reviewed and implications for classroom instruction presented. Several means available to the teacher for assessing children's interests are also described. The second major section of the chapter discusses techniques for helping children develop personal standards to guide their selection of books. Special attention is given in this section to book reports and children's classics.

CREATING AN INTEREST IN READING

Interest in reading does not develop in a vacuum but is instead founded on personal interests. For example, the boy who enjoys collecting insects will probably enjoy a good book on the same topic. A girl who loves and cares for a pet poodle will surely have a special interest in a book about grooming poodles for show. On the other hand, it may be much more difficult to interest a child in a book who has few personal belongings, hobbies, or special interests. The first step in creating reading interests is therefore to stimulate the child with life and the world around him. The home is a potent factor in this process, indeed, a factor that can predispose the child negatively or positively in his attitude toward reading.

The Home: Origin of Interest in Reading

Most children enter school with a broad variety of interests born of rich experiences during their earlier years. Typically they have enjoyed a circus and are looking forward to additional trips to the zoo. Their backgrounds may include a vacation touring Disneyland or exploring the wonders of Mammoth Cave. The vocabulary and concepts gained from such experiences are fundamental to readiness for learning to read (see Chapter 7). Perhaps even more important, however, is the desire created by these experiences to read about other vacation spots. Growth in reading interests is almost spontaneous with children of this sort.

Furthermore, the parents of children with a wide variety of background experiences are frequently anxious for their youngsters to learn to read. Usually there are many books in their homes—books owned by the child and shared frequently with his parents. The parents themselves probably read occasionally. The child often sees his father turn to the evening newspaper before dinner, read a book occasionally, and refer to the atlas when seeking information.

Reading is viewed as a desirable tool by the youngster from a background as rich as the one just described. Significant people in his life read; he associates enjoyment with books. An interest in reading is as natural to this child as watching television.

The recollections of an elderly well-read friend of the authors are helpful in describing the role of the home:

> My early days at home are a warm memory to me. I can remember well the winter evenings when the wind would tug at our roof and shutters while newly fallen snow drifted against the tool shed and animal shelters. My mother would wrap an afghan around her shoulders and invite me to squeeze with her into a big stuffed chair near the Ben Franklin stove. From that port we ventured off together on many journeys. We hunted with our young comrade in Prokofieff's tale of *Peter and the Wolf*, drifted over sleepy villages far below with *Peter Pan*, and scratched for our existence alongside *Robinson Crusoe*.
>
> Often in the spring of the year I would tag along with my father in the evening as he took our small herd of cows out to pasture. We shared the sight of geese heading north and bluebirds building their nest in our orchard. Later we might hunt in the *Audubon Handbook* for the name of a new bird we saw perched near the creek. Sometimes I sat on his lap listening to the late news broadcast wondering at how he could know so much about world events. He listened carefully when I ventured a comment and sometimes helped me look at another point of view.
>
> On Friday evenings we went to town for shopping and visiting. The county library stayed open until 8:00 p.m. and I worried

every week that we would be too late to get in. Somehow we always made it in time. I was permitted to search for new treasures while my parents completed their errands.

Grandpa Knippling was the best storyteller who ever lived, it seemed to me in those days. He always claimed to be fresh out of new stories, but remembered one when I begged him. I even loved to hear the same stories again and again. Later in life I discovered in books tales like those my grandpa told. It was like visiting an old friend to read them, but not quite the same as hanging on every word, hoping Grandpa would not run out of chewing tobacco and have to stop in the middle of an old favorite.

Those early days had a great deal to do with my fondness for literature and reading.

The rich background enjoyed by this individual was a significant factor in building his interest in reading. Tody the opportunities for extending a child's horizons are even greater.

The experiences that sensitize a child to his surroundings are certainly not limited to middle class homes. (Indeed, in some middle class homes parents are so involved with their own pursuits that their child is as deprived of enriching experiences as the child from a poverty-stricken home.) Many children from working class homes enjoy highly desirable experiences. A trip to the Grand Canyon may be impossible for such children, but the opportunity to see and experience the wonder of a constantly expanding world can be theirs. A walk around the block or through the park with a parent who explains, discusses, and listens can serve the same purpose as a trip to a distant place. Even a poor father can take his child to the public library and share a book they select and borrow. Without the attitude toward reading such experiences provide the child enters school with a severe handicap. Typically five or six years of influence by the home have transpired before the youngster enters school. The home is the child's first and most powerful influence with regard to creating an interest in reading.

Recently the importance of early childhood experiences as a prerequisite to success in school has been underscored by programs such as Headstart. Deprived children only three and four years of age are placed in an environment designed to provide the stimulation often lacking in their own homes. Teachers and trained parents read to these youngsters, listen to their ideas, teach them simple skills and concepts learned at home by more fortunate children, and generally enrich their backgrounds. Whether such programs are a satisfactory substitute for a rich home environment is difficult to determine, but certainly they are a desirable alternative to no stimulation at all. The teacher who tells his class a story or provides a field trip experience is

providing valuable experiences insofar as reading interests are concerned. While each child reacts individually to specific enrichment
experiences, a variety of activities offers something to spark the
interest of every child. One mechanically minded boy may be en-
thralled by a visit to the fire station where shiny trucks with chromed
engines wait. How eagerly he will listen to the story of *Engine No. 9*
(Hurd, 1961). Later, his own maturing reading skill can open many
paths to enjoyment and information, paths that might not beckon to
a youngster who regards reading and life in general as a dreary
imposition. A little girl may be fascinated by a film about raising
horses in Kentucky. Through such techniques as discussions of horses
and looking at picture books such a girl can develop an interest that
ultimately leads to the writings of Marguerite Henry. The joy of
knowing literature of this quality might mean for her the difference
between understanding love for an animal and never experiencing
such feelings.

What the Parent Can Do

Although this text is not written primarily for the lay public and
therefore is not likely to be read by many parents, a program for
building a powerful home environment for reading will be described
for two reasons: First, many teachers are parents and eager to know
what steps they should take to help their own child succeed in school.
Second, and more important, teachers often have the opportunity to
influence what goes on in the homes of their students. Many parents
would gladly help their youngster prepare for school if they only
knew how. The teacher can be a good consultant in this regard.

Books are an individual matter, and the parent who wishes to
encourage his child to read should know something about them
before he begins. Learning about books is not something that can be
done overnight. Even before the child is born the parent can begin to
explore what is available. A local bookstore or library is the logical
place to start.

In deciding what kind of book to choose, the parent should keep
several points in mind. First, the child can be read to long before he
can talk. Nursery rhymes and other short rhythmic pieces will be
enjoyed by the child who understands only the swing of the words and
the beat of the language. Second, the parent should select children's
books that he himself enjoys. The pleasure conveyed by the adult's
voice is an important factor in determining the child's response. Even
the best attempt at sharing a selection not enjoyed by the oral reader
is not likely to be successful.

The child's first books should be attractive ones that contain
accurate and colorful pictures. Children usually prefer uncluttered

drawings that highlight familiar objects such as animals and activities that they themselves enjoy. Cloth books that can be handled by the child can be an excellent investment, since small, uncoordinated hands are not likely to tear them. It is not possible or desirable to give a comprehensive list of recommended books, since personal taste should dictate actual choice. However, the following titles may serve as a point of departure:

AUTHOR	TITLE
Leslie Brooke	*Ring o' Roses*
Beatrix Potter	*The Tale of Peter Rabbit*
Ezra Jack Keats	*A Snowy Day*
Aileen Fisher	*In the Middle of the Night*
Robert McCloskey	*Make Way for Ducklings*
Wanda Gag	*Millions of Cats*

Also, *A Parents' Guide to Children's Reading* by Nancy Larrick (1964) is an excellent reference.

The parent should also know something about his child's interests. Learning about a child's interest is a matter of carefully observing his reaction to stories that are read and his choice of play activities. An appreciative response to a rhythmic poem such as "There Was a Crooked Man" calls for more of the same. Naturally, a solid diet of this fare is undesirable, but the child's favorable reactions provide a clue for future selections. Likewise, his attachment to stuffed animals may suggest stories that contain such characters.

As the young child becomes acquainted with picture books his taste in books and in other things will develop. His personal likes and dislikes will become evident. Opportunities for familiarity with a broad variety of books and topics are necessary to expand the child's horizons. However, the alert parent will not attempt to force the classics or other topics on the child if he shows a dislike for them. As a general rule, it is advisable to stop reading to a child when his attention or interest lags.

It is most important that books be available for the child to look at and "read" on his own. If possible, he should have personal copies of his favorite books. While he must be taught to treat books with care and respect, his fear of damaging books should not interfere with his desire to handle them. It seems better to risk a torn page than to keep books in perfect condition on a shelf inaccessible to the child.

Children who grow to school age in an atmosphere where books are a respected and familiar commodity usually have an early interest in reading. Most children even learn to read a few isolated words such as *milk* or *stop* before entering school, and have the necessary attitude and readiness to conquer the demands of reading in first grade. With this background, a few youngsters, such as those described by Durkin (1966), go far beyond acquiring a few sight words to the point of actually reading second or third grade material before they enter school. The rich home environment facilitates early reading when the child is ready to do so. Most children will not and should not be expected to read before entering school. The home that creates an interest in reading and a familiarity with books has indeed done its job well.

The Role of the School

Apparently children enter school with a broad range of home backgrounds. They include the fortunate youngster who has his own books, parents who read to him, and a wealth of enriching experiences, as well as the child who has never seen anyone read a book for enjoyment. The classroom teacher has responsibility for capturing and stimulating the interest of children in reading regardless of their home environment. In all instances experiences similar to those provided in a rich home environment are useful in school as well. Books can be shared, trips taken, discussions held, games played, poetry recited, and numerous other enrichment activities undertaken.

The same experiences, however, will not be appropriate for all children in a classroom. Thus differentiation of instruction to meet individual needs must begin immediately in the kindergarten and first grade. The deprived child who lacks even fundamental knowledge about books, their use, and the wonder they can provide requires a program of experiences designed to build the background a more fortunate child receives at home. The youngster who owns a personal library and already reads a few isolated words may rebel at participating in some of the same activities. His interest in reading can easily be dampened by too much repetition of the preschool activities shared with his parents. He is ready for new experiences that take him from his own level and broaden his world.

Some experiences are worth repeating, however. Most children desire and enjoy the retelling of a favorite story or hearing a familiar book read time and time again. There is little danger of destroying interest in reading under these circumstances. In fact, good literature wears especially well. However, there is a real possibility that exposure to certain picture books loved in the past but now regarded disdainfully as "baby books" by the mature child will turn him away from reading. The deprived youngster undoubtedly requires exposure to such material; therefore, the solution lies in differentiated instruction. While some children are sharing with their teacher a picture book such as *An ABC Book* by C. B. Falls, those with a fuller background can independently read a book more suitable to their own level.

In one case recently called to our attention the importance of differentiated instruction was reinforced. A very mature first grade boy read only two pages of a linguistically based primer, "Nan can fan Dan. Can Dan fan Nan? Dan can fan Nan," before indicating that he was bored with the book. A child less ready than he for more meaningful material might not find the nonsensical story so uninteresting. In fact, earlier in his young life this same first grade boy might have found the story about Dan and Nan very engrossing. To keep all children interested in reading the teacher must strive to provide individualized experiences geared to their needs.

This is not to say that whole-class activities that benefit each member of the group are not possible. Indeed, listening to the teacher read *The Biggest Bear* by Lynd Ward (1952) is an experience all the children in any primary class could share. Each child brings his own background to this activity and reaps personal benefit from participating. However, activities related to a story must take into account the range of backgrounds represented in a group. For example, in a discussion the teacher cannot assume that every child has been to a zoo or museum and actually seen a bear. A comment about *The Biggest Bear* that assumed such knowledge would only confuse some children. Some adjustment must be made for the range of the children's backgrounds. The rich experiences of some youngsters may be used to increase the understanding of others. Johnny, who has seen and touched a bear, can share his experience with the class. Johnny benefits from his opportunity to share and others learn from his description and personal reaction.

A field trip is another example of a whole-class activity that can mutually benefit each child by broadening his background. Suppose a class of second graders visits a local construction site. Juan may never have seen large machines such as a bulldozer and steam shovels at work. The opportunity to watch and hear their operation may arouse his interest in learning more about them. A book, carefully chosen by the teacher, or found by Juan with the teacher's guidance, such as *Mike Mulligan and His Steam Shovel* (Burton, 1939), might be the key to a new world. Another boy in the same class may be very familiar with construction machinery, but be intrigued by the scientific principles that enable a steam shovel to lift heavy loads. Again, a book on simple machines may be found, or the opportunity provided to read the directions in order to experiment with an erector set. In each case, the broadening experience of taking a field trip is valuable for the child. The follow-up to such a trip is even more valuable from the standpoint of stimulating reading interests. Only an alert teacher can know the distinct needs of his students and adjust accordingly.

The Classroom Atmosphere

Just as the parent's attitude toward reading is instrumental in molding the child's disposition toward reading, the teacher's attitude is also a significant factor. The child tends to imitate the attitude he perceives important adults displaying toward reading. Furthermore, the school environment, like the home environment, is a direct outgrowth of the adult's attitude. The parent who honors reading will buy and personally use books; the teacher likewise must procure, use, and respect books if his example is to be positive. Similarly, the parent who wishes to encourage reading will make books available for the child, as will the interested teacher. Finally, both the parent and teacher must take time to share books firsthand with the child. A parent can work one to one; the teacher usually must resort to sharing with a group. In short, the classroom environment must make it *easy* to read and the classroom atmosphere must make it *important* to read.

Making Books Available

It is a well-known fact that people tend to do what is convenient. The nearest market is usually the one we shop at; the closest gasoline station gets our business (provided we have their credit card — another convenience factor). The same is true of reading. People are more likely to read if it is convenient to do so. A book must be close at hand. This accounts in part for the popularity of paperback books that are displayed conveniently in nearly every drugstore and supermarket.

Burger, Cohen, and Bisgaler (1956) succeeded in tripling the amount of reading done voluntarily by a large sample of urban children. Their approach was simply one of making books available. Books were placed in classrooms, and during reading instruction children were encouraged to read them outside of school. A follow-up check noted that a year later the children were still reading voluntarily.

In a recent investigation Bissett (1969) worked with a suburban sample of fifth grade youngsters who were reading on the average only one half a book a week despite numerous advantages such as libraries, well-trained teachers, librarians, and reading specialists. Interesting books were added to the classrooms; the number of books voluntarily read increased by 50 percent. A program of stimulating reading through recommendations by teachers and peers was then instituted and the number of books read was tripled.

The habit of reading is founded in large part on simply that — reading. The availability of books is crucial in determining whether the habit will ever be acquired. An excellent means for making books available is by developing a reading corner in the classroom.

The Reading Corner

The reading corner is a place in the classroom where books and other reading materials are conveniently and attractively displayed for children's use. Ideally, the reading corner should be in a quiet and private location so that youngsters can enjoy reading uninterrupted by regular classroom activities. Classroom procedures should be instituted that encourage children to freely visit the reading corner whenever their time permits.

The selection of a suitable location for building a classroom reading corner involves first finding a quiet, relatively isolated area. Often a corner of the room provides these requirements. Low room dividers, shelves, or even tables may be used to shape the physical environment of the reading corner, helping to establish an atmosphere of privacy for the young readers. A good light source is an equally important consideration. The area may be made more inviting with plants, colorful book jackets, displayed books, and child-sized chairs. Some teachers prefer a rug or mats so that the children may sit on the floor as they read. Books on many levels of difficulty and covering a wide range of subjects should be made available. Children with free time or those pursuing special interests are then able to find books expressly for their needs. Class projects and reference work will be aided by a well-planned reading corner. Children who have had a part in the planning will be eager to add their own stories and poems to class collections which can be shared, enjoyed, and reread as part of the classroom library.

The children can adapt and employ a simplified cataloguing system for their books and stories. Children who finish a book can complete a card reporting the title and author, adding a short annotation and a recommendation for others. If books are brought from home, they may be catalogued also, perhaps including the owner's name.

Dioramas, posters, and attractive book displays should be a part of the reading corner. They can be frequently changed to reflect current units and incidental occurrences which have influenced class interests. The reading corner can contain filmstrips and a filmstrip previewer, a tape recorder and headphone set, a boxed reading laboratory, and literally dozens of other items. The creative teacher will think of many ways to make reading enjoyable and will use the reading corner as a marketplace of enticing activities.

Miss Dale, a second grade teacher, found a likely place for her reading corner directly beneath the windows in the back of her classroom. With low dividers, she separated the area from the rest of the room. Because no bulletin board was available in the reading corner, she fastened brightly colored corrugated cardboard to the wall and

FIGURE 13-1   Reading Corner.

Although he has trouble with classroom reading materials, this boy is fascinated by Hot Rod. *The teacher capitalized on this interest in cars by including many books and magazines on the subject in the reading corner. (Photo by Carl B. Smith)*

developed the first display: "Look, New Books!"—a collection of book jackets. The school librarian helped her choose a general selection of books geared for the interests and reading levels of second graders at the beginning of the school year.

Miss Dale felt that later more specific selections could be included and that her children could add and request books for their class library. She also planned to use the public library as a resource, especially for supplementary and enrichment materials for classroom units.

One child brought a rug from home for the corner and Miss Dale added two small rocking chairs and a small table. The children placed plants on the window ledge and began to take responsibility for the display board. Soon books were being brought from home to be shared in the free reading time. A shoe box covered with adhesive-backed paper became their card catalog. The children took turns being librarian.

Miss Dale made a "look it up" game for the corner as the year progressed. Since some of her second graders were beginning to use encyclopedias in conjunction with a social studies unit developed around "Our Country," she supplemented the activity with a question box. Cards drawn from the box by the children contained one question which directed them to a specific volume and page in the encyclopedia: What man became our sixteenth president after losing a race for senator? Look in "L," page 1435.

The children who found the answer wrote it on a separate paper to be checked by Miss Dale. Later, this activity was changed to reflect the growing independence of the children. Only the volume was given.

All through the year the reading nook was a source of pleasure, information, and a storehouse for creative writing. Miss Dale's children learned to use it efficiently and with enjoyment.

Making Reading Important

Too often reading for recreation is permitted in the classroom only "after all other work is done." This unfortunate policy discourages recreational reading by making it the last thing to be done — almost a last resort. Furthermore, this policy is shortsighted, since other work is often hurriedly and poorly done when the requirement is made that all else comes first.

There must be regular and lengthy opportunities to read for enjoyment *in the classroom*. It seems incongruous to urge children to read, or to make books readily available, and then not treat recreational reading as an activity worthy of valuable class time. As was stated earlier, an excellent grasp of reading skills is nearly worthless unless they are *used* by the reader. Therefore, it seems appropriate that some class instructional time also be devoted to recreational reading (a better label might be *practice reading*).

The authors recommend that at least once a week children be given the equivalent of a full reading period for recreational reading (not necessarily in one sitting). A logical time for providing some of this allotted time is immediately after the class has returned from the school library. Most elementary schools with a library arrange a schedule that reserves the facilities for each classroom for a half hour or so once a week. Book selections are made by the children during the time spent in the library and some skill instruction may be provided by the teacher or librarian. Upon returning to the classroom, interest in a new book just selected should be at its highest. What better time to provide twenty or thirty minutes of free reading? This brief period of time permits the child to get a good start on his new book and thus increases the probability that it will be read in its entirety.

As suggested in Chapter 5, recreational reading is an excellent independent activity for children not working directly under the supervision of the teacher during reading period. Several times a week each reading group can be given a fifteen or twenty minute respite from workbooks and other written exercises to enjoy the use of their growing skill through recreational reading.

Another activity that emphasizes the importance of reading is oral reading by the teacher. At opportune moments during the day the teacher can share a poem with the class or continue a story from the point where reading ended last time (see Chapter 12). The enjoyment evidenced by an enthusiastic teacher and the personal satisfaction gained by each child when a selection is shared orally emphasizes the contribution reading can make to one's well-being.

What Is Known about Children's Interests

The experience of growing up in the United States (or any other country, for that matter) teaches us that our society has certain expectations for us at specific stages of our lives. What we can do at three years of age (take something from a neighbor, for example) is severely punished at fifteen years of age. What a girl can do at seven years of age (play with a doll, for example) is regarded as strange behavior for a boy. Sociologists label this shaping of behavior *socialization*.

The socialization of children begins early and continues throughout their lifetimes. Just how early social pressures begin to shape the expressed interests of children was demonstrated in a recent investigation by Harris (1967). First grade children from low socioeconomic schools were asked to select illustrations of objects they liked. A booklet of illustrations was presented to the subjects and they were directed to indicate objects they liked best. Sharp differences between the choices of boys and girls were observed for 30 of the 42 objects illustrated. Six objects (soldier, football, rocket, spaceman, pistol, and airplane) were chosen by over 80 percent of the boys and less than 15 percent of the girls. Nine objects (fairy, purse, carriage, baby, dress, doll, playhouse, tea set, and ballerina) were chosen by over 80 percent of the girls and less than 22 percent of the boys. Only four objects (butterfly, crayons, kitten, and puppy) were chosen by over 60 percent of both sexes. A replication of this study with suburban first grade children found much the same separation of expressed interests for boys and girls (Braun, 1969).

King (1967) summarized the present state of knowledge on children's interests. She concluded that reading interests change as new personal interests develop. A child's need for information does not necessarily influence his reading interests. Audiovisual aids such as television and movies seem to play an important role in changing reading interests. Primary grade children prefer fairy tales, realistic stories based on everyday activities, and animal stories. Intermediate grade children prefer mystery, adventure, animal stories, family life stories, biographies, sports, science, and social studies. She also observed that children now appear to be maturing faster in their reading interests.

King also found that until age nine few sex differences in reading interest appear between boys and girls. After age eight boys read more nonfiction than girls; girls read more poetry; boys prefer stories of science, invention, and vigorous action; girls prefer stories of home and school life, sentimentalized fiction, and fairy tales; girls will read a book considered to be of interest to boys, but the reverse is seldom true. She also concluded that the reading interests of children who are higher in intelligence mature faster than those of lower intelligence.

Jefferson (1958) also found a sharp difference between the reading interests of intermediate grade boys and girls. Boys prefer stories about war, sports, science, invention, and exploration. Girls prefer stories of love and romance, feminine activities, school adventure, child life in other lands, and magic and fantasy. Some overlap in interest was found for stories about humor and whimsy, self-improvement, realistic animals, and money making.

Wolfson (1960) found the top six categories of interest among intermediate grade children. Boys chose adventure, sports, physical science, machines and applied science, social studies, and fantasy. Girls chose fantasy, personal problems, social studies, sports, adventure, family life, and children.

Studies by Taylor (1957), Rudman (1955), and Butler (1964) are largely in support of the findings reported above. Huus (1963) summarized the research on children's preferences with regard to age and sex as follows:

> Interests of children vary according to age and grade level.
>
> Few differences between the interests of boys and girls are apparent before age nine.
>
> Notable difference in the interest of boys and girls appear between ages ten and thirteen.
>
> Girls read more than boys, but boys have a wider interest range and read a greater variety.
>
> Girls show an earlier interest in adult fiction of a romantic type than do boys.
>
> Boys like chiefly adventure and girls like fiction, but mystery stories appeal to both.
>
> Boys seldom show preference for "girls'" books, but girls will read "boys'" books to a greater degree.

Sebesta (1968) suggests that the reading interests of children are greatly influenced by the reactions of adults to "perceived" interests. For example, parents and teachers think Marie enjoys mystery stories so they encourage and reinforce this perceived interest with discussions and books on the topic. Marie, who may or may not be especially interested in mysteries, responds to the expectations of those around her, not unlike the subjects in *Pygmalion in the Classroom* (Rosenthal and Jacobson, 1968). It is clear that differences in interests among the sexes are in part a product of fulfilling society's expectations.

The unfortunate aspect of the self-fulfilling prophecy is that children may read avidly on only those topics that teachers think interest them. Sebesta (1968, p. 21) states: "Interest studies generally describe preferences of the majority, while the child himself is a minority." The implications of this statement for teaching will be explored shortly.

A number of recent investigations have sought to explore the effect of television on the reading interests and habits of children. Witty (1960a,b, 1966) has pioneered in this area. Television has become children's favorite leisure time activity, with boys watching more than girls (Witty, 1960a). In 1966 the average number of hours per week spent watching television by elementary school children in the Chicago area was twenty. Reading was found by Witty to have relatively little appeal for children as compared with television. Of special importance was Witty's finding that television had a significant influence on children's choice of reading materials.

Flierl (1960) attempted to use children's television interests to build strong or recreational reading habits. Selecting several popular television programs, she arranged displays and bulletin boards with books matched to the content of the programs. She also motivated various language arts activities such as creative writing with tape recordings of the programs. Some increase was found in the number of books read with a corresponding decrease in hours spent watching television.

Sister Miriam (1960) conducted a similar experiment to determine whether children's television viewing habits could be improved along with a corresponding increase in the amount of personal reading. She concluded that by recognizing children's television viewing habits and taking advantage of them, it was possible to not only upgrade the quality of their choices, but also make them more aware of the importance of doing more reading.

Clearly teachers today cannot ignore television. By using the strong hold television has on children, teachers can build reading interests related to children's viewing interests.

The research evidence concerning children's interests is useful in a rather limited sense. While it is helpful to know that intermediate grade girls in general enjoy horse stories, a fifth grade teacher cannot assume that Jessie or Heather have either an interest in or the background for enjoying *Born to Trot* (Henry, 1950). As suggested earlier, generalizations about children's interests are simply that — generalizations. Each child is an individual that may or may not fit the usual pattern. Weintraub (1969) concluded from an extensive review of the literature on reading interests that no single category of books will supply all children of the same age with what they want to read about. He suggests that each teacher identify the unique reading interests of children in his own classroom and then try to supply the materials required.

Are we to conclude then that research findings on children's interests are not useful in the classroom? Not at all. A librarian or classroom teacher should build his book collection with an awareness of general interests. Research says that primary age younsters are more likely than sixth grade boys to be interested in fairy tales. Consequently a school library should contain fairy tales for children who have this interest. A first grade teacher should display fairy tales in her classroom collection for the same reason. In addition, both the librarian and classroom teacher should obtain many other types of books for youngsters who do not fit the pattern. More will be said later about the importance of broadening reading interests by making a variety of books available. In view of the fact that individual youngsters may not have reading interests that coincide with those identified by the research, some means for assessing children's interests are needed.

Assessing Interests

The best way of assessing a youngster's interests is to learn more about him as an individual. We know well the interests of our best friends and close relatives. Almost unconsciously we decide that Aunt Mary would enjoy seeing the latest play by Arthur Miller but that Uncle Alex would prefer to see the Yankees play the Orioles. Or we may realize that our roommate will not appreciate hearing the latest folk-rock record album. Our understanding of another's interests is based on our familiarity with his likes and dislikes, our knowledge of his disposition. Much the same is true of a teacher's ability to identify his students' interests.

The pupil-teacher interview is an excellent way to get acquainted and a good source of information on interests. It is a technique that should be employed as often as possible. Unfortunately, the time to conduct such discussions is severely limited by a busy schedule. Furthermore, one round of interviews would hardly be completed before another round would be required. Children's interests simply change too rapidly, especially in the primary grades, to depend entirely on this technique. Therefore, other means for gathering information on interests must also be used.

An informal questionnaire developed by the teacher can be used to gather more easily much of the information obtained in an interview. An example of an easily devised questionnaire that provides highly useful information is provided below. The teacher can easily keep up to date on current student activities with such data for each youngster. Providing the right book at the right time is more easily accomplished by having useful information about interests. For example, Jerry may report on an interest questionnaire that his hobby of collecting insects has taken a slightly different direction and now focuses more specifically on bees. The alert teacher makes direct application of information about Jerry's leisure time activity to recommend an appropriate book.

"LIKE TO DO" CHECKLIST

Name_____ Date_____

Age_____ Class in School_____

Directions: This is a list of things that some boys and girls like to do in their spare time. If you never do the thing shown, leave the line blank. If you like to do it, check once on the line; if you like to do it very much, check twice. If you check on the line, and a question is asked about it, please answer the question in the space.

Watching TV _____	Repairing things _____
Writing letters _____	Drawing and painting _____
Sewing or knitting _____	Driving a car _____
Dancing _____	Cooking _____
Hunting _____	Fishing _____
Loafing _____	Teasing _____

Singing or playing a musical instrument _____

Playing cards _____   chess _____   other games _____

What other games? _____

Collecting things _____	What do you collect?
Making things with tools ____	What do you like to make?
Experimenting in science ___	What kind of experiments?
Going to the movies _____	What kind do you like best?
Going for a walk _____	Where?
Talking _____	What do you like to talk about?
Listening to the radio _____	What programs do you like best?

Another type of information the teacher will find useful in assessing interest concerns the child's background of experiences. This information can also be obtained by a different type of questionnaire completed by either the child or his parents. Much the same information may also be obtained by asking the child to prepare an autobiography. Or the teacher may learn valuable information about the child's background from the cumulative record folder. Regardless of how the information is obtained, the teacher can use this knowledge to recommend books that he believes the child will enjoy. For example, a boy who has just moved to a community can be introduced to *Roosevelt Grady* (Shotwell, 1963), a story about a family that has just moved. Or a youngster who lost a parent might profit from reading *Rascal* (North, 1963), a story about a child who faced and overcame a similar tragedy. Crosby's (1963) *Reading Ladders for Human Relations* is a valuable resource for teachers who are seeking books with special themes.

Finally, through daily observation the alert teacher can obtain continuous information about a child's interests. The daily reading period offers an excellent opportunity to note the child's reactions to stories, characters, and topics. A story about a dog may elicit an enthusiastic reaction from Bill. The teacher should note his response and take the appropriate steps to introduce *Big Red* (Kjelgaard, 1945), *Silver Chief, Dog of the North* (O'Brien, 1933), or similar books about a dog. The teacher can also note special interests in other subjects, particularly social studies. For example, *Johnny Tremain* (Forbes, 1944) or *Caddie Woodlawn* (Brink, 1936) are excellent books that relate directly to our nation's history. In addition, children often reveal much about themselves and their interests during informal "show and tell" or group discussions. The teacher who watches for such information can do much to individualize the assistance he provides for children in selecting books.

Aids for selecting children's books are listed in Appendix C.

Expanding Children's Interests

It has been said by Dora V. Smith that when a child enters school his reading interests are the teacher's opportunity; when he leaves school they are the teacher's responsibility (Smith, 1964). The teacher has the responsibility for broadening and deepening the child's reading interests and making him more fully aware of what books are available. The surest method of achieving this goal is by creating a classroom environment that arouses the child's interest.

A bulletin board in the reading corner that asks, "How will Mafatu survive?" is almost sure to prick the curiosity of an intermediate grade boy. An illustration of Mafatu fighting a wild boar to defend his dog adds further interest. The final touch is to place a copy of the book *Call It Courage* (Sperry, 1940) on display with the recommendations of several classmates attached. Another excellent technique for advertising a book is reading an exciting part aloud to the class and displaying other books by the same author in the reading corner. By carefully "setting the bait" a creative teacher can entice many youngsters to try a book.

Many teachers have found it helpful to keep some record of each child's recreational reading choices. With guidance older children can easily do this themselves. Younger children may copy the title of a book or simply sign their name on a sheet attached to a book. Another approach is to fasten to the book slips of paper imprinted with the name of the author and title. When a child has read the book he can simply remove one of the slips and place it in his record folder. In any event, a record of the books each child has read enables the teacher to tell at a glance what kind of reading is being done. A steady diet of one type book may prompt the teacher to instigate a "sales campaign" on another category for Peter or Susie.

A chart like the one in Figure 13.1 is often helpful in tabulating the reading choices of children. A concentration of titles in one section of the circle may signal a need for greater variety in book selection.

Occasionally a child is encountered who will only read books of one type. One such youngster was Daniel, who refused to read anything except nonfiction science books, usually on rocks and minerals. When urged to try a good fiction book he responded, "I want to learn something when I read." How should a teacher react to this attitude? Daniel's motive for reading was certainly beyond reproach even if it was a bit limited. An older child of junior or senior high school age might be shown what can be learned about human nature from a well-written novel. Daniel may have been persuaded by this approach, too; however, a different tack was taken by his teacher. Using the highly effective technique of *gradually broadening* Daniel's current reading interests, he was led to try other topics. The teacher first suggested another nonfiction science book similar to those Daniel usually selected, but on plants rather than rocks and minerals. Next, a biography of a well-known botanist was recommended. After reading several biographies about scientists Daniel was ready to read some historical fiction that enabled him "to learn something" in a fictional setting. Eventually he began to read other fiction stories and soon had a well-balanced reading diet.

The case of Daniel is interesting for several reasons. First, we see how interests can be broadened gradually by finding topics related to a child's main interest. Second, the question of how much reading of one type can be permitted is implicit in Daniel's case. What if he had

Name _____

Age _____

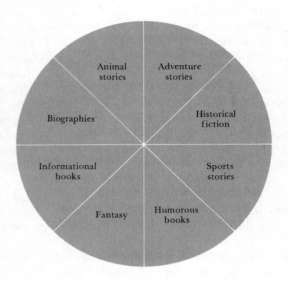

Directions: Write the title of your book in the space below and place the identification number in the proper category above.

Date	Identification Number	Book Title	Author
1.			
2.			
3.			
4.			
5.			

FIGURE 13-2   Checking Reading Interests

A simple record keeping device of this sort enables the student and teacher to note personal reading interests.

steadfastly refused to budge from his interest in rocks and minerals? The authors believe that reading even of a singular nature is preferable to no reading at all. There is always the chance that a habitual reader will change his interests but far less chance that a "nonreader" will pick up the habit of reading.

Another point to remember is that some of our most "unbalanced" citizens insofar as interests are concerned have been major contributors to society through their intense dedication to one pursuit. Einstein is the most obvious example, but others can easily be cited. It was discovered in a study of eminent scientists by Anne Roe (1961) that the vast majority of men studied were regarded by others as unbalanced and not well rounded in their youth. This is not to say that balanced reading fare is unnecessary for most children. However, we must keep in mind the youngster who rebels at external demands placed upon his reading. If well-planned guidance is ineffective in broadening the child's interests, it is advisable to stop short of badgering him to read more widely. He may be another Einstein or just a very stubborn child; in either case, we should be pleased that he reads at all.

But what about the child who will *not* read at all? For example, Mark reads very poorly and flatly refuses to take a book from the library. Teachers frequently ask how they can get a boy like Mark to read. There is no simple answer, of course. One surefire way to fail with Mark is to threaten or coerce him into reading. Nothing is gained, since Mark will never read outside the classroom if he is literally forced to do so in school.

Often refusal to read is simply the child's way of avoiding a highly frustrating experience. Nobody seeks out an activity in which they constantly fail. Therefore, the first step is to help a child like Mark succeed in reading. This usually means finding a book that the child can read without difficulty. Perhaps we will have to go as far back as a preprimer to locate such a book. It would be better if we could find an easy trade book, since the preprimer-primer route is often partially responsible for his lack of interest. After all, the failure to read probably started in these or similar materials.

Level of interest is a second factor to be considered in selecting a book for the child who refuses to read. Many easy to read books are now available on a variety of topics. Spache's *Good Books for Poor Readers* (1968) lists hundreds of them. Mark may be fascinated by submarines. The Harr-Wagner Deep Sea Adventure Series has a book titled *Submarine Rescue* written at a low level of difficulty that may meet his need.

A third thing to keep in mind is that Mark may need help even with easy books. A friend or teacher's aide may be able to read

through the book with him. The teacher or Mark's parents even may
be able to help him read it.

The key with most reluctant readers is helping them find success
in reading. Until the pattern of failure is broken, interest in reading
is unlikely.

THE ELEMENTARY SCHOOL LITERATURE PROGRAM

We have seen how the home and school environments are related to
children's interests in reading. We have considered various ways of
stimulating and assessing interests. Most would agree that without an
interest in reading skill instruction is largely futile. However, wanting
to read and having the skills needed to read and comprehend are
not enough; one additional element is missing: taste in reading.

Literature is the vehicle that carries young and old alike through
doorways they may never personally encounter. It has the capacity
to give sheer enjoyment, to provide new perspectives and vicarious
experiences. Literature can develop one's insight into human behavior and transmit the accumulated wisdom of mankind. Good literature provides beauty and inspiration. Because literature has so much
to offer it is essential that taste be encouraged so that young readers
may select the best that is available.

Reading interests determine what will be read, for example,
fairy tales or sports stories; reading taste determines the quality of
what is read, for example, *Sport* magazine or *All American* by John
Tunis. Taste in reading grows from the opportunity to read materials
of varying degrees of quality. Without adequate guidance children's
choice of books may be based on superficial and fleeting elements that
have little connection with good literature. But the teacher is not a
censor deciding what a child will or will not read. Only the child's
parents have the right to provide such supervision. Neither should the
teacher sit in judgment of what is and what is not good literature. It
is his responsibility to help the youngster develop his own standards
(Huck and Kuhn, 1968, p. 650).

Initiating Literature Instruction

Perhaps because of the difficulties involved in defining exactly what
constitutes a total literature program at the elementary school level,
no research has been done on the extent of such programs. We know
that the senior high school curriculum usually provides for the study
of literature in English classes. Some junior high schools have formal
literature study also. However, several factors operate to limit the
amount of time devoted to literature at the elementary school level.

First, most elementary schools in this country are without libraries (Austin and Morrison, 1963). Without adequate materials the literature program is often limited to the basal readers, not always a good source of quality literature. Second, the emphasis on teaching basic reading, writing, and computational skills is so great that little time remains for other pursuits. It is our firm conviction that literature instruction cannot be separated from effective reading instruction. The basics of literary analysis and evaluation can be introduced early in the primary grades regardless of the instructional system employed.

The work of Bruner (1960), Taba (1963), and Spodek (1958) is representative of an approach to the elementary school curriculum that emphasizes teaching the structure of the disciplines. The "new math" movement, Project English, and Project Social Studies sponsored by the U.S. Office of Education, were all predicated on the idea that the child is capable of learning the principles underlying the academic disciplines if the concepts are geared to his level of understanding. Thus calculus can be taught to the first grader, and the techniques of historical inquiry are useful in grade two. The same is thought to be true in the case of literature. Given a scheme for analysis and a basis for making judgments, the primary grade youngster can begin to evaluate the basic elements of literature. Indeed, he *must* be taught these skills or become a nondiscriminating consumer of trivial writings that do little more than occupy his leisure time.

Developing Taste

Our purpose in helping a child develop a taste for good literature is not to make of him a prig or a snob but rather to enable him to sort the meaningful from the empty, the rich from the bland. Whatever reading one does should be put in proper perspective. This is possible only through accurate analysis and evaluation of literature.

We all read material that is not great literature. It would be folly to suggest that we hold up for the elementary school child the unrealistic ideal of reading only great literature. However, by studying the elements that comprise good literature we provide the child with a means for making his own assessment. The following definition is helpful in setting our goal: good literature is language that "combines both intellectual and emotional responses. It [causes] the readers to perceive character conflicts, elements in a setting, and universal problems of mankind; it will help the reader to experience the delight of beauty, wonder, and humor; or the despair of sorrow, injustice, and ugliness" (Huck and Kuhn, 1968, p. 7). Good literature helps the reader to better understand himself, those around him, and his surroundings.

Having judged a book as one written without real purpose, the child can proceed to devote as much time to its consumption as he wishes; he does so by choice, however, not out of ignorance. In many ways such reading corresponds to the interest many adults have in James Bond. Ian Fleming hardly regarded his supersleuth as a Hamlet, yet millions have enjoyed *From Russia with Love* and *Thunderball* in book and movie form. An adult who finds Fleming's characters more real and more significant than Steinbeck's Jody in the *Red Pony* apparently lacks sufficient skills to critically evaluate what he reads. We believe that the classroom teacher has responsibility for guiding the child in the development of skills necessary for making such judgments.

Evaluating Books

The teacher has two primary roles with regard to evaluating books. First, he must generally appraise the value of a book and decide for which child the book is suited. In this process he uses the traditional criteria for literary assessment that will be described in this section. Second, he is responsible for teaching skills of literary analysis so that the child grows in his ability to independently apply personal standards of taste.

Criteria for Evaluation

Authorities in the field of children's literature classify books into a variety of categories, for example, fiction, picture books, biographies, and informational books. There is by no means complete agreement on which classification scheme is best. It is important to note that regardless of the scheme used, different criteria are required for evaluating types of books. It is beyond the scope of this text to present criteria for all types of books, so for purposes of illustration we will discuss the evaluation of books of fiction. The reader is referred to *Children's Literature in the Elementary School* by Charlotte Huck and Doris Young Kuhn (1968) and *Children and Books* by May Hill Arbuthnot (1957) for a more complete discussion of evaluating all types of children's books.

Even within the category of fiction, additional criteria are required to evaluate the various forms. Historical fiction, for example, cannot be judged according to the same standards as fairy tales or mystery stories. Evidently the first task of the teacher and the child is to identify the kind of book being evaluated in order to apply the appropriate standards. Again, the reader is referred to Huck and Kuhn and Arbuthnot for a discussion of the various types of children's books.

We suggest consideration of the following factors in evaluating books of fiction: theme, plot, setting, and characterization.

Theme

The theme of a book is the *idea* of the story; the author's reason for writing is revealed through the theme. Some themes may amount to little more than presenting a moral; others focus on the meaning of friendship or courage. For children the theme will have meaning only as it relates to their own experiences. Thus Cervantes' *Don Quixote*, which reveals that high ideals are the only goals in life worth pursuing, has little meaning and therefore little appeal to children in the primary grades. Yet the idea or theme of *Don Quixote* is a powerful one and most appropriate for older children.

A theme must be judged on at least two counts: (1) its worth for presentation to children and (2) the age level for which it is most appropriate.

Plot

The plot is the *plan* of the story. We can identify it by asking what happens in the story. What is the thread of events that carries the action forward? Good plots grow out of good themes. The actions in a plot normally progress in an interrelated fashion, leading to a climax.

For purposes of evaluation it is important to consider the credibility of the plot. It must not depend on coincidence or contrivance but instead grow logically and naturally from previous events of the story.

The plot of *Black Stallion* (Farley, 1941), for example, concerns a teenage boy who is marooned on a deserted island with a wild Arabian stallion. The boy tames the horse, is finally rescued, and returns to New York City with his horse. A special match race is arranged between the year's two greatest horses by a New York newspaper. The wild stallion is entered as a mystery horse and wins the race.

Some stories such as Mark Twain's *Tom Sawyer* succeed with practically no plot. In this instance a series of incidents is related in a loose fashion. Most books require a stronger plot to be successful.

Characters

The characters in a story must be *believable*. The author's ability to create individuals who possess strengths and weaknesses, who act in a manner that is consistent with their nature, determines the success of his characterization. Children can identify with believable characters. A story is carried by and comes alive through the characters.

In addition to determining the authenticity of characters, we should also assess their depth. To be true to life characters must be complex. Some facets of their character will become apparent only after getting to know them very well. Seldom will a person be all bad or all good. These principles also apply to animal characters such as Charlotte, the spider in *Charlotte's Web* (White, 1952), and humorous characters such as Homer in *Homer Price*.

Effective characterization is also dependent upon growth and development. As events occur, realistic characters often change in the course of a story. To be believable change will be gradual rather than instantaneous. Mafatu, for example, grew in courage as he proved to himself that he was capable of assuming the responsibility of a man in *Call It Courage*.

Setting

The *background* against which a story is set is called the setting. The time and place of the story comprise the physical setting; the religious, moral, social, and psychological conditions comprise the emotional or spiritual setting (Georgiou, 1969). All aspects of the setting should affect a story in an authentic way or not at all. *The Yearling* (Rawlings, 1944), for example, is set in the scrub land of Florida. Physically, the isolation of Jody from other youngsters his own age is an important factor in creating the boy's longing for a pet. The poverty of his family is instrumental in making the destruction of a new corn crop by his pet deer a genuine catastrophe. The time of the story, on the other hand, is insignificant, for the events and characters have almost no relation to the outside world.

Some stories such as *Mountain Born* by Elizabeth Yates (1943) have a physical setting of an almost incidental nature. The story revolves around a shepherd and his flock; it can be generalized to any setting given these few necessary elements.

Two additional factors may be considered by the teacher and perhaps by older students: *style* and *format*. When selecting books for a school or classroom library, for example, these matters are of some importance, since a variety of selections should be available for children to read.

Style is the author's particular way of expressing his ideas—his selection and arrangement of words. Just as different people speak with their own unique manner, writing styles also vary. Older children, perhaps in grades five and six, may enjoy contrasting the descriptive style of Mark Twain with the terse presentation of Armstrong Sperry. Huck and Kuhn (1968) suggest oral reading as an effective means for studying an author's style. While a child may not be able to identify the specific aspects of an author's style that appeal to him, he often prefers one author to another because of style.

Format concerns all physical aspects of the book itself, including size, shape, typography, quality of paper, durability, illustrations, and length. Today's books for children are especially attractive. The teacher will want to evaluate matters of format primarily to decide the appropriateness of a book for a particular child. A reluctant reader may require a book that looks "easy," with numerous illustrations and ample space on a page. A more able student may insist on books that have more of an adult book appearance.

Since children often choose a book by its cover if left to their own means, the teacher must also devote some attention to overcoming this tendency. Obviously the value of an attractive format must be balanced against the other factors previously mentioned. A good book in terms of theme, plot, setting, and characterization may lack a striking appearance. In this case children need to discover that it is necessary to look inside to judge its value. On the other hand, a striking book full of stereotyped characters and dull action cannot be saved by an attractive cover or glossy illustrations.

These criteria can be used by children in both the primary and intermediate grades. Naturally the kind of analysis and the depth of understanding will vary from grade to grade and among children in the same grade. Most younger children cannot be expected to discuss how the setting of a story influences the lives of the characters and thereby the plot. However, many older children in grade six, for example, could handle this relation. Thus, *Tom Sawyer* set in the middle of a large city would greatly change the events if not the actual personality of the main character. Speculation concerning the effect this totally different setting would have on Mark Twain's classic is both plausible and instructional for most sixth grade children. On the other hand, even the first grade child can be expected to tell what happened in a story (plot). He can also identify who is in the story (characters) and report where the story took place. Some evaluation is also possible: "Could this story happen?" "Could you ever take a trip like the boy in the book took?" "How did you feel toward the man in the story? Why?"

A planned program of literary criticism is an essential facet of the total reading program. An early start at identifying and evaluating the various aspects of a story is necessary for developing active, knowledgeable readers who rationally evaluate literature. One possible approach to organizing a program of literary criticism is described below.

Developing Evaluation Skills

The purpose for helping children analyze and evaluate books is to increase their appreciation, deepen their understanding, and relate literature to their own lives. By providing a system for studying the

TABLE 13.2 Sequential and Cumulative Literary Analysis Skills

Grade Level	Skill
1	Name characters, identify setting, retell story, identify conflict, tell solution
2	Identify beginning, middle, and ending of plot
3	Describe characters, identify climax
4	Discuss characterization, note cause and effect
5	Discuss mood through choice of words
6	Discuss style through sentence patterns and approach

elements of a story the teacher leads the child to gain as much as possible from reading. If the analysis of a story ever detracts from the child's enjoyment, the program of literary criticism has gone wrong. Analysis just for the sake of pseudointellectual discussion has no place in the elementary school, or any other school for that matter.

Developed with the proper perspective, literary criticism permits the child to compare and contrast one selection with others by the same author, with other similar works, or with literature in general. The criteria suggested here or those developed by others are helpful in considering specific aspects of literature in an objective fashion. For example, the development of a character can be studied for authenticity and consistency. However, some aspects of literary criticism are reserved to each individual reader. Children should be encouraged to develop their own standards for assessing literature. The opportunity to explore books with the teacher and other students is instrumental in helping the individual arrive at personal criteria. The object of our literature instruction is to encourage the *development* of standards, not to standardize children's standards.

Children's Classics

Certain children's books become classics because they have withstood the test of time; generation after generation of youngsters enjoy some of the same books. *Alice in Wonderland* is an example of a children's classic, as is *Heidi*.

Teachers often feel compelled to require that children read the classics. Others remember being bored by some so-called classics and are determined not to make the same mistake their teachers made. What is the place of classics in the elementary school literature program?

The fact that some books remain popular with children over long periods of time is a significant recommendation in their behalf.

Teachers should be familiar with such books and stand ready to suggest *The Jungle Book, Peter Pan,* or other classics to a youngster who is searching for something to read. But not all youngsters will enjoy those books. This reaction is understandable and acceptable. The teacher should not attempt to force a child to read any book including a classic. Instead, he must work very hard at enticing this student to personally select quality books.

The magnificence of *Treasure Island, Robinson Crusoe, Swiss Family Robinson, Tom Sawyer, Huckleberry Finn, Hans Brinker, or the Silver Skates,* and *The Secret Garden* guarantee that most youngsters will probably enjoy some if not all of these books. The teacher should read several of these books aloud in order to be sure that all youngsters have some exposure to them. The enjoyment these books provide should be experienced by all youngsters. Familiarity with children's classics is also important from the standpoint of providing children with a means for assessing other books. In a sense, children's classics can serve as a measuring device. For example, other books can be compared to *Charlotte's Web* for effective character development. Or the plot of *Treasure Island* can be taken as a measure of excellence that is useful for assessing other literature. The greatest danger in this approach is that dull, uninteresting books will be called classics and held up as exemplars for judging other books. Unfortunately, the *Award Books,* chosen by adult judges, are sometimes misused in this way. However, if children's classics are judged strictly on the basis of children's reactions over a long period of time, the danger is minimized.

Book Reports

Like children's classics, considerable difference of opinion surrounds the matter of book reporting. Properly handled, book reports can play a significant part in the literature program. Since a major goal of the reading program is to develop critical readers, the opportunity to analyze and evaluate books must be provided; book reports that focus on this goal can be productive of growth in critical reading skill.

Unfortunately, in their desire to interest children in reading, teachers occasionally conduct contests to see who can read the most books; they often require book reports as evidence of the children's accomplishments. Under these circumstances book reports as well as reading books can get badly out of perspective. No book report should ever be prepared simply to prove that a child has read a book. Furthermore, contests on the number of books are ill conceived. The means and ends have become confused in cases where either of the above occur.

The purpose for reviewing, analyzing, and evaluating a book is to increase one's appreciation and understanding of its contents. A book report should contain the reader's appraisal of a book according to some previously chosen guidelines. The goal is to maximize his learning, not to satisfy an external requirement. Thus, book reports are written to provide some evidence of the child's response to a book. The teacher should regard them as a means for evaluating the child's reading growth. His reading tastes and interests are reflected in the type of books he selects and how he reviews them. His understanding and appreciation are also evident through his report on a book.

In actual practice book reports often contain little that is analytic and nothing that is evaluative. Typically book reports are either written or oral summaries of the plot. Occasionally (if a teacher insists) the characters and the setting are mentioned. The results of this approach are often not happy ones. Teachers decry the inability of youngsters to think; youngsters moan about the necessity for rewriting every book they read. If anything, *less* reading and *less* study of literature probably result from this procedure. Therefore, several suggestions for improving book reports are in order.

First, teachers should encourage children to report their books through a variety of means. Permit and even encourage the use of various art projects for reporting on books. For example, dioramas, maps, murals, models, table displays, bulletin boards, and posters can be made about a book. Or puppet shows, flannel board presentations, mock radio broadcasts, and interviews with stand-ins for actual authors can be given. Book reports should be regarded as a means for encouraging children to *respond* to books. The more enjoyable they are for the reader and for an audience, the better the chance that they will encourage and reinforce reading.

Second, teach some skills of literary criticism. This can be initiated in a group setting after children have heard the teacher read a story aloud. The teacher can encourage critical thinking and direct attention to specific elements of the story. Characters can be evaluated for consistency, for example. The plot can be studied for conflict. Later, children can be asked to study many of these same factors in a story they are reading independently. The technique of comparing books can be introduced and encouraged by the teacher.

Third, do not require a report on every book that a child reads. Allow some books to simply be recorded by author and title. The child should have this option of choosing not to report on a book.

Fourth, do not use a standardized book report form unless the youngsters have helped design it. Even then only a few specifics such as author, title, characters, and setting should be included on the form. Other information should be voluntarily reported. Children's responses to books should be as individualized as possible.

Fifth, whenever possible use book reports to arouse the interest of other children in a book. Display them in the reading corner or on a bulletin board. One interesting approach is to have several oral reports given simultaneously. The teacher can announce what books are being reported and permit each child to attend the session that interests him the most.

Book reports are primarily a means for encouraging children to respond to books. They are only a means to this end and must not be regarded as an end in themselves. It is especially important that children be encouraged to respond to literature because both interest and taste in reading are predicated on the personal involvement of the reader.

SUMMARY

This chapter has made a case for the belief that lifelong reading habits are as important to a good reader as the ability to decode word symbols or comprehend an author's message. An interest in reading determines whether the basic reading skills will ever be used by an individual.

The home is the origin of interest in reading. Parents who value reading in their own lives and take the time to provide stimulating experiences for their children facilitate their offsprings' reading progress in school and promote healthy attitudes toward reading.

The school must build on whatever disposition toward reading the child brings to school. For some, interest need only be maintained and broadened. For others, a remedial program is necessary to build the attitudes and interests not created at home. The classroom atmosphere must make reading important and books accessible. A reading corner is highly recommended to provide these features.

Research abounds on the identification of children's reading interests. While some general sense of direction is provided by such evidence, the classroom teacher must still assess each child's interests individually. Providing appropriate reading materials and encouraging broadened reading interests are both the responsibility of the teacher.

The elementary school literature program is designed to help children learn to establish personal standards for guiding their selection of reading materials. Analysis of literature is helpful to the extent that it permits children to make more rational judgments about their reading fare. Book reports should also be regarded as a means to the end of selective reading and not as an end in themselves. Children's classics should be available to children but not assigned as required reading.

TERMS

interest inventory (questionnaire)	format
reading corner	children's classics
theme	Nancy Larrick
plot	Paul Witty
setting	George Spache
characterization	Charlotte Huck
style	Doris Young Kuhn

PART V

HIGHER COMPETENCIES IN READING

Reading is used to accomplish many purposes. To be used as a tool to gain knowledge, to analyze, and to interpret life it must bring along skills in analyzing, evaluating, and applying the ideas that are read. These reading-thinking skills enable an individual to study independently and to enjoy literature—indispensable competencies in a world of communication.

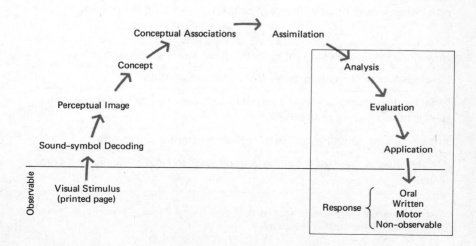

Chapter 14

Critical and Creative Reading *

The day will come when you ask a youngster to pretend that he is a critic of a story he has read, and he will say, "I can't criticize it. I like it too much."

Many people mistakenly believe that critical reading and thinking involve ripping and tearing and destroying. But that is a far cry from what is meant here by critical reading. You might very well have responded to the above comment: "I hope your judgment that you like the story is actually based upon critical reading; for reading critically doesn't mean disliking the story. It simply means you are reacting to it and judging it. Your judgment may be favorable."

Dispelling a false notion about the meaning of critical reading constitutes one instructional task, a fairly minor one. The teacher's major task is to conceptualize clearly what critical reading is so that he can describe it and lead his students to use critical reading skills. That task may not be quite so simple. If you had to answer the following questions right now, what would be your concept of critical and creative reading?

How does critical reading differ from literal comprehension?

How does critical reading differ from creative reading?

What kinds of questions would you ask a student in order to reveal whether or not he is reading critically?

Are certain students incapable of critical and creative reading?

Are there valid ways of teaching a youngster to read critically and creatively?

*Grateful acknowledgement is expressed to Dr. Nancy Roser, University of Texas, for her work in constructing this chapter.

Both critical and creative reading gained increased attention during the 1960s, but there was no agreement as to a precise definition of terms and the confusion was evident. Some writers have defined critical reading broadly, even including literal comprehension; others have preferred a more narrow approach (King, Ellinger, and Wolf, 1967). All the discussion and concern, however, have resulted in very little attention to developing critical and creative readers in elementary classrooms.

The reading-communication model of Figure 1.1 may help to focus on where critical and creative reading fit in the total reading process. Remembering from Chapter 11 that literal comprehension is the ability to identify the main idea in a passage or selection, recall fact and recount detail, note that critical reading begins with analysis of the author's form and organization and includes all parts of the model thereafter, including evaluation and synthesis or application. The focal point of reading critically rests on evaluation, that is, the application of criteria to a written passage. Creative reading in its initial stage begins with synthesis, or the point where the viewpoints of the reader and the author merge to create a unique communication. Creative reading implies the ability to internalize the written message and then to use it in some stimulating or artistic mode of expression.

Critical and creative reading lie along a continuum of skill development and are here artifically dichotomized for purposes of clear explanation.

This chapter defines critical reading, shows how to teach it through improved question patterns and through classroom exercises that focus on the way language is used to influence opinions, and discusses the need to select criteria for making judgments. Techniques for evaluating critical reading skills are also presented. Then creative reading is discussed and ways of developing it through oral, written, and artistic activities are described. Ways of appraising creative reading are presented in the concluding pages of the chapter.

IMPORTANCE OF CRITICAL READING

Even though the terminology and skills involved in reading critically may be somewhat elusive, the development of critical readers has come to be an undeniably important goal of the curriculum. The rapidly increasing volume of printed material to be read, assimilated, and evaluated, plus the constant propaganda that pounds on our senses, makes critical reading ability a workaday tool and a weapon. From the time we read the morning newspaper editorials to the commercials we watch on evening television, each day we are forced to read and react critically to the obvious and the obscure.

For example, readers will recognize the different approaches to a school tax hike taken by the bulletin of the chamber of commerce and that of the local teachers' association; will note inconsistencies between headline and text in a movie magazine; will question the advertisement that promises a bright future for using a certain toothpaste or cleansing cream. It is imperative that intelligent citizens read with care, and teachers need to be alert to daily opportunities to teach critical reading skills. More important than teaching a lesson in critical reading is developing a sensitivity to the opportunities to teach critical reading in daily situations. The teacher must work toward situations that cause pupils to go beyond recall to set other purposes for reading: to analyze, to draw inferences, and to make judgments on the basis of some criterion.

Definition of Critical Reading

Robinson (1964) has stated that critical reading is the ability to apply relevant criteria in evaluating a selection. It is the judgment of the "veracity, validity, and worth of what is read, based on criteria or standards developed through previous experience" (p. 3).

Russell (1956) has suggested four conditions essential to reading critically:

1. A knowledge of the field in which reading is being done
2. An attitude of questioning and suspended judgment
3. Some application of the methods of logical analysis or scientific inquiry
4. Taking action in light of the analysis or reasoning.

Neither teachers nor their students will meet all these conditions at all times. Neither adults nor children can possibly be armed with background knowledge in every field in which they must read. Today's world is too big and man's knowledge is too vast. It is necessary, therefore, to equip students with an attitude of general awareness so that they can detect unsupported statements, sweeping generalizations, and conclusions that have been drawn too rapidly. An attitude of suspended judgment may not always be possible. Previous biases and prejudices affect one's ability to read critically, as do such factors as age, sex, home background, and sociopolitical attitudes. As part of his training a student should be taught to recognize his biases and deal with them as a factor in the way he reacts to the printed word. The teacher should foster an attitude of inquiry when he teaches the techniques for critical reading. Against such a background children will develop higher and higher standards for judging what they read.

Neglect of Critical Reading in the Classroom

A study of teaching time and emphasis in U.S. schools (Austin and Morrison, 1963) indicated that more than half of the teachers questioned devoted "little or no time" to critical reading in the first and second grades. About one third of the third and fourth grade teachers allotted "little or no" instructional time for teaching these skills.

Research has indicated that even primary grade children can and do read critically. McCullough (1957) compared the abilities of first, second, and fourth grade children to answer questions of detail, main idea, and sequence with their abilities to answer questions in seeing relations, drawing conclusions, and passing judgments. She found that her cases experienced no special difficulty with higher-level comprehension tasks at any grade level. Similarly, a study by Covington (1967) indicated that children with below average intelligence and reading two years below grade level could read critically when materials were adjusted to their restricted proficiency.

It is likely that many students function at a constant level when it comes to determining author intent, detecting tone, differentiating fact from opinion, and so on. Consequently they attack every printed selection in the same way, satisfied with a literal comprehension of the main idea and pertinent details. It appears then that critical reading skills can and should be developed gradually from the early grades.

Perhaps with a better understanding of what is involved in the critical reading process, teachers would devote more teaching time to critical reading in the elementary grades.

Steps in the Critical Reading Process

Literal Comprehension

Before higher-level mental processes can function a student needs an understanding of the facts and ideas as the author presents them. An assessment of the student's ability to identify the main idea of the content and to recount important details is a check on literal comprehension. Basic comprehension skills were treated in a previous chapter. The reading-thinking skills more closely related to critical and creative reading move from a base of literal comprehension.

One task of the critical reader is to interpret the writer's message accurately, a process sometimes described as "reading between the lines."

Two levels of interpretation are presented here: (1) analytical interpretation and (2) inferential interpretation. These skills were presented in Chapter 11 and are discussed here in the light of the more complex reading selections found in the upper elementary grades. As reading material becomes more complex, the skills of analysis and inference involve broader concepts and more abstract relations.

Analytical Interpretation

As we noted in the reading communication-model of Figure 1.1, analysis follows literal comprehension. It involves an attempt on the part of the reader to secure from the printed material the logical unity of the presentation. At this point the reader begins mentally to manipulate the author's ideas for the purposes of perceiving relations and visualizing the structure of the selection. The reader asks, "What is the author's main thesis?" "How are main points supported by detail?" "How do major points within the selection relate?" "Has significant information been overlooked?" The process involves the reader in forming a mental outline, weighing points for their relation and strength.

Children who can underline key words and phrases in a selection, who can strike out irrelevant sentences in a presentation, or who can select appropriate titles for stories are involved in analysis of the author's organizational plan. Skill in analytical interpretation requires guided practice and practical illustrations.

Inferential Interpretation

Inference is an attempt on the part of the reader to secure from the printed material what the author has left unsaid or what he attempts to say without words. An interpolating process, it involves inferential leaps from what is literally stated to what is actually intended: "This is what the author has said, but what does he mean?" An example of this type of reading is found in Marc Anthony's funeral oration in Shakespeare's *Julius Ceasar*. Marc Anthony continually repeats, "But Brutus is an honorable man." What he states, however, is directly opposite to what he is implying, and his implied strategy is an effective one.

Inferential interpretations depend upon reader acuity and intuition. The reader must put several clues together in order to predict possible occurrences or behaviors. He needs to become adept at using context as a sounding board against which inferences can be tested. And he may need more information about the author: Is the author a satirist? Does he try to manipulate his reader? The reader is involved in bridging the gaps in an author's presentation; he gathers source clues as a springboard and then makes the inferential leap. These suggestions indicate a level of inference quite different from the inferences described in Chapter 11 on basic comprehension.

Evaluation

At the evaluation stage the reader is called upon to make judgments as to the worth of the ideas gleaned from print. Evaluation depends not only upon literal comprehension and interpretation skills but also upon the ability to employ successfully selected criteria for appraising the truthfulness, validity, and accuracy of the material. The reader attempts to determine the accuracy of presentation, the author's professional competence, and the relevancy of his thoughts.

Students who are asked to make judgments while reading need at times the aid of *external criteria*, or other references and sources. A pupil with no previous experience with a subject must suspend judgment until he can establish some criteria through the use of valid outside references. *Internal standards* may be all that are required by the student with a strong basis of experiences in the area in question. His task is simplified. Internal standards or criteria are also formulated as a result of societal role. Difficulty occurs when a pupil's internal criteria, the product of his culture, are strongly in conflict with the prevailing issue. Because of his emotional reaction the reader may not be able to suspend judgment until all evidence is presented on a subject. For example, a Quaker reading a plea to expand the offensive power of the military has strong cultural criteria that would direct him to reject the piece regardless of its logic or rhetoric.

It is the teacher's responsibility to aid the student in clarifying the assumptions he brings to the reading task, in analyzing and ascertaining the assumptions of the author, and in broadening the background of knowledge out of which more adequate standards of judgment may come (DeBoer, 1967).

Another aspect of evaluation that has come to be labeled critical reading is that of evaluating the worth of a poem or a prose selection. We have chosen to call this kind of evaluation literary appreciation rather than include it under critical reading because it is treated in courses on literary criticism. It is, of course, a form of reading critically, with criteria arising from the literary form and from the nature of the experience being described.

THE ART OF QUESTIONING

When a teacher asks questions to determine a child's grasp of content he not only gives the student a type of problem but also leads him to establish his own questions and set his own purposes for reading.

What questions might be asked about the following selection from a children's book? Formulate three questions you might ask a second-grade child concerning the story:

Susan and Billy watched Billy's new airplane sail through the air. "Look at it go, Susan!" Billy called. "It's as fast as lightning."

"Let me fly the airplane," begged Susan.

"No, you're too little," answered her brother.

"Please?" Susan asked again.

Billy handed the airplane to his sister. "Be careful," he warned. Susan raced across the yard. Gaining speed, she threw the plane into the air. It made a sudden turn and dropped to the ground in a nosedive. One of the bright red wings lay beside the plane.

What kinds of questions did you formulate? If you asked questions such as "What did Billy say when Susan asked to fly his plane?" or "What color was Billy's airplane?" you asked for literal recall or a restatement of fact. If you asked questions that required children to go beyond literal comprehension to interpretation you may have asked, "How do you think Billy feels toward his sister now?" or "What do you expect Billy to do now? What makes you think so?" Tapping critical judgment would require questions such as, "Would it have been better had Billy never shared his toy?" or "Could a toy plane fly as fast as lightning?" Ideally, questioning can also lead the child to see application of the story in his own life: "Have you ever had to share with younger brothers and sisters?" "How did you feel about it?"

Critical thinking does not take place automatically. Questions can lead pupils to become better readers. The teacher can guide an inquiring attitude by artful questioning. If posed questions seek only immediate recall, then reading for detail is reinforced and critical reading skills are neglected.

Wardeberg (1969) lists three qualities to which the artful questioner must give attention:

1. Questions that relate new ideas to the child's experiential background and personal involvement
2. Questions that develop critical thinking and the correct assessment of statements
3. Questions that integrate the structure of the disciplines in such a way that future learnings as well as past experiences can be encompassed in the structure.

Teacher questions leading to critical reading can be loosely categorized into three general areas—questions demanding (1) literal recall, (2) interpretation (analysis and inference), and (3) critical judgment or evaluation.

Questions for Literal Recall

Questions that ask children to recount or retell without necessarily involving them in any higher-level thinking demand *literal recall*. As discussed earlier, these types of questions are most valuable when they serve as checks to determine whether concepts are grasped firmly enough to be reproduced. These questions are the easiest to formulate and the easiest to answer. Often they are looked upon as the first step in a series of questions—necessary but not nearly as far as children need to climb for a rich experience in reading. They are often questions of (1) *detail* ("Who planted the flowers in the garden?"); (2) *sequence* ("What happened after the rain?"); and (3) main idea ("What was the story about?").

Questions for Interpretation

Interpretive questions require the reader to extend what is actually stated. He must use both subtle and obvious author cues to move beyond literal presentation. This is a gap-filling process. Interpretations can be checked for support or rejection against what is actually stated.

> In what season of the year might this story have taken place? What makes you think so?
> Why do you suppose these Plains Indians made their homes from buffalo hides rather than from bark or logs?
> Why was Mother eager for the rain to stop?
> How did the author really feel about animals? How could you tell?

The answers to these questions would not be directly stated but rather would depend upon reader interpretation and prediction.

Questions for Evaluation

Questions that demand critical judgment from the reader while using internal or external criteria force critical reading. Children are usually hesitant to question the printed word. They may view the author as the authority figure. Teachers who adhere to one textbook as the ultimate source of knowledge reinforce this attitude; so too do teachers who attempt to avoid controversial issues and debate in their classrooms (Heilman, 1961). A realistic attitude can be fostered through questions that ask children to distinguish fact from opinion, to recognize assumptions, and to judge author competence, for example.

> Was Billy's reaction the best one under the circumstances? Why or why not? How does this author know so much about Smokey the Bear?

Being a Critical Reader

As a mature reader you should be prepared to detect devices designed to influence a less perceptive reader. What kinds of questions come to mind as you read the following passage:

You know that I was born and raised in Austria. Do you know that there are no remedial reading cases in Austrian schools? Do you know that there are no remedial cases in Germany, in France, in Italy, in Norway, in Spain — practically anywhere in the world except in the United States? Do you know that there was no such thing as remedial reading in this country either until about thirty years ago? Do you know that the teaching of reading never was a problem anywhere in the world until the United States switched to the present method around about 1925? This sounds incredible, but it is true.*

Did you ask, "How is a remedial reader being defined by this author?" "Does the author refer to remedial cases or classes designed to handle such readers?" (refer to sentence four in the passage) Can you detect the cause against which the author is building his case — his purpose for writing? Did you question his field of interest, his specialization? Where are the supporting facts for these assumptions?

Although you may have no immediate knowledge either to substantiate or to refute this author's statements, you no doubt detected some sweeping generalizations and a rather hastily drawn conclusion. Note the last statement: "This sounds incredible, but it is true." The author appears to have foreseen disbelief and uses rhetoric to validate his argument. Maturity in reading tells you that something is not true just because someone says it is. Children can only be led to a similar type of intelligent inquiry by teachers who are first critical readers themselves and then ask questions to encourage evaluation (Meehan, 1970).

CLASSROOM EXERCISES IN CRITICAL READING

Truth versus Fantasy

In the primary grades one of the first critical reading skills the teacher attempts to develop is the ability to distinguish truth from fantasy. He is careful neither to discount fantasy nor to dismiss a story as unworthy because it is untrue. The teacher realizes that tales of fancy can spark imagination and elicit creative thought. Even first grade children, however, can learn to distinguish the difference. They become aware of fantasy signals such as "once-upon-a-time" beginnings and stories incorporating such traditional

*This selection was taken from *Why Johnny Can't Read* by Rudolf Flesch (New York: Harper & Row, Publishers, 1955), a book which stirred much controversy in the late 1950s because of its indictment of U.S. schools for the lack of attention they gave to phonics.

fantasy motifs as the beautiful princess, the aged king, the triumph of the younger brother or sister, and reliance upon magic powers and objects.

To initiate awareness the teacher may wish to start with isolated statements and have children respond with "yes" or "no" depending upon previously established criteria as to the truth or falsity of the statements:

> The moon is made of green cheese.
> A dog can fly.
> Apples grow on cherry trees.
> A kitten is smaller than me.
> A boy can run.

By indicating agreement or disagreement the children grow accustomed to meeting statements in print that are not true. Later, they can discuss the fantasy elements within stories with a "Could this have happened?" approach.

> Could the prince really have climbed Rapunzel's hair? Why or why not?
> Could a boy be as small as Tom Thumb?
> Could the cabbage leaves actually have grown as large as a barn? How do you know?

Very young children can also detect the difference between fantasy events and those that are plausible or might have happened. Direct the children to listen to two accounts of an event, one which is more true to life than the other. Encourage discussion as to which really could have happened.

> The puppy shivered from the cold. No one seemed to notice him on the sidewalk as last-minute shoppers hurried home with arms full of Christmas packages. He huddled against a tall building to avoid being stepped on.

> Oliver Puppy shivered from the cold. "Oh dear," he sighed, "Don't any of those people want a puppy to take home? I do *so* want a people." Just then he had an idea. "I'll ask one of them to belong to *me*!"

Children also enjoy changing a factual presentation to one of fantasy by incorporating talking animals or magic events or other fantasy elements. It becomes easier as children get older for them to draw from works of fiction the specific incidents that make the story depart from realistic fiction. They can also work successfully with tall tales and the works of humor writers to differentiate truth from fantasy when fantasy is presented as truth.

Denotative-Connotative Language

Awareness of the power of words is a crucial factor in reading critically. Words can comfort, coax, convince, and deceive. A first step toward intelligent and profitable reading results from the reader's ability to scrutinize a passage to determine what reaction the author is attempting to elicit through the use of words that appeal to the emotions, arouse sentiment, evoke sensory images, or incite to action. We can differentiate the dictionary definition of a word — its denotation — from the images and implication the word suggests — its connotation.

Consider, for example, your own reaction to the word *child*. Apart from the rather stark denotative definition, "offspring," the connotative implication calls to mind either the sum total of your experiences with children or isolated singular responses — perhaps your own childhood memories, the children you teach, the dimpled baby across the street, or the freckled little leaguer in your family. Your reaction to the word may be positive and pleasant. On the other hand, words such as *death, disease, poverty,* and *hell* evoke an opposite reaction. These are often called *loaded* words because whether you react positively or negatively, the author has intended to trigger a stereotyped response within you. Not all words have connotative power, but those that do can wield a tremendous influence on our lives. Becoming aware of the techniques of connotative language makes for more critical consumers of printed words.

The advertiser is aware of connotations as he markets his product, appealing to the vanity, desires, and weaknesses of his public. Editorials that take a decisive stand on a controversial issue are rich with "loaded words," which may either flatter the reader by appealing to his highest virtues or awaken fear and distrust for an issue that is new or different. Appeals from worthwhile charities make full use of connotative language for good causes. Election times provide an abundance of campaign material and speeches carrying loaded words which seek to win public approval for a cause or candidate. In descriptive writing words that appeal to the senses, evoke mental images, and provide literary effectiveness and vividness are used extensively.

Children who can recognize evocative language are better equipped to make rational judgments and to read critically. Exercises in the primary grades deal with identification of words with strong imagery. Guide the children to spot them through specific direction:

Find the words that make you able to almost feel the kitten: (*fuzzy, warm, rough, wet tongue*)

Find words that give clues to how Mrs. Hill's farm may have smelled. (*fresh-cut hay, newly painted fence*)

Similarly, allow the children to find examples of words that appeal to sight, sound, and taste. Many words appeal to more than one sense. Children with limited experiences have developed fewer connotations. Those that develop first center around sensory impression. The teacher should look for opportunities to build upon a child's storehouse of personal connotations: "Tell me what comes to mind when I say a word," "Describe what you see or think about." (Use words very close to the child such as "home," "mother," "love," and so on.)

It is not the teacher's purpose to develop his students' analytical reading to the point that they examine scrupulously each word in a selection for an expected connotation. Literary works are sometimes better appreciated as a Gestalt; newspapers, advertising, and political speeches provide excellent opportunities for working with connotative language in the intermediate grades.

Example: Have children underline the loaded words in a political speech as the following:

> Long have I been a citizen of our beloved community. I have watched my children grow here. But now I am deeply disturbed. Never have I witnessed a more tragic upheaval than our city has suffered under my opponent Mayor Davis. Taxes have skyrocketed, yet children lie awake at night too hungry to sleep. Our once fair city streets are littered and gutted. Graft and corruption have encamped at City Hall. But, my friends, there is hope. Beckoning us is a bright new horizon, involving us all as free Americans who want desperately to stop decay and begin anew. With a dependable team we can aim toward a better tomorrow. Continuing down the same path can lead only to certain civic death. The judgment is yours.

Lead children to note generalities, words with fuzzy meanings, and the ways in which words can be used to skirt issues and to embellish empty statements.

Discuss connotative words in advertising.

Find words the advertisement includes in order to appeal to your senses:

(*shampoo*)
"Hair that shines like the sun . . . soft and perfect all the time."

(*salad dressing*)
"with all the sassy flavor, tender garlic, and mild sweet peppers . . . oozing with twenty-three herbs and spices."

(*air freshener*)
"seeks out and eliminates cooking odor, musty odors, all kinds of household odors—leaves a fresh clean scent, but never a telltale odor of its own."

Discuss some words that advertisers avoid. See if you can determine why some words are chosen rather than others (for example, "scent" rather than "smell").

Pick brand names of products and try to determine why that particular name was selected (Joy, Thrill, Halo).

Find titles of books that have connotative power.

Think of words that have recently gained another connotation ("protest," "bohemian"). Which of these words have general connotation (eliciting similar response in the total populace) as opposed to personal connotation?

Write advertisements or editorials incorporating as many loaded words and words with strong imagery as possible.

Facts versus Opinion

Often it becomes the reader's purpose to distinguish statements of fact from statements of opinion. Factual statements are objective and can be verified, that is, measured in some objective fashion. "Johnny is seven feet tall" is a statement the truth of which can be determined by any number of observers using a metric instrument. "Johnny is extremely tall" is not verifiable but rests upon one's interpretation of *tall* or *extremely*, which may or may not coincide with another's viewpoint.

Consider the difference in presentation of facts and opinion in the following example:

1. The temperature and rainfall in the equatorial zone make living there an unpleasant experience.
2. Alabama was admitted to the Union in 1819.

Perhaps proof of these statements does not lie within our personal realm of experience. It is not difficult to ascertain, however, that the truth or falsity of the second statement may be readily checked with a reliable encyclopedia. The first statement depends upon personal background, tastes, and temperament. Certainly some native of the area may object.

Altick (1969) clarified the difference between fact and opinion by stating the contingency for factual presentation: "Where there is no commonly accepted measure of truth, there can be no objective fact; everything that is judged by the individual on the basis of personal standard is subjective."

This is not to suggest, however, that unless facts are obtainable we refuse our ear to opinion. Airing opinion is an important part of life. We depend upon the commentaries of experts and their opinions based upon facts. We expect a senator to interpret economic developments. We expect an editor to editorialize. The mature reader attempts to maintain critical awareness of the issues to weigh in relation to the opinions of others.

At times, however, facts are a necessity. We demand facts about daily occurrences in straight news reporting. We demand this same kind of factual presentation from textbooks.

Distinguishing fact from opinion is not always simple. Especially when his experience and background in a subject is weak, the reader must make use of outside criteria. When an author is giving opinion, he often sends out opinion signals. Children can be made aware of these just as they can be made aware of fantasy signals. Opinion signals include: "it seems to me," "although not necessarily proven," "in my opinion," "as I (we) see it," and so on. They indicate that someone's expert or inexpert opinion follows.

Children in primary grades may work with fact and opinion at a simple level. If the teacher makes sure that the children have internalized criteria for assessing the truth of *one* statement, he can teach them to watch for an obvious signal in another.

A dog is an animal.

I think dogs should be kept outdoors.

At an intermediate level isolated statements of fact and opinion can give way to materials taken directly from the content area. Truths may be rewritten as opinions, and vice versa. The teacher should help children to understand the importance of factual presentation in texts. For example, speculate as to how social studies books would reflect different views if written by strong Republicans, Democrats, segregationists, Englishmen, and so on. The teacher can give statements such as the following and ask the students to indicate which are facts (verifiable) and which are opinion.

Asia is the largest continent.

Asia is the most beautiful continent.

Thurgood Marshall became the first Negro to be appointed to the Supreme Court on June 13, 1967.

Thurgood Marshall deserved the honor of Supreme Court Justice.

Judging Author Competence

Teaching children to critically evaluate the printed word can also be extended to guarded acceptance of the author's right to speak as an authority on a topic. Again, judgment of the right need not be delayed until the intermediate grades.

Two third grade boys in a summer corrective reading class were involved in an animated discussion concerning the amount of gear needed by a deep sea diver.

"But I read it in a book!" Paul protested when his argument was disputed.
"Yes, but books say different things sometimes," David retorted.
"But Jacques Cousteau wrote my book!"

The point was won, both boys resting their case on their assessment of the competency of this hero.

A mature reader notes both the source of a publication and the author's background. Knowing something about an author's professional training and bias makes a reader more or less open to incorporate his viewpoint.

Children in primary grades can be asked:

Is this author writing about something or someone he really knows?

How can we find out? (Lead students to the jacket flaps of books, to reviews, to the school librarian)

Where might we look to check some of these facts? (encyclopedias and other references)

Children in intermediate grades can use such references as *Who's Who in America* and *American Men of Science* for biographical data. They can learn to check the card catalog and the *Reader's Guide to Periodical Literature* to determine the scope of an author's work. Children in the middle grades will also enjoy writing to publishers to obtain information about an author. They may seek information as to the extent which the author has pursued or studied in his field or determine the depth and breadth of his reporting.

Children in intermediate grades can also use sources such as *Junior Book of Authors* (edited by S. J. Kunitz and Howard Haycraft, Wilson and Company, 1951) or sections of the *Horn Book* or *Elementary English*. The school librarian may be an additional resource. How children learn about standard references is discussed in Chapter 16.

For middle graders practical examples of evaluating author background, education, reputation, and professional position can be profitable. You may, for example, read two blurbs about authors of science books. The first is head of a science department, director of research studies at a university, and has worked as consultant on several science textbooks. The second is highly interested in science, has read extensively, and is primarily a children's author. Ask the children:

Which of the two might have more background to write a book on leaf identification? What is their standard for selecting one over the other?

With your children try to determine whether publishing houses and book jackets have any reason to distort author expertness in the field. It may result in evaluating the source of the author evaluation.

Determining Author Purpose

Determining the intent of the author better enables the reader to evaluate the message. Does the author hope to inform, amuse, convince, or arouse? Does he wish to state facts, deprecate, or dispel doubt? The purpose of an author's work often determines where it is published. If he purports to substantially increase the knowledge in a certain field by reporting his research results, he may choose a more scholarly journal with a limited readership than, for example, the *Reader's Digest,* which appeals to a wider audience. Similarly, the *Congressional Record* may carry a more direct account of a Senate bill you are following than the editorial page of your newspaper. Author purpose was again different.

Children, too, can learn to become aware of how author purpose affects the slant of a presentation. For example, Robert Lawson's delightful *Ben and Me,* a fictionalized account of the scientific achievements of Benjamin Franklin, as "told" by a mouse who takes full credit, may be compared with the d'Aulaires' book *Benjamin Franklin* on the life of this famous inventor. Author bias is obvious in this example. Lead children to discern differences in account because of differences in purpose.

Stories can be assessed for author purpose. A simple classification scheme such as "fun" or "information" may be a good starting point for beginning the work. Newspapers and varied news accounts bring home the point for intermediate grade students. They may also engage in such activities as the following:

Reading selected paragraphs with readily determined purposes. For example, one paragraph may inform the children about the new school cafeteria—size, cost, seating capacity, and hours open. Another may urge the students to take care of the cafeteria, reinforcing the rules while appealing to school spirit.

Writing articles with different purposes. Using the same subject matter, have children write with different purposes in mind, that is, to amuse, to inform, and so on. Compare the different accounts.

Collect different accounts of the same event which occur in different newspapers or those which are presented in straight news style as opposed to feature presentation. Determine the slant of the articles, author purpose, and the way author purpose can be determined in the article.

Propaganda Techniques

In 1937 the Institute of Propaganda Analysis reported seven techniques whereby unwary readers could fall victim to propaganda. Since then, more than any other area of critical reading, identifying propaganda has received teaching emphasis. The original list has been expanded, interpreted, and repeatedly redefined by its users. Basically, it consisted of (1) bad names; (2) glad names; (3) transfer; (4) testimonial; (5) plain folks; (6) stacking the cards; and (7) band wagon.

Bad names is a method by which readers are encouraged to make a negative judgment about someone or something without examining the evidence cautiously. The writer intends to provoke an emotional reaction through use of words with unpleasant connotations. Avoidance behavior is sought by name-calling: "Relieve irritating itching"; "The situation is a rotten-smelling mess."

Glad names is also dependent upon the connotative appeal of words. In this case the propagandist appeals to our senses, our noblest ambitions, our feelings of love and of loyalty. "Lovers of justice," "seekers of truth and honor," "dedicated to democracy," and "delicate, demure beauty" are examples of the ways glad names are used to arouse a pleasant response and insure acceptance or approval before the reader scrutinizes the evidence.

Transfer is the utilization of long-standing feelings of admiration for something in an attempt to precipitate the same reaction toward another product or issue. Politicians cite their church affiliation, hoping for the transfer process. Beauty queens smile beside many different products and the public desires to emulate the queen who sells the product.

Testimonial involves citing an authority or some well-known person as endorsing or rejecting some product, service, charity, or issue. The propagandist attempts to play upon the name and fame of the individual in order to convince the public to react as this famous person does. Testimonial is similar to transfer; for example, "Janie Jansen, famous screen star, uses Tress, the shampoo of beautiful women."

Plain folks is the title given to the attempt, often by public speakers such as politicians, ministers, and businessmen, to gain favor and win confidence by feigning the speech patterns, dress, and interests of those whom they seek to impress.

Stacking the cards is a method of withholding some element of truth. Omission of truth or slanted judgment may make truth appear to be falsehood and vice versa; for example, "You know that Roosevelt was betraying us because he made secret deals with Communist boss Stalin."

Band wagon is a follow-the-crowd approach. All are urged to join with the masses and to team with a winner; for example, "More doctors use ____," "the number one selling brand."

Because there are so many categories of propaganda techniques, it is particularly important for the teacher to help children become aware of the technique itself rather than to become expert classifiers of such. A ready source for initial classroom work with propaganda is, of course, advertisements. They are easily obtainable and highly interesting to intermediate grade pupils. Newspapers and magazines are rich sources of advertisements. Ability to recognize propaganda is not a sure indicator of ability to resist it in its varied form (Nardelli, 1957). The teacher should strive to give as many concrete examples and applications to actual experience as possible.

EVALUATING CRITICAL READING

The child who becomes a critical reader can, in retrospect, judge the veracity, worth, and validity of what he reads. He brings critical judgment to bear upon the author's work; he can distinguish fact from fantasy, can determine author purpose and competency, can note instances of evocative language, and can incorporate outside resources to check facts.

He becomes aware of propaganda and the effect it can play in his life. He can successfully analyze arguments, aligning points and evaluating conclusions. The critical reader makes use of his skill daily in newspaper reading, incidental reading experiences, and in reading for pleasure. He is likely to become a more intelligent voter, citizen, and consumer as a result of this skill.

By using the ideas and the exercises described in this chapter a teacher can develop his own tests in critical reading. The question pattern provides a sound diagnostic technique, for it delineates the kinds of questions a child is able to answer. Through observation the teacher can likewise identify strengths and weaknesses. A short checklist such as the one shown helps the teacher structure his observations to collect more significant data.

CREATIVE READING

While reading critically demands setting a purpose for reading that involves evaluation of the author's words, creative reading occurs when the reader is able to extend the reading selection, to rearrange the ideas obtained into new thoughts and fresh ideas, and to express them in some creative fashion. Some authors prefer to use the terms *critical reading* and *creative reading* interchangeably, and indeed the overlap is indisputable. Creative reading is viewed here, however, as

CHECK LIST OF SKILLS IN CRITICAL READING	Always	Usually	Seldom	Never
Can the student do the following?				
a. Recognize the significance of the content				
b. Recognize important details				
c. Identify unrelated details				
d. Find the main idea of a paragraph				
e. Find the main idea of larger selections				
f. Locate the topic sentences				
g. Locate answers to specific questions				
h. Develop independent purposes for reading				
i. Realize the author's purpose				
j. Develop standards to determine the accuracy and relevancy of information				
k. Determine, judge, and draw conclusions from the author's interpretation of controversial issues				
l. Evaluate concepts gained by contrasting and comparing them with facts and opinions from several other sources				
m. Suspend judgment until sufficient data is gathered				
n. Visualize from a written or oral description				
o. Draw one's own inferences from the material and recognize the inference implied by the author				

a unique expression stimulated by the reading material, be it composition, dramatics, or art work. The objective is to transform the reading material into something highly personal.

The justification for including creative reading as part of the reading process is that it represents one kind of application and response to the material, similar to giving oral reactions to what has been read. Upon reading about Alice falling down the rabbit hole, one child says, "Oh, how scary!" and another draws a picture of Alice using an umbrella in the manner of Mary Poppins to drift into the land of make believe. Each response flows spontaneously from what is read and in that sense can be viewed as part of the continuous process of reading. In a guided reading lesson creative reading would take place in the segments referred to as follow-up discussion and developing related activities.

Torrance (1969) has summed up the necessity for creative reading:

> Until the ideas on the printed page become a real part of the reader — influencing his thoughts and actions, aiding his assessment of ideas and the way they are expressed, changing and reinforcing his point of view — until this material becomes a functioning part of his thinking and acting, the reading program has been only partially successful. It is not enough to read and react critically to the author's ideas. The ideas which pass the critical test of the reader's scrutiny must become a part of the reader's thinking and actions. For example, it is not enough to read and critically judge democratic ideals. These ideals must become an active ingredient of the reader's behavior.*

Refer again to the reading communication model of Figure 1.1. Note the point of synthesis — where the author's ideas are grasped cohesively and both imagination and background experience can be called into play. Here creative reading begins, new arrangements, applications, and relations are drawn. In a sense the child actually enters into a form of co-authorship, so engrossed does he become when encouraged by a teacher who also reads creatively. Thoughts and feelings spring up, ready to be channeled into a multitude of creative directions. This then is *application*, the final phase on the reading continuum.

Inherent in both synthesis and application is the building of a coherent unit. The reader employs a common foundation, the experience, upon which he can fashion a unique superstructure. In that way reflective thinking as well as the ability to react in the light of one's

*Torrance, E. Paul. Introduction, *Ginn 360 Reading Series* by Theodore Clymer. (Boston, Ginn and Company, 1969).

own experiences constitutes creative reading. Here it is valuable to emphasize that the desire to communicate a resultant creative product is a logical follow-up of any creative act. Indeed, the communication may itself be integral to the creative act, as in the spontaneous comment: "That poem makes me feel like a warm turtle dove."

CLASSROOM ACTIVITIES FOR CREATIVE READING

The teacher who realizes the value of creative expression senses that the satisfaction gained from the creative process lends new worth and a sense of individuality to each child. Teacher alertness to the many opportunities for creative expression will aid in developing youngsters who not only *experience* reading but also *expand* and *express* thoughts and feelings in a variety of modes. The three "E's" bear remembering in setting the stage for creative expression. First, the child must be open to experience and then drawn to reflect upon the situation and its consequences. Finally, he is encouraged to express his reaction in concrete images.

Sparking creative expression involves "expectation and anticipation" as the reading task is approached and then "doing something" with the story. For facilitating discussion, classroom creative activities have been grouped here into four categories: (1) oral activities; (2) written activities; (3) arts and crafts; and (4) dramatics.

Oral Creative Reading Activities

The activities discussed in Chapter 12 can be profitably incorporated by the teacher who seeks to set the stage for creative expression. Several additional activities are offered here.

Choral Reading

The enjoyment of poetry is heightened by sharing it aloud. Take advantage of the rhythm of the poet's words by having young children provide accompaniment with rhythm instruments or improvisation (sand blocks, dowel sticks, honey-locust seed pods, coconut shells, or bottles.) Children begin choral *speaking* almost naturally as they chime in on the chorus or a repeated line of a favorite teacher-read poem. From this simple beginning the rudiments for choral reading are formed. Older children can find natural divisions in favorite poetry for high and low voices, as well as locate parts that seem to require a solo voice or a sound effect. Thus, the way is paved for enjoying poetry together. Children hesitant to read aloud alone join in, not only to gain a sense of belonging but also to derive a thorough experience with tone and voice melody. Care should be taken to avoid sacrificing the satisfaction derived from choral reading for the sake of arriving at perfect rhythm and harmony. It is much more important to interpret the mood of the poem and to gain pleasure from group participation.

Supplying Different Endings through Discussion

An assumption that is too often made in many classrooms is that a story is completed when the final paragraph is read. Much like a musical sentence, the plot is resolved and the pupils must accept the resolution. This need not be the case. Rather, here is the opportunity for doing something with a story. Reopen it; provide new solutions; toss it about to the creative urges of each child. Stories incorporating a repetitive sequence provide a good beginning point. Instead of accepting the happily-ever-after dictum, why not conjecture what might happen to the *Gingerbread Man*? A whole new series of adventures can be built upon the story's structure, with the children becoming oral authors.

Modifying a crucial incident within the story may also lead to spinning new endings. The teacher who encourages divergent thinking of this sort is helping children to respond creatively. That is, they move out from the story, expanding to consider new aspects on what they have read. "The Valentine Box," a story by Maude Hart Lovelace, deals with the efforts of a lonely new girl at school to aid a classmate in recovering valentines blown from her hand by the winter wind. Children involved in divergent thinking could speculate about a change in decision on Jane's part. How would the story have changed if Jane had decided not to risk tardiness or the loss of her own valentines to help? Give opportunity for several children to finish the story in a different way.

Creative story ending can be begun with even prereaders listening to a story. One first grade teacher noticed a frown from a little fellow in the story circle as "Peter Rabbit" ended.

"What are you thinking, Danny?" she asked.

"Well, he shouldn't have left home in the first place!" he shouted defiantly.

Here was the chance to find out how Danny could reconstruct the story and draw new consequences. A lively discussion is certain to follow and result in a new twist to an old tale.

Dramatic Oral Interpretation

Oral interpretation helps children gain empathy for the characters they portray. Reading parts can put life into a story, aid in understanding motives, and offer a more direct experience with the story itself. Prior discussion about the kind of person a particular character is can lend a sense of reality to his life and may result in differing oral interpretations by students who view the character from different vantage points. Abraham Lincoln and one of his famous speeches, such as the Gettysburg Address, are favorites for dramatic interpretation.

Written Creative Reading Activities

Just as students can vitalize stories by orally providing new endings, they may also communicate those endings in writing. Especially since writing enables a direct visual comparison, the notion is fostered that stories need not be static but may involve fresh, dynamic thinking.

Parallel Stories

Parallel stories are those that grow from the original plot but may follow a minor character into full development or fan from a touched-upon but passed-over event. They can develop from such discussions as, "If I were Sarah," or from questions that draw speculation as to what must have happened before. Expanding a character provides opportunity for children to manipulate events and to ascribe characteristics, feelings, thoughts, and even environmental stimuli to enrich their reaction to the story. They are deeply drawn into discussions of two versions of a story prepared by their own classmates. Sharing a story on parallel planes adds richness to the reading experience. Other opportunities for building parallel stories include:

> Pretend to be a character who witnesses the action from a different perspective. Write this new interpretation.
>
> Describe the conjectured personality traits of a character if he could be met face to face today in your classroom.
>
> Pretend to be a certain character and keep a diary of his thoughts and feelings.
>
> Write a letter that one character in the story may have written to another describing some event and his reaction to it.

Writing Plays

Children can turn stories of all kinds into plays, whether dialogue based or straight narratives. The impetus for writing plays stems largely from the desire to participate actively in a story that lends itself to action. Aesop's *Fables* are a good start for the novice playwrights in the classroom. The action is simple; the characters are few; the dialogues are simple and straightforward. Fairy tales, legends, and favorite stories of individuals within the classroom also lend themselves to dramatization. The scripts prepared should be evaluated as any piece of creative writing in the class: check for clarity and structure but avoid filling the product with red pencil marks.

Poems and Songs

Both poetry and poetry set to music are possible when a child is caught up in a story or event. When neither is assigned but arises from spontaneous appreciation of a shared reading experience, the enjoyment is heightened. A first grade class finished a story about a snowstorm. Later that afternoon big flakes began to hit against the window. The children were excited to see the story come to life. The teacher sensed it. From the repetitive rhythm of one child's chant, "It's snow, it's snow, it's snow," the teacher followed the line on the piano, the first line resulting finally in a "many-composer" melody.

It has been said that every child is a poet; indeed, poetry arises spontaneously from children deeply excited by an experience and intent upon communicating it. To encourage the writing of poetry, a teacher should read poems to his class — lots of them and of all kinds — and should enjoy sharing his pleasure openly. He should be alert to the poetry in the language of children, taking it down when he hears it. The children's poems need not rhyme but rather should reflect and express innermost thoughts.

As a teacher, find descriptions in stories that lend themselves to poetry. Try poetry as a class project. Recognize that children's poems are sometimes lacking in elements considered valuable in adult writing and may be considered crude by some standards, yet children who write poetry as a reaction to what they have read gain confidence in their ability to communicate.

Letter Writing

As mentioned earlier, letter writing can be imaginary in nature, as, for example, a letter Jane and Michael Banks might have sent to Mary Poppins after her abrupt departure. Children also profit from writing letters to authors, expressing appreciation for a story, suggesting alternate solutions, or asking pertinent questions. Many authors respond to their small critics. Increased interest and an immeasurable sense of self-worth will result among the children.

Arts and Crafts

From children's illustrations of stories the teacher can learn much about what appealed to the child, what he remembered and considered crucial. More important, the child is offered opportunity to express himself in yet another way. Fingerpaints are effectively used to illustrate stories and poems of mood and mystery or those that draw upon the elements for special effect. With splashes of blue and swirls of white young artists can create wind and rain. "Plink Plink Goes the Water in My Sink" by Ethel and Leonard Kessler (Doubleday & Company, New York, 1954) lends itself to this type of expression. Encourage children to sweep their fingers and swirl their fists to create movement, excitement, and texture.

"The Beach before Breakfast" by Maxine W. Kumin and "Hide and Seek Fog" by Alvin Tresselt suggest by their titles the creative moods they elicit. Watercolors could be used effectively as background wash for illustrations of either of these books.

Crayon resist, a method whereby foreground figures are crayoned in and watercolor applied to the entire picture, with the crayoned part resisting the paint, is effective for depicting such graphic descriptions as the following:

> "But out of doors the fog twisted about the cottages like slow motion smoke.
>
> It dulled the rusty scraping of the beach grass.
>
> It muffled the chattery talk of the low tide waves
>
> And it hung, wet and dripping, from the bathing suits and towels on the clothesline." (Kumin, 1964)

Three-dimensional models are tangible results of a shared story experience. Models can be sculpted from paper, clay, toothpicks, or odds and ends. Children involved in a unit of stories dealing with pioneers may fashion an entire village as a class project or work on individual dioramas. Wire or pipe cleaner figures may represent the characters in the stories.

Dramatics

When children respond to a story they move wholeheartedly toward the reenactment of the same tale. "With wonderful abandon they throw themselves into the various parts and relive the events of the story or book" (Torrance, 1969). Through imagination the author's words are brought to life. Pantomiming, role playing, play acting, puppetry, and shadow plays are all methods for creative interpretations.

Pantomime

Playing out a story through pantomime is one of the simplest forms of creative dramatics. Variations on the pantomiming technique include acting the story while selected readers describe the action or free interpretation of favorite story parts. Instruct the children to use only gestures and movements to convey their character:

> Skip through the woods as Little Red Riding Hood
>
> Run home from the ball as Cinderella
>
> Be the crotchety grandfather or carefree Peter in "Peter and the Wolf"
>
> Huff and puff with the Big Bad Wolf
>
> As one of the seven dwarfs, discover the intrusion of the sleeping Snow White.

Role Playing

Role playing involves assuming a character's traits and playing out imaginative discussions or climactic scenes. Students from a third grade class read with interest stories of Christopher Columbus from boyhood to old age. Deciding to act out his life, they constructed his ships from tables and chairs, designated Spain as the chalkboard, and set sail. Similarly, other children, after following the moon flight through newspaper and television coverage, enacted the roles of the astronauts.

Play Acting

Play acting differs from the above in that parts are assigned and usually "learned" in one fashion or another. Often these plays are written, produced, and directed by students.

Puppetry

Simple puppets are a joy to all children. They especially help the shy child to project his feelings and to extend his verbal experiences. Activities with puppets spark language expression, broaden understanding, deepen feelings and emotion, and develop empathy with the characters of the story. Puppets can be formed from paper bags, from sticks, or with papier mâché heads and cloth bodies; they may be as elaborate as time and energy permit. In any case they serve the function of playing out stories in a projected role.

Shadow Plays

Performing a story behind a suspended sheet with a strong light directly behind the players calls attention to bodily movements and gestures. Shadow plays are an effective way to implement pantomime.

Dancing

Creative dance and rhythms are techniques whereby entire stories may be enacted or small portions fraught with emotion and movement. Forms of creative interpretation include:

Move like the saggy, baggy elephant. Bend and sway, slowly, slowly.

Be a tiny seed under the ground. Feel the warm sun on your back. Stretch to reach the sun. Grow. Grow.

Be the Indian Hiawatha. Greet the morning sun. Move to the beat of the Indian tom-toms. Dance a joyful dance.

EVALUATING PERFORMANCE IN CREATIVE READING

Creative reading activities need meet no established standards or levels of perfection. That each child experience creative expression in time set aside for this activity is an important goal. Keep in mind that the effort of each child should be as unique as the child himself. Guiding questions for the teacher include:

Did the creative activity achieve the purpose set for it?

Was the activity original, that is, a unique expression for the experience and age of the learner?

Have I led and encouraged children toward creative expression?

SUMMARY

Critical and creative reading were viewed as separate operations in the reading process, though the two cannot be sharply separated. Critical reading is concerned primarily with the reading-thinking skills that enable a reader to apply criteria to a selection and make judgments about it. Thus the skills of analysis, inference, and evaluation relate closely to critical reading.

Creative reading is concerned primarily with integrating the reading experience into the knowledge and affection of the reader and producing a response unique to the individual. The skills of synthesis and application also relate closely to creative reading.

A key factor in producing critical readers is the use of questions that lead the students from recall and restatement to classification of information and the application of criteria.

One of the major reasons for encouraging creative reading is that it fosters divergent thinking about what has been read, whether the creative results are expressed orally, in writing, through motion, or through a fine art form. In both critical and creative reading the attitude of the teacher concerning the analysis and interpretation of the reading material is crucial. The teacher who systematically moves the discussion toward evaluation and who encourages all forms of expression as an extension of reading is most likely to develop critical and creative readers.

TERMS

evaluation	connotative language
fact	propaganda
opinion	testimonial
denotative language	band wagon

Chapter 15

Concepts and Skills in Content Reading

When Tony was four years old, he brought home a pail of pond water in which there were some tadpoles. He was told to watch them to see what happened. He watched the tadpoles develop through a number of stages, and two of them survived as frogs. The day he got up and found that that's what happens to tadpoles, he commented, "Tadpoles make the nicest frogs."

What happened to Tony may provide some clues about reading in content fields. In a way, Tony went through the kind of thinking a scientist engages in when he looks at nature and tries to make some conclusions about what he has observed. That pattern of observing nature, of making some inferences about the observations, of classifying them, and of arriving at conclusions may provide some important clues as to how to read science content, as well as other content subjects. If the scientist's thinking is reflected in his writing, comprehending the writing could be aided by knowing about the scientist's typical thinking patterns.

Reading in any content field is different from reading in a basal reader. That is not a surprising statement, but it needs to be repeated and repeated loudly, because teachers do not often teach children how to handle expository writing—writing that is different from fiction and that has a different purpose from the basal reader.

To determine what content reading is and how to teach it, think about these questions as you read this chapter:

What is the difference between reading content material and reading basal reader stories?

Is there a visual difference in the content material?

What are the general skills needed to read content material efficiently?

What special reading skills are used to read specific kinds of content, such as science and math?

Are there instructional guidelines for teaching content reading?

Content reading is receiving considerable attention these days. Professional organizations are discussing the topic; publishers are producing reading series that contain an increasing volume of expository material, and teachers are listening to speeches about it at state conventions. The term "content reading" sounds like someone's double talk. After all, if you do not read content when you read, what do you read? Nonetheless, "content reading" is a term used to denote expository writing concerned with information subjects and the evaluation of that information. The term does not refer usually to the reading of a short story or a novel, that is, a selection which provides a vicarious experience or an emotional involvement in imaginative living.

One reason for isolating content reading in a text on teaching reading is that children need particular practice in reading content material. They have been systematically introduced to the short story and they spend most of their first six years in school learning to read short stories in their readers. Teachers and pupils spend much time building a short story vocabulary, analyzing plots, describing characters, interpreting actions, and applying morals to their own living.

TREND IN ELEMENTARY CURRICULUM

When it comes to the information subjects, such as social studies, most instructional emphasis goes to recalling specific information and gaining concepts. The students have to read in order to get these facts and these concepts, but since this activity is not called learning to read, many teachers seem to feel that no overt transfer of reading pedagogy is necessary. Even though the content subject has a new vocabulary, often no effort is made to get the children to analyze the vocabulary and develop automatic recognition habits as is always done in "reading" lessons; and even though content is organized differently, the writing is not analyzed as those hundreds of plots in the readers are. The attitude that creates a wall between learning to read and reading in the content subjects fails to understand what reading is. It is a tool or a process whereby a learner communicates with an author. Once the initial mechanics of learning the code of written English are conquered, reading becomes a combination of reading and thinking—an inseparable union when an individual is reacting to a printed message. He has to read some content; he cannot simply read reading. Consequently, the natural and relevant place for reading-thinking to take place is in conjunction with literature, science, math, and social studies. The question, then, is how does the teacher put the learner and the content author together so that the printed page communicates. Communication involves, among other things, a common vocabulary, a common interest, and the ability of the receiver of the message to follow the thinking of the writer of the message. Since individual writers have different thinking patterns, and since different content disciplines have different thinking patterns, the teacher has the responsibility of aiding his students to identify some of those patterns to open the channels of communication.

Comparison of Material

Consider some samples of writing from various subject areas.

There is a story in one of the basal readers that is called "A Kitty for Kathy." It is a typical primary grade story with characters and a situation or problem that the characters try to resolve. After the students read the story they are asked: "Who are the characters?" "What are they trying to do?" "How do they do it?" "Did they succeed?" Those are typical questions, because they indicate the organizational pattern of short story writing.

The story "A Kitty for Kathy" is representative of that pattern. Kathy finds a kitty on the way home from the playground and asks her mother if she may keep it. Mother tells her that they cannot keep the cat because they are going to grandmother's house for a week. They cannot take the cat with them nor can they leave it home alone. Kathy asks if she can keep the cat provided she finds someone to take care of it while they are away. Her mother consents to that plan. After a period of sitting on the door stoop Kathy has an inspiration. She goes next door and asks Mrs. Henrietta if she will babysit for her. Mrs. Henrietta says that she will be happy to babysit for Kathy anytime. Then Kathy explains that it is a cat she is to sit with. Mrs. Henrietta, being a nice neighbor, accepts the kittysitting job for the week and the problem is solved. That pattern is typical of the short stories that children continue to analyze for four, five, and six years in their basal readers.

The child has to read other types of material. In expository writing a character, a plot, a problem to be solved, or some interaction between characters may not appear. Then what does the child do? What kinds of questions does he ask when he approaches the material and tries to comprehend it? The structure of the selection is different from the short story. It is not sufficient to tell the child that he will have to discuss the topic; that he is to read the next several pages; and that he must answer several fact questions, such as: What is a tadpole? Where do tadpoles live? How do tadpoles develop? The child must recall many facts and details, but he also needs suggestions on how to analyze the author's purpose and thinking pattern.

Through a series of analyses of science, social studies, and mathematics texts the students can see that there are different structural patterns, or different organizational patterns in different kinds of texts. Science writing usually has an organizational pattern different from social studies, for example. If students were alerted to these patterns they would have a way of preorganizing themselves in order to increase comprehension.

To understand a selection a reader must have the main idea, know the important details, and see the interrelation of the parts. To analyze scientific data, classify them, and find some conclusion or resulting law, a reader must begin with literal comprehension. Beyond that he has to know what the various parts of the selection are, what relations exist among the parts, and how those relations lead to the conclusion. As important as that learning is, one wonders how often it occurs in schools where memorizing the content is stressed.

LEVELS OF DIFFICULTY IN CONTENT TEXTS

A child faces many problems when he comes to the task of reading science content. For example, in one science textbook he finds a selection that discusses how Mendel first discovered the laws of heredity. The teacher's guide states that the book was written for the lower track of junior and senior high school groups, but no specific grade or readability level is given. Evidently it is meant to be read at some reading level below grade seven. According to the Dale-Chall readability formula, it has a 7.8 reading level.* Thus, it would appear that some of the people for whom the book is intended will have considerable difficulty with it.

Another selection taken from a popular elementary school science text is designed for grade five according to the publisher. In the teacher's guide the authors say they were deliberately conscious of writing on a simple level so the book can be used by children whose reading skills are average or below. Using the Dale-Chall readability formula on that grade five text produced a grade readability of 9.1 (Smith, Carl, 1969a).

Why should the readability formula indicate a much more difficult level than the publisher and authors estimate? One reason is that the selections contain many difficult words, that is, words which do not appear on the list of easy words in the readability formula. The larger the number of difficult words, the higher will be the readability level. The list of easy words is composed of words that appear most frequently in basal readers. Therefore, through the basal reader children are trained to ready easy words, then are asked to read *heredity, Austrian, monk monastary, differed, traits, crosspolinated, resulting,* and *offspring* in the article about Mendel. All of these words appear in one paragraph of the text and are considered difficult words because they are

*Readability formulas include the number of difficult words and the length of the sentence combined with a mathematical formula to produce the grade equivalent of the material.

not commonly used. In the next paragraph are found the words *generation, pure-bred, produced, tallness, dominant, shortness, recessive, expressed.* One out of every eight words in the article is not regularly used in basal readers or language arts texts, and therefore children are not expected to be able to respond to them automatically. They have to stop and analyze them, provided they have sufficient word-analysis skills. But consider a word like *hybrid* in this sentence: "He prided himself in having both hybrid corn and hybrid chickens." What does *hybrid* mean? A child can analyze all day and not know what *hybrid* means unless he is from a farm region. Even then he may not know precisely, but know only that *hybrid* is a word used for a special kind of corn. He has to have some way to relate those words to his experience and some way of identifying them.

Look at the paragraphs on Mendel that follow. Every eighth word has been systematically blocked out. It is still fairly easy to read the passage and understand it. By systematically deleting words, form words like *a, the,* and *in* are likewise eliminated, and their omissions are usually rather simple to figure out. But block out *monastery, hybrid, crosspollination,* and *pure-bred,* as the child does when vocabulary is a problem, and see what happens to comprehension.

MENDEL FIRST DISCOVERED THE FACTS ABOUT HEREDITY

      _____ 1860, an Austrian monk named Gregor Mendel _____ to raise peas in the monastery garden. _____ found that they differed somewhat and was _____ as to why this was so. He _____ records of the traits of leaves, stems, _____, and seeds. He noted also the shape _____ color of the seeds. He crosspollinated _____ by hand and kept careful records of _____ resulting offspring. If the offspring were _____ result of crossing different kinds of peas, _____ called them *hybrids.*

      He crossed tall peas with short peas _____ found that the offspring were all tall. _____ when he crossed this generation of offspring _____ each other, he found that three fourths _____ tall and one fourth was short. When _____ crossed some of the tall peas with _____ tall ones, the offspring were all tall. _____ again, when he crossed tall and tall, _____ of the offspring were tall and some _____ short. So, he reasoned that some of _____ peas were *purebreds* which always produced because _____ and that all the short ones were _____ because they always produced short peas. But _____ of the tall plants must be hybrids _____ have the short trait hidden in them. _____ called these tall plants *pure tall* if _____ always produced tall offspring, and *hybrid tall* _____ they sometimes produced short offspring along with _____ tall ones. He also said that tallness _____ a *dominant trait.* And shortness was a _____ *trait,* because it was often hidden by _____ dominant.*

---

*Davis, Ira C., *et al. Science 3, Discovery, and Progress* (New York: Holt, Rinehart and Winston, Inc., 1965), p. 438.

The fifth grade text that was rated 9.1 on the Dall-Chall formula presents still further difficulty. The first paragraph contains *esophagus, stomach lining, soften, chemicals,* and *particles* — all words not found in the easy word list. Other difficult words are *completely, digested, moist, valve, coiled, tubes, liver, pancreas, intestine, glands, molecules, bloodstream, capillaries, gristle, stringy fibers.* One out of six of these words is not in the easy word list. Eliminate one sixth of the words in a passage and comprehension must suffer. Many words that are essential to comprehension cannot be identified. It is evident, therefore, that vocabulary and word recognition play key roles in reading content selections. In this example one sixth of the words have been blocked out, but they are the difficult words that are liable to cause the reader the most trouble.

THE DIGESTIVE SYSTEM

After you _____ the food, it passes down the _____ into your _____. Juices from the lining of your _____ mix with the food. The juices soften the food, and _____ in the juices break up _____ into even smaller ones.

Most food is not completely _____ in the _____. When the food is _____ and soft enough, a _____ at the end of the _____ opens, a little at a time. The partly _____ food flows into a long, _____ narrow _____ called the small _____.*

These examples indicate that content teachers need to know ways to teach vocabulary just as a reading teacher would. They have to build background so the child has the concepts to work with, and they have to present vocabulary in terms of concept development as well as in terms of word recognition.

In addition to vocabulary problems in content material, there are diagrams, charts, and tables that accompany the text, and usually it is rather essential to relate the text to those diagrams.

USING ILLUSTRATIONS

Here is the opening paragraph from a story entitled "From Tadpoles to Frogs"** taken from a second grade book:

When I first put my tadpoles into the bowl they were funny little things. I had never seen anything like them before. They stayed under water all the time.

A student living in a large urban center might not know what a tadpole is. For those who can find tadpoles in ponds and creeks near

*Schneider, Herman and Nina. *Science in Our World* Book 5 (Boston: D. C. Heath and Company, 1968), p. 185.
**Stratemeyer, C. G. and Smith, H. L., Jr. *Frog Fun*. Evanston, Harper & Row, 1963.

their home, this is no problem. But children in Cleveland and New York City may never have seen a live pig, much less a tadpole.

It is reported that an eighteen-year-old boy from Brooklyn, New York, took a train to go to school in the Midwest. When he arrived on campus he told his counselor that on the trip he had seen his first live pig and his first live cow. It is not unrealistic to say, therefore, that many second grade children do not know what a tadpole is.

That is the reason why teachers have to build concepts and relate the text to the illustrations. Look at the sample page from the "Tadpole" story. The science text gives a diagram, a picture, or an illustration. A child reads: "I'd never seen anything like them before. They stayed under water all the time." Without illustrations, what image would the second grade reader have? What has he seen on television that stays underwater and that he has never seen before?

The illustrations demonstrate the growth of a tadpole. The teacher must explain: "Look at the pictures and go back to the text." This seems quite elementary, but for the child who does not have the experience, the teacher has to show him how to relate illustrations to the text, especially since the illustrations may be quite different from the illustrations of people in the basal readers.

The tadpole story was a grade two science reading problem. In a grade four science text the subject may be the operation of a refracting telescope. The conceptual problem is compounded. Not only does the student not understand what a refracting telescope is but the teacher too must study diligently at night to relate an illustration of the telescope with the text that describes it. Relating the drawing to

The tadpoles are growing.
Oh how fast they grow.
They are turning into frogs.

Tell me, little frog,
what happened to your tail?

FIGURE 15-1   Illustrations from "Frog Fun"

From Sounds Around the Clock, *a Sounds of Language Series, edited by Bill Martin, Jr.,* © *copyright 1970. Reprinted by special permission of Holt, Rinehart & Winston, Inc.*

the text is a reading skill. It is a skill that is needed often in reading science, math, and social studies texts. Show the children how to move systematically through the diagram by locating the point where the text explanation and the diagram correspond. Remind children that reading the illustrations will help them visualize, conceptualize, and understand.

The primary goal of content reading is to teach the child how to comprehend the totality of the selection. He must comprehend what the science writer had in mind when he made an observation about nature. In a sense, the reader wants to know how the scientist thinks when he writes, and that is an excellent "handle" to give children: read like a scientist; read like a mathematician; read like a social scientist. By trying to identify the structure of the content discipline and typical patterns for presenting that information, the reader is prepared to comprehend.

READING SKILLS FOR CONTENT READING

If reading the expository material in the content subjects needs a different approach, what are skills needed in order to read if efficiently? Evidently most of the same skills that are used in reading narrative will also be used in reading content selections. Word-analysis and word-meaning skills and skills leading to a literal comprehension of the selection will be employed in all types of reading. In addition to those elements, however, there are skills related to using materials and skills of analysis and evaluation that apply most often to the format and organization of the selections usually found in the content subject texts and their related materials.

Underlying the reading of any selection are the general skills that enable a person to achieve literal comprehension. These include a basic reading vocabulary, the use of context to help determine the meaning of words within a given selection, and the use of phonics, structural analysis, the dictionary, and illustrations as other aids in deciphering the words that the reader does not respond to immediately. The reader asks himself these basic questions: What is the main idea? What are the major parts of the selection? What are the important or supporting details to the main idea? But in answering those questions the reader often finds himself faced with some of the problems that have already been identified as problems in content reading. *The vocabulary, format, references, point of view, and organization deviate from what he is familiar with.* Thus he needs to employ a number of procedural skills that will assist him in locating information, examining it efficiently, and adjusting his reading rate so that he can achieve his purpose for reading the selection. The common study skills, such as summarizing, outlining, using references and organizing time, play a role in comprehending content subjects. Study skills are treated in a succeeding chapter. How to teach the other skills for content reading is discussed here.

As a reader grasps the basic meaning of a selection he can analyze it and evaluate it. Involved in the task of analysis are classifying, categorizing, and identifying the principles of organization. Evaluating requires the reader to formulate some criteria for judging the relevancy, utility, and validity of the information. He has to make some decisions about the content. If nothing more, he has to decide whether to remember it or not, and whether or not to make it a part of his concept of the subject area. If his evaluation indicates that the selection yields little or no valuable information, he will decide not to integrate it with the knowledge he has stored concerning that subject.

Teaching Skills for Reading in Content Subjects

Knowing that content subjects require general reading skills, skills for using the specialized material, and analytic and evaluative reading skills does not make them automatically viable. Figure 15.2 indicates the variety and the levels of skills incorporated in reading content material. Each of the areas will be discussed in relation to teaching children how to read content material.

General Reading Skills

It is true that most children have the general reading skills to read content material, but they often do not realize it. The teacher, therefore, should demonstrate how those general reading skills can be transferred or applied to science, math, and social studies. He should tell his students that reading content material should be considered a continuation of their learning how to read. In one sense, reading of content material can begin as the child acquires the basic reading skills of word analysis and the recognition of a common vocabulary.

Because developing concepts and a specialized vocabulary are integral to reading, a specialized content instruction for reading in the content areas can be said to be always occurring. An eclipse of the moon is discussed in class in anticipation of the event. When it occurs, the students read about it in newspapers and magazines. With more attention to the purposes for which the student reads, learning content reading skills can be more naturally and easily achieved. Thus, instruction for content reading begins before the child can "read," continues as he goes through the process of learning to "decode," and progresses throughout his encounters with reading materials and other classroom activities.

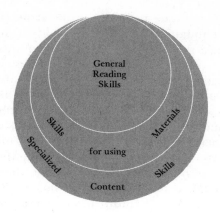

FIGURE 15-2 Skills for Reading Content Selections

Reading content subjects require general reading skills as well as other locational and thinking skills indicated by the format of the material and the presentation of the ideas.

Literal Comprehension

The focal point for the application of general reading skills is to assimilate the meaning of the passage, that which is usually called literal comprehension. In order to assimilate meaning the reader must have an understanding of the concepts contained in the passage and be able to identify the words used. He must likewise be able to follow the writing style and the organization of the writing—all of which sounds fairly simple until it is applied to reality. Earlier, a passage from a grade five science text on the digestive system was used as an example. The completed passage follows:

THE DIGESTIVE SYSTEM

After you swallow the food, it passes down the esophagus into your stomach. Juices from the lining of your stomach mix with the food. The juices soften the food, and the chemicals in the juices break up particles into even smaller ones.

Most food is not completely digested in the stomach. When the food is moist and soft enough, a valve at the end of the stomach opens, a little at a time. The partly digested food flows into a long, coiled, narrow tube called the small intestine.*

The concept-development problems, definition problems, and word-identification problems are considerable.

Concept attainment is, in itself, a complex task. What is meant

*Schneider, *Science in Our World*, p. 185.

by a "system," for example, a system for processing food? Vocabulary development (definition) is not necessarily a complete concept development, since the meaning to be used in a particular context may not require recognition of the total complex of characteristics and relations making up the "true" concept symbolized by a particular word, such as *esophagus*. In the classroom this is particularly true. Children's concepts develop over time and rely on their ability to perceive and understand the various components of a concept. The problem for the teacher is to identify the special words and the aspects of the total concept necessary for understanding the material. Those aspects can then be related to the knowledge the children have to help them obtain adequate meaning from the text. For example, consider this single sentence: "Landforms are closely and intricately related to man's use and occupation of the land." Special words to be defined and studied for continued recognition are *landforms* and *occupation*. The teacher may find it advisable to discuss *intricately* as well, not because of its special connotation but because it may not be a word in the children's reading vocabulary. Depending on the age and education of the children, the teacher then works to establish and clarify the concept. Perhaps there are local examples or experiences which show that river valley land (landform) is used for grazing cattle or mining coal (occupation). By establishing those contacts with the child's experience the teacher enables him to understand the sentence and probably the paragraphs that follow.

Developing Vocabulary and Concepts

A major problem with vocabulary and concept development is that the vocabulary assumes different technical meanings in different content. For example, *satellite* as an orbiting body around another body, as a country whose control comes from another country, and as a manmade object revolving around the earth makes it difficult to preview material and select at a glance the words that need concept development. Questioning the students about the material should provide information concerning their grasp of the meaning of a single word. Such questioning should be carefully planned, since reiteration of a statement in a book is no indication of understanding. The question should elicit explanatory, definitional, or application responses. Restating or defining are relevant to a specific concept, for example, "What does *satellite* mean in that passage?" Application questions test the ability of the child to generalize the meaning and thereby illustrate his competence in dealing with specific content concepts.

The problem of words with multiple meanings is clearly illustrated in "story" problems in arithmetic. Children need to acquire the skill of learning to translate words such as *is, more, less, times greater* as computational signals and as indicators of relations between quantities. Direct and explicit instruction often assists in the acquisition of this skill. Another means is to use "headlines." A mathematical equation is presented as a "headline" ($2 \times 3 = 6$ or $2 + 3 = ?$). The students are asked to tell a story that could be represented by the equation headline. That procedure reverses the translation process. Once the relation between story and equation is understood, the translation difficulty, or the reading problem, decreases.

The translation process is the underlying problem in literal comprehension. To help overcome the problem students need experiences equal to their grasp of concepts as well as experiences that expand the level of understanding. By planning instruction to draw on past experiences and concrete examples, vocabulary and concepts will usually develop routinely.

Vocabulary and concept development is critical across all grade levels. For some words, a simple explanation in context will suffice; for others, a special experience or set of experiences of varying degrees of "concreteness" is required. Picture dictionaries, flash cards, and word lists can be useful tools. If dictionaries and word lists are made, then occasional activities—even games—using the lists should be included in the curriculum. Referring to the dictionary or word list upon reencountering a word whose meaning is forgotten is essential for several reasons: meanings of words are usually forgotten until repeated encounters strengthen recall; the habit of relearning becomes established; and reluctance to use the dictionary can be diminished.

Word meaning in content subjects, then, can be developed by using such activities as:

1. Firsthand experiences
   a. Real situations involving contact with names, concepts, principles
   b. Dramatization of a real situation
   c. Construction of examples or models representing the concept
2. Relating to personal experiences or acquired concepts
3. Exhibits
4. Films, filmstrips
5. Pictures
6. Context clues
7. Dictionary
8. Word lists

Concept development can be promoted by guiding a student's analysis of ideas. This analysis should include:

1. Comparing and contrasting instances and noninstances of the concept
2. Extracting relevant criteria belonging to the set of ideas
3. Identifying the relation of the concept to others and to the problem being considered
4. Use of the concept in the immediate and extended situations.

Literal comprehension of expository material also demands the ability to cope with the structure of the content and the style of the author. To aid learning, the most plausible approach for the elementary teacher is to consider each reading activity as a relatively separate task and to make sure that the skills required for that task are available to the student. Comparisons are not possible without adequate familiarity with the characteristics of the different types of materials. In general, the teacher is the decision-maker who determines how explicit the instruction is to be with respect to attention to concept or vocabulary development and to structure and style of the reading material.

USE OF MATERIALS

The second general category of skills for reading content material contains all of the procedural skills one should have to handle efficiently the material he reads. Three sets of skills are found in this category: (1) locational skills, those procedures for efficiently using books and other materials; (2) study skills, those procedures that organize and direct efficient and effective learning from printed material; and (3) reading-rate adjustments. Each of these sets requires a knowledge of the skills, a demonstration of when to apply an appropriate procedure, and the actual implementation of the skills. Chapter 16 discusses these matters in detail. They will be treated here only as they affect content materials.

Knowledge about procedures can be learned through an explanation, but knowing when to apply and actually use the skills will remain at a quasilearned state unless a real need to use the skills is provided. Map reading, note-taking, or scanning material will not become real skills for the reader who has few occasions to perform those skills in order to achieve a goal. Having a variety of materials available will be of little use if the reader can answer all questions with one or two books and without using maps, charts, notes, and so on. Activities must be designed to include a variety of skills in a variety of materials. Efficient use of a skill, such as note-taking, takes practice and refinement. Refinement will not occur if the student can achieve a goal without even using the skill or using it poorly.

Locational Skills

Locational skills refer to the *skills one needs to find information.* There is, first, a body of knowledge to be learned. The reader needs to know the kinds of information obtainable from different types of books and reference guides. These include the characteristics of the following:

1. Textbooks
2. Dictionaries
3. Encyclopedias
4. Almanacs
5. Trade books

The reader also needs skills in locating and using:

6. Bibliographic references (authors, *Who's Who,* and so on.)
7. Table of contents
8. Indexes of books, encyclopedias, and periodicals
9. Card catalog
10. Bibliographies
11. Glossaries

Second, in order to use these resources, the following skills are needed:

1. Alphabetizing
2. Use of multiple classification
3. Use of pronunciation keys
4. Use of titles and major and minor headings.

In a developmental sense the first content activities in the primary grades may begin with locational skills:

1. Picture dictionaries: use of alphabetical knowledge and skill
2. Use of table of contents with all books used
3. Use of glossaries
4. Use of index in all books used
5. Use of headings, titles
6. Use of pictures and simple graphs and maps

Picture dictionaries can be made for primary science and social studies and, if needed, for basic arithmetic concepts. A table of contents can be used to find the specific location of a topic or to preview the contents of a section. In the primary grades the use of glossaries, some indexes, headings, pictures, graphs, and maps can be developed as part of the basal reading instruction as well as in the content curriculum. Index use and graph and map reading will need sufficient guidance.

In the upper grades as more reference material is required formal instruction should cover the details. Exercises that clearly call for the use of those details are essential. The desired skill should be called for frequently and demonstrated how that skill is used in a specific article. Most learners need assistance in seeing a transfer of learning from practice during the reading period to actually using the skill on science or math. For example, it is usually necessary for a reader to formulate the main idea. As a matter of habit, then, the teacher can ask for the main idea of a science selection, just as he would for a narrative. "You read the selection about Mendel and heredity. What is its main idea?"

Practice in specific locational skills can follow the same pattern: "Where can I tell if this book has a major section on heredity?" (Table of contents) "Let's look." "Where would I look for a definition of *heredity* as used by the author of this book?" (Glossary) "Let's see what it says."

The student's trained reaction to a new word, to scanning for an answer, and to finding information on a chart, and so on, depends on the patterns encouraged and developed by the teacher. No special tools are needed. It can be done with textbooks, since a table of contents, index, glossary, headings, pictures, graphs, charts, and maps are built into many texts. By employing these resources as one uses the text the students discover the usefulness of the skills in obtaining information quickly. Special exercises in using reference materials should be devised to lend weight and reinforcement to skills introduced functionally. These exercises should be brief (able to be completed in fifteen minutes or less). They could include problems such as:

1. Pick a topic about early American history. What books does our library have on this topic? List their names and authors.
2. After you have selected a book to read, check the card catalog under the author's name and list what the card tells you about the book. List other books written by the same author.
3. After you have selected a book to read try to find some information about the author. Check the encyclopedia, the bibliographies of authors, and the book itself.
4. Select a small topic and, using the index of three or four books, find the pages on which you find information about this topic.

Short problems such as these can be checked individually, and as each child indicates his ability to use the reference skill, he can be freed to explore a topic of interest. Children can, then, use the skill as situations arise. The more frequently the need arises, the more important the skill becomes.

Subject teachers cannot assume that all students have knowledge of or ability to use all of the skills effectively. By reviewing the skills needed to obtain information, those who have the skills will be ready to use them and those who do not can be identified for special instruction.

Study Skills

Study skills are those skills that enable a person to gather information and to organize it in such a way that recall, analysis, interpretation, and evaluation are facilitated. Some of these skills are:

1. Ability to arrange a proper setting in which to read, think, write, study
2. Ability to select the appropriate strategy to attain the purposes of study
3. Ability to take notes that can be used efficiently for review, recall, or writing
4. Ability to outline
5. Ability to summarize.

These are discussed in Chapter 16 on study skills, as is the question of adjusting reading rate to the purpose for reading.

ANALYTICAL AND EVALUATIVE SKILLS FOR CONTENT READING

A third set of skills applicable to content reading involves an analysis of the concepts and the organization of the selection as a preliminary to evaluating it, that is, to determine its veracity, relevancy, and utility.

Ordinarily a content teacher in a departmentalized staff organization will expect a reader to spend more effort in the areas of analysis and evaluation. The problem is, how does he teach and test for those higher-level reading skills. Since content material brings a heavier concept load, less easily identifiable organization or theme, and more inaccessible criteria for evaluation and use, a restatement and evaluation of the material is more difficult. The instructional conclusions are evident:

1. The student needs special assistance in gaining the basic concepts — vocabulary identification and associations for concept development.

2.   He must be given demonstrations and practice in analyzing, expressing the organizational unity, and evaluating selections from content books.

In a certain sense this is equivalent to asking the reader to think like the scientist, to think like the geographer, to think like the historian. It might be more accurate to say, "to think like the science writer."

Given that kind of orientation, the reader or the teacher first can pose comprehension questions that request the literal meaning; for example, ask about:

1.   The main idea of a paragraph, section, or chapter
2.   Factual support for the main idea
3.   Relation of fact to main idea
4.   Sequence of ideas, events, acts
5.   Organization of the presentation
6.   Author's purpose, point of view, and style.

Studies with adult readers have shown that the consistent asking of the same types of questions (factual, recall, main idea) tends to produce greater facility in retention of the type of material asked for in the questions. Thus, if instruction tends to be biased toward one type of thinking activity, that skill will be strengthened, with little effect on the level of ability in the other skills (Meehan, 1970).

At the beginning stages one skill may be emphasized, such as that of identifying the main idea. Recalling details, then, will be overlooked if it is always underplayed in pay-off situations in class assignments, as will the identification and recall of main ideas if detail is always rewarded. The development of each of the six comprehension skills mentioned above should be made methodically and regularly in view of the goal of the content area. The student needs to receive reinforcement and concrete satisfaction for each of the six skills, not recall of factual data only.

A second group of comprehension competencies includes these typical activities of analysis and evaluation:

1.   Relate past knowledge and/or events to present knowledge and/or events.
2.   Distinguish similarities and differences, fact from fancy and/or opinion and/or generalizations.
3.   Make predictions about the outcome of events.
4.   Draw conclusions or inferences.
5.   Organize the material obtained to suit the purposes for reading.
6.   Judge the relevancy, adequacy, authenticity, and utility of the information.

None of these abilities are mutually exclusive, and they presuppose abilities to isolate factors, discriminate among factors according to a variety of criteria, and apply new information through a set of criteria. In that way the reader prepares himself to make judgments.

To develop those higher competencies the reader has to be aware of the bases upon which to analyze and evaluate. Thus it is important that the criteria for making an analysis or evaluation be as clear as possible. For example, size, color, and weight may be criteria for analyzing and categorizing objects to determine similarities and differences; utility in an urban school may be a criterion for evaluating or judging a technique. Decisions for instruction, again, have to be made according to the reader's abilities, the purposes of the reading, and the necessary prerequisites for the reading. Instruction should be tied to specific content and activity: no one should presuppose that transfer of reading skills will occur until how to transfer the skill has been adequately demonstrated in one subject. That does not mean that the student will not recognize similarities between skills for reading narrative and skills needed to read in the content areas. Similarities will not be recognized without teacher demonstration. It simply means that research indicates that the process of thinking is modified by the organization of the material. Reading instruction in the content area, then, should take on a form that will produce the objectives of that area. Once the reading and thinking processes of the subject discipline have been acquired, the general reading skills will be more readily applied, with modifications to types of material.

Instructional procedures must look at both long-range goals, those that should be attained over the years, and at short-term goals, those to be attained within a particular unit of study. The short-term units need to include a variety of activities, including consistent question patterns for the different reading and thinking skills. Refer to the chapters on basic comprehension and on critical and creative reading for guidelines on question patterns to develop higher reading competencies. Also see Appendix G.

CONSIDERATIONS FOR DIAGNOSTIC TEACHING

The development of reading skills should be coordinated with the purposes and nature of the content material. The teachers of reading and the teachers of content areas should not operate separately. If they are two different teachers, they must work together to facilitate the reader's progress. Reading skills are not independent of the purposes for which the material is being read, nor are the purposes for reading independent of reading skills. A basic consideration for instruction in reading content material is the coordination of purposes of the content and the reading skills.

The coordination of content with reading skills requires the identification of several factors:

1. The structure of the content material
   a. What concepts does the author assume the reader knows?
   b. What concepts, generalizations, or processes does the author develop?
   c. What style of presentation is used?
   d. What is the order of presentation?
   e. What assumptions does the author make about background knowledge of the subject?
2. The purposes for which the material is to be read
   a. What should the reader be able to do when he has read the material?
   b. What concepts should he have? (before reading)
   c. What concepts should he obtain?
   d. What is the reader expected to do with the material?
3. The skills of the reader
   a. Can the student read the material and grasp the meaning of the vocabulary, concepts presented, and intent of the author?
   b. What concepts and reading and thinking skills should he have in order to read effectively and efficiently?
4. The conditions under which the material will be read
   a. Is the length of time adequate for achieving the purposes for reading?
   b. Are distractions minimized?
   c. What is the time lag between reading and implementation of the information gained?

Instructional decisions, then, rest on a set of teaching principles, which may be stated as follows:

1. The teacher has knowledge of the structure of the particular subject as well as specific concepts and generalizations to be promoted in that subject.
2. The teacher must grasp the concepts, their dimensions, or levels of abstraction and be able to break them down into components for learning.
3. The teacher must suggest appropriate learning activities which are suggested by the objective for that selection.
4. The teacher needs to tie a set of varied experiences to the concepts being developed.
5. Reading should be used as a medium of learning when it is the most effective method of achieving the teaching purpose.
6. The material used should be appropriate for the teacher. The teacher needs to know:

    a.   The reading ability as reflected by tests and observation.

    b.   The nature and extent of the student's specialized vocabulary.

    c.   The rate of the pupil's reading in different materials.

    d.   The nature and extent of each pupil's reading experience.

    e.   The interests, personal characteristics, and social adjustment factors which affect reading.

7.   Competence comes with practice and application in a variety of situations.

For a reader to cope with content reading his first problem is to identify the purposes of instruction in the content area. Then he must identify the reading and thinking skills required to achieve those purposes. Finally, he must isolate the skills that require development. That information provides a basis upon which to direct both the reading and the content instruction. If the skills are such that direct instruction and practice skills are needed in order to be applied successfully to the attainment of the content purpose, then the teacher should teach those skills in isolation. If the skill is such that it can be taught simultaneously with the work in the content area, then they should be worked on together. The development of a child's thinking skills for a content subject (science) should be integrated with the books he reads. Due to the recent publication of many trade books for the young reader a coordination can be accomplished more easily than before. Browsing tables can set conditions for exposure and provide an opportunity to become aware of a variety of books and materials. The following activities can provide for the thinking skills:

1.   Questioning the truth or fantasy of a situation
2.   Deciding if action is plausible in stories not labeled fairy stories
3.   Leading children to judge competence of the author
4.   Judging the fairness and justice of others
5.   Judging the characters as real or lifelike
6.   Appraising titles
7.   Judging pictures
8.   Judging likenesses and differences in books dealing with children of other lands
9.   Setting up various types of comparisons of sources of information: biographies of the same person, books versus filmstrips, books versus television
10.   Evaluating oral or written reports
11.   Detecting propaganda
12.   Being alert to figurative language
13.   Being alert to words that arouse emotion
14.   Selecting pictures according to preferences
15.   Listening to the teacher retell a story with incorrect information
16.   Looking at bulletin board displays of pictures with incorrect and correct titles and judging which are correct

17. Writing summaries of poems and making selections of correct and incorrect ones for a critique
18. Completing teacher-made exercises designed to develop selected thinking skills
19. Selecting relevant and irrelevant facts in a story
20. Interpreting character traits
21. Differentiating fact and fiction
22. Drawing conclusions and inferences from stories.

The primary grade teacher has an opportunity to exploit many activities to develop the skills the child will need in reading to learn. On a day when a youngster brings a caterpillar to school the teacher can ask: "Will someone read about the caterpillar and report to us on how he grows and develops? Where will you look for information? What kinds of things will help us understand the life of a caterpillar?" Whenever possible the use of locational and study skills may be introduced and illustrated. Deliberately planned activities that demand the use of a particular skill are essential. Singling them out for new learning gives them an importance that many children might miss if they are treated only incidentally. The art of directing questions and activities toward concepts, reading, and thinking skills must be included in the instructional repertoire of the primary teacher (Meehan, 1970).

SKILLS FOR SPECIFIC CONTENT SUBJECTS

Even if a student had a repertoire of all the skills discussed in the previous sections he would still have to be aware of the peculiarities of the disciplines of science, math, and social studies in order to move through their content with ease and competency. A number of suggestions have already been given on how to cue the student into the content material so that he knows how its structure differs from another subject. The student should be encouraged to read the selection as the scientist or the historian or the mathematician would. There are additional aids, much more specific than the general admonition "to read like a scientist." The items that follow attempt to list some more specific cues for reading math, science, and several kinds of social studies.

The classroom teacher can use these cues in a variety of ways. For example, the major headings under which the cues are given could act as a model for asking questions about content selections: "What is the special vocabulary? What can you learn from the graphs or charts?" Or the teacher can take one cue at a time and demonstrate to the class how they can use a cue to get a clearer understanding of the selection they are reading. There are sample selections on which you can try to apply some of the cues. Naturally not all cues will apply to every article. Children can be taught to look for the following cues as aids in reading specific content subjects.

MATH CUES

1. VOCABULARY CUES
   Essential key words or phrases help to determine operation or sets to be utilized:
   Addition: Total, sum, add, add to, in all, altogether, plus
   Subtraction: Difference, left over, minus, subtract, minus
   Multiplication: Total, times, how many times, product
   Division: How many times more, divided by, how many would

2. TYPOGRAPHICAL CUES (locational cues)
   a. Question mark (gives clue to the location of the question to be answered)
   b. Charts and graphs (give essential information for problem on page—often located in another area of the page)
   c. Illustrations may act as road signs or directionals for the problem.
   d. Signs (percent, decimal point, operational signs indicate categories and math operations)

3. KINDS OF READINGS—read for:
   a. Skimming for the purpose and over-all comprehension
   b. Question asked
   c. Key words or phrases
   d. Operation or operations to be utilized
   e. Key numbers (also eliminate extra numbers)
   f. Write equation
   g. Reread problems to justify equations—redo if necessary
   h. Solve problem

4. SPECIAL CONSIDERATIONS
   a. The same term is not always used to indicate the same operation (for example, and, added to, and plus are interchangeable)
   b. The same term can indicate different operations (for example, altogether could indicate either addition or multiplication)
   c. Several technical terms have different meanings in general conversation (for example, square, mean, product, and so on)
   d. Mathematics involves the understanding of the many terms that remind the student of absolutely nothing and must be learned by memorization (for example, multiplier, divisor, radius, diameter, circumference)

5. ORGANIZATIONAL GUIDES
   There is no specific order, but certain sections appear in most math problems:
   a. A situation is given
   b. A numerical question is asked
   c. An equation must be formulated from given information

Trial Math Selection

Look at the math problem given below. See how many of the cues listed above can be used to help read the problem more clearly and therefore arrive at a solution to the various problems posed.

CIRCUMFERENCE OF A CIRCLE

The circumference of the circle is 61/4. We often speak of the circumference of a circle as the "length" of the circle, or the "distance around" the circle.

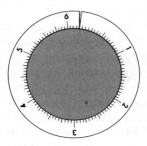

Since we cannot wrap our ruler around a circle, as shown above, we will look for other ways to find the circumference of a circle. Try this experiment:

1. Draw on cardboard a circle with a diameter of 3 centimeters. Cut out the circle carefully.
2. Draw a line 30 centimeters long on a piece of paper.
3. Mark a starting point on the circle. Use a pin and roll the circle along the line, marking the place where the starting point touches the line again.

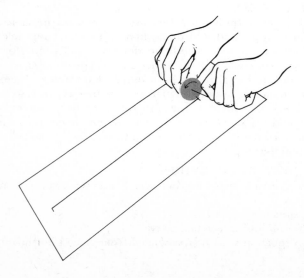

4. To find the circumference of the circle measure (to the nearest 1/10 centimeter) the segment along which you rolled the circle.
5. Use this method to find the circumferences of circles with diameters of 4, 5, 6, 7, 8, and 9 centimeters. Copy the table and record your results in the circumference column.

Special Factor		Diameter (cm)		Circumference
a	×	3	=	
b	×	4	=	
c	×	5	=	
d	×	6	=	
e	×	7	=	
f	×	8	=	
g	×	9	=	

Exercise:
After you have found the circumference of the circles with the diameters given, divide to find the "special factor" for each equation in the table. (Give the factor to the nearest hundredth.)*

SCIENCE CUES

1. VOCABULARY CUES
    a. There are certain words and related concepts that all pupils should know in order to read almost any science material above the primary level:
        1. Things "in common," "characteristics," "various," "classified," "similarities." An understanding of these terms is quite helpful in comprehending the data that follow the terms.
        2. Common Latin, Greek, or other derivations:
            a. *hydro*
            b. *electro*
            c. *photo*
            d. *un*
            e. *bi*
    b. Every new science lesson requires the teaching of terms pertinent to that selection.

2. TYPOGRAPHICAL CUES (locational skills)
    a. In most science textbooks there are good subtitles and chapter headings to use.
    b. Often there are good summaries at the end of chapters.
    c. Typographical cues are especially important in the first survey reading.

*Keedy, M. L., *et al. Exploring Elementary Mathematics*, 5. New York, Holt, Rinehart and Winston, 1970, p. 252.

3. KINDS OF READINGS — read for:
   a. Surveying the material.
      1. Attention to pictures.
      2. How many main parts? Use the subheadings.
      3. Read the first paragraph and the summary, if given.
      4. Formulate questions for reading from the survey.
   b. Answering the questions
      1. Appreciation of facts and objective data.
      2. Critical reading — what are the criteria?
   c. Reviewing the material read
      1. The discussion and evaluation of the reading is probably the most important part of the lesson.
      2. Pupils should be urged to report exactly what they have read. Precision.
         a. "*Most* kinds of bats are useful to mankind because they eat harmful insects."
         b. "*Some* scientists believe there is life on Mars."

4. SPECIAL CONSIDERATIONS
   a. Ability to read symbols. AuH_2O = goldwater.
   b. Ability to follow diagrams; for example, a student must understand the idea of completeness, as in an electrical circuit, or a chemical equation.

5. ORGANIZATIONAL GUIDES
   Various organizational approaches typical of science selections are:
   a. Generalizations are given first, then the examples and data. Deductive.
      1. All mammals have hair, bear young alive, and so on.
      2. The different kinds of mammals are listed.
   b. Examples and supporting data.
      1. Information on different mammals — their size, speed, and so on.
      2. In other selections — phenomena about light, heat, and so on.
   c. Classification of data.
      1. Different classes of mammals, stars, and so on.
      2. Differences and similarities among the classes.
   d. Often the data is given first, then the science writer builds up to classifying and generalizing. Inductive.

GEOGRAPHY CUES

1. VOCABULARY CUES
   1. Extend concept of a previously known word (for example, *range, mountain range*)
   2. Homonyms (for example, *plain, plane*)
   3. Refer to glossary
   4. Develop vocabulary in context (for example, Bananas are a *tropical* fruit)
   5. Use illustrations to create perception of vocabulary.

2. TYPOGRAPHICAL CUES
   a. Chapter headings, main headings, and subheadings are given.
   b. The format of the book includes illustrations, glossary, appendix, and index.
   c. The book is generally set up with two columns to make reading easier and to facilitate scanning.

3. KINDS OF READINGS
   a. Survey for overview.
   b. Read to answer specific questions.
   c. Skim to find specific answers and make generalizations (for example, What are the natural resources of Manitoba? How does this affect the industries of Manitoba?)
   d. Detailed reading of charts, graphs, maps, and so on.

4. SPECIALIZED CONSIDERATIONS
   a. Statistical reading: This type of reading is developed through repeated use of statistics (for example, present statistical data and provide an exercise for using the data such as comparing the area in square miles of several given countries)
   b. Symbolic language of maps (for example, a child's use of the map legend)
   c. Recognize that a map is a ground plan drawn to scale
   d. Interpret different kinds of maps (for example, population, political, rainfall, topographical)
   e. Reading graphs (for example, the reader learns to interpret data of various types of graphs — circle, line, bar, and pictorial)
   f. Authenticating facts (for example, the reader must verify the date of statistical information such as the population of a given area)
   g. The reader cuts across the author's organization and makes his own groupings of factual material for a given purpose.

5. ORGANIZATIONAL GUIDES
   The material in a geography book is generally organized in one of two ways:
   a. A specific area is given and all geographical aspects are examined. (for example, the New England states would be thoroughly discussed as to topography, climate, population, industries, and so on.)
   b. A geographical aspect is considered as it is found throughout the world.

BIOGRAPHY CUES

1. VOCABULARY CUES
   a. Pronunciation skills
      1. Multisyllabic words (for example, *as-tro-labe*)
      2. Foreign words (for example, *apartheid*)
   b. Meaning skills
      1. Technical words (*latitude*)
      2. Abstract words (*democratic*)

       3.   Concepts; abstractions (*tolerance*)
       4.   General terms (*elevator:* grain or passenger)
       5.   Mathematical terms (*ratio*)

2.   TYPOGRAPHICAL GUIDES
     a.   Headings and subheadings provide clues to location of responses to questions.
     b.   Use the parts of the book as reference tools.
     c.   Relate text and graphic content such as maps, graphs, and cartoons to corresponding text material

3.   KINDS OF READINGS — read for:
     a.   Main idea and supporting details
     b.   Use of key words, concepts, and literal facts
     c.   Read critically
         1.   Appraisals   2.   Conclusions and inferences
         3.   Propaganda   4.   Current events
     d.   Organize ideas to recognize relations and sequence of events; identify central issues
     e.   Graphic skills (maps, graphs, charts, diagrams, and pictures)
     f.   Related reference skills (table of contents, index, cross references, footnotes)
     g.   Related materials (periodicals and mass media such as radio, television, lectures, and field trips)

4.   ORGANIZATIONAL GUIDES
    General organization of the content:
     a.   Material in the social studies area is usually organized by the initial statement of a selection (for example, the current voter age limit), a practice (for example, selection of the President by an electoral college), an event (for example, passage of the Eighteenth Amendment), or a method (for example, representative democracy).
     b.   Often a point of view is presented, usually subtly (for example, private enterprise is best for the country), in some cases, overtly (for example, dictatorships are bad).
     c.   A relation often presented is one of conditions surrounding an effect: condition-effect relation.
     d.   Chronological order likewise often meets the organizational needs of social studies material.

"GO-GO" READING

Not all content reading is performed in textbooks. After a child is finished with school most of his reading will be content reading that may not include the contextual aids he found in his textbooks. Road signs, labels on bottles, newspapers, and magazines all demand content reading. Magazine and billboard advertisements require reactions that involve many of the same skills that have been proposed here for textbook reading and perhaps additional ones.

Tank trucks roll across the country bearing the red label *inflammable;* others, *flammable.* What is the difference between these two words? The reader of these signs had better not decide to drive his car into one of those tank trucks no matter what he decides about the spelling of truck signs.

Reading-on-the-go, or "go-go" reading requires quick reactions. The reader must apply his criteria for making immediate judgments. It is easy enough to decide not to drink a liquid when it has *poison!* stamped across it; but the reader with a sick five-year-old must bring other criteria to bear on his reading of the label that says: "Take one teaspoon four times a day. For children under six consult a physician before administering this medicine."

Though "go-go" reading does not occupy much classroom time, examples from the world of signs, television, the newspaper, and magazines afford excellent teaching examples of what reading-thinking skills must be used in examining content selections. Children will usually respond vigorously to exercises that have them examine popular commercials: "The computer confirms that Regi cigarettes give you whiter, brighter teeth"; "Senator Fogbound comes from the Midwest and knows the problems farmers face"; "Sandpaper tissue gives you more paper, more softness, and more color — buy the tissue with more of what you're looking for."

Each of these statements makes assumptions, some of them are quite misleading. In the first ad the reader must ask, "What do computers do?" They do not *confirm* anything. They simply report data. In the second statement the reader should ask, "What does coming from the Midwest teach you about farming?" A person could live his entire life in Indianapolis and not know how to milk a cow or disc a field. And in the third statement, the reader should ask, "More than what?" There are, of course, other avenues to explore with these statements, but these brief comments indicate ways to show youngsters how to apply content reading skills to the "go-go" world around him. Short examples like the above provide direct and pertinent demonstrations of some of the analytic and evaluative reading skills that are integral features of content reading.

APPRAISING CONTENT READING SKILLS

Chapter 14 discussed a means of asking graded questions to appraise the child's application of certain reading-thinking skills. The same method can be used in teaching the content material discussed in this chapter.

If the teacher expects the child to think like a scientist while reading science material, then the teacher should have a speaking knowledge of the structure of that discipline, too. The teacher should know that what is called the discovery method in education is akin to the scientific method; that is, there is observation of data, classification of the data, and a prediction or a conclusion that follows from the relations observed.

Story problems in math involve a problem description requiring a numerical solution. The specific problem question has to be identified, and elements in the situation have to be categorized in order that problem-solving operations can be established and the computation carried out. Various methods are applied in social studies, but they might be summarized under the broad category of conditions and effects. Social studies is most often concerned with observing effects and trying to determine the conditions surrounding and preceding those effects. Thus, time and space relations and people and government relations are conditions that surround important events that affect the lives of everyone.

Part of the teacher's preparation for an appraisal of content reading skills is to make sure that the background of the students warrants an appraisal. After all, an assessment means that the examiner expects to find some of the skills that he is looking for and that he is prepared to correct and develop the skills that need changing or adding. He might, therefore, use a checklist similar to the one below to appraise his own performance and the capability of the school system to carry out a program in teaching content reading skills.

These practices are often recommended for teaching special reading skills in the various content areas. A teacher should check off the items that apply to his teaching and make an appraisal of what has to be done to prepare his classroom to teach those skills.

Assuming, then, that the teacher has enough knowledge of the structure of the subject discipline, his next step is to get a broad picture of the skills the children have for reading content selections with comprehension. As was recommended for several other kinds of reading skills, careful observation of the children during the reading of the content may provide a picture of what the strengths and weaknesses are. The broad categories in the checklist below could guide the teacher in a general appraisal. A teacher would construct a checklist with a different set of skills if specific skills had been identified for individuals to achieve by the end of the term or the end of the school year. Nonetheless, the kinds of observations indicated on the checklist are essential in order to differentiate instruction.

In any fourth or fifth grade classroom the range of content reading skills is likely to be quite wide. Some children will have learned to respond to the cues on their own; others may not be consciously aware of them. Those that use the skills well, or at least know what to look for, will need only a minimum amount of instruction to maintain and improve what they already know. Students who have difficulty

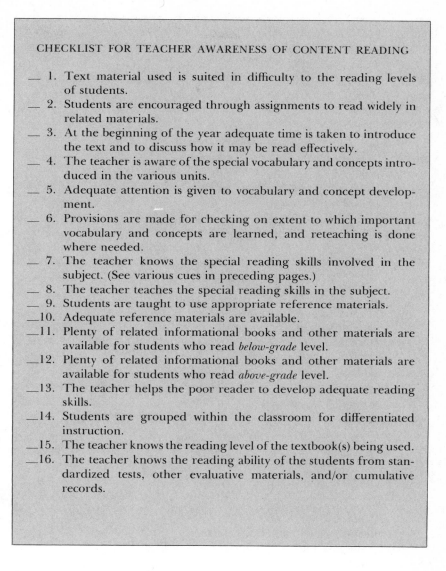

CHECKLIST FOR TEACHER AWARENESS OF CONTENT READING

___ 1. Text material used is suited in difficulty to the reading levels of students.

___ 2. Students are encouraged through assignments to read widely in related materials.

___ 3. At the beginning of the year adequate time is taken to introduce the text and to discuss how it may be read effectively.

___ 4. The teacher is aware of the special vocabulary and concepts introduced in the various units.

___ 5. Adequate attention is given to vocabulary and concept development.

___ 6. Provisions are made for checking on extent to which important vocabulary and concepts are learned, and reteaching is done where needed.

___ 7. The teacher knows the special reading skills involved in the subject. (See various cues in preceding pages.)

___ 8. The teacher teaches the special reading skills in the subject.

___ 9. Students are taught to use appropriate reference materials.

___10. Adequate reference materials are available.

___11. Plenty of related informational books and other materials are available for students who read *below-grade* level.

___12. Plenty of related informational books and other materials are available for students who read *above-grade* level.

___13. The teacher helps the poor reader to develop adequate reading skills.

___14. Students are grouped within the classroom for differentiated instruction.

___15. The teacher knows the reading level of the textbook(s) being used.

___16. The teacher knows the reading ability of the students from standardized tests, other evaluative materials, and/or cumulative records.

in using those special skills may need additional practice in supplementary materials.

Teach and Test for Specific Criteria

In assessing content reading skills it would be easy to slip into the practice of testing the child with a single selection and trying to estimate his use of all skills on the basis of a single response. Because so many factors are involved in demonstrating skills for reading con-

CHECKLIST OF READING AND STUDY SKILLS FOR CONTENT SUBJECTS	Bert Back	Tony Curt	Helena Rubin	Lyndon Bird
Word-Meaning Skills				
1. Understanding of technical terms				
2. Use of the dictionary				
3. Use of the glossary				
4. Use of new terms in speaking and writing				
5. Understanding of prefixes, suffixes, and roots				
6. Understanding of figurative language				
7. Understanding of personal and general connotations of words				
8. Understand of technical vocabulary related only to this subject				
Comprehension Skills				
1. Recognitions and understanding of main ideas				
2. Recognition of relevant details				
3. Recognition of relations among main ideas				
4. Organization of ideas in sequence				
5. Understanding of time and distance concepts				
6. Following directions				
7. Reading maps, tables, and graphs				
8. Distinguishing between facts and opinions				
9. Judging and criticizing what is read				
10. Reading widely to seek additional evidence				
11. Drawing inferences				
12. Listening attentively and critically				
Study Skills				
1. Familiar with many sources of information				

CHECKLIST (continued)	Bert Back	Tony Curt	Helena Rubin	Lyndon Bird
2. Using an index and encyclopedia efficiently				
3. Constructing a two-step outline				
4. Organizing and summarizing information				
5. Adjusting rate of reading to suit purpose and content				
6. Skimming with a purpose				

Use appropriate rating symbol.
+:Strong
—:lacking
?:unknown

tent material, the teacher's assessment and the child's progress are more likely to benefit from several tests on specific criteria. For example, the children should perform an exercise in which the teacher can observe their use of headings to determine the main parts of the article, or they should read a selection and then draw a map of what they read to test visualization and following directions; or, in reverse, from a map the children could describe what a region or a city is like.

The major headings under which a teacher should test a child are *vocabulary, using heads, charts, typographical cues,* and *organizational guides* to see if the child can get his facts straight, can identify the organizational pattern or principle of the selection, can state the conclusion or prediction, can apply criteria to evaluate the information and the selection, and can apply the information to the life that he knows.

On the basis of criterion tests about vocabulary, chart reading, organizational analysis, evaluation of information and procedure, and use of the conclusions to make predictions or to integrate the information, the teacher can form his instructional groups, place some children in study kits, and give some demonstrations to the entire class in his continuing process of making children aware of the power that they have over printed information once they develop a few key reading skills.

SUMMARY

There is a difference between content selections and narratives, especially the short stories typically found in basal readers. There is a vocabulary difference due to the technical terms in science, math, and social studies, but also because those disciplines have an organizational structure that often influences the way information about the subject is presented in the elementary school text. Thus, it seems important that teachers and children learn something about the way in which expository selections are written within specific subject areas.

There are various kinds of cues that a reader can use to assist himself in reading content material effectively. These cues relate to vocabulary, typography, expository writing patterns, and, in a sense, learning to read like the scientist or the mathematician who wrote the selection.

To teach content reading skills the teacher and student together should make a task analysis of the kinds of skills that are needed by the individuals in the class, then construct criterion exercises where needed. Content reading is a part of the notion of developmental reading. Content reading includes the reading of signs, ads, tables, editorials, and news reports. The skills that are needed for reading a content subject text must also be adjusted to reading-on-the-go. Verifying information, reading directions, knowing the vocabulary is just as important in our daily lives as it is in the more formal textbook arena.

Finally, an appraisal of content reading skills should start with the teacher's appraisal of his own knowledge of the structure of the discipline so he can teach the children to "read like a scientist"; continue through an analysis of the capability of the school to teach content skills and end with specific criterion tests—those to be used as a prelude to grouping and individualizing instruction in the skills of reading content selections.

TERMS

organizational pattern	expository writing
readability formula	translation
analysis	locational skills
evaluation	typographical cues
synthesis	criterion test

Chapter 16

Library
and Study Skills

Try to remember the last time you prepared a term paper for one of your college classes. Think for a moment about the skills you used to locate resources. Knowledge of the library and familiarity with various reference volumes determined in large part how efficiently you were able to go about discharging your task. In addition, you used a set of specialized skills in gathering and recording the pertinent information from each resource consulted. Later you organized and reorganized your ideas so that they might follow logically and be properly documented. In brief, you were utilizing library and study skills for the purpose of solving a problem.

Children also require specialized skills that enable them to gather and use information on a specific topic. This chapter discusses library and study skills and describes how the classroom teacher can provide children with the appropriate instruction.

As you read this chapter look for answers to the following questions:

What reference volumes should be introduced first?

What is a good technique for teaching children to outline and take notes?

Should the classroom teacher teach library usage skills?

What can be done to increase reading rate?

Why is it important to teach the parts of a book?

How can the classroom teacher identify individual needs with regard to library and study skills?

Reading is a skill needed for countless daily tasks. In a world as complex as ours it is not enough to simply read what is placed before us. We must also know where to look for a specific piece of needed information and how to use that resource once it has been located. Reading that helps us meet personal needs for information is dependent upon a specialized set of skills called *library* and *study skills*. Library and study skills enable the reader to apply and use his basic reading skills according to widely varied and constantly changing demands; in a real sense they make basic reading skills functional and give credence to the notion that we learn to *read* so that we may read to *learn*.

Four general types of library and study skills are discussed here. First, *reference skills* are needed for the reader to find the correct resource. Second, *locational skills* are needed for the reader to efficiently find his answer in the resource. Third, once the required information has been located, the reader must know how to *interpret* it. (Interpretation skills were given special attention in Chapters 11 and 14). Fourth, the reader must have some means for *organizing* the information in order to remember and use it.

This chapter will first discuss the teacher's role in teaching library and study skills. Next, specific library and study skills will be presented. Finally, the techniques and instruments for assessing children's progress will be presented.

PRINCIPLES FOR INSTRUCTION

As with any reading skill, development of library and study skills is a long-term undertaking that has its initiation in the primary grades. Eventual mastery of complex skills such as using an encyclopedia and writing an outline are built on numerous prerequisites — for example, alphabetizing and finding a specified page in a book. Thus the instructional program must be planned with reference to some over-all scope and sequence of skills. The introduction and systematic practice of skills must be planned to avoid a haphazard approach to teaching. No one can teach all these skills alone, of course. Planning is required on a school- or district-wide basis. Most basal reading programs provide some guidance in study skills, and many publishers have units available for guiding the sequential development of specific skills, such as dictionary usage or outlining (Smith, Batts, and Dunn, 1969).

The classroom teacher is responsible for demonstrating the actual use of reference materials and skills. Especially in the area of library and study skills, trial and error learning strictly on an incidental basis is most inefficient. Too often children are expected to grow in their ability to use an index by completing workbook pages or discovering for themselves how an index is organized. This should not rule out exploration and discovery learning. Indeed, it can be quite valuable to have children browse through a dictionary or other reference volume to note what information it contains. However, even in this case, some follow-up instruction is called for that leads children to understand when and how the various parts of a dictionary are useful. Clearly the teacher is just as responsible for planning and conducting lessons on library and study skills as he is for similar activities on word recognition and comprehension.

Children should be asked to apply library and study skills in true-to-life situations. This means that the teacher should frequently provide the opportunity for children to practice their skills through activities that are built on personal interests. Suppose a third grade boy is especially interested in stamp collecting. Preparing a report on stamps gives this boy a chance to apply study skills such as using an index and reading a chart in a highly meaningful setting. By way of contrast, an assignment from the teacher that provides practice on study skills by requiring a report on Brazil may be far less rewarding.

The teacher can also occasionally take advantage of classroom incidents to demonstrate or reinforce library and study skills. Suppose a third grade boy finds a frog on his way to school. The teacher might show the class how to use the subject index of a library card catalogue to locate a book on frogs. As stated earlier, all skill instruction cannot be incidental, but the interest generated by real events can be a powerful ally for the alert teacher.

Children should be provided with the opportunity to apply library and study skills in the content fields. They must be helped in transferring the use of their skills to social studies, mathematics, science, and language arts. For example, the dictionary is especially helpful when children encounter the specialized vocabulary of their history book. They should be encouraged to look up words that present special difficulties.

As with other reading skills, proficiency with library and study skills develops at varying rates among children. As much as possible the teacher must determine individual needs and plan activities that build on each child's current level of understanding. That is to say, not all nine-year-old youngsters have exactly the same awareness of how to use an index. Some may be totally ignorant while others demonstrate good understanding. The teacher must differentiate instruction on library and study skills just as he would on other, more basic reading skills.

REFERENCE SKILLS

Very early in their school careers children should learn that many books are not intended to be read from cover to cover. There are, in fact, over 5500 standard reference titles that cover a broad range of topics (Bond and Wagner, 1966). No child, indeed, no teacher can possibly know so many separate resources. Nonetheless, beginning in grade one children should become familiar with several standard reference tools. In each succeeding year their ability to use these references should increase just as their awareness of additional references should expand.

The dictionary, for example, is a tool children can begin to use as soon as reading instruction begins. At this early date they can begin to learn the functions of a dictionary and how to find the information it contains. Various publishers produce picture dictionaries such as *My Little Pictionary* (Scott Foresman, 1964) and *The Cat in the Hat Beginner Book Dictionary* (Random House, 1964) that introduce the child to this reference. Picture dictionaries should be included in every first grade book collection.

The organization and purpose of picture dictionaries is fairly simple. A picture is used to "define" each entry. In other words, the child knows what object is represented by a word from the picture that accompanies the printed symbol; thus *dog* is "defined" by a picture of a dog, *tree* by a picture of a tree, and so forth. Figure 16.1 is a sample page from a picture dictionary. In some editions guide words

asparagus
Asparagus is a
green vegetable.

astronaut
The astronaut guides
his space ship.

automobile
Our automobile has safety
belts in it.

FIGURE 16-1   A Picture Dictionary Page

Reprinted with permission from Rovers, Sister R. M., The New Picture Dictionary *(Dayton, Ohio: Geo. A. Pflaum, Publisher, Inc., 1965).*

appear at the top of each page and entries are alphabetized. Children can learn their first lessons about the dictionary from these simplified editions.

Another approach to introducing dictionary concepts is to have a group of children develop their own picture dictionary. As the children learn to recognize certain words they can make appropriate entries in their dictionary. A "shoe box" of words and corresponding pictures on 3 by 5 inch cards can be developed, or a looseleaf notebook can be used. (The form of the dictionary can vary; it is the understanding that comes from building this resource that is important.)

In addition to teaching children how a dictionary is developed, a self-made picture dictionary can be used by youngsters as a practice list of words they recognize at sight, or to check the spelling of a word for an experience story. A growing dictionary of "Words We Know" stands as proof of the progress a class is making in learning to read new words.

As children grow in reading ability new dimensions can be added to their personal dictionary. For example, entry words can be used in sentences; simple diacritical marks can be used for long and short vowels; definitions for words can be written; and multiple meanings for some words can be included. By studying other dictionaries children may discover additional features they would like to add to their own volume. Eventually a more sophisticated commerical edition will be appropriate. *The New Elementary Dictionary* (American Book Company, 1965) is an example of a simplified dictionary that children can use when a picture dictionary is no longer appropriate. *The Golden Dictionary* (Golden Press, 1944) combines some of the better features of a picture dictionary and a standard dictionary, thus making it especially useful as a transition vehicle.

Evidently children cannot learn all there is to know about the dictionary in grades one and two. What they learn in the primary grades is mainly a direct result of personal need. No formal instructional program on the use of the dictionary is usually undertaken until grade four. Prior to that time instruction is more incidental with the teacher presenting skills as they are required by the children. However, formal instruction on dictionary skills need be delayed only until the child has the reading techniques and abilities required for advanced dictionary use.

In the intermediate grades most children are ready to begin formal instruction on the use of the dictionary. Various publishers have units available on dictionary usage (Smith, Batts, and Dunn, 1969). It is not possible to explore here in detail all that constitutes such units. However, by the way of illustration a list of usual topics, not necessarily in the order given here, might include:

USING THE DICTIONARY

I. How To find words
    A. Guide words
    B. Finding the entry
    C. Different words with the same spelling
    D. Different spellings of the same word
    E. Words that sound alike
    F. Prefixes and suffixes

II. The main entry
    A. The entry word
    B. Pronunciation
        1. Accent marks
        2. Diacritical marks
    C. Parts-of-speech label
        1. Determiners
        2. Modifiers
        3. Intensifiers
    D. The definition
    E. Examples
    F. Definition by example
    G. Illustrations
    H. Labels
    J. Inflected Forms
        1. Plurals of nouns
        2. Comparative and superlative forms of adjectives
        3. Principal parts of verbs
    K. Idioms
    L. Run-on entries
    M. Usage notes

III. Pronunciation
    A. Accent marks
    B. Symbols for sounds
        1. Vowels
        2. Consonants
        3. Foreign sounds

IV. Abbreviations used in definitions

V. Special sections
    A. Persons and places
    B. Weights and measures
    C. Geologic timetable
    D. Foreign monetary units
    E. Presidents of the United States
    F. States of the United States
    G. Provinces of Canada
    H. Countries of the United Nations.

The term *formal study* indicates that planned instructional activities are conducted with reference to some over-all scope and sequence of skills. This is in contrast to the *informal* or incidental instruction. As much as possible instruction should include application of skills to actual everyday problems. For example, in making a current events report to the class a group of children should be asked to use their dictionary skills to check the pronunciation of certain words using the diacritical marking system contained in their dictionary. This procedure would be particularly effective following a lesson in which the diacritical marking system has been introduced or reviewed.

In addition to the dictionary, primary grade children should be introduced to the scope and use of an encyclopedia. Because of the reading difficulty of published encyclopedias for primary grade children, the teacher may find it worthwhile to develop his own encyclopedia. Bond and Wagner (1966) suggest that the primary grade teacher create a picture file arranged in alphabetical order according to index words such as *animal, city, farm, transportation, weather,* and the like. Materials, especially pictures, relevant to each of the topics are then placed for future reference in the appropriate file. The children should be largely responsible for finding useful items, classifying them, and filing them in the collection. Eventually cross references and other embellishments can be added as the need for them becomes apparent.

The value of this simplified encyclopedia is that through its development children begin to understand what an encyclopedia contains. Furthermore, they learn how such a resource is organized and how one analyzes a topic for entries of potential value. By asking, "What shall we look under to see what our resource file contains about animals on the farm?" the teacher initiates instruction at a fundamental level on a highly important aspect of encyclopedia usage.

As with the dictionary, in the intermediate grades children's reading skills and general knowledge are sufficiently advanced to make systematic instruction on using the encyclopedia profitable. Instruction should be based on a solid foundation of prerequisite skills learned in the primary grades and should proceed according to a sequential plan of skill development. A need to use the encyclopedia should be created to keep interest high and to give learning a goal. The teacher should demonstrate new skills and then provide for their immediate application in worthwhile projects. Exercises such as the one that follows provide an opportunity for the child to practice new skills and also yield diagnostic information for the teacher.

USING THE ENCYCLOPEDIA

Directions: Below is pictured a set of encyclopedias. By looking at the letters on the spine of each book it is possible to decide which one contains information we might need.

Indicate in column B which volume you would use to locate information about the topic in column A.

          Column A   Column B
 1. Brazil   _____
 2. Baseball   _____
 3. Measles   _____
 4. Horses   _____
 5. Colorado   _____
 6. Tropical fish   _____
 7. Beetle   _____
 8. Guitar   _____
 9. Knighthood   _____
10. Yellowstone Park   _____

The classroom teacher also has the responsibility for introducing children to other reference works such as almanacs, atlases,*Who's Who*, index volumes such as the *Reader's Guide to Periodical Literature*, newspaper and picture files, the telephone book, and special dictionaries. These and other reference tools will eventually be discovered by children as they mature and pursue varied interests. The teacher cannot possibly anticipate every resource that will be used, but he must introduce the major references mentioned here and arrange for their use by his students. Once found, the next concern is helping children learn how to use references, that is, applying *locational skills*.

LOCATIONAL SKILLS

It is apparent that reference skills cannot be developed in isolation from locational skills. Knowing which reference or resource contains the answer to a question is only half of solving a need; it is necessary to know how to locate the information within the correct resource. Locational skills can be roughly divided into two categories: library skills and book skills.

Library Skills

The library card catalogue is a resource that children must learn to use. They need to know that the card catalogue is a file containing title, author, and subject cards for every book in a library and how to find books through its use.

Various resources are available to help in planning the activities that build pupil understanding of the card catalogue (Aldrich, 1960). An excellent approach in grade two or three for developing the necessary knowledge is to construct a simple card catalogue for the classroom library.

The books housed in the reading corner can each be noted by author, title, and subject on a 3 by 5 inch card. As a first step students can be asked to decide how the cards might be arranged for easy retrieval. Alphabetizing the cards by author's name is a handy technique and entirely satisfactory as a first step. Later the students will discover that searching their card catalogue for an author is satisfactory when the author of a book is known. Occasionally only a title is known, however. The suggestion should be made, hopefully by a student, that a second card, filed by book title, might be added to the catalogue.

Subject cards can be added when the students are ready for that kind of classification. The fact that several subject cards might be made for the same book is a significant discovery for the children to make; this helps them understand the complexity of indexing. The suggestion can also be made (by the teacher, if necessary) that brief summaries or annotations added to the cards would be helpful to one who finds an interesting title but wonders about the exact nature of the story or the difficulty of the book.

Using the above approach, by the fourth grade a fairly sophisticated card catalogue can be evolved by the children themselves. Some of them will then be ready to learn about the card catalogue in their school and public library. (Of course, some children may be ready for this step as early as grade two. This sequence of steps illustrates only one possible approach. Other approaches and especially other chronologies will be appropriate in various situations.)

Various resources are available to help teachers plan a unit on library skills (Palovic and Goodman, 1968). In connection with the card catalogue, intermediate grade children should also be given instruction on the following points:

1. Specific abbreviations are used on catalogue cards. For example, © *1964* represents *copyright 1964*; *96p illus* means a book is 96 pages in length and contains illustrations.
2. Cross-reference cards direct the user to other potentially useful sources of information.

3.   Call numbers are listed on the cards in the card catalogue. These
     numbers are needed to find a book in the library.

As with reference materials, the best approach to teaching children how to use the card catalogue is to create a need for its use.
Careful attention must also be paid to the importance of prerequisite
skills, such as alphabetic skills and classification skills.

Dewey Decimal System

A second aspect of library locational skills is understanding the
cataloguing system, such as the Dewey Decimal System. Few people
have memorized even the main categories of the Dewey Decimal
System. This is not a goal of the instructional program. Rather,
children should learn the function of the system and how it is organized. They should also learn how the system has been employed in
their own libraries so that books of special interest can be located.

DEWEY DECIMAL CLASSIFICATION SYSTEM

000–099	General works
100–199	Philosophy
200–299	Religion
300–399	Social sciences
400–499	Language
500–599	Pure science
600–699	Applied science or technology
700–799	The arts
800–899	Literature
900–999	History

Several discovery techniques might be employed to introduce the
concept of a library classification scheme to children. For example, the
books housed in the reading corner could be catalogued with a
system devised by the class. Nonfiction and fiction books might be
separated and then alphabetized by author. All books written by
authors whose last name begins with *A* could be numbered (1A, 2A,
3A, and so on); the same numbering system would be used for books
by authors whose names begin with *B* (1B, 2B, 3B, and so on). Or
books might be grouped by geographic location of setting, type of
story, or even reading difficulty. The number assigned (1A, 3B, and
so on) to a book would also be written on the appropriate cards in the
catalogue and noted on the spine of the book.

A presentation of the organization and function of the Dewey
Decimal System by the classroom teacher or librarian might be just
as meaningful as a discovery approach provided the children are later
given an opportunity to study its application firsthand. Typically, the

major classifications and more commonly used subdivisions, such as fairy tales, reference volumes, and earth sciences, are introduced in the fourth grade. In later grades more specific categories may be presented.

Using the Public Library

Children normally learn to use their school and classroom library with relative ease. Daily activities familiarize children with these resources; the instructional program teaches them the skills needed to locate and use the materials the libraries contain. However, the objective of building lifelong reading habits requires that attention also be given to using the public library. It is human nature to avoid the unfamiliar. Consequently, the classroom teacher should introduce his students to the public library to increase the chances that they will utilize it, especially as adults.

First, the teacher should see that each child has a library card entitling him to borrow materials. Then the teacher can arrange for a class trip to the library. The trip might include a tour of the facilities and an opportunity to borrow a book, record, picture collection, or filmstrip. In conjunction with such a field trip a member of the public library staff might be invited to visit the classroom to make a presentation and answer questions.

Book Skills

Most nonfiction books contain a number of similar features. In addition to the preface, foreword, or introduction, where the author or editor describes his purpose for preparing a book, most reference volumes contain a table of contents; a list of illustrations; figures and maps; various chapter, section, and subsection headings; a glossary; and an index or indexes. Children need to know the purpose and use of these parts of a book.

Preface, Foreword, or Introduction

We often fail to recognize the importance of the preface, foreword, or introduction to a book. An attitude seems to prevail that the "important" part of a book begins with page one. The preliminary message wherein the author or editor of a book typically explains why the book was written and what unique contribution it makes to man's knowledge is frequently overlooked. The preface usually explains the organizational scheme of the book and gives acknowledgments to people who contributed to the preparation of the book.

Here the teacher's task is primarily one of demonstrating the wealth of information contained in a preface. Perhaps he might read a preface to the class. The forewords of several similar books might be contrasted for the purpose of determining what is unique about each volume. A follow-up assignment could be given to annotate various reference volumes on the basis of the information provided by the editors in the foreword.

Table of Contents

In contrast to the personal message often conveyed by the author in a preface, a book's table of contents is a structured outline of its contents. The table of contents may enumerate only the chapter titles and page numbers on which each chapter begins. In other books the table of contents may also list the major sections of each chapter. In either case the table of contents provides the reader with an overview of the book's contents and a general feel for its organization.

By reading the preface and studying the table of contents the efficient reader can quickly and accurately assess the appropriateness of a book for his needs. Naturally, youngsters must be led step by step to make judgments about the appropriateness of a book. Beginning in grade one the child must learn where to find a table of contents and how to interpret the information it contains. Gradually he must be shown the relation between chapters and units, the importance of chapter sequence, and how to identify where the needed information can be located.

List of Illustrations, Figures, and Maps

A list of illustrations, figures, and maps is not always included in nonfiction or reference books. When used, however, it is normally found in the front of the book just after the table of contents. A reader may consult this listing to determine what sort of graphic information is contained in a book. A reader may feel that a history book should contain a variety of maps or that a book about airplanes must have photographs of different models to be useful to him.

The history textbook used for the social studies class is likely to have such a listing. The teacher can demonstrate how to use it when the book is first introduced to the class. He might have several additional books with similar listings on hand to illustrate the use of this reference skill in other resources.

Chapter, Section, and Subsection Headings

Another procedure for locating information is to use the headings an author has given to divisions in his book. Chapter, section, and subsection headings (organizers) are frequently arranged in outline fashion with supporting ideas grouped as subsections under a section heading. Sections are then gathered into chapters and chapters into *parts*. This textbook, for example, has 17 chapters organized into 6 parts. By recognizing the organization of a book a reader can use these headings to identify where the information he needs is located.

The teacher can help his students develop the habit of using headings or organizers by paging through several chapters of a book with them and pointing out the relation between sections. The headings might be written on a chalkboard in outline form. Later the children could independently outline parts of a book as a written assignment to gain practice in correctly relating the sections of a book to each other.

Used in conjunction with skimming, organizers provide an excellent means for locating information in a book.

Glossary

The glossary of a book serves much the same function as a dictionary except that its contents are limited to entries taken from the book itself. Children with dictionary skills are thus able to use a glossary with only minimal additional instruction. The teacher's major tasks are demonstrating where in the book to find the glossary and providing practice in using this feature.

Index

An index is an alphabetical list of names, subjects, events, and so on, together with page numbers usually placed at the end of a book. By consulting the index a reader can locate exactly where in a book the information that he wants is located. Because of its utility the index is one of the most frequently used features of many reference volumes. The use of an almanac, for example, would be most unwieldy without an index.

By the intermediate grades the increased use of reading in the content areas will necessitate instruction on the use of the index. Instruction must begin with the simple and move to the more complex. At first, simply locating specific terms in the alphabetical index and noting a specific page number is appropriate. Later, using cross references, identifying entries that might provide information on a topic, and employing multiple indexes for the same book can be undertaken. The following exercise illustrates an activity on using the index.

USING AN INDEX

Listed below are the topics found in an index to a book on Egypt. Use the index to answer the questions that follow.

Alphabet, 31
Art, 15–17, 75, 76
  ancient, 43–45
  in tombs, 45
  recent, 113–115
Cairo, 13, 19–21, 25
  burning of (1952), 70
  government of, 140
Customs, 5, 57–59

Food, 48, 51
Islam, 99
Moslems, 95–98
  creed, 97
  laws of, 101
Nasser, Gamal Abdul, 117–121
  early life of, 117
  personality of, 123–125
Sports, 132–133
Villages, 17, 43, 83

On what page or pages in the book will you read about:

1. Islam? ____
2. Moslems? ____
3. Sports? ____
4. Early life of Nasser ____
5. Food? ____
6. Burning of Cairo ____
7. Customs ____
8. Moslem laws ____

How many pages are about:

1. Food? ____
2. Ancient art ____
3. Customs ____
4. Nasser ____

Guide Words

Guide words located at the top of a page of a dictionary, encyclopedia or other reference volume indicate the first and last entry on that page. A reader can quickly determine whether a word or topic he is seeking will be found on a given page by determining whether it falls alphabetically between the guide words.

Evidently a child must know the alphabet and have some skill in alphabetizing before he can use guide words. Furthermore, he needs a demonstration of where to locate guide words and how to use them to quickly narrow his search to the correct page in a book.

Numerous opportunities for learning and practicing all the locational skills discussed here are contained in the daily activities of social studies, mathematics, science, and other content areas. Teachers can teach the use of a glossary, for example, in connection with a textbook or reference book the students will use in studying American or state history. The value of integrating reading instruction with specific content areas is nowhere more apparent than in teaching the skills of organizing information.

ORGANIZING INFORMATION

A good many skills could be discussed under the heading *organizing information*; however, it is possible to treat only a few major topics here. They include: (1) outlining, (2) taking notes, (3) summarizing, and (4) making time lines.

Outlining

The ability to prepare an outline is a fundamental skill useful to many youngsters for organizing and writing a report. At the same time, outlining is a complex task demanding careful instruction and guidance from the classroom teacher.

The first step in teaching outlining skills is to demonstrate how to use the headings of a well-organized factual book or textbook. The teacher can place an outline of a selection on the board. After discussing the various elements of the selection and how they are related to each other the teacher should direct the children to read for the purpose of noting the author's organization of main points and supporting detail. A follow-up discussion can then focus on how the author builds his case by relating ideas to major points. The point can be made that the skeletal framework of ideas contained in the teacher's outline placed on the board earlier have been enhanced by the writer in sentence and paragraph form. Outlining is merely the reverse of the author's process, that is, identifying main ideas along with supporting detail and properly relating them to each other.

This introduction to outlining focuses children's attention on the organization of a selection. The teacher must also call children's attention to the use in an outline of Roman and Arabic numbers, large and small letters, and how points are grouped together by indenting them under a heading.

Armed with an understanding of how an outline is organized and the mechanics of listing ideas in their proper relation, children are ready to try some outlining on their own.

Special care should be taken in selecting the first material to be outlined independently by children. First, it should be well organized. Second, it should have sections that are clearly marked by headings. Finally, it should be fairly brief, probably not more than four or five pages in length. A chapter or part of a social studies or science book is usually suitable.

Harris (1961) suggests that at first children be asked to complete only the details of an outline that has been organized and developed for them through several levels. The following exercise illustrates this approach. A strategy can be followed by gradually withdrawing the amount of assistance provided. For example, in the exercise the number of points under each heading (A, B, C) is left for the child to determine. Next, the wording of each head is omitted so that only the number of headings is provided, and so forth. Through this approach the child is gradually asked to provide more and more of the outline until finally he can achieve the entire task by himself.

Procedure for Teaching Outlining Skills*

Directions: Provide the children with an outline that is complete through the first three levels. Their task at this stage is to compare the outline with the text, noting form and the relation among elements of the chapter.

Chapter 4—ANCIENT CULTURES IN THE RIVER VALLEYS
  I. The Tigris-Euphrates River Valley
      A. Conditions in the valley promoted settlement
          1. Rich soil (silt) was provided by the flooding rivers
          2. Rivers provided moisture for dry land
      B. The Sumerians were first to live in the valley
          1. Developed good water control system
          2. Irrigated dry land
          3. Built cities of sun-dried bricks
          4. Food surpluses led to specialization
          5. A way of writing was developed
          6. The Semites conquered the Sumerians
 II. The Nile Flood Plain of Egypt
      A. Physical features of the region
          1. Little rainfall in Egypt
          2. Flooding covered land with silt
          3. The Nile River begins in mountains of central Africa
      B. Economic importance of Nile

The second step in this procedure is to provide the children with an outline that contains labels for major sections and an enumeration of the number of points to be found under each label. The children must provide the information that is missing from the outline.

Chapter 5—CULTURAL GIFTS OF THE ANCIENT GREEKS
  I. Greek Lands
      A. Physical features
          1.
          2.
          3.
          4.
      B. Sources of food
          1.
          2.
          3.

*The outlines presented here were prepared from Kenneth D. Wann, Henry J. Warman, and James K. Canfield, *Man and His Changing Culture* (Boston: Allyn & Bacon, Inc., 1967), pp. 108–128.

II. A Scattered Nation
    A. Greek city-states
        1.
        2.
    B. Sparta
        1.
        2.

The third step in this procedure is to provide the children with an outline that contains only an enumeration for major sections and subsections. The child must complete the information that has been omitted.

Chapter 6—CONTRIBUTIONS OF THE EARLY ROMANS
  I. The Italian Peninsula
    A.
        1.
        2.
    B.
        1.
        2.
 II. The Early History of Rome
    A.
        1.
        2.
    B.
        1.
        2.
        3.

Next, the children can supply all of the labels for an outline. Only the form of the outline is provided with the number of points in each section indicated.

Chapter 7—CULTURAL HERITAGES FROM THE MIDDLE AGES
  I.
    A.
        1.
        2.
        3.
    B.
        1.
        2.
        3.
 II.

After leading children step by step through the elements of outlining, they should be ready to attempt an entire selection on their own. Children who experience difficulty may be taken through this sequence again with more teacher guidance.

The teacher will also need to provide instruction on how to condense a sentence into a few words that still manage to convey an idea adequately. Discussion and illustration of the fact that some words can be omitted from a sentence to produce a "telegram style" can be undertaken (Harris, 1961). For example, one could place an outline of complete sentences on the board. With the announced intention of deleting all unnecessary words, the teacher and class could jointly erase or cross out all but the essential words. The revised outline could then be contrasted with the original for clarity.

Taking Notes

Taking notes requires that a student be able to select the major ideas from a selection, decide what is worth recording, and state an author's ideas in a condensed but accurate form. Most note taking is done for the purpose of helping a reader understand and recall information he has read. Since note taking is an active process that requires a reader to restate an author's points, it can often help his comprehension. Notes are also taken to provide a record of what has been read for preparing a written or oral report.

Note taking and outlining are similar in many ways. It therefore often makes sense to correlate whatever instruction is undertaken relative to the development of these skills. In the previous section a procedure was discussed for gradually building independence in outlining. The reader's task was primarily one of recognizing main ideas and supporting detail. Note taking can be approached in much the same way. Initially the teacher might place notes on the board that he has taken while reading a selection. Following a discussion of the teacher's notes the children might be asked to read the same selection for the purpose of noting main ideas. Follow-up discussion could focus on how one determines what to record of an author's message as the main points. An outline of the same selection could be prepared and a comparison made between it and the notes taken. The similarity of outlining and note taking should be apparent.

As with most classroom activities, note taking, especially for the purpose of preparing a report, is more meaningful and better received by the child if he feels a personal involvement in his project. Simply assigning a written report on the Civil War may provide practice in organizing and recording information, but it runs the risk of becoming a dull, mechanical exercise. By using a child's personal interests the same practice can be provided, but in a setting that promotes more positive attitudes and a better chance for transfer of learning.

Summarizing

Anyone who has asked a child, "What is your book about?" or, "What happened in the movie you saw?" knows how difficult the task of summarizing can be. Many youngsters find it necessary to relate every detail in order to answer such a query. At the opposite extreme some children can summarize the most complex story in astonishingly few words, "It was about a horse," or, "Everybody gets killed." One of the problems confronting the classroom teacher is leading children away from these extremes to the point where their summaries include only pertinent information but in sufficient quantity to do a selection justice.

Outlining and note taking are actually specialized forms of summarizing. Skill in selecting major points is required for each of these tasks. Likewise, placing ideas in proper relation is also important when preparing an outline, taking notes, or writing a summary. The child's first opportunity to summarize is provided early in the developmental reading program. For example, he may be asked in grade one to recount the incidents from a story in his basal reader. Teachers are constantly refining the child's ability to summarize by discussing stories and daily events with him, and through their own example.

Formal instruction might well take advantage of the close relation between summarizing and outlining-note taking. For example, a chapter of a geography book might be outlined. Next, the sections of the outline might be translated into sentence form, thus producing a summary of sorts. Notes taken on the same selection could be used to expand the summary where needed. Such a procedure would effectively demonstrate for the child how a summary is comprised of the main points from a selection. It also illustrates the similarity of summarizing, outlining, and note taking.

Time Lines

The time line can be a highly useful device for organizing information. It also is a specialized means for summarizing information.

Children require help in learning to read time lines and later in preparing them. Preston (1968) discusses the preparation of time lines in some detail. He suggests the use of children's personal experiences as a meaningful introduction to time lines. For example, the teacher might introduce time lines by preparing one for the current school year. Special dates such as holidays, vacations, and the beginning and ending of school can be featured on the time line.

Next, each child might make his own time line. He can begin with the present and block off as many years as he has lived. Each birthday marks a milestone on his time line. Other significant events, such as the birth of a younger sibling, memorable trips, major news events, and events with special personal meaning can also be noted.

The next step might involve changing the scale from one-year intervals to five-year intervals. Events prior to the child's birth might be added. Children can interview their parents and other relatives for this information.

The final step is applying the newly acquired skills needed for reading time lines in a textbook or newspaper article. Children can also prepare their own time line for U.S. history or read the time lines provided by the authors of their textbooks.

IMPROVING READING RATE

To be functional, reading skills must be applied efficiently. In this regard it is essential that reading rate be maximized. Chapter 11 contained a discussion of how reading rate must be adjusted to one's purpose for reading. It was also noted that materials of greater difficulty must be read more slowly because of the reader's unfamiliarity with concepts and vocabulary. Chapter 11 stated that all reading should be as rapid as one's skill and purpose for reading will permit. Nothing has yet been said about the means for increasing rate of reading.

Commercial speed reading courses are designed to increase one's reading rate. Many such courses accomplish this objective by teaching correct study habits and helping the learner practice these skills until a high degree of efficiency is attained. Frequently the SQ3R method (survey, question, read, recite, review), EVOKER strategy (explore, vocabulary, oral reading, key ideas, evaluate, recapitulate), or other approaches to reading a selection are taught. These commercial reading courses help the reader become an active reader, one who previews what he intends to read, notes section headings, reads the first and last paragraphs of a chapter, and mentally predicts what a selection will contain. With such preparation the reading act becomes a process of verifying what one expects to read. The result is more rapid reading accompanied by satisfactory comprehension due to the active mental involvement of the reader. Needless to say, classroom teachers should and usually do teach these techniques as part of the developmental reading program. The guided reading lesson provides for these steps, but sometimes they are "lost" on youngsters who see little need for such preparation. Legitimate speed reading courses offer little that is new or unique but instead help the reader make more efficient use of his basic reading skills.

The popularity of speed reading courses—and their success— is probably due largely to the high motivation and goal orientation of their clientele. Many adults and older students desire to increase their reading rate to keep up with the demands of their job or studies. Research evidence indicates that the gains typically obtained in such courses are often eventually lost as personal motivation subsides and regular practice ends (Sosebee, 1963). Such findings indicate that the classroom teacher should begin early to promote rapid reading and continue practice over a long period of time. Only in this way can long-term gains in rate be realized.

Furthermore, the classroom teacher can borrow certain aspects of speed reading courses and adapt them for classroom use. For example, most readers do not read as rapidly as they can simply because they fall into the habit of reading slowly. Speed reading courses provide practice in reading at a faster pace, one that more closely approximates the reader's true potential. Various commercial pacing machines are available for pushing the reader along at a given rate. These machines teach nothing in the way of new skills; they merely help the reader to realize his potential. The photograph shows a reader using such a device.

A much cheaper and equally effective procedure that any teacher can use in his classroom is simply to provide practice ses-

FIGURE 16.2   Reading with a Radometer Pacer
Photo courtesy Audio Visual Research, Inc.

sions during which children are asked to focus their attention on reading rate. By providing the opportunity for children to consciously try to increase their speed, marked success can often be met. Each child should be given material to read that is written at his independent reading level. The teacher instructs the members of the class to consciously read faster than they normally read. At a signal the entire group begins simultaneously to read. The teacher stands at the front of the room where he can note the elapsed time and record each ten-second interval on the chalkboard. When a child completes his selection (usually one page of material 200 to 500 words in length) he notes the last number the teacher has written on the board (a 6 would indicate that 6 ten-second intervals have elapsed). While other children are completing their selection he can calculate his reading speed. The number on the board multiplied by ten reveals approximately how many seconds it took him to read his selection. The number of words in the selection can be counted and divided by the number of minutes to get the average words read per minute.

For example, suppose a youngster read a selection of 300 words in length in 15 ten-second intervals. The total time required would be approximately 150 seconds (15 intervals times 10 seconds per interval equals 150 seconds). By dividing 150 into 300 the number of words read per second is found to be 2. Multiplying this figure by 60 (the number of seconds in a minute) the number of words read per minute is found to be 120.

Step 1: $15 \times 10 = 150$

Step 2: $150 \overline{)300} = 2$

Step 3: $2 \times 60 = 120$ words per minute

Each child could keep a chart of his own reading speed. Comprehension questions can be asked to make sure the child is actually reading the material and not just running his eyes over the page. This exercise can be practiced several times a week with an emphasis on surpassing the previous effort without sacrificing understanding of what is read. Materials of varied difficulty and content can be selected to give a more accurate estimate of reading speed under varied conditions and to provide practices in adjusting rate according to the type of material read. Children can often give themselves added incentives if they know what to look for. A self-inventory on flexible reading, such as the following checklist, can be a stimulus to that end.

The act of trying to read faster frequently causes an increase in speed. Success with a more rapid rate proves to the child that he can speed up. Regular practice increases the chances that he will read more rapidly when he is not being timed.

MY READING SPEED

	Never	Some-times	Usually	Always	Unde-cided
1. I read easy books rapidly and with understanding	___	___	___	___	___
2. When reading rapidly I look for main ideas	___	___	___	___	___
3. Before reading I preview the material to see with what rate I will read	___	___	___	___	___
4. I change reading rate from one selection to another as needed	___	___	___	___	___
5. I skim when looking for a single fact, name, or number	___	___	___	___	___
6. When skimming I try a temporary meaning for a new word	___	___	___	___	___
7. I read silently without moving my lips	___	___	___	___	___
8. I read groups of words rather than one word at a time	___	___	___	___	___
9. I do not look back at words I have already read	___	___	___	___	___
10. I read without pointing with my finger	___	___	___	___	___

SQ3R

The comments about reading rate should not mislead you, for rate is important only in relation to the purpose for reading. A reader adjusts his speed depending on the difficulty of the content and the reason for reading it. The reader should have some method then for guiding him, especially when he reads to study.

One of the more popular methods proposed for developing study habits is that of the SQ3R (survey, question, read, recall, review). Attempts to present the entire process and to have children follow this procedure frequently meet with difficulty since children are impatient with activities that seem redundant. However, if reading assignments are consistently presented along the SQ3R lines, the procedure may become part of the child's skills due to repeated exposure to the model. Therefore, survey of a section noting its headings, pictures, and charts and listing questions that may be answered in the section as a group activity will prepare the children for reading and provide an example of how to proceed when they are reading on their own. The same procedure with recall and review can be directed by the teacher in the early stages of developing this study strategy. After some time the actual stages can be identified and explicitly discussed and evaluated by the class.

The key elements of the SQ3R method appear to be that of setting purposes for reading and for reviewing what was read. These two aspects require the stronger stress and in some instances it may be more economical from the point of view of time for the teacher to set purposes for reading and then to have the class set purposes for reading. In order to accomplish this they will have to survey. The same may hold true for the postreading activity. Asking for recall (or whatever relates to the purpose of the content) will lead to reviewing what was read when the child realizes he has forgotten or overlooked content. Because there is evidence to suggest that recall is strongest for that material one looks for while reading, care must be taken to set purposes that shape the reading behavior in the desired direction.

ASSESSING PROGRESS

When new library and study skills are introduced to children it is essential that feedback on student performance be obtained. The teacher must know who is ready to move ahead and who requires additional instruction. Misunderstandings must be caught before they are too well learned to be readily overcome. As much as possible the feedback needs to be frequent. Informal measures are usually quite valuable in assessing library and study skills. They will be presented first. Formal measures will then be discussed.

Informal Measures

One source of information on student progress that is available both immediately and on a daily basis is the written exercises such as those presented in this chapter. After teaching the use of guide words, for example, the teacher usually provides an opportunity for practice by means of an exercise. While the children are doing the exercise the teacher can circulate among them to check their work and correct apparent difficulties. These are criterion tests and the teacher can study the completed work of each child for errors and misunderstandings. Small instructional groups can be formed on the basis of common needs. Children who demonstrate a readiness to move ahead can be given advanced work. This differentiation of instruction is possible only if the teacher is aware of each child's progress. By regarding daily written work as a source of diagnostic data the teacher can build such an awareness. A checklist similar to the one that follows can be used to keep track of observations and to divide the children into groups with similar needs.

Student's Name WORK STUDY SKILLS	Great difficulty with this	Making progress but still in need of additional growth	Has a grasp of all essential elements	Completely independent of all assistance
I. Organization Can the student do the following? a. take notes b. determine relationship between paragraphs c. follow time sequences d. outline single paragraphs e. outline sections of a chapter f. summarize single paragraphs g. summarize larger units of material h. make generalizations i. draw conclusions j. derive "drift" of unit from table of contents, topical headings, topic sentences, etc.				
II. Knowledge and Use of Reference Materials Can the child do the following? a. place words in alphabetical order b. easily locate words in dictionary c. use table of contents d. use indexes of books easily and efficiently e. apply the above in the use of encyclopedia				

	Great difficulty with this	Making progress but still in need of additional growth	Has a grasp of all essential elements	Completely independent of all assistance
WORK STUDY SKILLS (continued)				
f. use library card catalogue				
g. use the telephone directory				
h. understand the purpose of foot- notes and bibliographies				
i. utilize the following sources to locate materials?				
1. Atlas				
2. World Almanac				
3. Glossary				
4. Appendix				
5. City directory				
6. Newspapers				
7. *Reader's Guide to Periodical Literature*				
8. *Who's Who*				
III. Following Directions				
Can the student do the following?				
a. follow one-step directions				
b. follow steps in sequence				
c. see the relation between the purposes and the directions				
IV. Specialized Skills				
Can the student accomplish the following graph and table skills?				
a. understand how to use the calendar				
b. interpret a table by reading across and down from given points				
c. understand the purpose of lines and bars in graph measurement				
Can the student accomplish the following map and globe skills?				
a. understand and interpret simple street or "landmark" type maps				
b. make practical use of a road map "key"				

WORK STUDY SKILLS (continued)	Great difficulty with this	Making progress but still in need of additional growth	Has a grasp of all essential elements	Completely independent of all assistance
c. use an air map; understand such symbols as railroads, boundaries, rivers, mountains, and lakes				
d. have the knowledge and ability to measure distance, area, and elevation, and locate certain points				
e. indicate ability to interpret the following:				
1. Outline map				
2. Population map				
3. Crops map				
4. Elevation map				
5. Mineral production map				
6. Rainfall map				
V. Other Specialized Skills				
Can the student do the following?				
a. Understand the significance of pictorial aids				
b. Observe and infer from picture representations				
c. Read and interpret charts				
d. Read and interpret cartoons				
e. Read and interpret diagrams				
f. Read and interpret scales				
g. React critically in content material				

Another source of information on pupil progress that has been mentioned in previous chapters is teacher observation. An alert teacher can gain insight into the skills and deficiencies of his students by observing their behavior in the library, for example. Self-directed youngsters who consult the card catalogue for books on their personal interests stand out in contrast to those who must ask the teacher, librarian, or a friend where to look. Children who know which reference volume meets their need for information may be observed in the process of answering a question or solving a problem. The teacher can also gain valuable information about a youngster's progress when special projects are assigned in one of the content areas. Again, self-directed students may be observed going about the job of completing their assignment; those with skill deficiencies will need special assistance.

TREASURE HUNT

Directions: Use whatever resources you need to answer the following questions. In addition to giving the answer, also describe where you found it.

1. Where and when was Charles Lindberg born? _____
2. Where can you find a map that shows the amount of annual rainfall in Arizona? _____
3. What is the latest population figure reported for Denmark? _____ What year was the last census taken? _____
4. What magazine in our school library recently contained an article on sugar beets? _____
5. What is the name and author of a book that would help you improve your table manners? _____
6. What is the origin of the word *city*? _____
7. To whom did the author of *Rasmus and the Vagabond* dedicate his book? _____
8. What chapter of your science book contains information about evaporation? _____
9. How deep is the Grand Canyon? _____
10. How many daily newspapers are now published in New York? What are their names? _____
11. What are the names of the books in our school library written by Marguerite Henry? _____
12. Does our school library have a picture of President Richard M. Nixon that can be checked out? If so, where is it kept? _____
13. How many phonograph records does our school library contain?
   _____
14. What magazines are available in our reading corner? _____
15. What is the largest bird in the world? _____

ARE YOU A GOOD STUDENT?

Name_____   Date_____

Good students know *where* to study and *how* to study. Are you a good student? Answer these questions *yes* or *no*.

Where I Study:

  1. I have a special place to study.   —
  2. My study area has pencils, paper, and
     other materials I need to study.   —
  3. My study area is quiet.   —
  4. I have plenty of light.   —
  5. I study at the same time and in the
     same place each time.   —

How I Study:

  6. I ignore noises.   —
  7. I work by myself.   —
  8. My work is done on time.   —
  9. I do neat work.   —
 10. I use a dictionary when I need one.   —

What is the one thing you need to work the hardest on to improve?

_____

_____

Occasionally a special task may be assigned specifically to serve as a test of students' library and study skills. A considerable amount of diagnostic information can be gained by this means. A "treasure hunt" can be created, for example, that requires students to locate pieces of information in various scattered resources. All those who successfully complete the hunt can be recognized in some way (with a paper cut-out of a treasure chest behind their name on a wall chart, for example). Those who have difficulty with the hunt may need help with library and study skills. An example of a treasure hunt is provided here.

A teacher-made test can also provide useful information on library and study skills. Questions can be asked concerning a variety of reference volumes, or one skill can be assessed in depth.

The classroom teacher can systematize somewhat his assessment of his students' skills by developing a checklist similar to that on page 429. The items on the checklist guide the teacher in his search for pertinent information. Through observation, checking daily work, giving special assignments, and so forth, a judgment can be made concerning each child's progress in various areas. Checklists can be prepared to focus intensively on specific skills or to cover a broad range of skills.

Children can also be asked to assess their own progress in library and study skills. A self-inventory that focuses on study habits is provided here. The information obtained with such a questionnaire can assist the teacher in planning appropriate instructional activities.

Formal Measures

Many achievement test batteries such as the *Iowa Test of Basic Skills* (Houghton Mifflin Co., 1964) and the *Stanford Achievement Battery* (Harcourt, Brace and World, 1964) include a section on study skills. Multiple choice questions in these tests require the child to indicate which volume of a set of encyclopedias he would consult for information on Chile, for example. Other questions test his ability to use and interpret an index, read a table of contents, select the correct reference volume, use a dictionary, and generally apply the study skills described in this chapter.

SAMPLE ACHIEVEMENT TEST ITEMS ON STUDY SKILLS

Directions: Choose the word that would appear first if the four words were arranged in alphabetical order.

A. 1.   flying
    2.   collar
    3.   pale
    4.   gym
B. 1.   chime
    2.   gold
    3.   basin
    4.   chip
C. 1.   smoke
    2.   slip
    3.   sky
    4.   shade

Directions: Answer the following questions by using the index provided. If you cannot answer the question by using the index, mark the fourth answer, "Not in index."

Index

Baseball, 24
Football, 17–19, 25
Diving, 48, 55, 78

Hockey. *See* Ice hockey
Ice hockey, 88
Ruth, Babe, early life of, 41;
    records of, 44–45

A. What page tells about baseball?
    1.   14   3.   41
    2.   24   4.   Not in index
B. What page might tell where Babe Ruth was born?
    1.   44   3.   41
    2.   44–45   4.   Not in index
C. What page might give you the rules for playing tennis?
    1.   9   3.   25
    2.   41   4.   Not in index

Directions: Answer the following questions:
A. If you wanted to read about the life of Winston Churchill, which of these
    would you use?
    1.   an almanac   3.   an encyclopedia
    2.   a dictionary   4.   an atlas
B. If you wanted to know on what page the chapter on the Civil War in a
    history book began, where would you look?
    1.   in the index   3.   on the title page
    2.   in the preface   4.   in the table of contents

The classroom teacher can gain some understanding of general class needs and the progress being made by individual youngsters from achievement batteries. For example, a fifth grade class that averages well above the national norms on spelling achievement and vocabulary but drops appreciably below the norms on study skills probably requires special attention in this area. In utilizing this information the teacher would first need to determine whether a few students greatly affected the class average or whether the whole group contributed to the situation. Depending on what is found, several alternatives might be appropriate. In the case of only a few students having low scores, special grouping on the basis of need might be called for immediately. Remedial instruction could be arranged for these students. A more wide-spread deficiency involving most youngsters in a classroom might call for a special unit on study skills which includes nearly the entire class.

The classroom teacher needs more specific information about his students' performance than what he can get from average scores, however. Whether only a few or many students need special instruction, the pattern of responses that determined each child's test score is important. By intensively studying a child's achievement test answer sheet much diagnostic information can be obtained. Errors of a singular nature point the way for remedial instruction on that skill— selecting the correct resource, for example. Widely varied errors suggest a general deficiency in study skills, thus indicating an instructional program of another nature. The patterns of errors revealed by studying students' answer sheets provides the teacher with the evidence needed to group students for instruction and also indicates where the instruction should begin.

SUMMARY

This chapter focused on how basic reading skills can be made functional. Library and study skills help the reader to meet personal needs for information by enabling him to select the correct reference, locate the information within the right resource, and organize the information he finds.

The teacher's role involves planning an instructional program that includes all necessary library and study skills in a sequence that facilitates effective learning. He is also responsible for demonstrating the actual use of reference materials and skills. Children require an opportunity to apply new skills to problems that are both real and interesting to them.

Children should know the dictionary and encyclopedia especially well. These resources can be introduced informally in the primary grades by having a class develop its own versions of a dictionary and encyclopedia. Other reference volumes such as an atlas, almanac, *Who's Who,* and the *Reader's Guide to Periodical Literature* are more specialized in nature and can be introduced as students find a need for them.

Locational skills include knowledge of the library and of the parts of a book. Children should be introduced to the card catalogue and the Dewey Decimal System in the intermediate grades. They should also learn to use a table of contents, list of illustrations, chapter organizers, glossary, book index, and other special features of a book.

Outlining, note taking, summarizing, and making time lines are skills needed to help the child organize and remember information.

Through daily assessment of progress the teacher determines how instruction should be differentiated according to individual needs. Informal and formal measures provide the teacher with the diagnostic information needed to properly adjust instruction.

TERMS

Dewey Decimal System	card catalogue
guide words	time line
glossary	SQ3R

PART VI

DIAGNOSTIC
TEACHING

Part 6 presents an over-all strategy for diagnosing a class group and for preparing an instructional plan that incorporates the needs of the individuals in the class. Chapter 17 gives recommendations for organizing all the individual knowledges and skills that have been discussed in the other parts of this book and provides a synthesis and a summary of the theme of this book: individualizing reading instruction through diagnostic teaching.

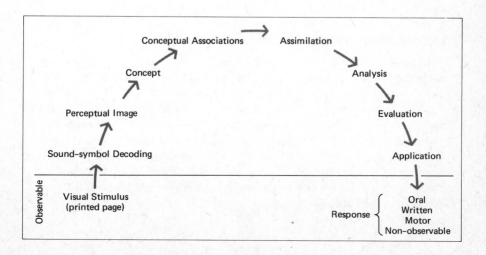

Chapter 17

Continuous Improvement in Reading

This book began with the idea that an important trend is taking place in reading education today. The special needs of children who enter school from widely disparate backgrounds, with different abilities, and a variety of learning styles require teachers to differentiate reading instruction. Technological and educational advances provide modern teachers with the means to individualize as they have never done before. Yet these factors influence learning to read only to the extent that the classroom teacher can accurately assess children's individual needs and match them with appropriate instructional activities. This book has turned on the idea that reading instruction can be individualized only to the extent that the teacher can diagnose reading behavior and plan continuous improvement.

INDIVIDUALIZE INSTRUCTION

Throughout this book we have focused on the means available to the teacher for diagnosing needs, for assessing progress, and for differentiating instruction. The reading process was represented in a model that suggested categories for diagnosing reading behavior—decoding, perception, association, and various levels of comprehension. The model artificially separates the elements of reading into a step-by-step sequence for the purpose of fostering diagnostic thinking. By identifying where in the process a child's reading breaks down a teacher can also prescribe appropriate instruction. This assumes that identifying the difficulty usually pinpoints the instructional need.

Systems and Materials

The major components of the reading program are described as: a system for instruction, arrangements for grouping, and means for assessing progress. In order to provide instruction some system is required. Four systems for teaching reading were described: the controlled vocabulary approach, the language experience approach, the programmed approach, and the individualized approach. No single instructional system has proved to be effective for all teachers or with all children. A program that borrows useful elements from each approach offers the teacher a greater chance to meet the needs of different children. Generally, teachers will move from a highly structured approach to a less structured approach as experience permits them to become more self-directed.

Instructional materials should be matched to the unique backgrounds and special needs of a school population. Core materials usually provide a developmental sequence of skills; additional materials should be available for encouraging greater individualization of instruction in independent work. Teachers must learn to evaluate instructional materials and identify specific children who might benefit from their use.

Classroom Arrangements

Armed with an instructional system and the necessary materials, the teacher must next organize himself, his classroom, and his students for instruction. Grouping alone cannot solve the problems of providing for individual differences, but it does permit the teacher to spend time in more direct contact with each child than does whole-class instruction. Once grouped, children retain their unique differences and must be taught as individuals. Flexible groups that are fairly small in size permit the teacher to differentiate instruction. Groups should be formed only after sufficient information regarding children's reading performance has been collected to provide the teacher with adequate guidance. Groups should be few in number until the teacher learns how to handle additional groups. When he sees a need for their formation, he can expand his grouping plan.

A variety of evaluation techniques were suggested so that the classroom teacher can gain sufficient information to provide a basis for differentiating instruction. Formal and informal assessment techniques were discussed as sources of diagnostic information. Throughout the book presentations on the various reading skills have been accompanied by suggestions to the teacher for assessing progress and identifying individual needs.

Specific Reading Skills

Reading skills were organized into three separate levels in this textbook: initial reading skills, primary reading skills, and higher competencies in reading. No attempt was made to equate these sections with
grade levels, since individual learners enter and complete each stage
at their own pace.

The initial reading stage corresponds to the child's first attempts
at learning to read. Auditory and visual discrimination were discussed
as prerequisite skills needed for perception, that is, associating meaning with oral and written symbols. The importance of environmental
factors in teaching auditory and visual discrimination skills were emphasized. The teacher must determine the child's stage of development and plan activities that overcome deficiencies in these fundamental areas. Furthermore, the teacher should emphasize the meanings of words encountered in daily activities so that sound and symbol
are not divorced from reality.

Sight Words

This textbook suggests teaching a small body of sight words as an
initial step in actual reading instruction. Whole words are the meaning-bearing vehicles of reading, and the child should see first that
reading involves a sequence of words just as speech does. Through
visual memory he learns to associate a printed symbol with its counterpart in his spoken language. In most cases the words he initially learns
to read are ones of great personal importance — his name, the names
of familiar objects, people, and places. He dictates language-experience stories about events that occur in school, at home, and on the
playground. A few printed symbols are thus learned at sight.

Decoding

Almost immediately the child also begins to learn a strategy for decoding word symbols. When he has learned to recognize several words
with the same initial letter at sight, the teacher calls his attention to the
similarity among the words. From that point a systematic decoding
program (phonics or linguistics) can be taught. The child gradually
learns to generalize about the sound-symbol associations found in the
words he can read. That constitutes a major step in enabling him to
read independently.

It is difficult to pinpoint the exact moment at which the child
leaves the initial reading stage and enters the primary reading stage.
Certainly when first learning to read most children require weeks and

months of drill to learn the association between sound and symbol. During this time their visual memory skills are also developed along with their decoding skills. Meaning is not neglected during these early days of reading instruction, either; the teacher constantly checks the understanding the child brings to the printed symbols and provides instruction to assure that meaning is present. Without question, however, the emphasis is on decoding during the initial reading stage.

Eventually the child is sufficiently skilled in the mechanics of decoding to enter the primary reading stage. While instruction on decoding continues, the scope of the instructional program broadens. Additional techniques for recognizing words are taught, comprehension is emphasized as the content of what is read becomes more difficult and more complex, oral reading skills are taught, and the child's reading interests are strengthened and expanded.

Word Analysis

The child must become independent in his ability to recognize words; therefore, expanding the child's sight vocabulary continues to be an objective. Until a word is recognized instantly it must be analyzed each time it is met. Some words can be broken into familiar parts; others must be reduced to syllables or even phonemic elements. The efficient reader has all these skills at his disposal. He is also able to use context clues in conjunction with word analysis to quickly unlock words not recognized at sight. The child learns a battery of word-recognition skills in the primary reading stage.

Literal Comprehension

At the primary reading level the child is asked to read increasingly more difficult material. At first he need do little more than add up the author's thoughts to understand the message contained by the printed page. Later he must follow more complex logic, restructure broken sequence, recognize sarcasm, and generally apply higher thought processes as he reads. In other words, the reader must be able to apply his thinking skills during the act of reading. In order to comprehend a written message the reader must have background experiences, real or vicarious in nature, that permit him to associate correctly meaning with the printed word. His language skills, including his vocabulary and grammar, must be equal to the task of correctly interpreting the author's thoughts. He must be able to adjust his reading for different purpose and according to the kind of material he is reading. Comprehension is the payoff in reading. Without understanding reading is an empty shell, a game of word-calling.

The primary reading skills also include oral reading. Many occasions occur where an audience depends on one who is reading orally for information. Consequently, the reading program must teach the skills necessary for effective oral reading. The teacher can also use oral reading as a means for assessing reading problems. This textbook also suggests that teachers regularly read orally to their students.

Interest in Books

Many children acquire an interest in books even before they enter school. The teacher has the responsibility for strengthening that interest when it exists and creating such an interest when it is missing. In addition, the teacher must expand children's reading interests by introducing them to new ideas and new topics. As children develop an interest in books they should be led to set personal standards for judging what they will read. They require instruction in the principles of literary analysis to the end of increasing their appreciation of what they read.

Again, for mere purposes of identification it is not possible or even desirable to determine with any accuracy when a child has "mastered" the primary reading skills. Oral reading skills, for example, are improved and refined even in adulthood. By the same token, higher competencies in reading are not delayed until a given date or grade level. It is not crucial that all primary reading skills be handled at a specified degree of sophistication before a higher-level skill (such as study skills) be introduced. In the general sequence of reading skills, however, the higher competencies of critical and creative reading, reading in the content fields, and study skills normally follow the primary reading skills. It is easy to see that the higher competencies are built on the foundation skills of the previous level.

Critical and Creative Reading

Nowhere is the dependence of a higher-order ability on a lower-order ability more apparent than in the areas of critical and creative reading. Without a solid foundation in reading comprehension the child is ill equipped to take on a critical reading task. Here critical reading has been identified as those reading-thinking skills that enable the reader to apply criteria to a selection and make judgments about it. In this process the skills of analysis, inference, and evaluation are crucial. Creative reading involves integrating the reading experience into the knowledge and affection of the reader and producing a response that is unique to the individual. Here the skills of synthesis and application are crucial. The teacher is responsible for leading the child to read critically and creatively, a task he achieves primarily through question-asking and follow-up discussion.

Study and Reference Reading

At the initial and primary reading levels most reading is done in a basal reader or fiction book. The reader's primary task is to learn to read; his basic skills are developed and practiced in these materials. When the child has sufficient skill to use reading as a tool he is ready to enter the content fields. He can read history and science books, follow mathematical problems, understand geography concepts, and so forth. The teacher is responsible for helping a child adjust his reading to the style, format, organization, and difficulty of expository materials.

Children also use reading as a tool when they apply their library and study skills. They must be familiar with standard reference volumes, know how to locate information in a library or book, and be able to organize information to solve a problem or answer a question. The teacher must demonstrate the use of these skills and provide children with the opportunity to use them in realistic situations. The close relation between reading in the content fields and library-study skills makes it highly desirable to integrate the instruction provided in these areas.

THE IMPORTANCE OF THE TEACHER'S ROLE

The above summary provides an overview of the teaching of reading. It is obvious from even this simplified description that the reading process is extremely complex and is replete with areas in which performance can go awry. In view of this complexity the teacher's task takes on special importance. In addition, the responsibility for properly individualizing instruction according to the needs of 25 to 35 children only intensifies the demands on the teacher.

We have suggested that a classroom teacher can effectively discharge his responsibilities for teaching reading by approaching the reading process diagnostically. First, he must organize the various reading skills into some logical sequence; he must then systematically determine where each learner stands in the sequence. He needs diagnostic tools and techniques to gather this information. But, perhaps more than anything else, he needs an attitude that causes him to approach every classroom activity with a diagnostic point of view. He is constantly on the alert for useful feed-back; he watches for patterns of behavior that indicate an instructional need; he classifies information and relates it to his conception (or model) of the reading act. Without such an approach the task of teaching reading can be overwhelming. The myriad of reading skills and sea of children's faces can cause even a conscientious teacher to look for an easy way out — usually whole-class instruction with standard assignments and activities for everyone.

EVALUATING READING INSTRUCTION

Suppose you want to teach diagnostically. How can you determine whether you are a successful diagnostic teacher or not? Obviously there is no simple way to decide whether such a complex task has been achieved. Information from a variety of sources is needed to provide a satisfactory answer.

Evidence concerning the success of the reading program can be gathered from the results of children's performance on standardized achievement tests, the number of children needing special remedial instruction outside the classroom, the attitude of children toward reading class, the quality of daily workbook assignments, and dozens of other sources. This text cannot begin to present an adequate discussion on the total evaluation of teaching; however, it is possible to describe several simple but useful means for teacher self-evaluation. Included will be interaction analysis, closed circuit television, introspective means, library usage, and student growth.

Interaction Analysis

Flanders (1965), Amidon (1967), and others have developed procedures for assessing the nature of classroom interaction. Somewhat over-simplified, the interaction-analysis technique requires that an observer classify the types of activities present in a classroom according to *who is speaking* (for example, teacher, student, or silence), the *nature of the talk* (for example, lecture, giving directions, or taking directions), and the *nature of the interaction* (for example, acceptance of feelings, praise or encouragement, criticism, or acceptance and use of ideas of students).

Interaction analysis can be an effective tool for appraising a teaching-learning situation. Interpretation of the results involves some subjectivity but generally reveals the degree of teacher dominance in classroom activities and the kind of intellectual tasks that children are asked to perform. From the standpoint of reading instruction, it is essential that children have numerous opportunities to talk, react, debate, and share. Insofar as the type of thinking taking place, higher-level tasks such as interpretation and synthesis are preferable to memorization or simple recall. An analysis of the type of interaction found in the classroom can provide feedback on how well the teacher is following good instructional principles. It is simple and highly desirable for the classroom teacher to tape record his own lessons and conduct an interaction analysis of his own teaching. Having assessed the type of classroom interaction taking place, a teacher can judge the desirability of his teaching and make efforts toward improvement.

Closed Circuit Television

Closed circuit television (CCT) and the use of video tapes can be a helpful tool for self-evaluation of teaching. The opportunity to see a lesson as an observer has several advantages. First, the teacher can focus on different aspects of the teaching situation and see the same lesson a number of times. Second, with the press of teaching responsibilities removed, the teacher can observe his own behavior with a degree of detachment not possible while a lesson is in process. For example, the number of students participating in a discussion can be noted or the adequacy of a phonics lesson can be checked. This technique enables the teacher to personally judge his performance and effectively plan a program of self-improvement.

Introspective Means

All teachers are constantly in the process of evaluating their performance by introspective means. As a lesson proceeds, for example, the amount of attention exhibited by the class is noted and serves as feedback for self-evaluation. Teachers have many daily opportunities for introspective self-evaluation. The sensitive and concerned teacher depends heavily on this useful approach to evaluation.

A more systematic approach to introspective evaluation is by means of checklists such as the one that follows. The items on a checklist can vary from straightforward questions requiring little or no subjective judgment (for example, Are reading skills presented so that one specific skill is developed in a lesson?), to very subjective questions requiring much self-analysis (for example, Are follow-up activities constructed to contain a balanced program of written and oral responses?). The greatest value of such checklists is that many aspects of the reading program are explored which might otherwise be forgotten or ignored. Introspection is highly suspectible to self-delusion. The teacher who wants to be completely satisfied can rationalize and explain away nearly any negative aspect of his teaching. The teacher intent on objective self-evaluation can learn much about himself from introspection.

Use of Libraries

An evaluation program that began and ended with a study of how the class and school libraries were being used by the children in a classroom would be incomplete but very meaningful, nonetheless. The finest reading instruction with regard to skill development, materials, tests, and the like might well be regarded as a failure if the children do not read widely for information and recreation.

TEACHER SELF-EVALUATION OF THE READING PROGRAM*

LOOKING AT MY CLASSROOM
I.   Are there evidences of my reading program around the room?
    A.   Charts
        1.   Primary:
            Are there evidences of experience charts?
            Are there charts relating to specific reading lessons?
            Are there vocabulary charts?
            Are there sound charts?
                Teacher made?
                Pupil made?
            Are there attractively arranged displays of pupil language efforts?
        2.   Intermediate:
            Are there charts to guide development of writing and speaking skills?
                Example: paragraphs, reports, letters
            Are there pupil-teacher made summaries?
                Example: social studies, science, health
            Are there charts to develop word meanings and concepts?
            Are there charts to illustrate principles of word analysis?
            Are there attractively arranged displays of pupil effort?
    B.   Additional Materials for Independent Reading
        1.   Are there books of varying levels related to *different topics* and of diverse types (textbooks, biographies, travel books, stories, and so on) attractively arranged and easily available to the children?
        2.   What provision do I make in my planning for:
            a.   Helping children develop an interest in independent reading?
            b.   Building cooperatively general but meaningful purpose for this reading?
            c.   Sharing the ideas, information, and enjoyment children gain from this activity?
II.   Does my classroom environment lend itself to individual and group work in reading?
    A.   Is there a library or reading corner which:
        1.   Displays books in an enticing manner?
        2.   Provides space for book reviews, book information, and pupil comments?
        3.   Provides a comfortable reading in terms of chairs, tables, adequate lighting?
    B.   Is the room so arranged that the group working with the teacher
        1.   Is compact enough to enable all to hear without using a loud voice?

*Prepared by John E. Connelly, Reading Center, State University College, Fredonia, N.Y.

    2.   Is far enough from those working independently so that it is not disturbing to the others?

    3.   Has sufficient space to work comfortably?

    4.   Is planned so that graphic materials used by the teacher are readily visible to all members of the group?

    5.   Is planned so the teacher has writing space available if the situation demands additional visual material?

LOOKING AT MY CLASS

I.   Is each person in my room at the same proper reading level?

    A.   Have I accurately assessed each child's instructional reading level and independent reading level through:

        1.   Studying the reading record card?

        2.   Analyzing objective test results?

        3.   Reading former teacher reports?

        4.   Administering needed informal inventories?

    B.   Have I utilized the above information in planning:

        1.   Other language activities?

        2.   Social studies?

        3.   Science, health, safety?

        4.   Mathematics?

II.   How have I provided for the group working independently?

    A.   Are the independent activities:

        1.   Reading or language centered?

        2.   Differentiated according to pupil abilities?

        3.   Related to previously taught reading skills?

        4.   The result of a directed reading activity follow-up?

        5.   An outgrowth of independent reading?

        6.   So constructed that there is an indentifiable learning purpose in them?

LOOKING AT THE LESSON

I.   Are my directed reading activities (developmental reading lessons) a strong part of my reading program?

    A.   Are the introductory phases planned so that they include:

        1.   Definite, precise, specific, attainable teacher purposes?

        2.   Adequate (neither too little nor too much) readiness in terms of theme, background knowledge, vocabulary, and concepts?

        3.   Necessary vocabulary presentation in context?

        4.   A check of individual pupil mastery of needed concepts and vocabulary?

        5.   Challenging, interest-provoking, attainable purposes set for the individuals in the group?

        6.   Silent reading to achieve purposes set?

        7.   A culminating activity in oral or written form?

        8.   An appropriate length of time for the particular group?

        9.   Suitable distribution of time among the various elements of such a lesson?

B.   Are follow-up lessons constructed to contain:
1.   Teacher-guided pupil recall of purposes?
2.   Activities appropriate to purposes set and material read?
3.   Opportunities for use of vocabulary and concepts introduced in the original presentation?
4.   Carefully constructed, preplanned questions, statements, or challenges to stimulate pupil reaction to material?
5.   A balanced program of written and oral responses?
6.   Approaches other than question and answer?
7.   Provision for ample opportunities for pupil self-evaluation and teacher-pupil evaluation?
8.   Reasonable time for these activities?

C.   Are reading skills presented so that:
1.   One specific skill is developed in a lesson?
2.   Children are helped to discover principles and generalizations *for themselves?*
3.   Children are helped to understand how and when the skill is applied in reading material?
4.   Sufficient practice items are used with the group?
5.   Individual written practice follows the group presentation?
6.   Situations are provided in which the skill is applied?
7.   The proper amount of time is devoted to each phase?

II.   Are oral reading activities given their proper place in the total program?

A.   Are oral reading activities planned so that:
1.   Children acquire the proper concepts concerning the value and place of silent reading and oral reading?
2.   The time devoted to oral reading is minor in scope and used for a specific purpose?
3.   Of those included, a major portion involves
    a.   An audience situation in which only the person reading has the book?
    b.   Reading to prove a point?
    c.   Reading to find a point of information?
    d.   Choral speaking?
    e.   Sharing poetry?
    f.   Dramatizations?

The number of books read by a class per week provides an excellent index of how successful the reading program has been in stimulating reading. More careful analysis might contrast fiction with nonfiction circulation, or note how many award books are being read. These and other factors might be helpful in determining what aspects of the total reading program need attention. But unless simple circulation figures indicate a healthy flow of books into the hands of children, more fundamental issues should be considered first.

The use of libraries is probably one of the best estimates available as to what attitudes toward reading are being nurtured in the reading program. Interests and tastes in reading can also be assessed by noting the types of books being read.

Student Growth

While it would be foolish to base self-evaluation solely on the reading achievement of students, some insight into the quality of instruction can be gained by studying student growth. Various means can be used to make such a comparison. For example, the year-end gain in raw score points (or grade equivalent) on an achievement test could be noted. Such gross measures are not likely to be as revealing as performance on informal measures. Suppose the child who could not use an index at the beginning of the school year can accurately complete an exercise on the use of an index at the end of the year. Growth of this sort is concrete evidence of teacher effectiveness. Systematic evaluation would require that evidence be gathered for all children in a class on a variety of reading skills. Nonetheless, mastery of a skill on an informal measure is excellent proof of progress.

A teacher who actually teaches diagnostically would have records of children's progress in any number of forms that could be used for evidence of growth. A checklist of skills mastered late in the school year could be compared with a similar checklist completed in September. The number and types of books read for pleasure per week by each child early and late in the school year could be contrasted. Teacher-made tests and basal reader tests can provide similar information regarding student growth.

SELECTED REFERENCES

Aldrich, Ella V. *Using Books and Libraries*. Englewood Cliffs, New Jersey: Prentice-Hall Inc., 1960.

Allen, Robert B. "Better Reading Through the Recognition of Grammar Relationships." *The Reading Teacher*, XVIII (Dec., 1964), 194–198.

Allen, Robert B. *English Grammars and English Grammar*. Nobb, 1967.

Altick, Richard. *Preface to Critical Reading*. New York: Holt, Rinehart and Winston, Inc., 1969.

Ames, Wilbur S. "The Development of a Classification Scheme of Contextual Aids." *Reading Research Quarterly*, 2 (Fall, 1966), 57–82.

Amidon, Edmund, and John Hough. *Interaction Analysis:* Theory, Research and Application. Reading, Massachusetts: Addison Wesley, 1967.

Arbuthnot, May Hill. *Children and Books*. Chicago: Scott, Foresman and Company, 1957.

Ashton-Warner, Sylvia. *Teacher*. New York: Simon and Schuster, 1963.

Austin, Mary C., and Carl B. Smith. *Study of Title I—Reading Programs for Fiscal Year 1967*. Final Report U.S.O.E. Contract #3-7-000168-0168. Cleveland, Ohio: Western Reserve University, 1967.

Austin, Mary, and Coleman Morrison. *The First R: The Harvard Report on Reading in Elementary Schools*. New York: The Macmillan Co., 1963.

Bailey, Mildred H. "The Utility of Phonics Generalizations in Grades One Through Six." *The Reading Teacher*, XX (February, 1967), 413–418.

Balow, Irving H. "Does Homogeneous Grouping Give Homogeneous Groups?" *Elementary School Journal*, LXIII (Oct., 1962), 28–32.

Baratz, Joan C. and Roger W. Shuy. *Teaching Black Children to Read*. Washington, D.C.: Center for Applied Linguistics, 1969.

Barrett, Thomas C. "Visual Discrimination Tasks as Predictors of First Grade Reading Achievement." *The Reading Teacher*, XVIII (Jan., 1965), 276–282.

Bateman, B. "Reading: A Controversial View, Research and Rationale." *Curriculum Bulletin*, XXIII (1967), 1–41.

Bernstein, Leonard, conductor and narrator. *Peter and the Wolf* (S. Prokofiev). New York Philharmonic Orchestra, Exploring Music 1. New York: Holt, Rinehart and Winston, Inc.

Betts, Emmett A. *Handbook on Corrective Reading*. Chicago: Wheeler Publishing Co., 1956.

Betts, Emmett A. "Structure in the Reading Program." *Elementary English*, XLII (March, 1965), 238–242.

Bissett, Donald J. *The Amount and Effect of Recreational Reading in Selected Fifth Grade Classrooms*. Ph.D. dissertation, Reading and Language Arts Center: Syracuse University, 1969.

Bloom, Benjamin S., ed. *Taxonomy of Educational Objectives Handbook I: Cognitive Domain*. New York: David McKay Company, Inc., 1956.

Bloom, Benjamin S., Allison Davis, and Robert Hess. *Compensatory Education for Cultural Deprivation*. New York: Holt, Rinehart and Winston, Inc., 1965.

Bloomer, Richard H. "The Cloze Procedure as a Remedial Reading Exercise." *Journal of Developmental Reading*, V (Spring, 1962), 173–181.

Bloomfield, Leonard and Clarence L. Barnhart. *Let's Read: A Linguistic Approach*. Detroit: Wayne State University Press, 1961.

Blumenfeld, Jacob, and Gerald R. Miller. "Improving Reading Through Teaching Grammatical Constraints." *Elementary English*, XLIII (Nov., 1966), 752–755.

Bond, Guy L., and Robert Dykstra. "The Cooperative Research Program in First Grade Reading Instruction." *Reading Research Quarterly*, II, no. 4 (Summer, 1967).

Bond, Guy L., and Leo C. Fay. "A Comparison of the Performance of Good and Poor Readers on the Stanford-Binet Scale, Forms L and M." *Journal of Educational Research*, XL (Feb., 1950), 475–479.

Bond, Guy L., and Miles A. Tinker. *Reading Difficulties: Their Diagnosis and Correction*. New York: Appleton-Century-Crofts, 1967.

Bond, Guy L., and Eva B. Wagner. *Teaching the Child to Read*. New York: The Macmillan Co., 1966.

Bormuth, John R. "An Operational Definition of Comprehension." *Psycholinguistics and the Teaching of Reading*. Edited by Kenneth S. Goodman and James T. Fleming. Newark, Delaware: International Reading Association, 1969, pp. 48–60.

Bormuth, John. "Cloze Tests and Reading Comprehension." *Reading Research Quarterly*, IV, no. 3 (Spring, 1969), 359–367.

Bormuth, John R. *Cloze Tests as Measures of Readability and Comprehension Ability*, Ed.D. dissertation, Indiana University, 1962.

Braun, Carl. "Interest-Loading and Modality Effects on Textual Response Acquisition." *Reading Research Quarterly*, IV, no. 3 (Spring, 1969), 428–444.

Brink, Carolyn. *Caddie Woodlawn*. Illustrated by Kate Seredy. New York: Macmillan Company, 1936.

Bruner, Jerome. *The Process of Education*. Massachusetts: Harvard University Press, 1960.

Burger, I. Victor, T. A. Cohen, and P. Bisgaler. *Bringing Children and Books Together*. New York: Library Club of America, 1956.

Burnett, Richard W. "The Classroom Teacher as a Diagnostician." *Reading Diagnosis and Evaluation*, XIII, Part 4 (1970). Proceedings of the Thirteenth Annual Convention of the International Reading Association, Newark, Delaware.

Buros, Oscar K. ed. *Sixth Mental Measurements Yearbook.* New Jersey: Gryphon Press, 1965.

Buros, Oscar. *Reading Tests and Reviews.* New York: Gryphon Press, 1968.

Burns, Paul C. and Alberta L. Lowe. *The Language Arts in Childhood Education,* Chicago: Rand McNally and Co., 1966.

Burr, Marvin G. "Study of Homogeneous Grouping in Terms of Individual Variations and the Teaching Problem." *Teachers College Record,* XXXIII (October, 1931), 63–64.

Burton, Virginia Lee. *Mike Mulligan and His Steam Shovel.* Boston: Houghton Mifflin, 1939.

Buswell, Guy T., and Wm. H. Wheeler. *The Silent Reading Hour.* Chicago: Wheeler Publishing Co., 1923.

Butler, James Orval. *Expressed Reading Preferences of Children in Grades Two in Selected Schools of Colorado.* Unpublished Ph.D. dissertation, University of Oklahoma, 1964.

Chall, Jeanne. *Learning to Read:* The Great Debate. New York: McGraw-Hill, Inc., 1967.

Cleland, Donald L. "A Construct of Comprehension." *Reading and Inquiry,* IRA Conference Proceedings, X (1965), 59–61.

Clymer, Theodore. "The Utility of Phonic Generalizations in the Primary Grades." *The Reading Teacher,* XVI (Jan., 1963), 252–258.

Clymer, Theodore. "Criteria for Grouping for Reading Instruction." Paper presented at twenty-second Annual Conference on Reading, University of Chicago, June 30, 1959.

Clymer, Theodore. "Research Design in the Language Arts." *Elementary English,* XXXIX (April, 1962), 349–354, 356.

Clymer, Theodore W. *The Influence of Reading Ability on the Validity of Group Intelligence Tests.* Unpublished Ph.D. dissertation, University of Minnesota, 1952.

Coleman, James C. "Perceptual Retardation in Reading Disability Cases." *Journal of Educational Psychology,* XLIV (Dec., 1953), 497–503.

Cook, Walter W., and Theodore Clymer. "Acceleration and Retardation." *Individualizing Instruction,* Sixty-first Yearbook of the NSSE, Part I. Chicago: University of Chicago Press, 1962.

Cooper, James David. *A Study of the Learning Modalities of Good and Poor First Grade Readers.* Unpublished Ed.D. dissertation, Indiana University, 1969.

Cordts, Anna D. *Phonics for the Reading Teacher.* New York: Holt, Rinehart & Winston, Inc., 1956.

Coulter, Myron L. "Verbal Problem Solving in the Intermediate Grades." *Reading and Inquiry,* IRA Conference Proceedings, Newark, Delaware, X (1965), 303–306.

Covington, M. V. "Some Experimental Evidence on Teaching for Creative Understanding." *The Reading Teacher,* XX (Feb., 1967), 390–396.

Crosby, Muriel, ed. *Reading Ladders for Human Relations.* 4th ed. Washington, D.C.: American Council on Education, 1963.

Cutter, Virginia. "And Beyond the Lines." *Vistas in Reading,* IRA Conference Proceedings, XI, Part I (1966), 64–68.

Davis, Frederick B. "Research in Comprehension in Reading." *Reading Research Quarterly,* III, no. 4 (Summer, 1968), 499–545.

Davis, Ira C., John Burnett, Wayne E. Gross, and L. Benton Prichard. *Science 3, Discovery and Progress.* New York: Holt, Rinehart & Winston, Inc., 1965.

Dawson, Mildred. *Developing Comprehension Including Critical Reading.* Newark, Delaware: International Reading Association, 1968.

Dawson, Mildred A. "Children's Literature — Lodestone in Children's Books." *Changing Concepts of Reading Instruction,* VI (1961), 183–186.

Dawson, Mildred A., and Henry Bamman. *Fundamentals of Basic Reading Instruction.* New York: David McKay Company, Inc., 1959.

DeBoer, John. "Teaching Critical Reading." *Critical Reading.* Edited by King, Wolf, and Ellinger. Philadelphia: Lippincott, 1967.

Deighton, Lee C. "Flow of Thought Through an English Sentence." *Vistas in Reading,* IRA Conference Proceedings, XI, Part I (1966), 322–326.

Deutsch, Martin. "Early Social Environment: Its Influence on School Adaptation." *The School Dropout.* Edited by Daniel Schreiber. Washington, D.C.: National Educational Association, 1964.

Dolch, E. W. *The Basic Sight Word Test.* Champaign, Illinois: Garrard, 1942.

Downing, John A. *The Initial Teaching Alphabet Reading Experiment.* Chicago: Scott, Foresman and Company, 1964.

Downing, John A., Daphne Cartwright, Barbara Jones, and William Latham. "Methodological Problems in the British i.t.a. Research." *Reading Research Quarterly,* 3 (Fall, 1967), 85–100.

Duker, Sam. "Basics in Critical Listening." *English Journal,* LXI (November, 1962), 565–567.

Durkin, Dolores. *Children Who Read Early.* New York: Teachers College Press, Columbia University, 1966.

Durkin, Dolores. *Phonics and the Teaching of Reading.* New York: Teachers College Press, Columbia University, 1965.

Durrell, Donald D. *Durrell Analysis of Reading Difficulty.* New York: Harcourt Brace Jovanovich, Inc., 1955.

Durrell, Donald D. *Improving Reading Instruction.* New York: World Publishing Company, 1956.

Durrell, Donald and Helen A. Murphy. "The Auditory Discrimination Factor in Reading Readiness and Reading Disability." *Education,* LXXIII (May, 1953), 556–560.

Dykstra, Robert. "Classroom Implications of the First Grade Reading Studies." *College Reading Association,* IX (Fall, 1968), 53–59.

Dykstra, Robert. "Auditory Discrimination Abilities and Beginning Reading Achievement." *Reading Research Quarterly,* I, no. 3 (Spring, 1966), 5–34.

Dykstra, Robert. "The Use of Reading Readiness Tests for Prediction and Diagnosis: A Critique." *The Evaluation of Children's Reading Achievement.* Edited by Thomas Barrett. Newark: International Reading Association, 1967. (Perspectives in Reading Series.)

Dykstra, Robert. "Summary of the Second Phase of the Cooperative Research Program in Primary Reading Instruction." *Reading Research Quarterly,* 4 (Fall, 1968), 49–70.

Eastman, P. D. *Cat in the Hat Dictionary.* New York: Random House, Inc., 1964.

Elkind, David, Margaret Larson, and William Van Doorninck. "Perceptual, Decentration, Learning and Performance in Slow and Average Readers." *Journal of Educational Psychology*, LXVI (February, 1965), 50–56.

Emans, Robert. "The Usefulness of Word Pronunciation Rules." Speech at AERA Convention. Chicago, 1966.

Emans, Robert. "History of Phonics." *Elementary English*, LV (May, 1958), 602–608.

Farley, Walter. *The Black Stallion*. New York: Random House, Inc., 1941.

Farr, Roger. *Measurement and Evaluation of Reading*. New York: Harcourt Brace Jovanovich, Inc., 1970.

Farr, Roger. *Reading: What Can Be Measured?* Eric/Crier. Newark, Delaware: International Reading Association, 1969.

Farr, Roger, and Nicholas Anastasiow. *Review of Reading Readiness Tests*. Newark, Delaware: International Reading Association, 1969.

Figurel, J. Allen. *Forging Ahead in Reading*, IRA Conference Proceedings, XII, Part I. Newark, Delaware, 1968.

Flanders, Ned A. *Teacher Influence, Pupil Attitudes and Achievement*. Superintendent of Documents, Catalog no. F. S. 5.225: 25040. Washington, D.C.: U.S. Department of Health, Education and Welfare, 1965.

Flesch, Rudolf. *Why Johnny Can't Read and What You Can Do About It*. New York: Harper & Row, Publishers, 1955.

Flierl, Nina T. "Using Television Interests to Build Reading." *New Frontiers in Reading*, V (1960), 121–124.

Forbes, Esther. *Johnny Tremain*. Illustrated by Lynn Ward. Boston: Houghton Mifflin Company, 1944.

Fries, Charles C. *Linguistics and Reading*. New York: Holt, Rinehart & Winston, Inc., 1962.

Fry, Edward. "Teaching a Basic Reading Vocabulary." *Elementary English*, XXXIV (November, 1957), 38–42.

Gagne, Robert M., and William J. Gephart, in collaboration with Eleanor J. Gibson. "Perceptual Learning in Educational Situations." *Learning Research and School Subjects*. Bloomington, Indiana: Phi Delta Kappa, 1968.

Gates, Arthur I., and David H. Russell. "Types of Materials, Vocabulary Burden, Word Analysis and Other Factors in Beginning Reading." *Elementary School Journal*, XXXIX (September, 1938), 27–35.

Gates, Arthur I., and Walter H. MacGinitie. *Gates-MacGinitie Reading Tests*. New York: Teachers College Press, Columbia University, 1964.

Georgiou, Constatine. *Children and Their Literature*. Englewood Cliffs, New Jersey: Prentice-Hall Inc., 1969.

Gibson, Eleanor J. "Perceptual Learning." *Annual Review of Psychology*, XIV (1963), 29–56.

Gibson, Eleanor J. "Perceptual Learning in Educational Situation." *Learning Research and School Subjects*. Edited by Robert M. Gagne and William J. Gephart, Itasca, Illinois: Peacock Publishers, 1968, pp. 61–86.

Gibson, Eleanor J., James J. Gibson, Anne D. Pick and Harry Osser. "A Developmental Study of the Discrimination of Letter-Like Forms," *Journal of Comparative and Physiological Psychology*, 55 (November, 1962), 897–906.

Gilmore, J. V. *Gilmore Oral Reading Test.* New York: Harcourt Brace Jovanovich, Inc., 1952.

Goldberg, Miriam L., Harry A. Passow, and Joseph Justman. *The Effects of
Ability Grouping.* New York: Teachers College Press, Columbia University, 1966.

Goodman, Kenneth S. "A Communicative Theory of the Reading Curriculum." *Elementary English,* XL (March, 1963), 290-298.

Goodman, Kenneth S. "Analysis of Oral Reading Miscues: Applied Psycholinguistics." *Reading Research Quarterly,* V, no. 1 (Fall, 1969), 9-30.

Goodman, Kenneth, et al. *Choosing Materials to Teach Reading.* Detroit: Wayne
State University Press, 1966.

Goodman, Kenneth S. "Dialect Barriers to Reading Comprehension." *Reading and Inquiry,* IRA Conference Proceedings, X (1965), 240-242.

Gordon, Edmund W., and Doxey A. Wilkerson. *Compensating Education for
the Disadvantaged.* New York: College Entrance Examination Board,
1966.

Gray, Lillian, and Dora Reese. *Teaching Children to Read.* New York: The
Ronald Press Co., 1957.

Gray, William S. *Gray Oral Reading Test.* Indianapolis: Bobbs-Merrill Company, Inc., 1963.

Griffin, Margaret May. *Identifying Unknown Words Through Association with
Known Words: Consonant Substitution as a Technique in Word Identification.*
OEG-6-9-009029-0063 (010), Ed.D. dissertation, Univ. of Missouri,
Columbia, Missouri, August, 1969.

Guilford, J. P. "The Three Faces of Intellect." *American Psychologist,* XIV
(1959), 469-479.

Guszak, Frank J. "Questioning Strategies of Elementary Teachers in Relation
to Comprehension." Speech given at IRA Conference in Boston, Massachusetts, April, 1968.

Hackett, Alice P. *Seventy Years of Best Sellers: 1895-1965.* New York: R. R.
Bowker Co., 1967.

Hall, Robert A., Jr. *Linguistics and Your Language.* New York: Doubleday
Anchor, 1960.

Harris, Albert J. *How to Increase Reading Ability.* New York: David McKay
Company, Inc., 1970.

Harris, Albert J. *How to Increase Reading Ability.* New York: Longsmans, 1961.

Harris, Larry A. *A Study of the Rate of Acquisition and Retention of Interest-
Loaded Words by Low Socioeconomic Kindergarten Children.* Unpublished
Ph.D dissertation, University of Minnesota, 1967.

Harris, Larry A. *Guide to Materials for Reading Instruction.* Eric/Crier Reading
Review Series, Bloomington, Indiana: Indiana University, 1968.

Hay, J., and C. Wingo. *Reading with Phonics.* New York: J. B. Lippincott Co.,
1960.

Heilman, Arthur. *Phonics in Proper Perspective.* 2d. ed. Columbus, Ohio:
Charles E. Merrill Publishing Co., 1967.

Heilman, Arthur W. *Principles and Practices of Teaching Reading.* Columbus,
Ohio: Charles E. Merrill Publishing Co., 1967.

Henry, Marguerite. *Born to Trot.* Chicago: Rand McNally, 1950.

Hildreth, Gertrude. *Teaching Reading: A Guide to Basic Principles and Modern Practices.* New York: Holt, Rinehart & Winston, Inc., 1958.

Hildreth, G. H., and N. L. Griffiths. *Metropolitan Readiness Tests.* New York: Harcourt Brace Jovanovich, Inc., 1965. (Metropolitan Readiness Test Series.)

Hillson, Maurie. *Change and Innovation in Elementary School Organization.* New York: Holt, Rinehart & Winston, Inc., 1966.

Holt, John. *How Children Fail.* New York: Pitman Publishing Corp., 1964.

Huck, Charlotte, and Doris Kuhn. *Children's Literature.* New York: Holt, Rinehart & Winston, Inc., 1968.

Huhkins, F. P., and P. Shapiro. "Teaching Critical Thinking in Elementary Social Studies." *Education,* LXXXVIII (Sept.-Oct., 1967), 68-71.

Hull, Clark L. "Variability in Amount of Different Traits Possessed by the Individual." *The Journal of Educational Psychology,* XVII (1927), 97-104.

Hunt, Mabel Leigh. *Ladycake Farm.* Illustrated by Clotilde Embree Funk. Philadelphia: J. B. Lippincott Co., 1952.

Hurd, Edith Thacher. *Engine, Engine #9.* New York: Lothrop, Lee and Shepard Co., Inc., 1961.

Huus, Helen. "Developing Interest and Taste in Literature in the Elementary Grades." *Reading as an Intellectual Activity,* VIII (1963), 46-50.

Ilg, Frances L., and Louise Bates Ames. *School Readiness:* Behavior Tests Used at the Gesell Institute. New York: Harper & Row, Publishers, 1965.

Ives, Sumner. "Some Notes on Syntax and Meaning." *The Reading Teacher,* XVIII (Dec., 1964), 179-183, 222.

Jefferson, Benjamin F. "Some Relationships Between Parents' and Children's Preferences in Juvenile Literature." *Elementary School Journal,* LVIII (Jan., 1958), 212-218.

Jenkinson, Marion E. *Selected Processes and Difficulties in Reading Comprehension.* Unpublished Ph.D. dissertation, University of Chicago, 1957.

Jennings, Frank. *This Is Reading.* New York: Teachers College Press, Columbia University, 1965.

Karlsen, Bjorn, Richard Madden, and Eric F. Gardner. *Stanford Diagnostic Reading Test.* New York: Harcourt Brace Jovanovich, Inc., 1966.

Kasdon, Lawrence M. "Oral Versus Silent-Oral Diagnosis." Paper presented at IRA Conference Proceedings, Boston, Massachusetts, May, 1968.

Katz, Phyllis, and Martin Deutsch. *Visual and Auditory Efficiency and Its Relationship to Reading in Children.* Cooperative Research Project No. 1099. Washington: Office of Education, Department of Health, Education and Welfare, 1963.

Keedy, Mervin L., Leslie K. Swight, Charles W. Nelson, John Schlvep, and Paul A. Anderson. *Exploring Elementary Mathematics.* Vol. V. New York: Holt, Rinehart & Winston, Inc., 1970, pp. 252-253.

Keislar, E. R., and J. D. McNeil. "Oral and Non-Oral Methods of Teaching Reading; Replicative Study." *Educational Leadership,* XXV (May, 1968), 761-764.

Kelly, Madden, Gardner, and Rudman. *Stanford Achievement Test.* New York: Harcourt Brace Jovanovich, Inc., 1964.

Kephart, N. C. *The Slow Learner in the Classroom.* Columbus, Ohio: Charles E. Merrill Publishing Co., 1960.

Kerfoot, James F. "Problems and Research Considerations in Reading Comprehension." *The Reading Teacher,* XVIII (Jan., 1965), 250-256.

King, Ethal M. "Critical Appraisal of Research on Children's Reading Interests, Preferences, and Habits." *Canadian Education and Research Digest,* VII (1967), 312-326.

King, Martha L., Bernice D. Ellinger, and Willavene Wolf, eds. *Critical Reading.* Philadelphia: J. B. Lippincott Co., 1967.

Kjelgaard, Jim. *Big Red.* New York: Holiday House, 1945.

Krathwohl, David R., et al. *Taxonamy of Education Objectives, Handbook II: The Affective Domain.* New York: David McKay Co., Inc., 1964.

Kumin, Maxine W. *The Beach Before Breakfast.* New York: G. P. Putnam's Sons, 1964.

Kunitz, S. J., and H. Haycraft, eds. *Junior Book of Authors.* New York: H. W. Wilson Co., 1951.

Labov, William. "Some Sources of Reading Problems for Negro Speakers of Nonstandard English." *New Directions in Elementary English.* Edited by A. Frazier. Champaign, Illinois: National Council of Teachers of English, 1967, pp. 140-167.

Labov, William, and Clarence Robins. "A Note on the Relation of Reading Failure to Peer-Group Status in Urban Ghettos." *Linguistic-Cultural Differences and American Education. The Florida FL Reporter,* Vol. VII, no. 1 (Spring, Summer, 1969), 66-67.

Laird, Charlton. *The Miracle of Language.* New York: World Publishing Company, 1953.

Lamb, Pose. *Guiding Children's Language Learning.* Dubuque: William C. Brown Company, Publishers, 1967.

Lamb, Pose. *Linguistics in Proper Perspective.* Columbus, Ohio: Charles E. Merrill Publishing Co., 1968.

Larrick, Nancy. *A Parents' Guide to Children's Reading.* New York: Doubleday, 1964.

Lee, Doris, M., and R. V. Allen. *Learning to Read Through Experience.* New York: Appleton-Century-Crofts, 1963.

Lefevre, Carl A. *Linguistics and the Teaching of Reading.* New York: McGraw-Hill Book Co., 1964.

Loban, Walter. *The Language of Elementary School Children.* NCTE Research Report No. 1. Champaign, Illinois, 1963.

Lorge, Irving. "The Teacher's Task in the Development of Thinking." *The Reading Teacher,* XIII (Feb., 1960), 170-175.

McCloskey, Robert. *Homer Price.* New York: The Viking Press, 1951.

McCullough, Constance M. *McCullough Word Analysis Tests.* Boston: Ginn and Company, 1963.

McCullough, Constance M. "Recognition of Context Clues in Reading." *Elementary English Review,* XXII (Jan., 1945), 1-5.

McCullough, Constance M. "Responses of Elementary School Children to Common Types of Reading Comprehension Questions." *Journal of Educational Research,* LI (Sept., 1957), 65-70.

McKenzie, Edwin. "Reading Interests of Pupils in the Intermediate Grade in the Public Schools in a Small Urban Center." *Alberta Journal of Educational Research,* VIII (March, 1962), 33–38.

Marcus, Marie. "What Would You Choose? Gum." *Elementary English,* XLV (Nov., 1968), 987–988.

Marsh, R. W. "The London i.t.a. Experiment: A Rejoinder." *Reading Research Quarterly,* 4 (Fall, 1968), 120–123.

Mathews, Mitford M. *Teaching to Read:* Historically Considered. Chicago: The University of Chicago Press, 1966.

May, Frank B. *Teaching Language as Communication to Children.* Columbus, Ohio: Charles E. Merrill Publishing Co., 1967.

Meehan, Trinita. *The Effects of Instruction Based on Elements of Critical Reading Upon the Questioning Patterns of Pre-service Teachers.* Unpublished Ed.D. dissertation, Indiana University, 1970.

Mills, Robert E. *Mills Learning Methods Test.* Fort Lauderdale: Mills Center, Inc., 1954.

Mills, Robert E. *The Teaching of Word Recognition including The Manual of Directions for the Learning Methods Test.* Fort Lauderdale: The Mills Center, 1964.

Monroe, Marion. "Necessary Preschool Experiences for Comprehending Reading." *Reading and Inquiry,* IRA Conference Proceedings, X (1965), 45–46.

Monroe, Marion, and W. Cabell Greet. *My Little Pictionary.* Chicago: Scott, Foresman and Company, 1964.

Muehl, Siegmar, and Ethel M. King. "Recent Research in Visual Discrimination: Significance for Beginning Reading." *Vistas in Reading,* IRA Conference Proceedings, XI, Part 1 (1966), 434–439.

N.S.S.E. Yearbook. Chicago: University of Chicago Press, 1961.

Nardelli, Robert R. "Some Aspects of Creative Reading." *Journal of Educational Research,* L (March, 1957), 495–508.

Niles, Olive S. "Comprehension Skills." *The Reading Teacher,* XVII (Sept., 1963), 2–7.

North, Sterling. *Rascal.* New York: E. P. Dutton & Co., Inc., 1963.

O'Brien, Jack. *Silver Chief: Dog of the North.* New York: Winston and Co., 1933.

Palovic, Lora and Elizabeth B. Goodman, *The Elementary School Library in Action.* West Nyack, New York: Parker Publishing Co., Inc., 1968.

Parsons, R. B. *A Study of Adult Reading.* Unpublished Master's thesis, Department of Education, University of Chicago, 1923.

Peoster, Minnie. *A Descriptive Analysis of Beginning Reading, Combining Language Experience, Story Writing, and Linguistic Principles.* Unpublished Ed.D. dissertation, Indiana University, 1970.

Piaget, Jean. *The Language and Thought of the Child.* 3d. ed. New York: The Humanities Press, Inc., 1959, pp. 288.

Platts, Sister Mary E., Rose Marguerite, and Esther Shumaker. *Spice.* Benton Harbor, Michigan: Educational Service, Inc., 1960.

Pratt, Edward. "Reading as a Thinking Process." *Vistas in Reading,* IRA Conference Proceedings, Newark, Delaware, XI, Part 1 (1966), 52–55.

Preston, Ralph C. *Teaching Social Studies in the Elementary School.* New York: Holt, Rinehart and Winston, Inc., 1968.

Rawlings, Marjorie Kinnan. *The Yearling.* New York: Scribner, 1944.

Rinsland, Henry D. *A Basic Vocabulary of Elementary School Children.* New York: The Macmillan Company, 1945.

Robertson, Jean E. "Pupil Understanding of Connectives in Reading." *Reading Research Quarterly,* III, no. 3 (Spring, 1968), 387–416.

Robinson, Helen M. "Developing Critical Readers." *Dimensions of Critical Reading,* XI (1964), 1–11. Edited by Russell G. Stauffer. Proceedings of Annual Education and Reading Conferences. Newark: University of Delaware.

Roe, Anne. *Making of a Scientist.* New York: Apollo Editions, Inc., 1961.

Rosenberg, Phillip E. "Audiologic Correlates." *"Dyslexia" Diagnosis and Treatment of Reading Disorders.* Edited by Arthur Keeney and Virginia Keeney. St. Louis: The C. V. Mosby Company, 1968, pp. 53–59.

Rosenthal, Robert, and Lenore Jacobson. *Pygmalion in the Classroom.* New York: Holt, Rinehart and Winston, Inc., 1968.

Ruddell, Robert B. "The Effect of Oral and Written Patterns of Language Structure on Reading Comprehension." *The Reading Teacher,* XVIII (Jan., 1965), 270–275.

Rudman, Herbert C. "The Informational Needs and Reading Interests in Grades IV Through VIII." *Elementary School Journal,* LV (May, 1955), 502–512.

Rusnak, Mary. "What Happens Next?" *Elementary English,* XXXVIII (April, 1961), 225–226.

Russell, David H., and Etta E. Karp. *Reading Aids Through the Grades.* Columbia University: Teachers College Press, 1951.

Russell, David Harris. *Children's Thinking.* Boston: Ginn and Company, 1956.

Russell, D. *Children Learn to Read.* Boston: Ginn and Company, 1961.

Russell, David H. "Personal Values in Reading." *The Reading Teacher,* XII (Oct., 1958), 3–9.

Russell, David H. "Research on the Processes of Thinking with Some Applications to Reading." *Elementary English,* XLII (April, 1965), 370–378, 432.

Sanders, N. *Classroom Questions, What Kinds?* New York: Harper & Row Publishers, 1966.

Santos, Natividad Alejandre. *Provisions for Critical Reading in Phillipine Basal Readers: An Analysis of Reading Questions Based on a Classification Scheme of Cognitive Skills.* Unpublished Ed.D. dissertation, Indiana University, Bloomington, Indiana, 1968.

Sartain, Harry W. "Organizational Patterns of Schools and Classrooms for Reading Instruction." *Innovation and Change in Reading Instruction.* Edited by Helen M. Robinson. Sixty-seventh Yearbook of the NSSE, Part II. Chicago: University of Chicago, 1968, pp. 195–236.

Schneider, Herman, and Nina Schneider. *Science in Our World.* Boston: D. C. Heath, 1968.

Schneyer, J. Wesley. "Use of the Cloze Procedure for Improving Reading Comprehension." *The Reading Teacher,* XIX (Dec. 1965), 174–179.

Seashore, R. H. and L. Eckerson, "The Measurement of Individual Differences in General English Vocabulary." *Journal of Educational Psychology,* 31 (Jan., 1940), 14–38.

Sebesta, Sam L. "Literature in the Elementary School." Speech given at IRA Conference Proceedings in Boston, Massachusetts (April, 1968).

Severson, Eileen E. "The Teaching of Reading-Study Skills in Biology." *The American Biology Teacher,* XXV (March, 1963), 203–204.

Shaw, Phillip. "Achieving Personal Maturity Through Reading and by Recognizing and Constructing Meaning." *Developing Comprehension Including Critical Reading.* Edited by Mildred A. Dawson. Newark, Delaware: International Reading Association, 1968, pp. 55–57.

Shaw, Phillip. "Rhetorical Guides to Reading Comprehension." *The Reading Teacher,* XI (April, 1958), 239–243.

Sheldon, William D., and Mary C. Austin. "The Airport." *Town and Country.* Boston: Allyn and Bacon, Inc., 1968, pp. 46–52.

Shotwell, Louisa R. *Roosevelt Grady.* Cleveland: The World Publishing Company, 1963.

Shuy, Roger W. "Bonnie and Clyde Tactics in English Teaching." *Linguistics Cultural Differences and American Education. The Florida FL Reporter.* Vol. VII, no. 1 (Spring, Summer, 1969), 81.

Shuy, Roger W. "Language Learning and Reading Among Disadvantaged Blacks." Speech. Language Learning Institute, IRA Convention in Anaheim, California, May, 1970.

Silbiger, Francene, and Daniel Woolf. "Perceptual Difficulties Associated With Reading Disability." *College Reading Association Proceedings,* VI (Fall, 1965), 98–102.

Silvaroli, Nicholas J., and Warren H. Wheelock. "An Investigation of Auditory Discrimination Training for Beginning Readers." *The Reading Teacher,* XX (Dec., 1966), 247–251.

Sister Mariam. "Can the Teacher Improve Pupil Discrimination in TV and Reading?" *New Frontiers in Reading,* V (1960), 124–129.

Skinner, B. F. "The Science of Learning and the Art of Teaching." *Harvard Educational Review,* XXIV (January, 1954), 86–97.

Skinner, B. F., and James G. Holland. *The Analysis of Behavior.* New York: McGraw-Hill Book Company, Inc., 1961.

Smith, C. B. *How to Read and Succeed,* Essandess Special Edition, New York, 1967.

Smith, Carl. "Tadpoles Make the Nicest Frogs." *Bulletin of the School of Education, Indiana University,* XLV, no. 6 (Nov., 1969), 113–125.

Smith, Carl B., E. Batts, and M. K. Dunn. *Library Reference Skills,* Teacher Guide. Chicago: Encyclopedia Britannica, Inc., 1969.

Smith, Carl B., and Mary C. Austin. "Conducting a National Study of Title I Reading Programs." *Reading Research Quarterly,* IV, no. 3 (Spring, 1969), 323–341.

Smith, Dora V. *Selected Essays.* New York: The Macmillan Company, 1964.

Smith, Helen K. *Perception and Reading,* Proceedings of the Twelfth Annual IRA Conference, XII, Part 4. Newark, Delaware, 1968.

Smith, Lillian H. *The Unreluctant Years.* Chicago: American Library Association, 1953.

Smith, Nila B. "Relative Emphasis on Oral and Silent Reading in the School

Program." *Oral Aspects of Reading. Supplementary Educational Monographs.* Vol. LXXXII (Dec., 1955), 71-76.

Smith, Nila B. "The Many Faces of Reading Comprehension." Speech. Distinguished Leader Presentation at IRA Conference. Kansas City, Missouri, May 2, 1967.

Smith, Nila B. "Reading for Depth." *Reading and Inquiry,* IRA Conference Proceedings, X (1965), 117-119.

Smith, Nila B. *Reading Instruction for Today's Children.* Englewood Cliffs, New Jersey: Prentice-Hall, Inc., 1963.

Smith, Nila Banton. *American Reading Instruction.* Newark, Delaware: International Reading Association, 1965.

Sochor, E. Elona. "Literal and Critical Reading in Social Studies." *Journal of Experimental Education,* XXVII (Sept., 1958), 49-56.

Sosebee, Allen Louie. *Four Year Follow-Up of Students in the Indiana University Reading Program, 1958.* Unpublished Ed.D. dissertation, Indiana University, 1963.

Spache, G. D. *Spache Diagnostic Reading Scales.* Monterey, California: California Test Bureau, Del Monte Research Park, 1963.

Spache, George. *Good Books for Poor Readers.* Champaign, Illinois: Garrard Publishing Company, 1968.

Spache, George D. *Reading in the Elementary School.* Boston: Allyn & Bacon, Inc., 1964.

Spache, George David, and Evelyn B. Spache. *Reading in the Elementary School.* Boston: Allyn & Bacon, Inc., 1969.

Sperry, Armstrong. *Call It Courage.* New York: The Macmillan Company, 1940.

Spitzer, H. T., in collaboration with Ernest Horn, Maude McBroom, H. A. Green, and E. F. Lindquist. *Iowa Every-Pupil Test of Basic Skills.* Boston: Houghton Mifflin Company, 1964.

Spodek, Bernard. "Developing Social Science Concepts in the Kindergarten." *A Look at Continuity in the School Program.* 1958 Yearbook, ASCD. Washington, D.C.: National Education Association.

Staiger, Ralph. "How Are Basal Readers Used?" *Elementary English,* XXXV (Jan., 1958), 46-49.

Stauffer, Russell G. "Reading As A Cognitive Process." *Elementary English,* XLIV (April, 1967), 342-348.

Stevens, Martin. "Intonation in the Teaching of Reading." *Elementary English,* XLII (March, 1965), 231-237.

Stone, Clarence R. "Measuring Difficulty of Primary Reading Material: A Constructive Criticism of Spache's Measure." *Elementary School Journal,* 57 (October, 1956), 36-41.

Stone, David R. and Vilda Bartschi. "A Basic Word List from Basal Readers." *Elementary English,* XL (April, 1963), pp. 420-427.

Strang, Ruth. *Diagnostic Teaching of Reading.* New York: McGraw-Hill Book Company, 1964.

Strang, Ruth. *Diagnostic Teaching of Reading.* New York: McGraw-Hill Book Company, 1969.

Strang, Ruth. *Reading Diagnosis and Remediation.* Eric/Crier Reading Review Series. Newark, Delaware: International Reading Association, 1968.

Strickland, Ruth. "Building on What We Know." An address to IRA Convention. Boston, Massachusetts, 1968.

Strickland, Ruth. *The Language of Elementary School Children: Its Relationship to the Language of Reading Textbooks and the Quality of Reading of Selected Children. Bulletin of the School of Education.* Bloomington: Indiana University, July, 1962.

Strickland, Ruth G. *The Language Arts in the Elementary School.* Lexington, Massachusetts: D. C. Heath & Company, 1969.

Taba, Hilda. *Thought Processes and Teaching Strategies in Elementary School Social Studies.* AERA paper presented in Chicago February 13, 1963.

Taylor, Marion W., and Mary A. Schneider. "What Books Are Our Children Reading?" *Chicago Schools Journal,* XXXVIII (Jan., 1957), 155–160.

Templin, Mildred C. *Certain Language Skills in Children: Their Development and Interrelationships.* Minneapolis: University of Minnesota Press, 1957.

Thompson, Bertha Boya. "A Longitudinal Study of Auditory Discrimination." *Journal of Educational Research,* LVI (March, 1963), 376–378.

Thorndike, Edward L. "Reading as Reasoning: A Study of the Mistakes in Paragraph Reading." *Journal of Educational Psychology,* VIII (June, 1917), 323–332.

Tiedt, Iris M., and Sidney W. Tiedt. *Contemporary English in the Elementary School.* Englewood Cliffs: Prentice-Hall, Inc., 1967.

Tiegs, E. W., and W. W. Clark. *California Reading Tests.* Monterey, California: California Test Bureau, 1963.

Tinker, M., and C. McCullough. *Teaching Elementary Reading.* New York: Appleton-Century-Crofts, Inc., 1962.

Tinker, Miles A. *Bases for Effective Reading.* Minneapolis: University of Minnesota Press, 1965.

Torrance, E. Paul. "Introduction," *360 Reading Series* (Boston: Gibbon Co., 1969).

Veatch, Jeanette. *Individualizing Your Reading Program.* New York: G. P. Putnam and Sons, 1959.

Vernon, M. D. "The Perceptual Process in Reading." *The Reading Teacher,* XIII (Oct., 1959), 2–8.

Vernon, M. D. *Backwardness in Reading.* London: Cambridge University Press, 1960.

Vygotsky, Lev Semenovich. *Thought and Language.* Tr. by E. Haufmann and G. Vakar. 1934. Cambridge, Mass.: M.I.T. Press and New York: Wiley, 1962.

Walcutt, C. *Tomorrow's Illiterates.* New York: Little, Brown & Company, 1961.

Ward, Lynn. *The Biggest Bear.* Boston: Houghton Mifflin Company, 1952.

Wardeberg, Helen. "The Art of Questioning." Mimeograph. Cornell University, 1969.

Weintraub, Samuel. "Children's Reading Interests." *The Reading Teacher,* XXII (April, 1969), 655–659.

Wepman, J. M. "Auditory Discrimination, Speech, and Reading." *Elementary School Journal,* LX (Mar., 1960), 325–333.

Wepman, Joseph. "The Modality Concept—Including a Statement of the Perceptual and Conceptual Levels of Learning." *Perception and Reading.* Edited by Helen K. Smith. Newark, Delaware: International Reading Association, 1968.

White, E. B. *Charlotte's Web*. New York: Harper & Row Publishers, 1952.

Witty, Paul. "Studies of the Mass Media, 1949–1965." *Science Education*, L (1966), 119–126.

Witty, Paul A., et al. *A Study of the Interests of Children and Youth*. Washington, D.C.: U.S. Office of Education, 1960.

Witty, Paul, et al. "Studies of Children's Interests — A Brief Summary." *Elementary English*, XXXVII (Nov., 1960), 469–475.

Wolf, Willavene, Martha L. King, and Charlotte S. Huck. "Teaching Critical Reading to Elementary School Children." *The Reading Research Quarterly*, III, no. 4 (Summer, 1968), 435–498.

Wolfson, Bernice J. "What Do Children Say Their Reading Interests Are?" *The Reading Teacher*, XIV (Nov., 1960), 81–82, 111.

Yates, Elizabeth. *Mountain Born*. New York: Coward-McCann, Inc., 1943.

Appendix A

Primer

MR. AND MRS. GEOGRAPHY*

Hints
1. New sentences begin flush left.
2. New words are underlined.

Rules Which Illustrate Poor Teaching Procedures
1. No looking ahead.
2. No looking back.
3. No helping each other
4. Do not mark in books.
5. Keep your place in the story.

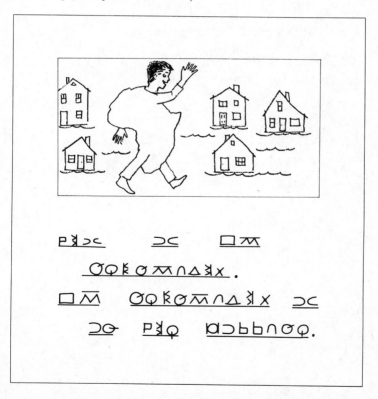

*Solution: This is Mr. Geography. Mr. Geography is in the village.

ᑭᘔᑐᑕ ᑐᑕ � ᒻᑕᓕ
ᐅᑫᐱᓯᒻᐅᐊᘔᕽ.
ᒻᑕᓕ ᐅᑫᐱᓯᒻᐅᐊᘔᕽ ᑐᑕ
ᑐᕮ ᑭᘔᕿ ᕼᑐᑉᑊᐅᕿᕞ.
ᒻᑕᓕ ᐅᑫᐱᓯᒻᐅᐊᘔᕽ ᑊᑐᕮᕞ
ᑭᘔᕿ ᕼᑐᑉᑊᐅᕿᕞ.
ᒻᕮ ᐅᑫᐱᓯᒻᐅᐊᘔᕽ ᑊᑐᐊᕞ
ᑭᘔᕿ ᕼᑐᑉᑊᐅᕿᕞ.

Solution: This is Mrs. Geography. Mrs. Geography is in the village. Mrs. Geography likes the village. Mr. Geography likes the village.

Appendix B

Materials and Programs

SUMMARY OF THE ECONOMY PROGRAM

Grade Range
Pre-primer to grade 6

Skill Range
Begins with long vowel sounds.
Critical thinking exercises are emphasized in the 6th grade.

Special Features
Phonic cards (grades 1, 2, 3)
Picture cards (grade 1)
Phonic charts (grade 1)

SUMMARY OF THE LIPPINCOTT PROGRAM

Grade Range
Pre-primer to grade 8

Skill Range
Grade 1
Auditory and visual discrimination of *a*. (Lippincott maintains that readiness is a fundamental part of the pre-primer.)

Grade 8
Comprehension activities or questions for discussion emphasize interpretation.
Activities also emphasize recognition of sentence patterns, punctuation, and function of sentence parts.

Characteristics of Content
Grade 1
Stories about children and animals.
Numerous pages are filled with words that contain a common element; aim, raise, rain, waist.

Grade 4
Story units are: Interesting Animals, Adventure, Science and Geography, Famous People, Fanciful Stories, and Favorite Tales.

Special Features of Series
Workbooks
Correlated filmstrips
Word cards for pre-primer and primer.
Tapes for teaching phoneme–grapheme relationships.

Reading Goals—program for extending reading work.

Phonics workbooks for grades 4–6.

Designed primarily to help those who did not use the Lippincott series as they began reading.

SUMMARY OF MERRILL READERS

Grade Range

Readiness to grade 2

The manual suggests some children may finish the program in one year while others may need two or more years to complete it.

Skill Range

Learning letters of the alphabet

Ability to recall facts, organize material, and draw conclusions

Characteristics of Content

No specific grade levels are designated for any one book; however, consideration might be given to the following:

Reader 3

Characters are children, a mother and father and animals.

Stories are constructed to accommodate linguistic word patterns.

Example: Dan looked into the pan and did a little jig. "Six thick chops, Mother." But his mother is big and Dan is little. He had to kiss her on the chin.

Reader 6

Stories are related to activities of urban, middle-class children.

Sentences still accommodate words with particular spelling patterns, but story content is much more involved and sentences seem more natural.

SUMMARY OF HARPER & ROW LINGUISTIC READER

Grade Range

Readiness through grade 2

Skill Range

Readiness

Language training to grade 2

Some comprehension questions require interpretation, but more require recall of information in the story; however, greatest emphasis is placed upon the word structure.

Characteristics of Content

Grade 1

Pre-primers All relate to animals: frog, puppy, kitten, etc.

Primer Many of the stories relate to nature: animals, wind, fish, etc.
First reader Animals play a prominent role in stories that happen on a farm.

Grade 2
Fantasy and realism are included. For example, Queen Notnote lived on the planet Sweetlode and was extremely fond of sweets; Kim Kong was a war orphan who was finally adopted by Mr. and Mrs. Sam who were Red Cross workers.
Awareness of word structure is also included in stories.

SUMMARY OF MCGRAW HILL PROGRAMED READING

Grade Range
Readiness
Upper reading level is approximately 5.5, but average children are usually expected to complete the program in grade 3.

Skill Range
Names of upper and lower case letters of the alphabet.
Emphasis seems to be on literal comprehension with some opportunity for interpretation.

Content Characteristics
Grade 1
Book 4–Content is developed to accommodate words fitting a particular pattern. There are no stories with titles; however the same characters, Ann and Sam, appear throughout the book (as well as the whole series, 1 through 7).

Special Features
Storybooks, Series 1 and 2. Storybooks correlated to corresponding programmed texts.
Duplicating masters for supplementary exercises for Storybooks 1 through 7 and for Series 1 and 2 of the programmed text.
Vinyl overlays for pupils' books
Duplicate response pages for pupils' books
Filmstrips for books 1 through 7
Vowel chart
Pupil Progress Charts
Character posters and sound-symbol chart

Appendix C

Selection Aids for Children's Books*

Arbuthnot, May Hill, *Children and Books,* Scott, Foresman & Company, Glenview, Illinois, 1964.

The author reviews books for children by main characters and plot and suggests ways of using some of them for reading aloud and storytelling. She also discusses illustrations and illustrators of children's books and criteria for judging illustrations, as well as, lists extensive reference materials at the end of each chapter. An excellent guide for any teacher or parent interested in presenting his students or children with better reading material.

Brewton, John E. and Sara W., comp., *Index to Children's Poetry,* Wilson, Chicago, 1954, pt. suppl. 1954, 2d suppl. 1965.

A title, subject, author, and first line index to poetry in collections for children and youth. Information about the poems is given in the title entries, with cross-reference to 130 books of poetry. This listing gives author(s), name of book, approximate price, a very brief summary, and the suggested grade level of the book. An excellent resource for finding known poems or to discover unknown poems for a specific grade level.

Crosby, Muriel, *Reading Ladders for Human Relations,* American Council on Education, Washington, D.C., 1963.

The author has grouped books around six themes: growing up; individual and group; search for values; feeling at home; change; and freedom. Materials were chosen for development and self-insight, sensitivity, and expectation of differences among people, and to extend insight into different value patterns. Includes information about recordings, films, and other supplementary materials.

Contains brief discussions of the books, indexes for locating them, ways to use short stories, and classification by grade level.

Eakin, Mary K., *Subject Index to Books for Intermediate Grades,* American Library Association, Chicago, 1963.

————, *Subject Index to Books for Primary Grades,* American Library Association, Chicago, 1967.

These two indexes to books for children list approximate prices and grade levels by subject; poetry, folk, or fairy tales are not included.

---

*Prepared with the assistance of Flossie Perkins, Assistant Professor of Library Science, University of North Dakota.

References to text books are made only when the subject coverage is inadequate in trade books. Especially helpful to teachers searching for related curricular material.

Eastman, M. H., *Index to Fairy Tales, Myths, and Legends*, Faxon, Boston, 1926, 1st suppl., 1937, 2d suppl., 1952.

Lists fairy tales, myths, legends, and stories in alphabetical order by title, with location or author. Author or book title is also listed in a second section with date of publication, publisher, and approximate price. Asterisks indicate good books for the primary level. Authors by geographical location and a directory of publishers are included.

_____, *For Storytellers and Storytelling: bibliographies, materials, and resource aids*. American Library Association, Chicago, 1968.

Includes versions of stories expressed in other art forms such as poetry, dance, music, the cinema, and recordings. This bibliography is for the experienced storyteller or the beginner.

Gaver, Mary, ed., *Elementary School Library Collection*, a guide to books and other media. Bro-Dart Foundation, Newark, New Jersey, 1968, supplement 1969.

Lists and annotates basic print and nonprint materials in classifications of reference materials, non-fiction, fiction, easy books, periodicals and professional tools for the teachers. Contains an author, title, subject index with a graded listing, a classified listing of audio-visual materials, one of large print materials, and a directory of publishers.

Guilfoile, Elizabeth, *Books for Beginning Readers*

_____, *One Hundred More Books for Beginning Readers*, National Council Teacher of English, 1962.

Discusses useful books and indexes them by author, title, illustrator, publisher, date of publication and appropriate grade level. The discussions of the characteristics of these books, their content, and what they offer for first grade would be most helpful for the teacher who is trying to start a good classroom library. A list of publishers is a potential source of newer books printed since this reference material was published. *One Hundred More Books for Beginning Readers* is an alphabetized list by author of books, also giving the vital statistics of the titles.

Gillespie, John T. and Diana L. Lembo, *Introducing Books: A Guide for the Middle Grades*, R. R. Bowker Co., New York, 1970.

A book talk manual for the educator to use with ages 8 through 12. Eighty-eight books are concisely described and analyzed for use as book talks. Suggests themes (and related book and nonbook follow up) that reflect needs and concerns of the intermediate group's growing social and ethical awareness: family, friends, physical problems, values, adult roles, reading for fun.

Green, Ellin, *Stories: A List of Stories to Tell and to Read Aloud,* New York Public Library, New York, 1965.

Divided into two main parts: list of stories to be told, stories and poems to be read aloud. An added section includes a list of recordings by well-known storytellers or authors reading from their own works. Name and subject indexes.

Heller, Freida M., *I Can Read It Myself,* Ohio State University, Columbus, Ohio, 1965.

Independent reading for primary grades graded from easiest to more difficult. Includes a publishers' directory. Self-explanatory titles of the bibliography sections are: I'm Just Beginning to Read by Myself; I'm Reading a Little Better; Now I Can Read Real Good.

Huus, Helen, *Children's Books to Enrich the Social Studies: For the Elementary Grades,* National Council for the Social Studies, Washington, D.C., rev. 1966.

A major topic is presented such as Times Past with subtopics such as The First Settlements, Toward Independence, under which are listed the books by title, author, illustrator, publisher, city of publication, year of publication and appropriate grade level, and a brief paragraph summarizing the content. A good reference for discovering books to use as supplementary material for social studies.

Hodges, Elizabeth D., comp. and ed., *Books for Elementary School Libraries; An initial collection.* American Library Association, Chicago, 1969.

Over 3000 books, catalogued by subject, with brief descriptive annotations and complete bibliographic information. Quality collection of basic books for K–8. Closely geared to the elementary school curriculums and needs and interests of children.

Keating, Charlotte Matthews, *Building Bridges of Understanding,* Palo Verde Publishing Co., Tucson, Arizona, 1967.

Lists fully annotated ethnic stories to help children gain insights into the contribution of different ethnic groups: Negroes, American Indians, Spanish-speaking, Chinese-Americans, Japanese-Americans, Hawaiians, Jews, and others. These books contribute to acculturation and to the student's personal development. Arranged by author under each subject. Pre-school to high school.

Kunitz, Stanley J. and Howard Haycraft, eds., *The Junior Book of Authors,* Wilson, Chicago, 1951.

Gives brief biographical and autobiographical sketches about various authors and illustrators of books. Useful for the teacher suggesting a particular author's books, and for students seeking more information about the author of a book they enjoyed.

Mahoney, B. E., and Elinor Whitney Field, eds., *Newbery Medal Books, 1922–1955*, Horn Books, Boston, 1955.

Presents brief comments about each year's Newbery Medal winner given to exceptional children's books, with a short excerpt from the book, a biographical note about the author or other qualified person, and the author's paper of acceptance, and illustrations from some books. Could help guide the teacher in selecting good books for his students or helping the students choose outstanding books to read.
Newbery and Caldecott Medal Books, 1956–1965, edited by Lee Kingman, 1965, brings these award books up to date.

Mahoney, B. E., Louise P. Latimer, and Beulah Folmsbree, eds., *Illustrators of Children's Books, 1744–1945*, Horn Books, Boston, 1947.

Describes the history and development of the use of illustrations in children's books. Includes illustrators from many countries and describes various procedures used for printing illustrations. Also includes a bibliography of illustrators and authors.
Same format is continued in *Illustrators of Children's Books: 1946–1956, Illustrators of Children's Books, 1957–1966.*

Miller, Bertha Mahoney and Elinor W. Field, eds., *Caldecott Medal Books: 1938–1957*, Horn Books, Boston, 1957.

Complete data on each medal-winning book and its illustrators from beginning of award to 1957. Includes name of author, book note concerning artist's techniques, the artist's acceptance paper and a biographical paper for each winner. Teachers will appreciate the value of distinctive art examples that are available for use by and with children.

Perkins, Flossie L., *Book and Non-Book Media: Bibliography of Selection Aids*, National Council of Teachers of English, Champaign, Ill., 1970.

An annotated selection aid of book and nonbook media with emphasis on school library materials. Listed by title with complete bibliographical data for ordering. The purpose and scope of each aid is noted, as well as the subject headings, similar tools, special features, usefulness and cost. Over 300 references are described. Divisions include: Aids for Elementary Schools, High Schools, Colleges; Teacher-Parent Backgrounds; Librarians and Adults; Author-Publisher Index.

Phelps, Jennifer L., ed., *New Educational Materials*, Scholastic Magazine, Inc., Englewood Cliffs, N.J., 1970.

Designed to aid teachers in making knowledgeable recommendations to their media specialists and librarians for books and other media. Pre-K through Grade 12 covered. Professional information is included for the teacher in addition to the annotated bibliography on books and other media such as study prints, tapes, teaching-learning games, posters, recordings, and films. Listed mainly by title under broad subject areas covering language arts, social studies, science, professional materials, references and guides. Sources of educational materials are cited.

Rollins, Charlemae, *We Build Together: A Reader's Guide to Negro Life and Literature for Elementary and High School Use*, National Council of Teachers of English, Champaign, Ill., 1967.

Lists many books now available that show Negroes honestly not as a stereotyped people. For all age groups except adult. Includes annotated bibliography on biography, poetry, folklore, history, picture-books, fiction and nonfiction. Directory of publishers.

Sell, Violet, Dorothy B. Frizzell Smith, Ardis Sarff O'Hoyt, and Mildred Bakke, *Subject Index to Poetry for Children and Young People*, American Library Association, Chicago, 1957.

Designed to help the librarian, teacher, pupil, and general reader locate quickly and easily the poems under a wide-ranging variety of subjects, on specific topics, universal concepts, persons, places, and things, as well as for poems for special occasions or programs. The first section of the book is a listing of books indexed. The second section is a subject listing under which the title of the poem and the author are given, together with the page and coding for the compilation in which the poem may be found.

Shor, Rachel and Estelle A. Fidell, eds., *Children's Catalog*, Wilson, Chicago, 11th ed., 1966 with four annual supplements, 1967–1970.

Designed to serve as a basic selection aid for elementary schools. In three parts: classified (subdivided by Dewey Classification, fiction, easy books, and story collections) with full bibliographical data for each book, plus an annotation and excerpts from review(s); author, title, subject and analytical index; directory of publishers and distributors. Teachers could use the subject guide to find related curricular material.

Spache, George, *Good Reading for Poor Readers*, Garrard Publishing Company, Champaign, Ill., 1970.

Describes the "psychological interaction of a child and a story." Lists trade and library books, and also adopted and simplified materials, textbooks, workbooks, games, magazines, newspapers, series books, and book clubs, with suggested grade levels. A comprehensive resource material for selecting material for poor readers.

Subject and Title Index to Short Stories for Children, American Library Association, Chicago, 1955.

An index according to subject of many short stories for children from grade 3 through junior high school with a code reference that describes the authors, book title from which the story was taken, publisher, and suggested grade level. A good reference for the teacher to use in selecting suitable short stories.

Appendix D

Word List*

PRE-PRIMER (1) WORD LIST

a	and	are	away	be
big	boat	but	can	come
did	do	down	eat	for
fun	get	go	good	has
have	her	here	him	his
house	I	in	it	know
like	little	look	make	my
no	not	of	one	play
put	run	said	the	then
this	three	to	too	two
water	we	what	where	who
will	you	your		

PRIMER WORD LIST

about	after	all	am	an
around	as	baby	back	bay
bed	blue	by	cake	call
came	could	day	find	fly
from	front	funny	give	gone
green	had	he	hello	help
how	hurry	is	jump	let
man	may	me	milk	mother
night	now	of	old	on
other	over	pet	ran	red
ride	sat	saw	see	she
so	some	stay	stop	story
street	take	that	them	there
they	time	toy	tree	up
us	very	want	was	way
went	when	would	yes	

FIRST READER 1

afraid	again	airplane	any	ask
at	ate	bad	bake	ball

David R. Stone and Vilda Bartschi, *Elementary English*, Volume IV, No. 4, April, 1963, pp. 420–426

basket	been	before	began	better
black	book	boy	brown	buy
car	cat	chair	children	city
cold	color	cry	dog	door
duck	far	fast	father	feet
five	flew	four	garden	girl
goat	got	gray	guess	heard
hen	hide	high	horse	if
into	just	laugh	light	long
lost	more	morning	much	must
name	never	new	noise	nose
or	out	please	pocket	pretty
pull	puppy	rain	read	ready
road	room	sang	seen	shall
side	sleep	snow	soon	stand
store	summer	sun	surprise	tell
then	thank	their	these	think
thought	through	together	tomorrow	took
town	train	truck	under	wagon
walk	well	were	wet	white
why	window	with	work	yellow

READER 2

above	almost	along	always	animal
another	apart	apple	aunt	balloon
bear	beautiful	because	behind	bell
best	birthday	blew	both	box
bread	breakfast	bring	bump	cage
care	carry	catch	chicken	circus
clean	climb	close	corn	corner
count	country	cow	cut	dig
dinner	dish	does	dress	each
ear	earth	egg	elephant	else
end	enough	even	ever	every
eye	fall	fed	fell	fence
field	fine	fire	first	fish
floor	flower	follow	food	found
friend	full	game	gave	glad
goodbye	grass	ground	grow	hair
hand	happen	happy	hard	hat
head	hear	hill	hold	hole

Appendix E

Useful Reading Tests

GROUP READING READINESS TESTS

Name of Test and Publication Date	Grade	Subtests	No. of Forms	Time in Minutes	Author(s)	Publisher and Address
Gates-MacGinitie Reading Tests—Readiness Skills (1939, rev. 1968)	K-1	Listening; comprehension; auditory discrimination; visual discrimination; following directions; letter recognition; visual-motor coordination; auditory blending; word recognition	1		A. I. Gates and W. MacGinitie	Teachers College Press Columbia University 525 West 120th Street New York, N.Y. 10027
Harrison-Stroud Reading Readiness Profiles (1949, rev. 1956)	K-1	Using symbols; making visual discriminations; using the context; making auditory discriminations; using context and auditory clues; giving names of letters	1	80-90	M. L. Harrison and J. B. Stroud	Houghton Mifflin Co. 110 Tremont Street Boston, Mass. 02107

GROUP READING READINESS TESTS Continued

Name of Test and Publication Date	Grade	Subtests	No. of Forms	Time in Minutes	Author(s)	Publisher and Address
Lee-Clark Reading Readiness Test (1931, rev. 1962)	K-1	Letter symbols; concepts; word symbols	1	20	J. M. Lee and W. W. Clark	California Test Bureau Del Monte Research Park Monterey, Calif. 93940
Metropolitan Readiness Tests (1933, re. 1964, 1965, 1966, & 1969)	K-1	Word meaning; listening; matching; alphabet; numbers; copying	2	65–75	G. H. Hildreth, N. L. Griffiths, and N. E. McGauvran	Harcourt Brace Jovanovich Test Dept. 757 Third Avenue New York, N.Y. 10017
Murphy-Durrell Reading Readiness Analysis (1949, rev. 1964, 1965)	K-1	Phonemes; letter names; learning rate	1	80	H. A. Murphy and D. D. Durrell	Harcourt Brace Jovanovich

INDIVIDUAL READING TESTS

Name of Test and Publication Date	Grade	Subtests	No. of Forms	Time in Minutes	Author(s)	Publisher and Address
Auditory Discrimination Test (1958)			2		Joseph M. Wepman	Language Research Assoc. 300 N. State Street Chicago, Illinois

Name	Grade range	Areas measured	No.	Time	Author	Publisher
Botel Reading Inventory (1961, 1966)	1–12	Phonetics mastery (consonants, vowels, syllabication, nonsense words); word recognition; word opposites	2		M. Botel, C. L. Holsclaw, and G. C. Cammarata	Follett Publishing Co. 1010 West Washington Blvd. Chicago, Illinois
Diagnostic Reading Scales (1963)	1–8	Word recognition; oral reading; silent reading; auditory comprehension	1		George D. Spache	California Test Bureau
Durrell Analysis of Reading Difficulty (1937, rev. 1955)	1–6	Oral reading; silent reading listening comprehension; word recognition and anlysis; naming letters; identifying letters; matching letters; visual memory of words-primary; hearing sounds in words-primary; learning to hear sounds in words; sounds of letters; learning rate; visual memory of words-intermediate; phonic spelling; spelling test; handwriting	1	30–90	D. D. Durrell	Harcourt Brace Jovanovich

INDIVIDUAL READING TESTS Continued

Name of Test and Publication Date	Grade	Subtests	No. of Forms	Time in Minutes	Author(s)	Publisher and Address
Gates-McKillop Reading Diagnostic Tests (1926, rev. 1962)	2–6	Mispronunciation; omissions; additions; repetitions; words-untimed presentation; phrases-flash presentation; recognizing and blending common word parts; giving letter sounds; naming lower case letters; recognizing the visual form of sounds; auditory blending; spelling; oral vocabulary; syllabication; auditory discrimination	2	30–60	A. I. Gates and A. McKillop	Teachers College Press Columbia University
Gilmore Oral Reading Test: New Edition (1951, rev. 1968)	1–8	Accuracy; rate; comprehension	2	15–20	J. Gilmore and V. Gilmore	Harcourt Brace Jovanovich
Gray Oral Reading Test (1963, rev. 1967)	1–16+		4		W. S. Gray	The Bobbs-Merrill Co., Inc., 4300 West 62nd Street Indianapolis, Indiana 46206

Roswell-Chall Diagnostic Reading Test of Word Analysis Skills (1956, rev. 1959)	2–6	Simple consonants and combinations; short vowel sounds; rule to – silent e; vowel combinations; syllabication	2	510	F. G. Roswell and J. S. Chall	Essay Press P. O. Box 5 Planetarium Station New York, N.Y. 10024
Standard Reading Inventory (1966)	pp–7	Recognition vocabulary; oral errors; comprehension; speed	2		Robert A. McCracken	Klamath Printing Co. 320 Lowell Klamath Falls, Oregon 97601

GROUP READING TESTS

California Achievement Tests – Reading (Form A available now; Form B available in 1971)						
Level 1 (1970)	1.5–2	Vocabulary; comprehension; word attack skills	1	46	E. W. Tiegs & W. W. Clark	California Test Bureau
Level 2 (1970)	2–4	(as above)	1	40	(as above)	(as above)
California Reading Test Lower Primary (1957, rev. 1963)	1–2	Vocabulary; comprehension	2	23	E. W. Tiegs & W. W. Clark	California Test Bureau

GROUP READING TESTS Continued

Name of Test and Publication Date	Grade	Subtests	No. of Forms	Time in Minutes	Author(s)	Publisher and Address
California Reading Test, continued						
Upper Primary (1957, rev. 1963)	2.5–4.5	(as above)	2	40	(as above)	(as above)
Elementary (1957, rev. 1963)	4–6	(as above)	2	50	(as above)	(as above)
Junior High Level (1957, rev. 1963)	4–6	Vocabulary; comprehension	3	68	E. W. Tiegs & W. W. Clark	California Test Bureau
Advanced (1957, rev. 1963)	9–14	(as above)	3	68	(as above)	(as above)
Classroom Reading Inventory (1969)	2–8	Word recognition; independent reading level; instructional reading level; frustration level; hearing capacity level; spelling	2		N. J. Silvaroli	William C. Brown Book Co. 135 South Locust Street Dubuque, Iowa

Developmental Reading Tests					
Lower Primary Reading (1965)	1–2.5	Word recognition; comprehending significant ideas; comprehending specific instructions	2	40	G. L. Bond, B. Balow, & C. J. Hoyt	Lyons & Carnahan 407 East 25th Street Chicago, Illinois 60616
Upper Primary Reading (1965)	2.5–3	(as above)	2	40	(as above)	(as above)
Intermediate Reading (1968)	4–6	Basic reading vocabulary; reading for information; reading for interpretation; reading for appreciation	2	50	(as above)	(as above)
Diagnostic Reading Tests					
Diagnostic Reading Test (1957, rev. 1963 & 1966)	K–4	Survey; word attack	2		F. Triggs	The Committee on Diagnostic Reading Tests, Inc. Mountain Home, N.C.
Lower Level (1947, rev. 1963, 1966, 1967, 1969, & 1971)	4–8	(as above)	2		(as above)	(as above)

GROUP READING TESTS Continued

Name of Test and Publication Date	Grade	Subtests	No. of Forms	Time in Minutes	Author(s)	Publisher and Address
Diagnostic Reading Tests, continued						
Upper Level (1947, rev. 1956, 1963, 1965, 1966, 1967, 1970, & 1971)	7–13	Survey; vocabulary; comprehension (silent & auditory); rate of reading; word attack	2		(as above)	(as above)
Iowa Silent Reading Tests						
Elementary (1933, rev. 1939, 1942, 1943, & 1948)	Pre–K to 3	Rate; comprehension; directed reading; word meaning; paragraph comprehension; sentence meaning; alphabetizing; use of index	4	60	H. A. Greene & V. H. Kelley	Harcourt, Brace Jovanovich
Advanced (1927, rev. 1931, 1939, 1942, & 1943)	9–14	Rate; comprehension; directed reading poetry comprehension; word meaning; sentence meaning; paragraph comprehension;	4	60	(as above)	(as above)

Test	Grade		Skills	Author	Publisher
			use of index; selection of key words		
McCullough Word Analysis Tests (1960, rev. 1963)	4–6	1 70	Initial blends and diagraphs; phonetic discrimination; matching letters to vowel sounds; sounding whole words; interpreting phonetic symbols; dividing words into syllables; root words in affixed forms	C. M. McCullough	Personnel Press, Inc. 20 Nassau Street Princeton, N.J. 08540
Stanford Diagnostic Reading Test					
Level 1 (1966)	2.5–4.5	2	Comprehension; vocabulary; auditory discrimination; syllabication; beginning and ending sounds; blending; sound discrimination	B. Karlsen, R. Madden, & E. F. Gardner	Harcourt, Brace Jovanovich
Level 2 (1966)	4.5–8.5	2	Comprehension; vocabulary; syllabication; sound discrimination; blending; rate	(as above)	(as above)

INDEX